COMPARATIVE RELIGION

A comparative study of the History of
Religion intended primarily as a textbook
for students, with references and full bibliography of relative literature. It is also designed to give the general reader an
account of religious thought and practice
in the light of recent research from rudimentary beginnings, through the great
religions of antiquity (Egypt, Babylonia,
Greece, Rome) to the higher living religions
of to-day (Hinduism, Buddhism, Confucianism, Judaism and Christianity).

UNIVERSITY PAPERBACKS
U.P.32

Comparative Religion

AN INTRODUCTORY

AND HISTORICAL STUDY BY

E. O. JAMES

D.Litt., Ph.D., F.S.A., Hon.D.D.

*Professor Emeritus of the History and Philosophy of Religion
in the University of London
Fellow of University College, London
Fellow of King's College, London
Chaplain of All Souls College, Oxford*

UNIVERSITY PAPERBACKS

METHUEN : LONDON
BARNES & NOBLE : NEW YORK

First published 1938 by Methuen & Co
First published in this series (revised edition) 1961
© 1961 by E. O. James
Printed and bound in Great Britain by
Cox & Wyman Ltd, Fakenham, Norfolk
Catalogue No (Methuen) 2/6782/27

University Paperbacks are published by
METHUEN & CO LTD
36 Essex Street, Strand, London, WC2
and BARNES & NOBLE INC
105 Fifth Avenue, New York 3

Preface

As the occupant of Chairs devoted to the study of the History of Religion I have long felt the need of a text-book written according to the methods of modern scientific inquiry covering the whole ground as an *introduction* to the more detailed and specialized treatises. Such a work to fulfil its purpose should be eclectic; a statement of ideas which have become or are becoming the common property of all serious students of the subject. However difficult this may be to achieve when much of the data available does not admit of precise determination, a text-book should not represent the findings of any particular school of thought, so that the student and general reader are left free to come to their own conclusions where expert opinion is divided. I have endeavoured, therefore, to set forth the evidence from as detached a standpoint as possible, though, of course, a writer who is himself engaged in independent investigations must in some measure be influenced by the direction taken by his own researches.

In the study of the higher religions the problems are very different in character from those which arise in connexion with the more rudimentary cults, and presuppose a difference of method. Nevertheless, the thought and practice of civilized peoples cannot be cut off as with a knife from the underlying customs and beliefs which have played a determining part in shaping the resultant products, however much subsequent knowledge and ethical evaluation may have modified and transformed the earlier notions. As Robertson Smith pointed out at the end of the last century, when evolutionary ideas were still very suspect in theological circles, 'it is a law of science that, to know a thing thoroughly, we must know it in its genesis and in its growth. To understand the ways of God with man, and the whole meaning of His plan of salvation, it is necessary to go back and see His work in its beginnings, examining rudimentary stages in the process of revelation.'[1] This principle applies whatever view may be taken of the ultimate character of any given

[1] *The Old Testament in the Jewish Church* (London, 1892), p. 192.

religious system. The most primitive human efforts in the establishment of a charter of faith and practice are relevant after their own fashion as part of a common culture pattern consolidating society and determining morality, conduct, and social structure. Therefore, in the study of the history of religion there should be no radical cleavage between the higher systems, ancient or modern, oriental or occidental, and the ritual and belief which constitute a common possession of mankind in a primitive state of culture.

In the long and chequered career of the human race certain elements in the religious, ethical, social, and technical equipment have been found to have survival value, and in order to separate the permanent from the temporary, it is necessary to engage in a comparative study of the available evidence. In the sphere of religion, where fortuitous variation is more apparent than intrinsic similarity, in the determination of the fundamental nature of the phenomena a common stratum, *quod ubique, quod semper, quod ab omnibus,* must be sought. But if Man is to be set down as everywhere and always religious, a generous attitude must be adopted towards the extent to which genuine religion occurs amongst mankind. This involves the framing of the most inclusive of definitions, and an evaluation of the function of religion as a universal feature in every known human culture, primitive or developed. In estimating the quality and value of types of behaviour which legitimately may be designated religious, it is a help rather than a hindrance to be able to view them from within—that is to say, from the standpoint of the religious man—provided that the scientific temper and method be rigidly maintained. Few to-day would deny that the ultimate truths of religion transcend their apprehension by any theological or ethical system, though it may reasonably be argued that they may be manifest more fully and completely under certain conditions than others. The question of validity lies outside the scope of this volume, but throughout the inquiry the needs of those who are engaged in the important work of interpreting the facts in terms of values in relation to real existence have been kept in mind.

A synoptic view of religion, or indeed of any other department of human experience, can only be obtained when the several parts making up the complete whole are 'fitly framed together'. To the anthropologist and the historian belong the task of supplying the data of the philosophy of religion. They must supply also the facts which the theologian endeavours to correlate with the philosophical interpretations in an attempt to render explicit religious experience in terms of faith and thought based on certain fundamental realities guiding human life and conduct. That this volume may help to these ends is my hope, and for the guidance of the student in a more detailed study of the material here described in outline, a full bibliography of the relevant literature is given, together with numerous references in the text.

To this distinguished army of workers in a vast field of research I should like to take this opportunity to express my indebtedness, since without their labours this book could never have been written. My devoted wife, as on so many former occasions, has given her valuable aid in proof-reading, together with my late friend, Mr H. Coote Lake, formerly Hon. Secretary of the Folk-lore Society, and the Rev. J. N. Schofield, Lecturer in Hebrew and Old Testament Studies in the University of Cambridge. To these, one and all, I desire to express my sincere thanks. Some of the material incorporated in this volume was collected in the first instance for a course of lectures given by invitation of the University of London at King's College in 1936, while a subsequent request for a similar course at University College, Bangor, in the University of Wales, led me to a further examination of the problem of sin and salvation in relation to theism. On both these occasions a stimulating discussion followed which helped to clear up certain points in my mind. Furthermore, the visits were rendered extremely pleasant as well as enlightening by the delightful hospitality I enjoyed from my friend Professor Oesterley in London, and from Dr. W. C. H. Simon, now Bishop of Llandaff, Warden of the Hostel at Bangor.

E. O. JAMES

ALL SOULS COLLEGE, OXFORD
February, 1961

Contents

ABBREVIATIONS

B.B.A.E.	*Bulletin of the Bureau of American Ethnology*
E.R.E.	*Encyclopaedia of Religion and Ethics* (Hastings)
G.B.	*The Golden Bough* (Frazer)
J.E.A.	*Journal of Egyptian Archaeology*
J.R.A.I.	*Journal of the Royal Anthropological Institute*
J.H.S.	*Journal of Hellenic Studies*
R.B.A.E.	*Report of the Bureau of American Ethnology*
S.B.E.	*Sacred Books of the East*

Introduction

From the time when religions mingled in the Graeco-Roman world thinkers have been compelled to evaluate their own beliefs and practices in relation to those of other peoples and races, but it was not until the latter part of the nineteenth century of our era that a serious attempt was made to apply scientific principles to the comparative and historical study of the subject. The Renaissance, it is true, revived interest in classical thought and mythology, but the recovery of an appreciation of the glories of ancient Greece and the splendours of pagan Rome was quickly followed in Northern Europe by the narrowing influence of the Reformation with its return to a circumscribed theological outlook. A fresh impetus was given to Biblical studies and a knowledge of Hebrew, but the Calvinistic doctrine of the inherent depravity of unredeemed humanity reacted against a sympathetic understanding of pagan religion. Nevertheless, although this opinion was widely adopted alike in Protestant and Catholic circles, isolated individuals took a broader view, as, for example, Joseph Scaliger who in 1583 treated the Old Testament as an integral part of ancient history. John Selden's *De dis Syris syntagmata duo,* published at Leipzig in 1672, reveals some critical understanding of Semitic mythology, while in 1678 Cudworth argued in his *True Intellectual System of the Universe* that Plato's 'trinity' was derived from Hebraism. In 1685 Dr John Spencer, Master of Corpus Christi College, Cambridge, produced a Latin work on the ritual laws of the Hebrews which Robertson Smith somewhat optimistically described as laying 'the foundations of the science of comparative religion'.[1] In France about this time a Jesuit, Lescalopier, and a Benedictine, Calmet, were working along the same lines.

[1] *The Religion of the Semites,* 3rd edition (Lond., 1927), p. xiv.

RELIGION, NATURAL AND REVEALED

Meanwhile the voyages of the early explorers were bringing to light new continents, and in an age of discovery knowledge of the religious ideas and systems current in different parts of the earth rapidly increased and called for some interpretation. In the seventeenth and eighteenth centuries, in opposition to the intolerant attitude of theologians, the Deists made some attempt to meet the situation by postulating a primeval revelation of 'five catholic truths' concerning the existence and worship of God as original religion pure and undefiled which was subsequently perverted by the ritual and superstition invented by a hypothetical order of 'priests' to exercise a stranglehold on the lives of their fellows. This approach, though wholly unscientific and unwarranted in fact, was part of a new critical movement which prepared the way for an unbiased empirical investigation of the phenomena.

For a while a sharp distinction continued to be made between 'Natural' and 'Revealed' religion, but on further examination this antithesis has been found to be one which is very difficult to maintain. Whether 'Natural Religion' be interpreted as the religious beliefs and practices of mankind apart from any reference to an alleged special revelation given to Israel and the Christian Church, or a knowledge of God gained from observation of the physical universe independent of any divine self-disclosure vouchsafed through the Bible, in either case the distinction cannot be upheld on philosophical or theological grounds.[1] But, moreover, so long as this scholastic doctrine of the existence of God as a truth of Reason attainable without supernatural aid as opposed to the revealed truths of the Incarnation and the Trinity was maintained, a scientific investigation of religion as a whole was impossible. Thus, for instance, in Sectarian Hinduism and Mahayana Buddhism ideas occur which, though very different in origin and character from the Christian conceptions, have certain points of contact with them ruling out a clear-cut division between ideas of Deity reached by reason and speculation and knowledge disclosed by a process of revelation. It is not ready-made theologies that are revealed at any time or in any place. If a process of revelation is discernible at all, it must be sought in human personalities and the movements of history

[1] cf. C. C. J. Webb, *Problems in the Relations of God and Man* (Lond., 1915), pp. 49 ff.

initiated and directed to specific ends, though, of course, this is not to deny that the ways of God may be manifest in Nature and purposive activity expressed in the physical universe.

It follows, therefore, that if the phrase 'revealed religion' is to have any significance to-day, it cannot be associated with any system of theology assigned to a separate category opposed to 'natural religion' as a distinct type of knowledge. That all religions have certain common features is now generally recognized, and no serious theologian would contend that the Hebrew and Christian Scriptures, however unique as a vehicle of divine self-disclosure, can be set apart from all other records of religious beliefs and spiritual experience. On the contrary, modern Biblical scholarship freely employs the material collected from other sources and contemporary cultures to elucidate its own specialized data.

THE EVOLUTIONARY IDEA

All this, though familiar to us to-day, did not become apparent till the veil had been lifted, disclosing the evolutionary process in its amazing complexity. But before the time of Darwin thought in Germany was beginning to take a new direction. The idea of evolution implicit in the Copernican astronomy assumed a dominant position in the philosophy of Kant (1724–1804) and Schelling (1775–1854), and in the skilful hands of Hegel (1779–1831) it became the key to world-history. As humanity is one progressive and perfectible being or organism, which advances by becoming more complete and reasonable, and as history is not merely one event after another, but the dialectic expressed in time, so 'the religious relation is a process within the mind, developing itself from lower to higher stages and forms according to immanent laws, laws which are essentially the same in the macrocosm of humanity as in the microcosm of the individual'.[1] Thus, Hegel opened the way to the understanding of the history of religion. With the aid of a monistic definition which described religion as the 'Divine Spirit's knowledge of itself through the mediation of finite spirit', he made an extended survey of the religious systems of the world, so far as they were known in his day. If he accommodated the facts to his scheme, and in the light of present-day knowledge his definition is no

[1] O. Pfleiderer, *The Philosophy of Religion* (Lond., 1887), vol. II, p. 80.

B

longer tenable, like the modern anthropologist, he showed development to be an integral element in the life of mind and in the religious aspect of experience. For him the history of religion was the evolution of the divine in the soul to higher self-consciousness, and from this point of view he set forth the sequence of the development of religions.[1]

But inasmuch as religion on this hypothesis was an atittude towards the Absolute in its unity, it constituted an expression of reality belonging essentially to the domain of philosophy rather than to that of science. Furthermore, apart from the difficulties raised by the ambiguity involved in Hegel's position concerning the Absolute in philosophy and the concept of God in theology, the study of religion could never come into its own so long as it was subordinated to any system which used the facts of religion to establish its own doctrines. Religious phenomena as distinct from spiritual experience must be investigated on their own merits historically and comparatively independent of any preconceived theories or accepted loyalties.

It was this formidable task which was undertaken by anthropologists after the great revolution in thought and knowledge initiated by Charles Darwin in 1859 had shown that the workings of the human mind as they find expression in social organization, moral and legal sanctions and magical and religious beliefs and practices are amenable to scientific treatment. As Dr Marett has said, 'anthropology is the child of Darwin',[2] and as such it is primarily concerned with the development of mankind and of human institutions. 'Reject the Darwinian point of view and you must reject anthropology also.' In other words, the application of anthropological methods to the study of religion presupposes at once a scientific and, in its broadest sense, an evolutionary standpoint in the investigation of the phenomena. Thus, those sections of the human race which have remained throughout the ages in a primitive state of culture are selected for special consideration on the supposition that they represent to some degree the condition in which the human race existed prior to the rise of civilization.

[1] Hegel, *Philosophy of Religion,* Eng. Trans. by E. B. Speirs (Lond., 1895), vol. I, pp. 79 f., vol. II, pp. 10 ff.

[2] *Anthropology* (Lond., 1911), p. 8.

THE STUDY OF ORIGINS

But, as Renan recognized,

the attempt to solve the problem of origins requires a keen eye to discri-
minate between things certain, probable and plausible, a profound sense
of the realities of life, and the faculty of appreciating strange and remote
psychological situations. And even with all these rare qualities it is very
difficult to attain certitude in the problem's solution. There must be
always wide gaps and interspaces where one can only measure possibilities, draw certain inferences, not half-seen indications, and where,
after all, one can but choose the least unlikely clue among many.[1]

This warning was never more needed than when an attempt is
made to explain the origin of religion in evolutionary terms since
the data available only admit of a choice of 'the least unlikely clue'
by reference to probabilities. In the absence of any positive record
to guide us, all that can be done is to piece together the few scraps
of archaeological material and interpret them by the aid of the
customs and beliefs that have survived on the fringes of the world,
far from the great centres of civilization, among culturally stagnant
people who appear to have remained little changed in their habits
and ideas from Palaeolithic times, when they were cut off from more
progressive cultures.

In the long period of their isolation, however, they have had to
adjust themselves to their particular environment, and in the process
they have developed cultural techniques, and undergone some measure of disintegration and degeneration. But essentially they seem
to be what they have always been, viz. primitive populations, and
as far removed in thought as in practice from the more progressive
races. Therefore, inasmuch as in no department of life is conser-
vatism so manifest as in matters concerning religion, it is reasonable
to surmise that in their ritual and belief they have been no less static
than in the rest of their cultural equipment.

Nevertheless, if the aim of historical investigation is to give an
accurate description of a people, society or series of events at a
given time, and to estimate chronologically the changes that have
occurred therein, as soon as either written records or archaeological
strata fail to supply the necessary material, it might seem that the
inquiry becomes impossible. Clearly what the study of modern

[1] Quoted by Sir A. Lyall, *Asiatic Studies* (Lond., 1899), vol. II, p. 285.

savage races yields is not a history in this sense so much as 'a number of pictures of given peoples each taken as it were by an instantaneous photograph at a given time'.[1] To turn these snapshots into a cinematograph film of a historic sequence of events is to confuse the issue, since before customs and beliefs manifesting a superficial resemblance to one another can be compared chronologically, all the factors have to be determined which have led to the precise course of the development.

But the word 'history' is employed in two ways. It may mean either the record of events or the events themselves. In its broadest sense history presupposes that 'there is something going on' and not merely that certain things happened in the past. In a dynamic universe continually undergoing change activity is a universal phenomenon, and since human society is part of this ceaseless process anthropology is an aspect of the universal history of mankind. As such it is concerned with the conditions under which thought and culture have developed, and as a product of the Darwinian movement its outlook has been evolutionary. Moreover, in its formative period the science was influenced by the positive philosophy of Auguste Comte (1798–1857) who, in endeavouring to establish the 'Law of the Three States' of intellectual development from the theological through the metaphysical to the positive or scientific, was led to consider the principal forms of society in relation to the laws governing human thought and behaviour. Taking social organization as a whole he recognized a nexus between each leading group of phenomena and other leading groups so that the early stages of civilized groups may be observed among primitive peoples.[2]

Thus, before *The Origin of Species* appeared with its inevitable repercussions on ethnology, Comte had laid the foundations of the Comparative Method in the study of social and religious institutions, though he realized that it did not explain the sequence of evolution or the co-ordination of the social system.[3] To overcome this difficulty he sought to determine an 'ideal series', or successive modifications of mental outlook, in the 'three stages' of intellectual

---

[1] Hobhouse, Wheeler and Ginsberg, *The Material and Social Institutions of Simpler Peoples* (Lond., 1930), p. 2.

[2] *Cours de philosophie positive* (Paris, 1877), 4th edition, IV p. 317.

[3] op, cit., p. 319.

progress.[1] Every group, he assumed, was bound to pass through these states by the same steps at varying rates, but uniformly independent of diversities of race or environement because the human mind is invariable in its operations.[2]

The elaborations of these ideas in relation to the history of civilization at a time when the scientific study of social phenomena was beginning to take shape, could hardly fail to have far-reaching effects, and the influence of Comte on anthropological theory at the end of the nineteenth century is manifest in the comparative investigation of similarities between the products of culture, such as beliefs, institutions, customs, implements, weapons and other objects of human design. Like the biologist, the sociologist and scientific student of religion had to devise a system of classification in order to explain the similarities and distinction manifest in the data in terms of origin and development. Moreover, since the time of Descartes the doctrine of the invariability of the laws operative in nature and in human life had become an established principle in philosophical thought, though it overlooked the fact that Man is a law unto himself.

THE COMPARATIVE METHOD

The first systematic attempt to explain the similarity in beliefs, customs and culture was made by Sir Edward Tylor in 1865 when in his *Researches into the Early History of Mankind* he affirmed that

> sometimes it may be ascribed to the like working of men's minds under like conditions, and sometimes it is a proof of blood relationship or inter-course, direct or indirect, between the races among whom it is found. In the one case it has no historical value whatever, while in the other it has this value in a high degree, and the ever-recurring problem is how to distinguish between the two.[3]

If it has been produced more than once under like conditions in two widely separated places such as Asia and Africa, in his opinion intercourse is improbable, but, on the other hand, a custom prevalent in two districts comparatively near suggests historical connexion.[4]

[1] p. 322.   [2] pp. 318 f., 343.
[3] *Researches* (Lond., 1865), p. 5. cf. pp. 175, 376 ff.
[4] pp. 274 f.

Having worked out a technique of the diffusion of culture and developed a theory of the borrowing of myths and folk-tales, six years later (1871) in his great treatise on *Primitive Culture* he turned to the investigation of the laws of human nature along the lines laid down by Comte, though he never lost sight of the use of correspondence in traits as a means of tracing lines of connexion and intercourse between ancient and remote peoples.[1] 'The notion of the continuity of civilization is no barren philosophical principle,' he affirmed, 'but is at once made practical by the consideration that they who wish to understand their own lives ought to know the stages through which their opinions and habits have become what they are.'[2] Comte, he believed, scarcely over-stated the necessity of this study of development when he declared that 'no conception can be understood except through its history', and the 'history of culture began with the appearance on earth of a semi-civilized race of men, and from this state of culture has proceeded in two ways, backward to produce savages, and forward to produce civilized men'.[3]

Thus, he recognized growth and decline in all states of human development, but living when the evolutionary idea was predominant, he was mainly interested in tracing progressive processes in custom and belief on the assumption that everywhere and at all times the human mind operates according to specific laws of thought and action rather than as a result of cultural connexions. This was also the view of T. H. Huxley who declared that 'the minds of men being everywhere similar, differing in quality and quantity but not in kind of faculty, like circumstances must tend to produce like contrivances; at any rate the need to be met and conquered is of a very simple kind'. But he doubted whether such a complicated apparatus as a boomerang or a bow, pile dwellings or outrigger canoes, was invented independently in several localities.[4] Similarly, the devoted Tylorian Andrew Lang, who with E. S. Hartland and J. G. Frazer laid the foundations of the scientific investigation of folklore as a 'study of survivals', in a series of essays published in 1884 set out to compare the myths and customs of various

[1] *British Association Report*, 1894, p. 774.

[2] *Primitive Culture* (Lond., 1871), vol. I, p. 19.

[3] op. cit., p. 35.

[4] *Collected Essays* (Lond., 1894), pp. 213, 225.

peoples who have never been in actual contact 'so far as history shows us'.

According to this view there is no necessity to establish

some sort of genealogy between the Australians and the Greek narrators of a similar myth, nor between the Greek and Australian possessors of a similar usage. The hypothesis will be that the myth, or usage, is common to both races, not because of original community of stock, not because of contact and borrowing, but because the ancestors of the Greeks passed through the savage intellectual condition in which we find the Australians.[1]

He does not deny for mythology the significance of race and migration, but his concern is with 'the mental condition of savages' and the 'common simple ideas' of humanity.

Sidney Hartland, again, in his *Mythology and Folk Tales* argued for the unity of mental process behind all the diversities of expression based on the fact of similarity,[2] while Sir J. G. Frazer acknowledged his profound debt to Tylor who, he said, 'opened up a mental vista undreamed of by me before'.[3] More than any other modern writer Sir James has perpetuated the Comparative Method by placing on record vast stores of invaluable material and deducing from the data thus collected an evolutionary development in human ideas and customs comparable to that exhibited in biological sequence and the stratigraphical history of the rocks. 'If there is one general conclusion which seems to me to emerge from the mass of particulars', he says, 'I venture to think that it is the essential similarity in the working of the less developed human mind among all races, which corresponds to the essential similarity in their bodily frame revealed by comparative anatomy.'

Nevertheless, he realizes that 'while this general mental similarity may be taken as established, we must always be on our guard against tracing to it a multitude of particular resemblances which may be and often are due to simple diffusion, since nothing is more certain than that the various races of men have borrowed from each other many of their arts and crafts, their ideas, customs and institutions'.[4]

The fundamental difficulty in this method of approach lies in the

[1] *Custom and Myth,* new edition (Lond., 1904), pp. 25 f.
[2] 2nd edition (Lond., 1914), p. 32.
[3] *Golden Bough,* Preface to 1st edition (Lond., 1890).
[4] 'Balder the Beautiful', vol. I (Lond., 1913), pp. vi f. (*G.B.,* pt. XI).

fact that customs and beliefs manifesting a superficial resemblance to one another tend to be brought together regardless of the non-comparability of the actual occurences. Nevertheless, if priority in type has often been confused with priority in time, in other departments of scientific investigation it is generally recognized that a genetic series is determined by the sum of internal resemblances, and simplicity in form usually indicates earlier occurrence. In a sense Tylor was correct in regarding the history of mankind as part of the history of nature, but the workings of the human mind cannot be explained in terms of natural laws since the personal experience of the individual introduces important modifications in his reactions to his environment and the circumstances that make up his life not present in the growth of plants and animals. It should be recognized, therefore, that the study of primitive psychology and the historical investigation of the development of human institutions and their contents, while closely related, are actually two distinct aspects of the science of man. The fact that this distinction was often confused in Tylor's methodology doubtless accounts for certain unwarrantable conclusions that sometimes have been drawn from the evidence by social anthropologists and students of comparative religion, which it has been the function of a more strictly historical method to correct.

THE HISTORICAL METHOD

Early in the nineteenth century an attempt was made in Germany to explain the irrational element in mythology philologically by etymological analyses of the names of gods in the hope of being able thereby to discover the origin of religion. The chief exponent of this hypothesis was Max Müller who with A. Kuhn made Aryan mythology the special field of research, and followed Grimm in regarding myth as rooted in the heart of the folk as completely as language. Mythological figures were personifications of natural objects, notably the sun, whose origin could be deduced from the character of human speech, its capacity for poetic interpretation, its polyonymy and homonymy. This theory derived its inspiration mainly from the Rig Veda, together with the Iranian Avesta,[1]

---

[1] The Avesta had been translated by Anquetil-Duperron and then by Burnouf as early as 1771 and 1833–5 respectively, while Indian research was revolutionized at the beginning of the nineteenth century by the work of the Asiatic Society. Bopp. Hodgson and Burnouf in connexion with the Vedic texts.

Homer and the Edda, and it only required the production of anthropological evidence from peoples in a primitive state of culture to show how inadequate were its foundations. But while it collapsed before the attack of Tylor and Lang, it at least made some attempt to investigate the problem of religious origins along historical lines, namely, to find a way back to prehistoric times by the aid of a specific cultural trait of a given people (i.e. language). As Harnack says, 'it needs but little consideration to recognize that the study of each single religion ought by no means to be separated from the study of the *history* of the people concerned. . . . To try to study the religion alone is a more childish undertaking than to examine only the roots or the blossoms instead of the whole plant.'[1]

A more serious effort to grapple with the problem than that of Max Müller was made by Friedrich Ratzel in 1886 and his pupil Frobenius (1895) who endeavoured to establish a series of culture-horizons (*kulturkreise*) within which human institutions were thought to have developed, and in the skilful hands of Graebner, Ankermann and Schmidt, a number of 'spheres' have been worked out chronologically as culture-strata. According to Ratzel all human groups are 'historical' and the similarities in their culture are to be attributed to geographical environment and the transmission of traits from certain centres. This theory was expanded by Frobenius into a complex system of *kulturkreise* with genetic connexions, so that whole cultures were supposed to have migrated from one area to another. Numerous 'spheres' of this nature were worked out chronologically in Africa and the Pacific by Graebner and Ankermann, while Schmidt and his followers have carried the method a further stage in the hope that thereby they may be able to establish their contention concerning primeval monotheism.[2]

At the base of the 'horizons', it is claimed, lies an archaic foundation represented by the very simplest peoples, such as the Pygmies, the Bushmen of South Africa, the Andaman Islanders, the Semang of the Malay Peninsula and the natives of South-east Australia.

[1] *Die Aufgabe der theologischen Fakultäten und die allgemeine Religionsgeschichte* (Berlin, 1901).

[2] Graebner, *Methode der Ethnologie* (Heidelberg, 1911). Ankermann, *Zeitschrift für Ethnologie*, 1905, XXXVII, pp. 28 ff. (cf. 54 for bibliography). Schmidt, *Der Ursprung der Gottesidee* (Münster, 1912–36). *Origin and Growth of Religion* (Lond., 1931), pp. 220 ff.

Upon this common substratum diverse structures have been erected
in mutual independence: the totemic, the horticultural and the
pastoral aspects of society. The scheme, however, lacks confirmatory
archaeological evidence, and our knowledge of the 'archaic'
peoples is very far from complete. Of the Tasmanians we know
little, and the information concerning the Pygmies, the Semang
and the most primitive North American tribes is either insufficient,
or the testimony is too conflicting to be adequate for the purposes
of the hypothesis. Furthermore, it is by no means clear that the
alleged 'archaic substratum' is composed of the same elements
among all the peoples included in the group (i.e. Bushmen, Andamanese, Fuegians, etc.). At any rate, marked differences of opinion
exist among the various workers in these respective regions concerning the character and significance of many of the cultural traits,
notably the religious beliefs, current in the areas.[1] Moreover, the
latest conclusions of ethnologists do not substantiate the contention
that the Pygmies represent a distinct race of 'dawn men'. On the
contrary, they seem to be merely dwarf varieties of existing races
resembling in all essential points the tall types, and reduced in
stature by geographical conditions governing the food supply and
similar biological factors producing arrested development.[2] It
cannot be maintained, therefore, that they are older than the tall
peoples of the same ethnological group, as Schmidt and his school
suggest. While, as Rivers,[3] Clark Wissler,[4] Lowie[5] and Kroeber[6]
have shown, it is possible to work out historical reconstructions of
culture by means of the distribution and spread of given traits, and
Sir Lawrence Gomme has demonstrated a similar historical approach to the study of folklore,[7] however intensively and analytically
primitive institutions and beliefs are studied they cannot be shown
to be really primeval.

[1] Brown, *The Andaman Islands* (Camb., 1922), pp. 136 ff., 354 ff.

[2] E. F. von Eickstedt, *Rassenkunde und Rassengeschichte der Menschheit* (Breslau), p. 226 ff.

[3] Speiser, *Anthropologische Messungen aus Espiritu Santo* (Neue Hebriden) Basel 1928, *History of Melanesian Society* (Camb., 1914), II, p. 585.

[4] *The American Indian* (New York, 1922).

[5] *Primitive Society* (Lond., 1921), pp. 6 f.

[6] *Anthropology* (Lond., 1923), pp. 199 ff.

[7] *Folklore as an Historical Science* (Lond., 1908), pp. xii, 110.

DIFFUSION OF CULTURE

The recognition of this fact has led the more recent exponents of
the historical method to discard the study of origins altogether and
concentrate on the spread of culture from given centres. Thus, Mr
Hocart says, 'we know nothing, absolutely nothing, about the
thoughts of primitive man or how he expressed them, how he be-
haved towards his fellows, and what was his attitude towards nature
and death. . . . All that side of his existence is a perfect blank.'[1] The
line of division, it is urged, runs not between one area and another.
It does not divide hunters like the Veddas and Feugians from
Aryans and Incas, but India from South America.[2] The isolation of
one part of the earth from another is denied, and in place of the
theory of independent invention, the widespread similarities of
culture are explained by a series of migrations through an extensive
system of ancient navigation and movements of peoples, which, it
is alleged, has been responsible for carrying ideas and customs from
one centre to another.[3]

While it cannot be maintained that Early Man was cultureless
and devoid of religion before a hypothetical 'archaic civilization'
called into being the whole complex scheme which on this hypothesis is held to have followed in the wake of migrating 'children
of the sun', nevertheless, as we have seen, the term 'primitive' is a
purely relative one. What lies behind the ancient civilizations of
Egypt, Mesopotamia, Crete and the Aegean, and the Indus valley
can only be conjectured from such evidence as is available from
Palaeolithic sources, though for reasons which have already been
considered it is difficult to believe that culturally stagnant races on
the fringes of civilization have not survived throughout the ages
little changed in their customs, habits and beliefs, if due allowance is
made for modification in adjustment to a particular environment,
and possible degradation and disintegration. It may be true that
religious development does not necessarily correspond with progress in mechanical arts,[4] but, if a food-gathering people such as

[1] *Hibbert Journal,* XVIII, 2, 1920, p. 379.

[2] Hocart, *Kingship* (Oxford, 1927), p. 143. cf. Rivers, *Ethnology and History* (Lond.,
1922).

[3] G. Elliot Smith, *The Migrations of Early Culture* (Manchester, 1915), *Human
History* (Lond., 1930). W. J. Perry, *Children of the Sun* (Lond., 1926), 2nd edition
Growth of Civilization (Lond., 1924). C. Daryll Forde *Ancient Mariners* (Lond., 1927).

[4] Hocart, *Kingship,* p. 143.

the aborigines of Australia who are unacquainted with agriculture, domestication of animals (except the dog), pottery-making, weaving, metal-working, and the erection of permanent houses, do not reflect the conditions that prevailed at the threshold of the human race, at least they have preserved many of the features that characterized the prehistoric past. The mere fact that this type of culture is essentially stagnant and inclined to retrogression, as the British school of diffusionists insists, suggests the probability that in thought and faith it has not moved far from its original moorings. In this sense it may be reasonably described as 'primitive'.

When we pass from the food-gathering to the food-producing stage of human development civilization may be said to have begun, and the centre in which this epoch-making event occurred is unquestionably the region known as the Ancient East.[1] In the fourth millennium B.C. (*c.* 3400) agriculture was in operation in the valleys of the Nile and the Euphrates, and gave rise to a new type of culture which spread rapidly through Anatolia to Cyprus, Crete and the Aegean region, penetrating Thrace, Macedonia and the Mediterranean littoral, while another stream passed up the Danube to Central Europe, eventually reaching Britain by way of the Rhine and Elbe.[2] The eastern Mediterranean appears to have been the nursery for navigation, and was well adapted for the purpose both as regards its relatively calm waters free from tidal currents and the nature of its shores,[3] just as the banks of the Danube and the lakesides in Switzerland became the home of peaceful farmers. Perhaps only the more venturesome spirits passed through the Straits of Gibraltar to negotiate the mighty waves of the ocean in their frail craft, but the civilization that flourished in Spain and Brittany, Britain and Ireland, Holland and Scandinavia apparently owed its origin to immigrants from the Ancient East, whatever may have been the quest of the ancient mariners. Moreover, it is now becoming clear in the light of recent excavations at Mohenjo-daro and Harappa in the Indus valley, that there was an easterly cultural drift which was responsible for the introduction of a pre-Aryan

[1] Perhaps the earliest phases of agriculture occured in the fertile oases of Western Asia from 8000 to 6000 B.C. cf. R. E. M. Wheeler, *Antiquity,* 1956. pp. 132 ff.

[2] G. Childe, *New Light on the Most Ancient East* (Lond., 1934). *The Dawn of European Civilization* (Lond., 1925). *The Danube in Prehistory* (Oxford, 1929). cf. Peake and Fleure, *Corridors of Time,* Parts III and IV (Oxford, 1927).

[3] cf. J. H. Rose, *The Mediterranean in the Ancient World* (Camb., 1934), pp. 3 ff.

civilization in north-west India having contacts with Mesopotamia and Elam.[1]

While it is theoretically possible to account for this distribution of food-producing civilization as a spontaneous growth independently evolved in each separate area, as Professor Gordon Childe says,

> practically, in the case of the Old World where the first metal-using civilizations had such wide foreign relations and were bound together by so many common traits, no one, unprejudiced by the passions evoked by a perverse diffusionism, will suggest that all the complex processes involved were elaborated separately at two or more comparatively adjacent points in Eurasia. Really the question resolves itself into one of the comparative claims of Egypt and the Asiatic cultural province designed 'prediluvian'.[2]

Granting that the human mind reacts in a similar manner to a stable or changing environment, or even that certain innate elementary ideas exist which are due to the uniformity of mental constitution, it is an indisputable fact, as Professor Karsten affirms, that 'the various human races have borrowed from each other many of their beliefs, customs, arts and crafts'.[3] Thus, for example, while the religions of Egypt, Mesopotamia, Palestine and the Aegean differed widely in many respects, each developing its own peculiar traits, collectively they possessed certain fundamental characteristics suggestive of a common pattern of myth and ritual centring in a particular attitude to the king in the community. Furthermore, as Sir Ernest Budge remarks, 'the similarity between the two companies of gods in Egypt and Sumer are too close to be accidental'. In his opinion, 'it would be wrong to say that the Sumerians borrowed from the Egyptians, or the Egyptians from the Sumerians, but it may be submitted that the litterati of both peoples borrowed their theological systems from some common but exceedingly ancient source'.[4] The question of origins is usually more difficult to determine than that of diffusion in a given area, and at present the evidence is insufficient to settle the relative claims of Egypt and Higher Asia as the common centre of the spread of

[1] J. Marshall, *Mohenjo-Daro and the Indus Civilization* (Lond., 1931).
[2] *The Bronze Age* (Camb., 1930), p. 24.
[3] *The Origins of Religion* (Lond., 1935), p. 7.
[4] *From Fetish to God in Ancient Egypt* (Oxford, 1934), p. 155.

the basic ideas upon which civilization and its earliest magico-religious systems are founded. But it is in the Ancient East of the fourth millennium B.C. that the cradleland and region of characterization must be sought.

THE RISE OF THE WORLD RELIGIONS

Arising out of this new cultural movement a ritual order was established as the consolidating force and dynamic of the agricultural and urban communities which constituted the first phase of civilized society. The cycle of seed-time and harvest, and the associated operations, were brought into the closest relation with the supernatural sanctions controlling the processes of vegetation and fertility, and only so long as man lived in harmony with the cosmic powers was his well-being secured. Around this central religious idea material culture was built up, till in the second half of the third millennium B.C. a period of decline began out of which eventually emerged a new cultural movement by a remarkable change in thought and outlook. From the Mediterranean to Persia, India and China in the first millennium B.C. ideas began to take shape of a God rising out of Nature and transcending it, of a moral purpose and a moral order. The ancient ritual organization remained in the background, and still dominated the structure of society and religious cultus, but prophetic intuition, philosophic speculation and mystical experience penetrated beyond the continual flux of the phenomenal world and its processes to an unchanging Reality. Many and various were the ways followed and the means adopted, as we shall see, by those who set out in quest of the ultimate cosmic principle, or the sole Creator and Sustainer of the universe, but whether it be along the path of Orphic mysticism, of Platonic philosophy, of Zoroastrian dualism, of Oriental pantheism, or Hebrew ethical monotheism, in each and every case it was a spiritual goal that was sought. Out of this revolution the world religions arose and continue to this day.

The remarkable achievement was largely the work of certain individuals possessed of outstanding gifts of leadership, and either a deep spiritual insight or a profound philosophical understanding which enabled them to pursue a path which more and more prepared the way for the break-up of polytheism as a possible belief for thoughtful and religiously-minded men. Nevertheless, they were essentially the products of their own age, and debtors to the general progress of civilization and knowledge that made possible the emergence. Thus, for example, in Greece, the material unity— water, air, fire—proclaimed by the Ionian scientists, the logical unity asserted by Parmenides, the pupil of Xenophanes, the deistic unity asserted by Anaxagoras, all alike attest a disposition which could not rest content with pluralism, and either ignored the evidence of the Many or else relegated it to the sphere of unreality and opinion. In this atmosphere we are far removed from the Olympian theology of Homeric mythology: the problem of Being has ousted the problem of the gods: even in Anaxagoras the Mind which ordered Chaos in the beginning has no role in things to play. It remained for the genius of Plato to give expression, first in the *Republic* and its correlative dialogues, later with greater precision and critical analysis in the *Timaeus* and the *Laws*, to a philosophical monotheism, and to gather up into all that the poetical imagination, moral earnestness, and metaphysical subtlety which his predecessors had portended.

Or, again, in India the new type of religion that found expression in the Upanishads, according to which man realized his end by the identification of his true self with the Supreme Self of the universe, was the work of many thinkers, who, while they broke away from the old paths and made others for the emancipation of their disciples, started from the Vedic concept of 'Brahma'. This term which formerly meant 'prayer', 'sacred utterance', 'divine knowledge', was associated with one pantheistic principle so that all the gods of the Veda came to be regarded as manifestations of the one Power at the heart of the world, absolute, infinite, eternal, omnipresent and impersonal, with which the human spirit is merged. Henceforth, amid all the various currents and cross-currents of religious tendency that prevailed in India between 800 and 600 B.C., the immanence of God in the universe became an axiom, and thought moved in the direction of monistic idealism, despite polytheistic and pluralistic deviations. In an atmosphere heavy with the burden of its heat, and morbid with its weariness, men's minds were inclined to spend themselves in over-subtlety of speculation, and Jainism and Buddhism represent revolts against the complexity of the current tradition. Both are really merely phases of a long Hindu development dominated by the speculations of the Upanishads as they had passed through the minds of their respective founders and their followers.

In Buddhism the ethical tendencies of the new movement of religious thought reached their height in world-renunciation and nihilism. In China, however, it reappeared in the form of Taoist quietism under the guidance of Lao-tze, with the same pantheistic strain, in contrast to the ethical positivism of Confucius. Both these leaders of thought, though diametrically opposed to one another, in their turn made their appeal to certain fundamental qualities in the existing mentality, culture and religious outlook. To one section of the community the universal order appeared as a metaphysical and transcendental concept (*Tao*); to the other as the principle of moral and social conduct, the ethics of a dignified aristocracy with a long-established lineage.

Similarly in Palestine, behind the Hebrew prophets lay the cultural background of Israel, so that Amos, Hosea and Jeremiah in the eighth and seventh centuries B.C. represented the period of Moses in the desert as the Golden Age in the nation's history, while the post-exilic community rested its theocratic priestly organization on the same foundations. But unlike the Greek philosophers and the Indo-European mystics, the pre-exilic religious leaders in Israel were in opposition to the indigenous culture of the land their forefathers had occupied, and in their endeavours to establish ethical monotheism they were compelled to maintain a hostile attitude to ritual in every form, including sacrificial worship and seasonal festivals, so that Jeremiah even rejected the Temple cultus at Jerusalem, and the ark of Yahweh. But they never ceased to see in the vicissitudes of their national history a divine process working towards specific ends, and when a complete break with the past had been made by the Exile, the priestly school were able to restore the worship of the Temple in its fullness as the dynamic centre of the religious life of the nation till it was finally destroyed in A.D. 70.

It was out of the welter of religious movements, Jewish and pagan, that Christianity arose, and if Christ was represented as the emergence of the divine on the plane of history, the Head of a restored humanity, and the first-born of a new creation, it was as the fulfilment of the hopes of Israel that He was either accepted or rejected in His own day and generation. Similarly, the society that arose to perpetuate His claims regarded itself in the first instance as the fulfilment of the promises made to Israel during its chequered career as the chosen nation of God. Again, it was essentially a social Gospel which found expression eventually in a Church-State as visualized by St Augustine and Hildebrand, in which spiritual values and realities constituted the dynamic. Henceforth European culture was dominated by a religious tradition till new forces arose in the fifteenth century which subsequently gave rise to Humanism and the modern secularization and mechanization of civilization.

THE FUNCTION OF RELIGION

Throughout the whole of this complex process of development which we have to examine in some detail in the forthcoming pages, religion can only be rightly understood if it is placed in its proper cultural setting and viewed as the spiritual force holding society together and growing out of the necessities of life. By assigning man his place in the universe, supplying him with a means of making contact with and deriving strength from its ultimate realities, which determine his destinies, it provides a system of values relative to the fundamental requirements of the individual and the community. At every crisis, personal or collective, it is called in aid to prevent disintegration, strengthen the bonds of human cohesion and co-operation, and sanctify human life and conduct. Consequently, when supernatural sanctions are removed disintegration invariably results.

Since religion is primarily the expression of the forces by which human groups maintain their solidarity and ensure thereby their continuity as well as their unity, it follows, as Professors Malinowski and Radcliffe Brown insist,[1] that attention should be focused on the function which every custom and belief, like every material object of human design, fulfils within the social structure of which it is an indispensable part. 'The function of any recurrent activity is the part it plays in the social life as a whole, and therefore the contribution it makes to the maintenance of the structural

[1] cf. Malinowski, *The Sexual Life of Savages in North-Western Melanesia* (Lond., 1932), pp. xxviii ff. *Encyclopaedia of the Social Sciences* (1931), vol. IV, pp. 641 ff. A. R. Brown, *British Association Report,* 1931, pp. 145 ff.

continuity.'[1] Historical and psychological factors are relevant inasmuch as they determine conditions, and the associations and connexions of events are in the past as much as in the present,[2] but if the study of the age-long quest of the immortal spirit cannot be confined to any one phase of culture or period of time, neither can it be cut off from the social order of which it is an integral part, from the emotions in which it is grounded, or the necessities of life out of which it grows.

[1] A. R. Brown, *American Anthropologist*, XXXVII, 1935, p. 396.

[2] Lessing, op. cit., p. 390.

CHAPTER I

Religious Origins

In an article in the *Fortnighly Review* in 1866, the year after the publication of *The Researches into the Early History of Mankind*, Tylor made the first attempt to investigate the problem of religious origins in the light of the anthropological data. In determining the part played by images in primitive worship he came to the conclusion that idols obtained their sanctity from the fact that they were regarded as animated by a human soul or divine spirit, and, therefore, were magically efficacious. Furthermore, they enabled man to give a definite existence and a personality to the vague ideas of higher beings which his mind can hardly grasp without some material aid.

ANIMISM

In this article he employed the word 'animism' to describe 'the theory which endows the phenomena of nature with personal life'.[1] In opposition to the German philologists of the school of Adalbert Kuhn and Max Müller, who sought to discover the origin of religion by an etymological analysis of the names of gods in Aryan mythology, Tylor argued that it is not the language that need be called in to explain how the sun, rain or a river were conceived of as animated beings. 'The simple anthropological view is itself', he claimed, 'the fundamental principle of mythology, and while it concerns itself with such visible, palpable, active, individual objects as these, language only needs to accompany and express it.' Similarly, the term 'fetishism', which Comte, following Ch. de Brosses, had adapted to denote the idea of 'all external bodies as animated by a life analogous to his own, with differences of mere intensity', was 'utterly inappropriate and misleading' as a

[1] *Fortnightly Review*, VI, 1866, p. 84.

description of the animistic hypothesis since it was restricted to objects used in witchcraft by sorcerers wrongly regarded as idols.[1]

Having thus opened the discussion, in *Primitive Culture* he endeavoured to establish the 'belief in spiritual beings' as 'the minimum definition of religion'. Men everywhere distinguish the human soul from the body, he contended, and by analogy project their own personality into the order of nature. Therefore, beginning with the soul, the whole complex phenomenon of religion can be explained as a process of evolution and growth in conception of personality, human and divine. In its full development animism includes belief in souls and in a future state, in controlling gods and subordinate spirits, these doctrines practically resulting in some kind of active worship. 'The ancient philosophers probably took the first step', it is suggested, 'by the obvious inference that every man has two things belonging to him, namely a life and a phantom.' These two are evidently in close connexion with the body, the life enabling it to feel and think and act, the phantom as being its image and second self; both, also, are perceived to be things separable from the body, the life as able to go away and leave it insensible or dead, the phantom as appearing to people at a distance from it. The second step, which is said to be also easy for savages to make, consists in the combination of the life and the phantom.

In this way the conception of the *anima*, or ghost-soul, is supposed to have arisen as a separable vital principle with a form of its own—

> a thin substantial human image, in its nature a sort of vapour, film or shadow; the cause of life and thought in the individual it animates; independently possessing the personal consciousness and volition of its corporeal owner, past or present; capable of leaving the body far behind, to flash swiftly from place to place; mostly impalpable and invisible, yet also manifesting physical power, and especially appearing to men waking or asleep as a phantom separate from the body of which it bears the likeness; continuing to exist and appear to men after the death of that body; able to enter into, possess, and act in the bodies of other men, of animals, and even of things.[2]

Similarly, 'the sun and stars, trees, rivers, winds and clouds became personal animate creatures, leading lives conformed to human

[1] op. cit., pp. 81, 84.
[2] *Primitive Culture,* vol. I, pp. 428 f.

or animal analogies and performing their special functions in the universe with the aid of limbs like beasts or of artificial instruments like men'.[1] In this way Tylor and his distinguished disciple Sir James Frazer, peopled the world with a multitude of individual spirits in 'every nook and hill, every tree and flower, every brook and river, every breeze that blew and every cloud that flecked with silvery white and blue expanse of heaven'. From this unlimited number of indwelling spirits a limited pantheon of deities emerged, believed to control the various departments of nature. 'Instead of a separate spirit for every individual tree, they came to conceive of a god of the woods in general, a Silvanus or what not; instead of personifying all the winds as gods, each with his distinct character and features, they imagined a single god of the winds, an Aeolus, for example, who kept them shut up in bags and could let them out at pleasure to lash the sea into fury.' By a further generalization 'the instinctive craving of the mind after simplification and unification of its ideas', as polytheism had evolved out of animism, the many gods were deposed in favour of one supreme deity, the maker and controller of all things, as polytheism passed into monotheism.[2]

ANCESTOR-WORSHIP

On the same animistic stratum Herbert Spencer rested his ghost theory in the belief that the idea of God and religion as a whole could be derived from the propitiation of the other-self of distinguished ancestors. In a sense, however, he made animism derivative rather than original, inasmuch as it represents a generalized form of the conception of the spirits of dead ancestors associated with certain natural objects.

Anything which transcends the ordinary a savage thinks of as supernatural or divine; the remarkable man among the rest. This remarkable man may be simply the remotest ancestor remembered as the founder of the tribe; he may be a chief famed for strength and bravery; he may be a medicine-man of great repute; he may be an inventor of something new. And then, instead of being a member of the tribe, he may be a superior stranger bringing arts and knowledge; or he may be one of a superior race predominating by conquest. Being at first one or other of

[1] op. cit., p. 427.
[2] Frazer, *The Worship of Nature* (Lond., 1926), pp. 9 f.

these, regarded with awe during his life, he is regarded with increased awe after his death; and the propitiation of his ghost, becoming greater than the propitiation of ghosts which are less feared, develops into an established worship.

There is no exception, then. Using the phrase ancestor-worship in its broadest sense as comprehending all worship of the dead, be they of the same blood or not, we reach the conclusion that ancestor-worship is the root of every religion.[1]

This far-reaching hypothesis, like that of the development of monotheism from animism, was in line with the evolutionary thought of the last century, and gained a considerable measure of recognition though actually it was merely the re-statement of the Greek philosopher Euhemeros (320–260 B.C.) who urged that the gods originally were distinguished warriors or benefactors venerated as deities after death. But ancestor-worship is too narrow a basis on which to erect a theory of religious origins, and like all animistic conceptions, is really a rudimentary philosophy rather than the beginnings of religion itself. This indeed Tylor recognized in the case of animism which he describes as 'the groundwork of the philosophy of religion, from that of savages up to that of civilized men'.[2]

ANIMATISM

As Dr Marett has pointed out, 'savage religion is something not so much thought out as danced out, that, in other words, it develops under conditions, psychological and sociological, which favour emotional or motor processes, whereas ideation remains relatively in abeyance.'[3] Belief in spirits and separable souls implies a realization of personality, a conceptual attitude, which hardly can have arisen till the individual became conscious of himself as a human being. Behind these philosophizings there is a more fundamental reaction of which animism, theism, ancestor-worship and similar beliefs are specialized and intellectualized interpretations.

If it is not possible to establish a preanimistic stage at the threshold of religion in the chronological sense, it is nevertheless true that

[1] *Principles of Sociology* (Lond., 1885), 3rd ed. vol. I, p. 411.
[2] op. cit., pp. 426 f.
[3] *Threshold of Religion* (Lond., 1914), p. xxxi.

rudimentary religion is 'at once a wider and in certain respects a vaguer thing than "the belief in spiritual beings"'.[1] Before man began to speculate about dreams and visions, and formulate ideas concerning heroes and ancestors, he appears to have been aroused by deeper emotions in the presence of inexplicable and awe-inspiring phenomena. Whether or not this 'animatistic' reaction be associated with the widespread notion of a mystic impersonal force connected with mysterious persons, objects and situations, variously called *mana* by some Melanesians, *orenda, wakan, manitu* by certain North-American Indians, *arungquiltha* among the Central tribes of Australia, and *baraka* in Morocco, the type of experience which finds expression in religious behaviour belongs essentially to the realms of the sacred. Religion as such, independent of any particular theoretical, philosophical or theological interpretations, evaluations and cult elaborations, is primarily *a recognition of a sacred order of reality which transcends the ordinary and commonplace and is responsive to human needs.* To enable man to gain some measure of control over the unpredictable and inexplicable elements in his everyday experience, a technique has been devised with which certain beliefs have become associated, to establish an efficacious relationship with the sacred. Thus have arisen myth and ritual.

In a primitive state of culture the entire magico-religious equipment is directed primarily to certain specific ends concerned with urgent problems connected with the particular nature of the environment and circumstances of daily life consequent upon the limitations of human knowledge respecting cause and effect. Any inexplicable occurrences which arrests attention tends to be attributed to supernatural agencies and influences imperceptible to sense but tremendously real and operative in fact, regarded with awe and respect as partaking of sacredness and mystery. Thus, birth, puberty, marriage and death, the sowing of the crops and the ingathering of harvest, or plague, pestilence, famine, drought and similar misfortunes, are the occasions of elaborate rites and festivals having as their purpose the driving away of evil and the promotion of health, wealth and prosperity.

In every community there are a few deeply religious people who are capable of first-hand spiritual experience independent of the traditional channels, but in the case of the majority it is only at those

[1] op. cit., p. viii.

critical junctures in their private or public life that religious reactions
are aroused to an appreciable extent. Thus, startling phenomena
such as thunder and lightning, volcanoes or peculiar mountains or
trees, curiously shaped rocks, bubbling streams, strange animals or
herbs, tend to be regarded as sacred, and not to be lightly approached (i.e. taboo). To the same category belong dead bodies,
dwarfs and deformed persons, chiefs and kings, powerful medicine-
men and priests, and those who have come in contact with a source
of sacredness, e.g. mourners, women in childbirth and their atten-
dants, a newly-born infant, an adolescent at the time of initiation,
or a bride.

THE CONCEPT OF 'THE NUMINOUS'

Something more than fear is involved, however, in this attitude
towards the abnormal, uncanny, or mysterious, because this emotion is too negative to call forth a positive response in an elaborate
protective cultus frequently destined to become a permanent institution, and assimilate to itself fresh elements of human experience.
But before anything can be venerated as an object of worship it
must acquire a religious significance, that is to say, condition
religious behaviour. Now according to Otto religion is a category
sui generis, like beauty, truth, and goodness, not reducible to any
ordinary intellectual or rational 'knowing'; a 'unique original
feeling-reponse, which can be in itself ethically neutral and claims
consideration in its own right'. To this purely religious state of
mind he applies the term 'numinous'[1] and equates it with the
recognition of a 'Something, whose character may at first seem to
have little connexion with our ordinary moral terms, but which
later becomes charged with the highest and deepest moral significance'. The nature of this 'Something' is only gradually learned,
but from the beginning it is felt as a transcendent presence standing
over against the individual self-consciousness—the feeling that there
is another out beyond human consciousness, even when it is also
felt as 'the within' man. In its presence the sense of 'creatureliness'
is produced, of 'self-abasement into nothingness before an over-
powering, absolute might of some kind'. But this *mysterium tre-*

---

[1] In the cult of ancient Rome the *numen* was an undistinguished supernatural power
hardly personal at all, though it called forth the emotion of awe and *religio* (taboo).
Therefore, as 'omen' has given us 'ominous' so 'numen' becomes 'numinous'.

mendum as over-powering mystery has also within it the element of 'fascination', and so draws men towards it in mystical experience and communion. 'The daemonic divine object may appear to the mind an object of horror and dread, but at the same time it is no less than something that allures with a potent charm, and the creature who trembles before it, utterly cowed and cast down, has always at the same time the impulse to turn to it, nay even to make it somehow his own.'[1]

As the 'tremendum' develops concrete forms emerge as 'numen loci', el, baal and the like, and become the centres of worship, arousing in their devotees the numinous attitude of mind which finds expression in the cry 'how dreadful is this place'. In this way a rationalized cultus arises in connexion with localized sanctuaries, and animistic and theistic systems of theology. But 'all ostensible explanations of the origin of religion in terms of animism or magic or folk psychology are doomed from the outset to wander astray and miss the goal of their inquiry' unless they recognize 'the basic impulse underlying the entire process of religious evolution—primary, unique, underivable from anything else'.[2]

To make the numinous state of mind irreducible to any other is, however, to eliminate the psychological conditions that call it into being. Actually it is not an 'unnamed Something' which stimulates the reaction to the mysterious, but anything that is uncanny, abnormal, awe-inspiring and beyond human control. Such an object or event appears to the primitive mind to belong to an order of reality outside its limited range of experience and understanding, and therefore to be approached with caution and reverence. But the domain of the sacred is neither 'wholly other' nor 'non-rational'. If it were completely transcendent it would not be within the reach of man at all, and consequently it would be useless to attempt to establish beneficial relations with it which is the essential aim of the religious reaction.

Again, if a supra-rational evaluation is given to that which cannot be grasped by ordinary processes of reasoning and controlled by empirical methods, it does not follow that the numinous is non-rational unless the term 'rational' be restricted to conceptual thinking. The religious thought of Plato according to Otto is non-rational

[1] *The Idea of the Holy* (Oxford, 1928), pp. xvi, 7, 15 ff., 31 ff., 228 ff.
[2] op. cit., p. 6.

because the objects of religion are grasped by the 'ideograms of myth, by enthusiams or inspiration, "eros" or love, "mania" or the divine frenzy', not by conceptual thinking.[1] But intuition cannot be opposed to intelligence in any valid theory of knowledge, and the intuitions of religion, though in their original strivings they may be incapable of description in intellectual terms, spring from the intellect no less than those of art or poetry. As Otto himself admits, these beliefs and feelings are 'peculiar interpretations and valuations at first of perceptual data, and then—at a higher level—of posited objects and entities, which themselves no longer belong to the perceptual world, but are thought of as supplementing and transcending it'.[2] The numinous, in short, must become articulate to produce religious behaviour, and it is difficult to understand how it could ever be clothed with intelligible ideas if it were strictly non-rational. On his hypothesis 'non-rational knowing' is practically self-contradiction and his use of 'cognitive' and 'reason' results in a confusion of the primary psychological categories, just as Kant's schematism, to which he appeals, involved an abstraction which rendered impossible the middle term to connect universal categories with sense-data.

So far as our knowledge of primitive reactions to the sacred bears upon this analysis of the primal contents of religious experience, no support is given to the theory of a non-rational numinous faculty, a state of mind perfectly *sui generis* and irreducible to any other. The awareness of mystery is not confined to the religious consciousness since not all baffling situations or uncanny objects produce this effect. Furthermore, something more than 'a feeling of dependence', as Schleiermacher supposed, is required to account for the reaction. The sense of awe and reverence must awaken the realization of a relationship with an 'other than itself' responsive to man's needs; a 'beyond which is within' and around and above. Moreover, this conception of sacredness must be brought into association with the facts and requirements of everyday life and experience to become articulate and given a religious evaluation.

LIFE VALUES AND ECONOMIC DETERMINANTS

Faith and practice in primitive society are always definitely connected with the preservation of life values. Thus, as Dr Radin points

[1] op. cit., p. 98. 　　　[2] op. cit., p. 117.

out, among the Winnebago Indians, religion is not a phenomenon distinct from mundane affairs, but

> one of the most important means of maintaining social ideals. What these are can be gleaned from practically every prayer; they are success, happiness, and long life. The vast majority of investigators are often surprised at the intense religious life which, among the North American Indians, exists side by side with an intense realism and a clear understanding and appreciation of the materialistic basis of life. The explanation, to judge from the Winnebago data, is simple enough. The Indian does not interpret life in terms of religion, but religion in terms of life. In other words, he exalts the world around him and the multifarious desires and necessities of the day, so that they appear to him bathed in a religious thrill. At least that is what the devoutly religious man does, and most of the religious data presented in this volume emanates from him.[1]

If religion grows out of the necessities of human experience and the continuity of the race, the scientific study of the phenomenon involves an analysis of the situations in which it takes its rise. Everywhere and at all times food and children are the two chief concerns of a primitive community. 'To live and to cause to live, to eat food and beget children, these are the primary wants of man in the past, and they will be the primary wants of man in the future so long as the world lasts.'[2] Thus, the primitive religious impulse seems to be directed primarily to one end, viz. the conservation and promotion of life so that the good is food and fertility, and evil is hunger and barrenness.[3] It was this urge doubtless that led the Aurignacians in palaeolithic times to fashion female figures with the maternal organs grossly exaggerated, as in the statues of the Mother Goddess in Crete, the Aegean, Malta, Egypt and Western Asia. At first, in fact, the Great Mother may have been little more than a life-giving amulet in the form of a cowrie-shell with only vaguely defined life-giving traits; a symbol which Elliot Smith would have us believe was probably 'the first deity that the wit of man devised to console him with her watchful care over his welfare in this life, and to give him assurance as to his fate in the future'.[4]

---

[1] 37th *Report of the Bureau of American Ethnology,* p. 278.

[2] Frazer, *Golden Bough,* pt. IV ('Adonis', I), p. 5.

[3] J. Harrison, *Epilegomena to the Study of Greek Religion* (Camb., 1921), p. 1. *Themis* (Camb., 1912), pp. 139, 280.

[4] *The Evolution of the Dragon* (Manchester, 1919), pp. 143, 150 f.

SEX AND REPRESSION

If this can hardly be regarded as an adequate basis of the idea of God, propagation and the production and maintenance of the food supply have been the two vital concerns of man and, therefore, integral elements in religion and magic throughout the ages. Religion, however, is not based upon the sex instinct, be it in the form of a mother symbol or, as the psycho-analytical school imagines, in a hypothetical Oedipus complex. There is no anthropological evidence for 'a dislocation in the family life of the primitive horde' as a result of the sex urge, the sons slaying their father in order to secure the women for themselves, and then inventing a ritual device to expiate and commemorate their crime.[1] If a 'primal state of society' ever existed characterized by a 'father horde' in contrast to a 'son horde' of expelled bachelors, at least no traces have been left of its occurrence in any known state of culture, and it has yet to be shown that religion in practice is an attempt on the part of the individual to be reconciled with his infantile father image. Actually sex *quâ* sex plays an insignificant part in the practice of religion,[2] for while sexual symbolism abounds in myth and ritual and ceremonial licence is prominent at seasonal festivals, both are directed primarily to specific ends, viz. the promotion and conservation of life, not the satisfaction of repressed erotic desires. Religion, in fact, has always endeavoured to exercise a regulative control over the instinct of sex by means of the elaborate system of taboos and sanctions with which it has controlled relationships within the kinship group, and inculcated within given limits the virtue of chastity.

THE CONTROL OF THE FOOD SUPPLY

The main link between man and his environment is food, and, as Professor Malinowski says, 'by receiving it he feels the forces of destiny and providence'.[3] Dependent as he is in a primitive state of culture on the precarious resources at his disposal, the maintenance of an adequate supply of the necessities of life is an ever-present

[1] Freud, *Totem and Taboo* (New York, 1918).

[2] cf. Malinowski, *Sex and Repression in Savage Society* (Lond., 1927).

[3] Malinowski, *Science, Religion and Reality* (Lond., 1927), p. 42.

problem taxing to the utmost his ingenuity at every turn and creating an intense emotional situation. Hence the prominence given to
this aspect of the struggle for existence in the round of fast and
festival and in myth and ritual. To eat is to live, and since it is to a
beneficent providence that man looks for his 'daily bread', it be-
hoves him to be at one with the powers and forces controlling the
supply. But food is not usually sent down from the heavens to be
collected at will, like the manna in the desert. In the natural order
the Pauline precept obtains: 'If a man will not work neither shall
he eat.' Consequently, to partake of providential bounty hunting,
fishing, the cultivation of crops and the domestication of animals
play an integral part, and when economic insecurity prevails it is
these operations which are given a magico-religious significance.

Thus, for example, when Palaeolithic man went on a hunting
expedition he was not content apparently to trust solely in his own
prowess and skill, great as these may have been. To re-enforce his
own efforts with supernatural power he (or possibly one of his
fellows adept in the magic art) appears to have resorted to the inner
recesses of a sacred cave where figures of the animals sought were
drawn and marked with spear-heads in the neighbourhood of the
heart, or, as at Niaux in Ariège, depicted in the act of dying. This
was thought to bring success to the chase by reason of the spell cast
upon the species, on the principle that 'like produces like'. Furthermore, in addition to these simple magical devices, it would seem
that on occasions more elaborate rites were performed, as, for
instance, in the cavern called Les Trois Frères near St Girons in the
French Pyrenees, where in a small alcove amid an array of engrav-
ings, a figure known as 'the Sorcerer' has been found. Probably this
represents a man clothed in an animal disguise so that the head was
hidden under a mask with a long beard and great antlers, while a
horse's tail was attached in the rear of the skin covering the rest of
the body. In front of the figure is a balcony where possibly an
audience assembled to witness the rite.[1] Similar masked dancers
occur in other Palaeolithic sites, such as those at Lourdes, Abri
Mège, Marsoulas, Tuc d'Audoubert and Mas d'Azil, pointing to
an established cult in which instead of a mimic slaying by magical
means, animal-headed men sought to become *en rapport* with the

[1] Luquet, *The Art and Religion of Fossil Man* (Oxford, 1930), pp. 96 ff. Burkitt, *Our
Forefathers* (Lond., 1924), pp. 208 ff. *Prehistory* (Camb., 1925), pp. 192 ff.

creatures by masks, gestures and dances in order to make them fruitful and multiply, very much as American Indians believe that fertility is promoted by similar ceremonies in caverns decorated with mythological animals.[1] Or, again, in Central Australia the men of the kangaroo totem in the Arunta tribe repair to certain rocks which they believe to be full of the spirits of kangaroos awaiting reincarnation in kangaroo bodies. These they decorate with vertical stripes of red and white to indicate the red fur and white bones of the kangaroo. Young men then sit on a ledge, open veins in their arms and allow the blood to fall over the edge of the rock on which they are seated to drive out the spirits of kangaroos in all directions, and so to increase the number of the animals. Meanwhile other men sit below watching the performance and sing songs about the multiplication of the species.[2]

In rites of this nature the intention is the reproduction rather than the hunting or collection of the sources of supply. Thus, to take another example from Central Australia, before the beginning of the rains the men of the witchetty grub totem leave the camp early, taking care not to be seen by any who do not belong to the food group. Surreptitiously they make their way one by one to Emily Gap near Alice Springs, a district associated with the ancestors who in the *Alcheringa,* or dream-time of long ago, produced a shallow cave high up on the western wall of the ravine containing a large block of quartzite surrounded by small stones. These represent the *maegwa,* or fully-developed witchetty grub, and its eggs. On the rock face on the western side of the Gap there are sacred drawings which it is said were originally placed there by Numbakulla, the First Creator, during his wanderings over the country, 'making' it and settling the sacred places. When the company has duly assembled, appropriate songs are sung inviting the grub to lay eggs, and the stones are tapped with the twigs the men are carrying. The leader then takes up one of the smaller stones, called *churinga unchima,* and says, 'You have eaten much food', as he rubs the stomach of each man with it. Despite the fact that actually they have eaten nothing this formula is repeated over and over again at some of the other sacred spots, the aim of the rites being to produce abundance symbolized and ritually expressed by the notion of much food.

[1] Bourke, *Folk-lore, II,* 1891, p. 438. *9th R.B.A.E.* (1892), pp. xliii f.
[2] *Natives Tribes of Central Australia* (Lond., 1899), pp. 193 ff., 199 ff., 206 ff.

On the way back to the camp, a halt is made before entering for
the party to decorate themselves with the sacred designs of the
totem, hair-strings, nose-bones, bunches of feathers and twigs of
the Udniringa bush. A long narrow structure of branches having
been set up during their absence to represent the chrysalis stage of
the grub, the performers enter it while the men and women of the
other moieties in three groups lie face downwards outside till they
are told to arise. Those inside sing of the insect in its various stages,
of the stone and the great *maegwa* at its base. Then they shuffle out
in a squatting posture singing of the emergence of the creature from
the chrysalis. This is thought to produce the multiplication of the
grubs. The performers now break their fast by receiving food and
water inside the hut brought to them by the old man who erected
the wurley. At dusk they all leave their retreat, a large fire is lighted,
and around it they sit till daybreak singing of the witchetty grub,
while the women of the right moiety keep watch to see that their
sisters of the other moiety continue to lie down, peering about as
did the women in the Alcheringa. Suddenly the singing ceases, the
fire is quickly extinguished by the leader, the men of the other
moiety of the tribe spring to their feet and run away to the main
camp. The section engaged in the *Intichiuma* (food-producing)
ceremony remains at the hut till daybreak, when the men strip
themselves of their ornaments and throw away the twigs. The
leader then exlaims, 'Our Intichiuma is finished, the *Mulyanuka*
(men of the other moiety) must have these things or else our Intichiuma would not be successful, and some harm would happen to
us.' They all reply, 'Yes, yes, certainly.' The ornaments are then
handed over to the Mulyanuka, the sacred designs and paintings on
the face are obliterated by rubbing red ochre over the bodies of the
performers, and having put on their arm-strings and other ornaments, they return to their respective camps.[1]

The aim of these ceremonies is clearly to exercise a magico-
religious control over the food supply by a dramatic representation
of the principal events in the sacred lore of the tribe or group, and
the repetition of the processes upon which its production is thought
to depend. The actions are made to suit the words and intentions
of the performers as the reincarnations of the ancestors, repeating

[1] Spencer and Gillen, *Native Tribes of Central Australia*, pp. 170 ff. *The Arunta*
(Lond., 1927), vol. I, pp. 148 ff.

what they are supposed to have done in the Alcheringa, when they lived on earth and 'gave the blackfellow all that he has'. As Spencer and Gillen point out, 'every prominent feature in the landscape of the Arunta country, whether it be a solitary mulga tree on a stony plain, a water-hole, a low ridge or high mountain peak, is associated with some *Knanja* or totem group'. Thus, for example,

> a gaunt old gum-tree, with a large projecting bole about the middle of the trunk, indicates the exact spot where an Alchera (Alcheringa) man, who was very full of eggs, arose when he was transformed out of a witchetty grub. When he died his spirit part remained behind along with his churinga[1] and used especially to frequent this tree, and therefore when that spirit went inside a woman of the local group and was reincarnated in the form of a man who died a few years ago, that special tree was the Knanja tree of that man.[2]

Since the natural environment is impregnated with the vital forces upon which the people depend for their sustenance, and the father of the present leader is regarded as the reincarnation of the great Alcheringa ancestor of the Witchetties who, with his companions, are represented by the sacred stones at Emily Gap, the intichiuma rites are essential to the maintenance of life. If they were not fully performed, fertility would cease.

TOTEMISM

In Australia, however, this supernatural economic system is organized on a totemic basis. Each tribe, that is to say, is divided into small social groups, or clans, descended from, or in some mystical alliance with, an animal or vegetable species or inanimate object, regarded as its sacred ally. So intimate is this association between the totem and the totemites that it constitutes a 'blood relationship'; the sharing of a common life-principle, so that all members of the same group are 'one flesh'. Therefore, they are forbidden to inter-marry, and are subject to various other taboos, including usually the eating of their ally, if it be an animal or plant. Consequently, since normally the clan itself is forbidden to partake of the totem except sacramentally on certain ceremonial occasions,

[1] The term *churinga* is applied by the Arunta to sacred stones or sticks, and certain objects such as bull-roarers associated with the totems.

[2] *The Arunta*, pp. 88, 327.

and then only sparingly, the performance of intichiuma rites, and their equivalents, in practice become part of a co-operative system by which each group promotes the fertility of its own sacred species on behalf of society as a whole; that is to say, for the benefit of its neighbours who may eat it freely.

Now this complex and altruistic organization can hardly be genuinely primitive in the sense of being rudimentary. Behind it doubtless lies a much more direct method of exercising supernatural control over the source of the food supply which has been brought into conjunction with a doctrine of reincarnation and economic social organization involving the practice of exogamy, or marrying outside the clan. The Australian evidence, in fact, coming into prominence as it did when a former generation of anthropologists were still inclined to over-emphasize the part played by totemism in religious origins, led astray Professor Durkheim and the French school of sociologists, as previously it had caused Robertson Smith to develop his theory of the 'theanthropic animal', at once god and kinsman as the originating cause of sacrifice.[1]

In 1886 J. G. Frazer was invited to write the article on Totemism for the Ninth Edition of the *Encyclopaedia Britannica* in which he suspended judgement on this derivation of animal sacrifice in general from a totem sacrament on the ground that no conclusive evidence was available of the custom of killing and eating the sacred ally as a ritual meal. But once the rite was discovered by Spencer and Gillen in Central Australia, he welcomed the discovery as a very striking proof of the sagacity of his brilliant friend who had anticipated conjecturally 'what it was reserved for subsequent research positively to ascertain'. Nevertheless, he recognized that from 'the practice of the rite by a single set of tribes it is still a long step to the universal practice of it by all totem tribes, and from that again it is a still longer stride to the deduction therefrom of animal sacrifice in general'. Of the universality of the institution he was not convinced, and he did not think either that sacrifice and the whole worship of plants and animals were derivatives from it, or that 'the cradle of totemism' was 'the cradle of humanity'.[2]

F. B. Jevons, on the other hand, maintained that 'in the most primitive form of society men were divided into clans or tribes;

[1] *Religion of the Semites* (Lond., 1903), p. 409.
[2] *G.B.,* pt. I, pp. xxii ff.

C

these tribes were usually hostile to one another, but might by means of the blood-covenant make alliance with one another', and enter into friendly relations with animal or vegetable allies. That a pre-totemic stage existed in human society he does not deny, but 'the nature of religious belief' that then obtained is 'entirely a matter of conjecture'.[1] As animals and plants are grouped into genera and species very much as men are organized in clans and families, an alliance between human kins and animal or vegetable species was readily formed, it is alleged, having the effect of making all the members of the two contracting parties blood-brothers. In this way all over the world society was constituted on a totemic basis, and 'probably every species of animal has been worshipped as a totem somewhere or other, at some time or other'. In consequence of the respect paid to them those animals which were capable of domesti-cation became gradually tame, and finally as totemism and the taboo on the flesh of the totem faded away, the habit of eating those domesticated animals which are good for food grew up gradually.[2] Similarly, food-plants originally adopted as totems and eaten only once a year ceremonially, were worshipped as sacred allies. Then the totem-god was conceived as having human shape; and at last the anthropomorphic god became so detached from the species that his origin was quite forgotten, the plant like the animal being merely sacred.[3] Traces of the original taboo, he thought, are to be found in the reluctance to eat the new corn until the rites have been performed with the first-fruits to make it safe for human consump-tion. Since the breeding of cattle and the cultivation of cereals made man dependent on the forces of nature, regarded as supernatural powers, he was led to worship them with the same ritual as he had 'worshipped his animal and plant totems'. In short, 'totemism, which is at least the worship of one god, declines into the worship of many gods', one people alone on the face of the earth having preserved 'this simple and amorphous monotheism', and developed it into 'something higher'. Everywhere else it 'degenerated into the grosser form of animal-worship'.[4]

This ingenious theory of the origin and development of religion is based so completely upon totemism that once these foundations

---

[1] *Introduction to the History of Religion* (Lond., 1896), p. 413.

[2] op. cit., p. 117.

[3] op. cit., p. 213. [4] op. cit., p. 395.

are undermined it falls to the ground. Moreover, as Frazer says, 'in pure totemism, such as we find it among the Australian aborigines, the totem is never a god and is never worshipped. A man no more worships his totem and regards it as his god than he worships his father and mother, his brother and his sister, and regards them as his gods'.[1] Totemism is essentially an institution through which a social group establishes an intimate relationship with the sacred regarded as a providential source of the food supply variously personified. Like ritual in general, it is a particular and specialized technique for controlling the forces of destiny which transcend his natural unaided powers, and call for reverential regard, coupled with a sense of kinship and affinity. Indeed, it is primarily a primitive system of economics governed by religious sanctions rooted in the desire to secure adequate means of sustenance for the community. That it is deeply laid in the history of the human race cannot be denied, but its absence among such very primitive peoples as the Veddas of Ceylon, the Punan of Borneo, the Andaman Islanders, the Pygmies of the Congo, the Bushmen of South Africa, and in the New World the clanless inhabitants of the north-west Pacific coast and the low Brazilian tribes shows that it is by no means universal in distribution, or a constant feature in the lowest cultures.

THE GROUP MIND

Equally untenable, therefore, is Durkheim's contention that religion is essentially the explanation of the idea of a mysterious impersonal force, or *mana*, controlling life, derived from the authority of society over the individual and concentrated in the totem as the visible emblem of this power. 'In a general way a society has all that is necessary to arouse the sensation of the divine in minds, merely by the power that it has over them; for to its members it is what a god is to his worshippers.' The totem, it is true, on this hypothesis, is not an anthropomorphic divine being approached by prayer and sacrifice, and the recipient of worship, because it is not an individual animal or plant that is regarded as the ally, but the species as a whole; that is to say, the life-principle permeating the entire group. It is at once the symbol of the god and of the society because the god and the society are one. 'The god of the clan, the totemic principle, can

[1] *Totemism and Exogamy*, vol. IV, p. 5.

therefore be nothing else than the clan itself, personified and represented to the imagination under the visible form of the animal or vegetable which serves as totem.'[1] Thus, what man really worships is society divinized, and since the totemic principle is the god of the clan, the totemic sign is the rallying-point of collective emotion.

In other words, religion is essentially a sociological phenomenon, 'a unified system of beliefs and practices relative to sacred things, that is to say, things set apart and forbidden—beliefs and practices which unite into one single moral community called a Church, all those who adhere to them'.[2] It is merely a subjective reflection of society; the expression of the forces by which a social group imposes its will upon the constituent units in just the same way as that imposed by the gods, to secure thereby its own continuance. But while it is true that religion functions as an integral element in the preservation of social structure, to make it only a symbolic representation of the organization and group consciousness of the community evades completely the objective validity of its beliefs in their cosmological character as apprehensions of a Reality transcending alike the human and the natural order.

As we have seen, the primitive mind reacts in a religious manner quite as readily to the mystery revealed in natural phenomena as to the stimuli within society, and it is certainly not correct to limit the practice of religion to the great seasonal ceremonies like Intichiuma marked by a social 'effervescence' out of which, according to Durkheim, 'the religious idea seems to be born'.[3] This is to overlook the numerous occasions in the career of individuals marked by *rites de passage* when the principal person frequently is required to retire in silence and solitude to make a 'private retreat' in the bush, where he undergoes a profound spiritual experience.

Behind these rites there are of course strong social sanctions, and the youth at his initiation is fitting himself for his life as a member of the adult community. But, nevertheless, he is acting as an individual and often receives some particular totemic name or sign during the process. Thus, among the Ibans of Borneo a secret helper, or *ngarong*, in the form of the spirit of some ancestor or dead relative, is attached to an individual as his special protector to whom he manifests himself in a dream. Sometimes the *ngarong*

[1] *Elementary Forms of the Religious Life* (Lond., 1915), p. 206.
[2] op. cit., p. 47. [3] op. cit., pp. 218 f.

takes on the guise of an animal, and then all individuals of the species become objects of special regard to the Iban under his protection.[1] To contend that 'the religious forces to which he addresses himself are only the individualized forms of collective forces'[2] is to lose sight of the fact that religious behaviour is very largely the expression of private spiritual experience before any attempt is made to give it intellectual evaluation in terms of 'collective representations' or individualized concepts.

Some form of interpretation is essential before religion can become a social phenomenon, and it is personal as well as corporate experiences that lead men to seek to establish a relationship with a reality transcending the natural order of which human society and its collective representations are a part. Social sanctions by themselves are insufficient to explain this reaction. Therefore, the group like the individual looks to an 'otherness' beyond itself in response to numinous stimuli. It is not true to say that 'society had all that is necessary to arouse the sensation of the Divine in minds merely by the power it has over them', or that 'the god of the clan can be nothing else than the clan itself'. As Dr C. C. J. Webb says in criticism of these group theories, religion is essentially cosmological in character. 'The notion of the Divine is no mere mirage of social facts: it is an implicit theory of the universe. The human mind necessarily conceives itself with the All, though it always starts in doing so with its immediate social environment, and only gradually realizes that this is not the dominant fact in the universe.'[3]

Again, religion cannot be resolved into a 'collective consciousness' peculiar to a so-called prelogical type of mentality, as Lévy Bruhl and the French sociologists contend,[4] as a corollary of their categories. Having divided society sharply into two divisions, the sacred and the profane, and made the supernatural the negation of the natural, the primitive is said to make 'no distinction between this world and the other, between what is actually present to sense, and what is beyond. To him it is these that are real and actual. His

---

[1] C. Hose, and W. McDougall, *The Pagan Tribes of Borneo* (Lond., 1912), II, pp. 90 ff.

[2] Durkheim, op. cit., p. 425.

[3] *Group Theories of Religion and the Individual* (Lond., 1916), p. 151.

[4] *Les Fonctions dans les Sociétés Inférieures* (Paris, 1915). *La Mentalité primitive* (Paris, 1921).

faith is expressed in his most insignificant as well as in his most important acts. It impregnates his whole life and conduct.'[1]

In short, in *les sociétés inférieures* mentality is of a character essentially prelogical and mystical, having a different orientation so that its collective representations are governed by the law of participation, and indifferent, consequently, to contradiction, and united with each other by connexions and preconnexions which are disconcerting to our logic. Everything is permeated by forces, influences and actions which, though imperceptible to sense, are so real that all things are fused. Exactly how this is brought about is not very clear except that they are supposed to be a product of the group mind as the source of all religious evaluations. But having evolved within the collective mental life of the community they are governed by the 'law of participation' so that all the objects and entities of the natural world are not divided from one another, but are united in a bond so intimate that each participates in the other, making a thing what it is not, and enabling the same entity to be present simultaneously in many places. In this way is explained how one object can act on another by imitative magic, and why a member of the witchetty grub clan in Central Australia regards himself as a witchetty grub and not merely as being 'one flesh' with it. In civilized society, on the other hand, the 'law of contradiction' prevails; that is to say, that nothing can be at once A and also B (which is other than A). A man does not imagine he is an ostrich, a witchetty grub or a macaw. But while it is true that the primitive mind is prone to mystical relationships and collective representations, it cannot be maintained that the 'law of contradiction' is thereby excluded. In point of fact it is only among certain individuals and under certain conditions that thought of this nature prevails in any society, usually as a result of a particular kind of spiritual experience. Thus, to suppose that a human being becomes an animal after death is not peculiar to primitive man being widely held among highly civilized people in India, while the idea of kinship between a human group and its sacred ally is not very different in mental process from the widespread Christian belief concerning the mystic relationship between Christ and the faithful. Both involve the idea of 'participation' but not to the exclusion of the laws of logic. The same is true of the modern child born of sophisticated

[1] *Primitive Mentality* (Lond., 1923), p. 32.

parents who solemnly asserts itself to be an engine, a tiger or an elephant, according to the mood of the moment. Feelings and movements may predominate over thought and produce a realization of unification with an object or unseen force, together with the sense of power that comes from the union, without any violation of logical processes common to human mentality as a whole.

Emotion qualifies the intellectual operations of every human being irrespective of the state of culture which constitutes his social and mental environment. In the presence of that which has acquired sacredness and traditional sentiments the reaction is the same however much the behaviour may be rationalized. It is only because critical reflection and scientific analysis are less developed in a primitive community that custom and belief appear to the civilized detached observer to be devoid of a rational basis. But 'it is fortunately only a rare individual here and there among us', as Dr McDougall says, 'who in considerable degree emancipates himself from the influence of such representations and becomes capable of confronting all objects about him in a perfectly cool, critical, logical attitude—who can "peep and botanize upon his mother's grave"'.[1] Idea and practices which may seem naïve and absurd viewed in the light of empirical knowledge are rational and intelligible enough once the premises are granted, and it is possible of course to reach erroneous conclusions without violating any of the rules of logic. A fallacy is an error in reasoning, but not necessarily in the principles of logical thought. False premises and inaccurate observations inevitably produce faulty inferences, and it is not lack of logic that characterizes the primitive outlook, but a different attitude to cause and effect. Things to us which seem mutually exclusive are identified owing to the absence of a conception of the universality and continuity of natural causation. But the mental life of civilized man is also largely dominated by 'ideas of objects to which traditional sentiments, sentiments of awe, of fear, of respect, of love, of reverence, are attached'.[2] Logical reasoning cannot be narrowed down to a positivistic materialism, as Lévy Bruhl imagines, in which everything that implies the existence of an unseen order of reality and spiritual powers external to man belong to a mystic prelogical mentality peculiar to primitive society.

[1] *The Group Mind* (Camb., 1927), p. 75.
[2] op. cit., p. 74.

Thus, for example, in Europe in the Middle Ages the group spirit was dominant and the unifying force was a transcendent theology interpreted in terms of Aristotle, who has been called 'the father of the science of logic'. Little attention may have been given to inductive reasoning, but few logicians would affirm with John Stuart Mill that the syllogism is not a valid instrument for the attainment of truth. Emphasis at certain times in the history of ordered thinking has been given to induction and at other times to deduction, but both are essential elements of the same reasoning process. Neither one can function independently of the other and both need to be supplemented by the creative work of the imagination. The emphasis on deduction in primitive society, as in medieval Europe, was due to the spirit of the times, but whether we start with particular facts and from these draw a universal conclusion, or, conversely, begin with a universal and proceed to some particular proposition, the mental processes involved are not 'prelogical' in the sense of being oblivious of the principle of contradiction.

There is no evidence that at any period in the history of the human race of which we have knowledge the ordinary processes of reasoning were in abeyance, either in the collective consciousness or in the individual members of society. If many elements of religious belief and practice are social in origin the categories of logic are not thereby excluded, any more than in other products of the group mind. The savage and the civilized alike are at once rational and mystical in their outlook and reactions to their environment according to the particular circumstances of a given situation. The distinction between the sacred and the profane does not belong to the categories of logic or rationality any more than the workings of the human mind are governed exclusively by the principle of 'participation' in opposition to that of 'contradiction'. The essence of religion in its most rudimentary form is to be sought not in the rival claims of society and of the individual and a wholly mystical collective consciousness, nor in crude philosophic speculations concerning souls, ghosts and ancestors, but in the recognition of a transcendent order and the elaboration of a technique to enable man to deal with the unpredictable and inexplicable elements in human experience, whether individual or collective, in this world and beyond the grave.

CHAPTER II

The Magic Art

Closely allied to the belief in a transcendent order of reality controlling human destinies from without is another technique employed for similar purposes but exercised from within. While the Hegelian contention that the true nature of religion is a purely immanent principle implying no recognition of a reality beyond this world cannot be maintained, the doctrine of immanence has its roots in 'the common plasm of crude beliefs about the awful and occult', out of which magic and religion have emerged. Does it therefore follow that the two disciplines have a common origin?

The more intensively magic is studied, the more apparent it becomes that it is a highly specialized system limited in its operation and carefully restricted in its performance. Unlike religion it has no transcendental reference to external supramundane powers superior to man and controlling the processes of nature. It is distinctively a human art inasmuch as while it involves the recognition of a supernatural order it always works through the agency of man. Furthermore, as Malinowski says, 'not only is magic an essentially human possesion, but it is literally and actually enshrined in man and can be handed on only from man to man, according to very strict rules of magical filiation, initiation and instruction'.[1] The virtue of magic is embodied in spell and in specific rites performed and mystic formulae pronounced for the express purpose of bringing about some practical result, such as making rain or sunshine, giving stability to a house or canoe, wounding an enemy or attracting a loved one to her lover. Thus, it differs fundamentally from the concept of *mana* from which, in common with religion, it has been said to be derived.[2]

[1] *Science, Religion and Reality* (Lond., 1927), p. 71.

[2] Marett, *Threshold of Religion,* pp. 60 ff. Hubert and Mauss, *L'Année Sociologique,* VII, 1904, pp. 14 ff., 138. Hartland, *Ritual and Belief* (Lond., 1914), pp. 26 ff.

MAGIC AND 'MANA'

According to Codrington, 'this supernatural power or influence' attached to certain sacred objects in Melanesia 'is always connected with some person who directs it : all spirits have it, ghosts generally, some men'.

> If a stone is found to have supernatural power it is because a spirit has associated itself with it. A dead man's bone has with it *mana*, because the ghost is with the bone ; a man may have so close a connexion with a spirit or ghost that he has *mana* in himself also, and can so direct it to effect what he desires. All conspicuous success is a proof that a man has *mana* ; his influence depends on the impression made on the people's mind that he has it.

In short, it is 'a force altogether distinct from physical power, which acts in all kinds of ways for good and evil, and which it is of the greatest advantage to possess or control'.[1]

> If a man has been successful in fighting, it has not been his natural strength of arm, quickness of eye, or readiness of resource that has won success ; he has certainly got the *mana* of a spirit or of some deceased warrior to empower him, conveyed in an amulet of a stone round his neck, or a tuft of leaves in his belt, in a tooth hung upon a finger of his bow hand, or in the form of words with which he brings supernatural assistance to his side. If a man's pigs multiply, and his gardens are productive, it is not because he is industrious and looks after his property, but because of the stones full of *mana* for pigs and yams that he possesses. Of course a yam naturally grows when planted, that is well known, but it will not be very large unless *mana* comes into play ; a canoe will not be swift unless *mana* is brought to bear upon it, a net will not catch many fish, nor an arrow inflict a mortal wound.[2]

Now, it is clear that this occult power as it is understood to-day in Melanesia is neither the prototype of magic nor of pre-animistic religion. On the contrary, as Hocart says,

> so far from being pre-animistic the word is out-and-out spiritualistic : it is almost, if not entirely, confined to the action of ghosts and spirits who, whatever their origin, now go under the same name as the ghosts : *tomate* in Mandegusu, *kalou* in Fiji, *atua* in Wallis Island, *aitu* in Samoa.

[1] *The Melanesians* (Oxford, 1891), pp. 118 f.
[2] op. cit., p. 120.

It would seem that the word is simply a technical term belonging to a spiritualistic doctrine which it is the task of ethnology to reconstruct.[1]

Magic, on the other hand, is confined to human beings and operates as a simulation of a real act, a ritualized expression of an emotional desire on the part of the performer enacted by word and deed in the belief that through the utterance of the spell and the accompanying action the result will follow automatically. The efficacy resides in the things done and said, not in any intervening supernatural agent, be it a ghost, spirit, ancestor or god. Therefore, it is not the common possession of supernatural beings and men, neither can it be 'conveyed in almost anything' like *mana*, because it is tied to its own formulae and rites. Being limited by its specified tradition it does not 'show itself in physical force'.[2]

The same is true of the corresponding terms in other parts of the world. Thus, for example, in North America the Iroquoian *orenda* is analogous to will and intelligence rather than to magic. It gives greatness and power to the shaman, skill to the hunter and cunning to his quarry, supernatural insight to the prophet and soothsayer, and equally potency in sacred rocks, rivers, plants, trees and animals; it is behind 'the efficient cause of all phenomena, all the activities of man's environment'. Everything and everybody partakes of *orenda* in greater or less degree, though it is the particular possession of medicine-men and wizards. Sometimes it works automatically, but generally it represents personal activities such as the exercise of will and intelligence, including prayer.[3] The Siouan term *wakonda*, 'the power that moves', is ascribed anthropomorphic attributes and prayers are addressed to it.[4] *Wakan,* which also has a parallel meaning as 'the power which makes or brings things to pass', is only assigned to objects or functions which come from *wakan* beings.[5] The term *manitu* is applied by the Eastern Algonquians to sacred objects, such as an arrow, into which a spirit, or *genius loci*, has transformed itself.[6]

Behind all these quasi-impersonal conceptions there is the

[1] *Man*, 1914, vol. xiv, No. 46.

[2] Malinowski, op. cit., p. 71.

[3] J. N. B. Hewitt, *American Anthropologist,* New series, IV, 1902, pp. 38 ff.

[4] Fletcher, *27th R.B.A.E.* (Wash., 1911), pp. 134, 597.

[5] W. Jones, *Journal Amer. Folk-lore,* xviii, 1905, p. 183.

[6] op. cit. XVII, 1904, pp. 349 ff.

shadowy form of a personal transcendent being or power external to man, and therefore the mystic force which is frequently described under the generic term *mana* is not magical in its operation any more than it exactly represents what is connoted by 'the numinous', though it is frequently used in this sense by anthropologists. In Melanesia the *mana* which gives sacredness to stones also equips chiefs for their office, so that in the Eastern Solomons hereditary chieftainship appears to rest on the belief that a particular person has inherited from the *tindalo,* or ghosts, sufficient *mana* to qualify him for the post.[1] Similarly, in Morocco the sultan, who is regarded as the viceregent of God, owes his position to the *baraka* which he inherits, or appropriates, from his predecessors.

Here, again, as Westermarck points out, there is a certain 'confusion of categories'[2] since *baraka* is at once the 'holiness', or sacredness, attributed to chiefs and 'saints' (*síyid*), and to natural objects and places; the animating principle, or soul-substance, in blood poured out in sacrifice, or employed to convey a conditional curse (*'ar*); the benign virtue of a sacrificial feast; and the source of life-giving potency. 'When it is strong and unpolluted the crops are abundant, the women give birth to children, and the country is prosperous in every respect', while, conversely, when it is weak drought and famine result, and the fruit falls from the trees before it is ripe. It is not the peculiar property of the sultan or of any individual, though he has it in an exceptional degree by virtue of his office as a descendant in the male line of the daughter of Muhammed, who of all men was filled with 'blessed virtue' (*baraka*).[3]

As a sacred contagion it is capable of transmission to any object or place connected with a saint, such as wells, springs, trees, rocks and caves, which as charged with mystic power are rendered taboo, and ascribed fertilizing and medicinal properties.[4] Anything, in fact, which gives evidence of having a mysterious inherent vitality is permeated with it, and is, therefore, sacred. The last portion of the crop on a field is left untouched for a while in order that its *baraka* may be transmitted to the crop which is thought to be reborn from

[1] Rivers, *History of Melanesian Society* (Camb., 1914), II, pp. 101 ff.

[2] *Anthropological Essays presented to Tylor* (Lond., 1907), p. 368.

[3] Westermarck *Ritual and Belief in Morocco* (Lond., 1926), I, pp. 39 ff.

[4] op. cit., pp. 66 ff.

this 'bride of the field' at the next season. That the *baraka* in the old grain may be transmitted to the new crops, the threshing-floors are left unswept.[1]

Baraka, therefore, like *mana* has a dual character. On the one hand it is in the nature of an inherent, impersonal, vital essence, as in the case of the seed-corn, and, on the other hand, it has a personal significance as the soul-substance and divine element in the sultan, a saint or shereef, capable of transmission from one generation to another. But in neither capacity does it fulfil the normal functions of magic. It is not confined to human beings since the quality is assigned to animals, birds, and inanimate objects, and its ultimate source seems to be in some transcendent reference, the sultan being a quasi-divine king who elsewhere is the priest *par excellence*, performing mediatorial functions between the gods and the community,[2] assisted by a hierarchy partaking in some measure of his supernatural powers.

Taking this evidence collectively it would seem that magic and religion have not a common root in the generalized conception of the power attributed to spiritual beings and sacred persons and things for which such terms as *mana*, *baraka*, *orenda* and the like have been used for the purposes of anthropological terminology. This is not to deny that on psychological grounds, as we have endeavoured to show, there is reason to believe that religion took its rise in an awareness of 'otherness' stimulated by the sense of awe and mystery before it became intellectualized in animistic and theistic concepts. But *mana* and its equivalents seem to be themselves part of this crude philosophic process of reasoning and rationalization, while magic represents another and distinct discipline.

MAGIC AND RELIGION

Since both magic and religion are specialized types of behaviour directed towards those elements of human experience which fall outside man's empirical mastery of his surroundings and destinies, they obviously have much in common. Indeed the various attempts to give chronological priority to the one or the other have proved as abortive as those which have tried to reduce them to a common

[1] op. cit., p. 106.
[2] cf. Chap. IV, pp. 102 ff.

source. Thus, Jevons maintained that 'belief in the supernatural', which he made the characteristic mark of religion, 'was prior to the belief in magic, and that the latter whenever it sprang up was a degradation or relapse in the evolution of religion', though he also regarded the two as having different origins, and being 'always essentially distinct from one another'.[1] But if magic is different in origin and kind it can hardly be a degenerate form of religion like polytheism or nature-worship.

Sir James Frazer, on the other hand, regards magic as older than religion, but he is in agreement concerning the fundamental distinction and opposition in principle between the two techniques. Like Hegel, he thinks that in the mental development of the human race an age of magic preceded an age of religion, and that whereas magic aims at controlling nature directly by 'the sheer force of spells and enchantments', religion endeavoured to control it indirectly by mollifying 'a coy, capricious or irascible deity by the soft insinuation of prayer and sacrifice'.[2] Though the two are now fused, this amalgamation is not primitive, and a time existed when a man trusted solely in magic for the satisfaction of the wants which transcended his immediate cravings.

In its fundamental conception it postulated like modern science the order and uniformity of nature, but it was ignorant of the particular laws which govern the sequence of natural events. This flaw, due to a misapplication of the association of similar ideas, was detected in course of time by the acuter minds and then recourse was made to 'the propitiation and conciliation of powers superior to man which are believed to direct and control the course of nature and of human life'. Thus, 'the age of magic' passed into 'the age of religion',[3] the magician giving way to the priest who, renouncing the attempt to control directly the processes of nature for the good of man, sought to attain this end by appeals to the gods to do for him what he no longer fancied he could do for himself.[4] But even at this early stage of the development the functions of priest and sorcerer were often combined, magical and religious rites being performed simultaneously. Prayers and incantation were uttered

[1] *Introduction to the History of Religion*, p. 25.

[2] *G.B.*, pt. I ('Magic Art', I), pp. 234 ff. Hegel, *The Philosophy of Religion*, vol. I, pp. 290 ff.

[3] *G.B.*, op. cit., pp. 220 ff.

[4] Frazer, *Early History of Kingship* (Lond., 1905), p. 127.

almost in the same breath with an inconsistency characteristic of the emotional reactions of the primitive mind.[1]

Now it is certainly true that a sharp distinction between a magical and religious traffic with the supernatural cannot be drawn where any external source of strength is involved. Thus, in the 'Ages of Faith' in medieval Europe the Black Mass was attributed to demons who employed human agents to perform their nefarious functions by occult methods which were indistinguishable from magic. Conversely, the ceremonial interments in Palaeolithic caves at Le Moustier, La Farrassie and La Chapelle-aux-Saints in France suggest that Neanderthal Man was religious in his attitude to the dead inasmuch as he made provision for the well-being of his comrades beyond the grave. Moreover, the Aurignacians and their successors in Palaeolithic Europe appear to have sought to establish right relations with sacred species superior to themselves upon which they depended for their subsistence, by means of masked dances and similar rites.

Therefore, as far back as the archaeological evidence takes us, magic and religion appear to have been very closely related, and there is nothing to suggest that originally one discipline had priority over the other either in time or importance. It is impossible to assume strata in the development of human thought and institutions comparable to the geological record of the earth, and in the case of magic and religion the two disciplines are at once so distinct and so intermingled that they cannot be kept in watertight compartments. Neither in the past nor in the present is there any indication that the one has existed to the complete exclusion of the other. Thus, for example, in Central Australia if actual deities play no part in the Intichiuma ceremonies, the intention of the rites is the control of the food supply by a dramatic representation of the acts by which in the beginning the supernatural ancestors and totems brought all things into existence. The chief actors perform their functions as the incarnations of the beings on whom the group depends for the maintenance of life, just as the *churinga* and similar objects gain their sacredness and significance from the belief that they enshrine their spirits or potency. All this can scarcely be reconciled with Frazer's conception of magic as a system by which early man controlled the course of nature directly for practical ends by spell and rite without

[1] G.B., pt. I ('Magic Art', I), pp. 226 ff.

the aid and intervention of any higher power. The introduction of spirits, ancestors and totems, quite as much as gods, marks the passage of magic to religion, but we know nothing of a time when such beings were non-existent in some hypothetical 'godless age' of pure magic. Ceremonies like the Intichiuma do not fall within a domain of this character, however prominent the magical element may be in them. Therefore, Frazer is not correct in saying that 'among the aborigines of Australia, the rudest savages as to whom we possess accurate information, magic is universally practised, whereas religion in the sense of a propitiation or conciliation of the higher powers seems to be nearly unknown'.[1]

Even if religion be narrowed down to this definition, if the native tribes of Australia are to be taken as a criterion it cannot be maintained that the phenomenon is almost absent among them. On the contrary, it is as fundamental as magic. Granted that the All-Fathers, or tribal High Gods, are seldom if ever the recipients of offerings and petitions, nevertheless they seem to occupy very much the same position in the mysteries in the south-east region as that of the Alcheringa ancestors and totems in the Central tribes. The Yuin, for instance, prepare a figure of their Supreme Being, Daramulun, and solemnly show it to the youths at their initiation,[2] just as the Arunta make known to their initiates after their circumcision the nature of the sacred bull-roarer, which originally appears to have been the outward and visible sign of a being named Twanyirika. It is commonly assumed that this is merely a bogey to frighten the women and children, but the evidence suggests that actually it is the symbol of a nebulous sky-being, so that as soon as a youth is initiated his elder brother goes to him with a bundle of *churinga* saying, 'here is Twanyirika of whom you have heard so much, they are *churinga* and will help to heal you quickly'.[3] He is also told that should a woman see them she would be killed at once, while in the neighbouring Unmatjera tribe it is explained to the candidates that should they reveal any of the secrets made known to them during the initiation ceremonies Twanyirika will carry them away. After the sub-incision operation they have to swing bull-roarers

[1] op. cit., p. 234. *Totemism and Exogamy,* vol. I, pp. 141 ff.

[2] Howitt, *Native Tribes of South-East Australia* (Lond., 1904), p. 540.

[3] Spencer and Gillen, *Northern Tribes of Central Australia* (Lond., 1904), p. 497.

while they are recovering in the bush lest a mysterious being known as Arakurta 'who lives up in the sky' should capture them.[1]

The bull-roarer being the outward and visible sign if not actual the embodiment of the ancestral souls and tribal All-Fathers, it is endowed with *mana* emanating from the supernatural being with whom it is associated, and so intimately is it connected with its ancestral prototype that it has 'feelings just as human beings have'.[2] Thus, bull-roarers, and similar *churinga*, are more than objects having *arungquiltha* (the Australian equivalent of *mana*) inasmuch as they contain the spirit-part either of the ancestors who lived in the Alcheringa or of the High God who presides over the mysteries, and acts as the external soul of the individuals with whom they are associated at birth. Their totemic counterpart appear to be the *nurtunga*, or sacred pole, on which *churinga* are hung, signifying apparently the relation of the individual to the group, and the transference of a man's soul temporarily to his totem.[3] In addition to these two sacred emblems a third object known as *Kauaua* plays a prominent part in the concluding rites at Arunta initiations. This consists of another pole smeared all over with human blood and ornamented with eagle-hawk feathers, head-bands, tail-tips and a nose-bone, together with a few *churinga*.[4] Of its origin and meaning the natives are ignorant, but its form is common to all the totems, and since it resembles a human being in appearance, it may correspond to the figure of Daramulun in the Yuin ceremonies. In that case it is a further indication of a High God lurking in the background of the initiation rites of the Central tribes, comparable to the All-Fathers in the South-eastern region, where the bull-roarer is so intimately connected with the Supreme Being as the producer of thunder which is the voice of the god.

Moreover, the Kaitish to the north of the Arunta recognize a High God called Atnatu, unknown to the women and children, who 'arose up in the sky in the very far past, farther back even than the Alcheringa', which in fact he created. He made himself, gave himself his name and rejoices in the noise of the bull-roarers when they are swung during initiation ceremonies. In the Alcheringa he

---

[1] op. cit., pp. 338, 343.

[2] Hartland, *British Assoc. Report,* 1906, p. 684.

[3] Spencer and Gillen, *Native Tribes of Central Australia,* pp. 122, 362, 627.

[4] op. cit., pp. 370 ff., 629.

dropped on the earth two *churinga* (bull-roarers) which became
men, and it was they who first made these sacred instruments of
mulga wood to imitate the sound of Atnatu's bull-roarer in the sky
(i.e. the thunder). If this sacred instrument is not sounded at initiation, he hurls down spears and drags the men and boys up to the
sky.[1] Atnatu, in short, is an almost identical counterpart of the
All-Fathers recorded by A. W. Howitt among the South-eastern
coastal tribes. These sky-gods preside over the tribal mysteries where
their symbols, attributes and functions are first revealed to youths
at the time of initiation. The thunder is their voice, the bull-roarer
their visible embodiment, or sometimes their 'son', as among the
Kurnai who regard 'Tundun' (which is also the name of the bull-
roarer) as the 'son' or 'boy' of Mungan-ngaua, the All-Father.[2]

The primary purpose of initiation being to effect rebirth by the
aid of a death and resurrection symbolism in order that youths may
take their proper place and part in society and be incorporated into
the mystical fellowship of the ancestors, totems, spirits and, where
he exists, the god of the mysteries, the rites can hardly be described
as magical in intention. If prayers and sacrifices are absent, the drama
as a whole belongs to the domain of religion rather than to that of
magic since it is supposed to have been instituted by the legendary
ancestors or tribal All-Father whose voice is heard in the hum of the
bull-roarer and who is sometimes thought to kill the initiates and
restore them as fully grown men. By means of sacred symbols and
emotional rites charged with supernatural potency proceeding from
an external unseen world, the novice is brought into union with the
higher powers, and he may even receive a personal visitation from
a tutelary divinity who henceforth becomes his guardian-spirit.
The physical ordeals, such as circumcision or the knocking out of a
tooth, by which the actual initiation is effected, are usually associated
with the idea of rebirth to a higher life on a higher plane, and frequently performed by persons symbolizing or impersonating ancestors or totems, while the gradual unveiling of the esoteric lore of
the tribe is as different from the tradition of magic as the *churinga*
and bull-roarers are from spell and incantation. Therefore, it cannot
be maintained, if the Australians are to be taken as a typical case,

[1] *Northern Tribes of Central Australia,* pp. 498 ff.

[2] The other bull-roarer in this tribe is called 'Wehntwin', or grandfather. Howitt,
op. cit., pp. 488 ff.

that 'in the most backward state of human society now known to us we find magic conspicuously present and religion conspicuously absent' and infer therefrom that 'the civilized races of the world have also at some period of their history passed through a similar intellectual phase'.[1]

Unquestionably magic plays a more prominent part in primitive society than in a modern civilized community, and when it is encountered to-day it is not infrequently a survival from an earlier state of culture. It can hardly be doubted that the spiritual experience of a worshipper kneeling before an altar in a Gothic cathedral or an Italian basilica is more strictly religious than were the emotional reactions aroused by a pantomimic dance in a Palaeolithic Pyrenean cavern, or in those displayed in an Australian intiation ceremony. Nevertheless, while magic may be largely an ancient and primitive heritage which has gradually given place to religion and science, notwithstanding fundamental differences in origin and technique that each displays, in practice the two attitudes to the sacred and occult converge so that it is often difficult to separate the one from the other. This is the justification for the use of the cumbrous and question-begging expression 'magico-religious' as a working principle to describe cult-practices which occupy a border-line position about which the framers of general theory are in dispute, and involving distinctions that may be ignored for purposes of description.[2]

For example, in a complex sacrificial rite the disposition of the blood and of special parts of the victim, the wearing of the skin by the officiant, and similar elements in the ceremonial, are efficacious by virtue of the actions performed, or through an inherent potency, while it can hardly be denied that they have a sacredness independent of 'powers superior to man' as integral parts of the rite as a whole. If the purpose of the sacred drama is, let us say, a re-enactment of an explanatory myth performed according to a prescribed usage approved by society, directed to beneficent ends and addressed to a divine being upon whom the worshippers depend for their life and sustenance, it belongs to the category of religion. Therefore, separated from their ritual context the several elements

[1] *G.B.*, pt. I ('Magic Art', I), pp. 234 f.
[2] *Notes and Queries on Anthropology* (Lond., 1912), p. 251.

may be more akin to magic in their mode of operation, but collectively they constitute a religious action.

THE MAGIC ART

The magic art as such, however, is a very different procedure. It is neither science, religion nor *mana*, but a technique of its own with its proper rules, laws and tradition. To equate it with pseudo-science is to lose sight of the fact that it lives and moves and has its being in the domain of the 'supernatural' rather than the 'natural', so far as such a distinction can be made in primitive society. It is at the point where empirical knowledge and experience fail that magic is called in aid. It may assume that one event follows another necessarily and invariably without the intervention of any personal agency, as Frazer maintains,[1] but if the magician believes the same causes will always produce the same effects, it is the spell and the incantation he employs that override the normal workings of natural law and rational knowledge in the profane order of empirical fact. He performs his functions in the domain of the sacred as completely as the priest, though he trusts to his own inherent supernatural powers rather than those of beings external and superior to himself over whom he has no direct control.

Working strictly within his own circumscribed tradition and technique he expresses in words and actions (i.e. by incantation, rite, and spell) an emotional reaction to a given situation and set of circumstances which he, and those who resort to his art, believe to be efficacious in bringing about the desired result. The methods adopted are usually simple, direct, expressive and highly practical, performed for the most part in secret for specific ends and private gain. In love magic an object representing the beloved is fondled with endearing terms, or attractive scents are used, while to wound an enemy a dagger or pointed bone is projected towards the victim with an intense fury and appropriate twists, accompanied by exclamations of vengeance. To remove the evil wrought by such a rite, the medicine-man extracts from the bewitched person by suction or a similar action that which has been projected. Thus, in cases of this kind it becomes a struggle between two practitioners,

[1] G.B., op. cit., pp. 220 ff.

the one endeavouring to inflict injury, and the other trying to counteract the nefarious operation.

The potency of the spell lies in the things done and said according to the ancient tradition of the magical art handed down from one generation to another. Consequently, any deviation from the prescribed actions or formulae breaks the spell and renders the rite null and void. Hence the insistence on correct formulation and performance. Moreover, since success depends very largely on the skill of the operator, who is the actor rather than the agent of the occult power, it is incumbent upon the magician to practise his art with the utmost skill and by the observance of taboos to keep himself free from supernatural influences which might negative the magic localized in himself and under his control by virtue of the tradition in which he stands as a practitioner.

The technical equipment required by a successful medicine-man is often considerable. Not only is it necessary for the correct incantations to be performed, but not infrequently a secret archaic language or cryptic terminology has to be learned, together with some knowledge of such subjects as meteorology, the processes of vegetation and folk medicine (herbs, leechcraft, poisons, &c.), primitive therapeutics and surgery (trephining, ligatures, &c.), massage, bleeding, childbirth, and the principles of auto-suggestion. Sometimes subterfuges involving sleight of hand, ventriloquism and so on are adopted, but while devices of this kind are not uncommon, normally the magician is a genuine 'medicine-man' who unquestionably believes firmly in his own creative powers. If this were not the case the very considerable measure of success which attends his efforts would be inexplicable.

SHAMANISM AND THE MEDICINE-MAN

There is, however, another important factor in the methods employed in the practice of the magic art. In addition to this specialized knowledge the most efficacious practitioners are not seldom in possession of very real psychic qualities, so that, for example, among certain Siberian tribes only a person who can show the right disposition can hope to find a vocation as a shaman. This functionary combines the office of priest, prophet and medicine-man, and exercises his powers by virtue of a first-hand acquaintance with

the occult. When the hereditary principle is maintained, the father
selects from his sons the one who displays the right symptoms
(fainting, excitability, moroseness, love of solitude), and the youth
then has to do everything in his power to foster a neurotic condition
in himself. No one, in fact, in this area becomes a shaman of his
own free will; it comes to him, as Miss Czaplicka says, *nolens
volens*, like a hereditary disease.[1] The office depends on the acquisi-
tion of occult supernormal powers regarded as a *sine quâ non* in the
performance of shamanistic functions.

This aspect of the technique, however, frequently introduces a
transcendental reference inasmuch as recourse is made to the spirit-
world to assist in exorcism, the cure of disease, or search for a
wandering soul. Therefore, at this point again magic enters the
borders of religion, the shaman performing his operations partly as
a result of his own inherent gifts, and partly as the agent of the
spirits with whom he is *en rapport*. Among the Transbaikalian Tun-
guses a man who desires to enter the sacred profession explains that
a certain deceased shaman has visited him in a dream and commanded him to be his successor. He then shows himself 'weakly, as
if dazed and nervous', and suddenly utters incoherent words, falls
unconscious, runs through the forest, lives on the bark of trees,
throws himself into fire and water, lays hold on weapons, wounds
himself, and generally behaves in a crazy manner. Having thus revealed the necessary symptoms, an old shaman is summoned to
instruct him in the lore of the spirits, and acquaint him with the
mode of invoking them.[2] During this period of training tutelary
spirits help him in his struggles with disease, and appear to him in
various forms, sometimes as men and sometimes as birds, to endow
him with power and reveal to him the mysteries of his art. But it is
very important that he comes into contact with the right spirits and
therefore he has to learn to test them.[3]

On the more practical side he has to acquire the art of beating the
drum accurately, a task requiring considerable skill. He must sing
in the approved manner and dance ceremonial dances. When all
this has been accomplished, after a period of fasting, and dietary,
the candidate is ready for initiation. Among the Yakut this takes the

[1] *Aboriginal Siberia* (Oxford, 1914), pp. 169 ff., 177 ff.

[2] V. M. Mikhailowsky, *J.R.A.I.*, xxiv, 1895, pp. 85 ff.

[3] W. Jochelson, 'The Koryat', *Jesup. N Pacific Expedition* (New York, 1905–8), p. 47.

form of being led up a mountain or into an open field by the old shaman who has been responsible for his training, and clothed in the appropriate vestments, given a tambourine and drumsticks, made to repeat certain words and promise allegiance to his tutelary spirit. After further instruction concerning the spirits and their propitiation, an animal is slain, his clothing is sprinkled with the blood, and a feast is held on the flesh.[1] Thus, duly installed in his office, and fully equipped with his technique, he is ready for any eventuality, but only as the agent of the higher powers with whom he is in constant converse.

Even in Australia, where the magic art might be expected to be practised in all its pristine simplicity and perfection, out of the three representative methods of initiation two involve the intervention of spirits. Among the Arunta, when a man feels he is capable of becoming a medicine-man he may go to the mouth of a cave in a range of hills to the north of the Emily Plain, 14 miles from Alice Springs, which is supposed to be occupied by *Iruntarinia,* or spirit individuals, who are doubles of the Alcheringa ancestors, and there lies down to sleep. At daybreak a spirit emerges, throws an invisible lance at the sleeper which pierces his neck from behind, passes through the tongue making a hole which is regarded as the sign of his having been duly initiated. If the hole should close up, his magical powers depart from him, and however it may be made in actual fact, normally he retains this mark of his office for the rest of his life. A second thrust from the lance is supposed to pierce the man from ear to ear so that he falls dead, and is immediately carried into the depths of the cave (which is thought to extend for miles far under the plain) where the spirits live in perpetual sunshine among streams of running water. There his body is cut open, the viscera extracted and replaced by a new set of organs in which magic stones (*atnongara*) are inserted to be the source of his miraculous powers. He comes to life in a state of temporary insanity. When he is in his right mind again he paints a broad band across the bridge of his nose to indicate that he has graduated, though he does not practise for a year, and should the hole in his tongue have closed up by then, as is sometimes the case, he does not pursue his profession. In the interval he reflects on his recent occult experiences and learns his craft from other medicine-men. If at any time he

[1] Mikhaïlowsky, op. cit., p. 86.

loses the *atnongara* stones his powers at once depart, and occasionally a former practitioner is discovered who has fallen a victim of this fate. To prevent such a calamity he has to abstain from certain kinds of food, such as fat or warm meat, he must avoid being bitten by a 'bull-dog' ant, inhaling the smoke from burning bones, or hearing the loud barking of the camp dogs, lest the stones take flight.

The second method of initiation is similar, but instead of the man being taken into a cave, he is thought to descend to the bowels of the earth at a sacred spot inhabited by a special class of Alcheringa spirits called *Aruncha*. On the rare occasions when women are admitted to the craft, this is usually the way they obtain their powers. Quite a different procedure, however, is frequently adopted in which spirits play no part. The candidate is taken to a secluded spot by other medicine-men, called *Nung-gara* and sworn to secrecy. A number of stones are then extracted from their own bodies by the initiators and placed one by one in the hollow of a spear-thrower. Some of them are pressed along the front of the leg and up the body to the sternum. Others are projected into his head by magic passes, and a crystal is pressed hard on the cranium. A hole is made under the nail of the first finger of the right hand into which a crystal is supposed to be pressed. The rest of the day is spent in further scoring of the man's body with stones between intervals of sleep. In the evening he eats meat and drinks water containing crystals. On the third day the tongue is pierced with a flint, and his body decorated with the sacred designs of the *oruncha* spirits. Fur string bands are put on his head, and he is required to keep a strict silence till the wound in his tongue is healed. He must also keep his thumb pressed against the wound in his finger till it is healed to keep the magic stone from escaping. On his return to the camp he is only allowed to talk a little, he must abstain from fat, fish and the flesh of wild dogs, and sleep with a fire between him and his wife in order to make him visible to the *oruncha*, and keep him aloof from mundane and carnal distractions. If he fails to observe these rules he is in danger of losing his powers.[1]

While each tribe has its own peculiarities, these three methods, broadly speaking, are typical of the making of medicine-men in Australia. It will be seen, therefore, that in a state of culture in which magic is alleged to be predominant, spiritual beings superior to man

[1] Spencer and Gillen, *Native Tribes of Central Australia,* pp. 522 ff.

are largely responsible for the bestowal of the marvellous powers, since it is they who endow new wizards with the stones, crystals and internal organs by means of which they exercise their functions.[1] Here, again, then, as in the case of the Intichiuma and puberty rites, magic and religion converge, though when it comes to effecting a cure the technique adopted is usually definitely magical in its method and operation. The patient is made to lie down while the medicine-man bends over him and sucks vigorously at the spot where the seat of the trouble is thought to be located, spitting out pieces of wood or bone which he supposedly extracts as the cause of the malady. In serious cases, after a solemn diagnosis, in which other practitioners assist, the services of a renowned member of the craft may be sought. The eminent doctor first gazes at the patient intently; he then recedes a few yards and looks at him fiercely, bends slightly forward and repeatedly jerks his arm outward at full length in order to project some of the *atnongara* stones into the sick man's body in order to counteract the evil magic at work in him. He repeats this movement with dramatic action, and finally comes close again, cutting the malign cord of the *ullinka* (i.e. short barbed stick attached to an invisible string) which he alone can see. To complete the restoration, once more he projects the *atnongara* stones, and then places his mouth on the effected part and sucks until the *ullinka* is removed.[2]

The patient and spectators having no doubts concerning the cause and nature of the trouble, and perfect faith in the ability of the medicine-man to locate and remove it, a real cure is not infrequently affected by means of auto-suggestion, if the actual disease is amenable to such treatment. If he is successful, the reputation of the doctor is enhanced, but should the operation fail it is believed that he has been thwarted by more powerful magic exercised by a spirit or rival medicine-man. So in either case the magic art as such does not suffer. A success or failure is explained in terms of magical efficiency in one direction or another, and one gain, as Malinowski points out, easily outweighs several losses, a positive case always overshadowing the negative one.[3]

[1] In the South-east area initiates are often thought to go to the camp of the High God in the sky to be invested with their powers. cf. Howitt, op. cit., pp. 404 ff.

[2] Spencer and Gillen, op. cit., pp. 531 f.

[3] Malinowski, *Science, Religion and Reality,* p. 76.

MAGIC, BLACK AND WHITE

Moreover, in primitive society belief in the power of magic is fundamental, and to disturb the conviction would necessitate a complete re-orientation of mind towards the forces of the external world and the chances and changes of this mortal life. Disease and death can only be explained in relation to the machinations of some person or persons unknown who have set in motion sinister forces and malignant agencies which have to be counteracted by appropriate spells and incantations if the evil is to be frustrated. Magic, therefore, is at once licit and illicit; it may be used to save life or to destroy it, to cure or to wound. Consequently, there is a so-called 'black art' comprising these vicious practices in contradistinction to the beneficent rites designed to help and heal in time of need; to promote and conserve life and health, love and felicity. The same person adopting similar methods may exercise both these types of the same power, sometimes to one end and sometimes to the other, but the exercise of the black art is normally done in secret, being illicit and anti-social. Love-magic, again, though not of vicious intent, will hardly be performed in public, otherwise it would defeat its end. Furthermore, it may be anti-social inasmuch as it may contravene the established laws of the community and lead to a quarrel between two local groups and subsequent bloodshed. But Hubert and Mauss are not justified in contending that magic is the illicit set over against the accepted order of society. Thus, rain-making and food production are licit acts highly beneficial to the community at large, and such ceremonies, like Rogationtide processions, constitute public rites.

RAIN-MAKING

Among the Arunta, for example, it is the duty of the members of the water-totem, to whom the secret of rain-making was imparted in the Alcheringa, to hold an Intichiuma at the spot set apart for the purpose by an ancestral being called Irtchwoanga. When this is to be done the head of the group, himself a celebrated rain-maker, sends messengers to the surrounding people to inform them of his intention and call together the men of the totem from the neighbouring groups. When all are assembled they go to the selected place in the Rain Country (*Kartwia quatcha*), a district about 50 miles east of Alice Springs, and having painted themselves with red and yellow ochre and pipeclay, and put bunches of eagle-hawk feathers on their heads, they sit down in a line and sing. At a given signal from the leader they all jump up and march in single file to a spot some 20 miles off where they spend the night. At daybreak they scatter to search for game which is cooked and eaten, but on no account must any water be drunk or the ceremony would fail. The meal over, they decorate themselves afresh, this time with broad bands of white bird's down, while the elder men erect a shelter of boughs near the main camp. At sunset they march back silently in single file to this hut, and on reaching it the young men go in first and lie face downwards at the inner end, while the older men outside decorate the rain-maker with pipeclay designs and patches of white bird's down. When he has taken up a position near the opening of the shelter, the old men sing till at length he emerges and walks slowly twice up and down a shallow trench which has been prepared near the entrance, quivering his body and legs in an extraordinary manner. While this is being done the young men get up and sing, but resume their former prostrations as soon as he re-enters the wurley. The performance is repeated at intervals throughout the night until, just before daybreak, he gives a final and prolonged quiver, which exhausts his strength and brings the rite to a close. The young men rise and rush out of the hut, scream-ing in imitation of the spur-winged plover, a bird regarded as a harbinger of rain. The cry is immediately taken up by the men and women in the camp. On the next night an ordinary rain-dance is held by the men.[1]

This ceremony is a typical example of imitative magic. Frazer is probably correct in describing it in terms of a rising storm. The hut represents the vault of heaven, he thinks, from which the rain-clouds, depicted by the patches of white bird's down stuck on the leader's body, come forth to move across the sky, as he struts and quivers across the trench. The other performers play the part of birds supposed to bring rain.[2] In support of this interpretation is the fact that similar rain-making rites occur in Australia and elsewhere

[1] Spencer and Gillen, op. cit., pp. 189–93.

[2] *G.B.,* pt. I ('Magic Art', I), p. 261.

in which clouds and a storm are enacted. On the principle that 'like produces like' rain is made by imitating the processes of nature, in a series of symbolical actions, often accompanied by appropriate exclamations, calculated to bring about the desired results. But the rite is more than mimicry because the performers believe that the effect is actually transmitted to the real object, and, therefore, by reproducing the natural conditions (i.e. the sky and clouds, the birds, &c.) and creating the proper emotional atmosphere for the discharge of magical potency, the end will be achieved by the utterance of the spell and the action of the rite. All this is magic pure and simple performed in public for the well-being of the community. There is, therefore, corporate and licit magic just as there is individual and illicit religion.

Magic cannot be distinguished from religion merely as a private affair, any more than religion can be identified with a particular attitude to society. Both are techniques for gaining a measure of control over human life and its environment and destinies. But magic is restricted in method and tradition, and is essentially practical in its endeavour to produce definite results within its circumscribed field of operation. In practice it is often fused with religion because the two disciplines deal with allied phenomena, and the primitive mind is not prone to make and maintain clear-cut distinctions in its traffic with the sacred and occult. Therefore, while *mana*, in the scientific use of the term, is not the common root from which both have sprung, it may be one of the connecting links inasmuch as it is an 'ambivalent' concept, implying alike the beneficent and malevolent effects of supernatural efficiency, and is at once a personal possession and an impersonal force inherent in certain aspects of sacredness. But if it has elements in common with the 'numinous' and the 'magical', magic is not born of the conception of *mana*, any more than it is the disreputable sister of religion. It is essentially the child of its own tradition, living its own life and effective in its own pedigree. It is not bastard science because it is directed towards the world of the supernatural and it is only when empirical knowledge concerning cause and effect fails that resort is made to supercausation by means of spell and rite. In short, the magic art belongs to its own peculiar domain in which it takes its rise as a specialized mechanistic technique exercising compulsion over natural processes in a passive universe. But although it is governed by its own laws and traditions, and fulfils its own proper functions, not infrequently its influence is felt in adjacent emotional spheres, as is shown in cult-practices which reasonably may be described as 'magico-religious'.

CHAPTER III

The Ritual Organization

Since religion and magic represent alternative techniques for dealing with the unpredictable element in human experience and the control of the external world in relation to a system of supercausation or transcendental references, both inevitably find expression essentially in action. Man 'dances out his religion' and manipulates his magic by rite and spell. True, behind these activities there are intense emotional reactions to an order of sacredness believed to be responsive to human needs, which in the case of that aspect of the experience which may be called genuinely religious are evaluated in terms of powers and entities superior to man, but ritual is nevertheless more fundamental than belief being the outward and tangible form of the inmost desires of the soul.

As we have seen, the quest of life is man's chief preoccupation, and in those states of culture in which the means of subsistence are none too secure the food supply is a constant source of anxiety and produces a perpetual state of emotional stress. In a modern civilized community these cares have been very largely eliminated by a scientific control of the supplies which at any rate have left a section of the population free to concentrate on other aspects of human thought and existence. Civilization, in fact, is in great measure the outcome of emancipation from the precarious conditions which made mere keeping alive the overwhelming burden of the daily round. But as long as life depended solely on the chase and the maintenance of crops in a given locality by adequate rain and sunshine, little time or thought could be expended on other matters, such as living well and progressively. All the resources of society had to be directed to one end, and every man assigned his own proper part in the elaborate magico-religious scheme to conserve and promote the means of subsistence. Within the limits of available knowledge the methods were rational and empirical, but when

these failed, or proved to be insufficient, a complex ritual organization, partly magical and partly religious, was employed either to
coerce or assist the processes of nature by supercausation exercised
by human agents, or to seek the aid of intervening beings responsive
to the entreaties of struggling humanity.

THE MEANING OF RITUAL

To secure rain in the Arunta country, for example, certain members
of the tribe who are experts in this particular type of ritual are
summoned to hold an Intichiuma ceremony in the manner that has
been described in order that refreshing and life-giving showers may
fall on the parched ground and the desert be made to blossom as the
rose. For a different purpose (e.g. the multiplication of the totems),
other groups are assembled to perform the rites appropriate to the
occasion and its demands. The procedure is an imitation of the
processes of nature, such as the gathering of rain-clouds, or of the
habits of sacred species, but only because the savage is a man of
action who utters and represents his inmost desires and longings in
outward and visible signs. Ritual thus becomes a vent of pent-up
emotions and activity, the desire to act discharging itself on the
efficacious symbol with which the performers identify themselves.
To complete this identification they disguise themselves as the thing
represented and behave as though they were actually that which
they impersonate, or else they wear objects charged with its potency,
and frequently partake sacramentally of some part of the sacred
species in the case of totemic rites. By these means a vital relationship
is established with the source of strength calculated to bring about
the desired results, or in a more strictly magical operation, a realistic
reproduction of some practical activity in order to establish an *ex
post facto* efficacy by imitative causation.

The primitive mind is not concerned with how this is accomplished. The ceremonies 'work' and that is all that matters. There
are no carefully-thought-out theologies, or systems of belief, no
clear distinctions between magic and religion as separate disciplines,
but absolute faith in magico-religious ritual. Some rites are known
to be anti-social and illicit, others are for the well-being of society
or the individual, but in either case the efficacy is not questioned,
be it to promote life and prosperity, or sickness and death, or yet

again, to avert evil. At no cultural level is *genuine* ritual mere commemorative ceremonial, still less hocus-pocus, for when a rite ceases to be efficacious it is no longer ritual. Similarly, pageantry is not ritual unless it is in the nature of a sacred drama, like the Mass which in Catholic theology is nothing less than the reiteration of the redemptive process in which Christ Himself is born anew to bestow His grace and the bliss of immortality on those who receive Him devoutly in faith and penitence. Thus, Dr Frere is correct when he says 'it is a form of blindness, not common sense, that prevents a man from recognizing that behind ceremonies there lie realities—principles, doctrines and states or habits of mind. No one can hope to judge fairly matters of ceremonial who does not see that the reason why they cause such heat of controversy is that they signify so much.'[1]

In the case of the rite it is not what lies behind the actions performed, but what it essentially is and does that give it its significance. The Eucharistic offering, for instance, is regarded as the re-enactment in time and space of the sacrifice of Calvary, and according to the Tridentine definition, in the consecrated elements 'the body and blood of our Lord Jesus Christ together with His soul and divinity are contained truly, really and substantially, and not in sign, figure or virtue'.[2] As Professor Malinowski says,

> The invisible grace makes the sacrament of transubstantiation the very epitome of everything that the Catholic believes: the incarnation of the Second Person of the Trinity, His Sacrifice on Calvary, and the institution of the sacrament by which He perpetually reappears on earth and unites Himself with every believer in the Sacrament of the Communion.[3]

Therefore, whether it be an Australian Intichiuma ceremony or the central mystery of Christianity, the principle is the same so far as the essential meaning of ritual is concerned.

To attempt to intellectualize, rationalize or to pour scorn on what is fundamentally an emotional reaction to the supra-sensible is to miss the point and confuse the issue. Miss Evelyn Underhill is nearer to a correct analysis of the situation when she says that

[1] W. H. Frere, *Principles of Religious Ceremonial* (Lond., 1928), p. 9.

[2] Council of Trent, Sess. xiii, can. i.

[3] *The Foundations of Faith and Morals* (Oxford, 1936), p. 49.

man's response to Reality with its myriad graded forms of expression, some so crude and some so lovely, some so concrete and some so otherwordly, but all so pathetic in their childishness,

affords a clue to

the real significance of those rituals and ceremonies common to almost every creed, which express the deep human conviction that none of the serial events and experiences of human life are rightly met, unless brought into relation with the Transcendent: that all have more than a natural meaning, and must be sanctified by reference to the unseen Powers.[1]

TRANSITIONAL RITUAL

It is especially at times of crisis when the necessities of life, physical or spiritual, demand supernatural intervention that the individual or the group endeavours to establish ritual relations with the sacred order to safeguard and consecrate birth, adolescence, marriage, death, seed-time and harvest, and the turn of the year. In primitive society life and health are synonymous ideas as are death and disease. In both man and nature the same process of decay and regeneration is manifest; a perpetual dying to be born again, and so arises the notion of a kind of never-dying spirit in all things, the clan becoming a continuous cycle of existence comparable to the succession of the seasons; birth, life, death and rebirth. It is the occasions marking these events that are singled out for the performance of rites of transition.

(a) *Birth Rites*.—When the human embryo begins its independent career it undergoes what Van Gennep describes as a *rite de passage* in which the creative process is repeated often by means of life-giving lustrations. Behind this ritual is a complex theory of generation and status requiring some explanation. It has frequently been suggested that primitive people are ignorant of the physiological facts of paternity[2] since among certain tribes such as the Arunta it is commonly supposed that a woman conceives by some spirit child entering her at a sacred spot where she first becomes conscious of pregnancy. In consequence, the infant when born is regarded as the reincarnation of one of the ancestors associated with the place.[3] The

[1] *Worship* (Lond., 1936), pp. 11 f.

[2] E. S. Hartland, *Primitive Paternity* (Lond., 1909–10).

[3] Spencer and Gillen, *Northern Tribes of Central Australia*, pp. 150, 606.

D

Melanesians think that sexual intercourse is the means of opening the way for spirits to enter a woman in order to produce a child, but the fertilizing properties of semen are apparently not understood. This explains why in the beginning the first woman conceived without a male partner, as the myths often assert, any act such as falling rain being sufficient to enable her to lose her virginity. The entrance having been unbarred the rest followed. Therefore, while it is freely admitted that pregnancy is possible without intercourse, piercing of the hymen is regarded as essential to motherhood, otherwise the tiny spirits could not enter the uterus. When the child is born it is the duty of the husband to protect and cherish it rather in the capacity of a guardian and benevolent friend than of a father, since he had no share in its procreation. Indeed, real paternal authority is exercised by the mother's brother as *potestas*, while kinship is strictly matrilineal.[1]

Such a theory of generation as this can hardly fail to have a profound effect on the whole notion of human origins, especially in view of the general laxity in the matter of pre-nuptial chastity. In a matrilineal society where 'fatherless children' are as universal as virgins are rare, the question of paternity raises many difficulties, and facilitates a supernatural interpretation of the causes of conception and birth. Actually, however, the number of illegitimate children in primitive communities usually is not large, for reasons which have never been very satisfactorily explained, and the misapprehensions concerning the physiological facts of paternity do not necessarily rule out altogether the function of a human progenitor. In ancient times and during the Middle Ages there was much speculation concerning the origin of the soul and its relation to the body and the sexual act,[2] and this same problem regarding the ingress of the incarnated spirit from the transcendent world appears to lie behind both primitive theories of generation and birth rites.

If the infant is a denizen from another sphere, a reincarnation of the spirit of an ancestor, or a dualism composed of a mortal body enshrining an immortal rational soul produced by special creation when the organism is sufficiently developed to receive it, something

---

[1] Malinowski, *The Father in Primitive Psychology* (Lond., 1927), pp. 28 ff., 43 ff. *Sex and Repression in Savage Society* (Lond., 1927), pp. 9 ff. *J.R.A.I.,* xlvi, 1916, p. 353.

[2] cf. Aeschylus, *Eumenides,* 658 ff., C. Singer, *Fom Magic to Science* (Lond. 1928), p. 222.

more than human paternity may seem to be required to explain its genesis. Hence the introduction of spiritual agencies either to the exclusion of the physiological process altogether, or, as is more usual, to supplement it where it fails to afford an adequate interpretation of all the sources of the new life. These beliefs are generally vague, uncertain and contradictory, but in primitive society they are very frequently associated with the notion of reincarnation so that new babies are really either old souls rejuvenated and reborn in new bodies of the right clan, or spirit children emanating from the never-dying spirit of the ancestral stock destined to enter women of the proper totem when the time for their return to earth has come.

Whatever may be the precise form of the belief in a particular case, the fact that the infant enters this world from the 'beyond' renders it at once sacred and an object of ritual regard to everybody immediately concerned with its birth. The mother, being the principal agent, is subject to taboos from the early stages of pregnancy until the child is weaned, designed for the most part to prevent supernaturally dangerous contacts, and reinstate both herself and the child in society. But the husband is also required to undergo similar restrictions, in some cases even to the extent of himself 'lying-in' at the time of the birth while the wife goes about her usual business. This custom, known as *Couvade*, is clearly a ritual institution. The process of parturition generally does not involve much if any interruption in the normal routine among primitive women apart from the self-imposed taboos. Thus, in British Guiana

> before the child is born the father abstains for a time from certain kinds of animal food. The woman works as usual up to a few hours before the birth of the child. At last she retires alone, or accompanied only by some women, to the forest, where she ties up her hammock; and then the child is born. Then in a few hours—often less than a day—the woman, who, like all women living in a very unartificial condition, suffers but little, gets up and resumes her ordinary work.

Her husband, on the other hand, takes to his hammock as soon as the event has occurred, and

> abstaining from every sort of work, from meal and all other food, except weak gruel of cassava meal, from smoking, from washing himself, and,

above all, from touching weapons of any sort, is nursed and cared for by all the women of the place.[1]

This period of quiescence in the case of the father is clearly magico-religious in significance. By it he affirms his paternity of the child and shares in the process of delivery, even to the extent of imitating the movements and groans of a woman in travail.[2] But it has no possible relation to the physiological condition of the mother, and in some measure the same may be true of the lying-in of the wife where nature does not require a protracted 'confinement', a word suggesting the real purpose of the custom; i.e., to exclude from society. Under conditions of modern civilization, childbirth, of course, makes much heavier demands on the strength of a woman, but even so the widespread custom of a mother remaining indoors until she has been 'churched' is a European survival of the earlier ritual seclusion. By this ceremonial act she is restored to the normal relationships of everyday life, just as in primitive states of culture the parents undergo a ritual re-admission to the community at the conclusion of the birth ceremonies consisting of lustrations, anointings, cutting of hair, visits of friends, offering of rice and various articles, and similar rites.

For example, after a birth among the Hopi, on the fifth day the wife is allowed to put on her moccasins and see the sun for the first time since her confinement. She then bathes her head and that of the baby's with amole, and is at liberty to resume her household duties, but she may not eat meat or salt, and is compelled to drink only warm water or juniper-tea till she has completed a series of bathings on the tenth and fifteenth days, culminating in a vapour bath on the twentieth day. The house has to be thoroughly cleansed, and the child bathed and rubbed with corn-meal, given its name and presented to the sun by the mother. The rites conclude with a feast and the giving of presents to the guests in return for those made to the wife during 'the event'.[3]

Mother and child, in fact, are similarly treated because both are

---

[1] Everard im Thurn, *Among the Indians of Guiana* (Lond., 1883), p. 217. cf. W. R. Dawson. *The Custom of Couvade* (Manchester, 1929), for recent discussion. The practice of Couvade still lingers in England, cf. *Man.*, 1930, 28, 62; 1931, 16; 1932, 288, 338. *Folk-Lore*, XLV, 1934, p. 158; XLVII, 1936, pp. 310 ff.

[2] Radin, 'Winnebago Tribe' in 37th *R.B.A.E.* (Wash., 1915–16), p. 126.

[3] *Journal of American Ethnology and Archaeology*, II, p. 165.

undergoing the same process of initiation into society; the mother, especially in the case of a first confinement, being raised to a higher status, and her offspring undergoing the initial *rite de passage* into this life. To this end it has to be desacralized, put into a right relationship with the spiritual world, and given its place in the family and the community. The lustrations and anointings affect at once a ritual purification and renewal, bestowing vitality on the new life and strength to combat the forces of evil with which man has to contend at critical junctures. Presentation to the spirits, totem or gods, establishes a communion with the transcendent order, and the solemn bestowal of a name, often connected with the ancestor from whom the individual is supposed to be derived, has a like effect inasmuch as the name is an integral part of the personality. By it the child is linked with his ancestry human and divine, and given his status in society (the family and the clan). Because of its sacred character and intimate connexion with his personality, the real name, sometimes revealed by his tutelary genius or in a dream, is kept strictly secret lest harm should be worked on him through it.

Besides the more generic name of the social or religious group, or that made known secretly on some specific occasion, a man has his personal name in everyday use. To this is often added a 'status term' indicating the stage of initiation he has reached. Thus, in Central Australia he is called *Ambaquerka* until he has been thrown up in the air during the initiation ceremony. He then becomes *Ulpmerka* till he is taken to the circumcision ground, after which he is called *Wurtja* while awaiting the operation, and *Arakurta* between circumcision and subincision, emerging finally as *Urliara*.[1] In this region each man has his personal name, his secret name (associated with his *churinga-nanja*), his 'status term' acquired during the initiation rite, his class or sub-class name, his totemic name, and sometimes a nickname. But while the designation of human beings in primitive society is very complex and regarded as a matter of great importance in view of the ritual and social significance of the titles, the actual naming ceremony is usually simple, and it does not necessarily take place at birth. Sometimes it is part of the puberty rites, or it may be deferred till some sign is given by astrological or divinatory means. Being intimately connected with status and

[1] *Native Tribes of Central Australia,* pp. 218, 249, 638.

personality, it is not confined to the opening phase of the earthly career, and in the course of a lifetime a man or woman may change his or her name many times as circumstances and occasions demand.

(b) *Initiation Rites*.—The next stage in the progressive status of the male is the attainment of adolescence marked by solemn induction into the full privileges and responsibilities of the community, religious, social and administrative. This involves a process of rebirth or transition from the family circle to active membership in the tribal fellowship. First, childish things have to be put away by a series of 'separation rites' which usually include fasting, tests of endurance or ordeals, circumcision (sometimes subincision) and a protracted period of isolation in addition to lustrations and numerous taboos. The proceedings are strictly secret, and during the ceremonies detailed explanations are usually given of the esoteric tradition, as well as long exhortations on correct social behaviour and religious practice. To reveal to the uninitiated anything said or done in the course of the mysteries involves instant death by natural or supernatural agencies, so great is the gulf separating those who have passed through the rites from those who have not.

In order that the past may be completely cut off, a pantomimic drama of death and rebirth is usually enacted. Thus, in the Yuin ceremonies witnessed by Dr Howitt, after the cardinal sins had been rehearsed before the boys in a kind of burlesque, and they had been instructed concerning Daramulun and their moral duties, a figure of the High God was dug in the ground, a grave was prepared with digging sticks into which a man was placed with his hands crossed holding a Geebung tree and covered with leaves, grass, sticks and plants in a realistic manner. Beside it the novices were placed while dirges were sung in procession invoking Daramulun. On reaching the grave the singers ranged themselves in front of the novices. The Geebung tree began to quiver, and the dead man rose up from beneath his covering and danced on the grave, displaying the magic quartz in his mouth which he is alleged to have received from Daramulun.[1]

In Fiji a more realistic ceremony of the same nature is held on the fifth day of the rites. The heads of the novices are shaved for a second time and their bodies arrayed in the largest and best folds of cloth. Carrying in their hands their choicest weapons, they enter

[1] Howitt, op. cit., pp. 554 ff.

the inner sanctuary of the sacred stone enclosure (*nanga*), where before their startled gaze they behold a row of dead men covered with blood and their bodies apparently cut open so as to reveal their entrails. Stepping over these ghastly relics, they form a line in front of the high priest who suddenly utters a great yell. Thereupon the dead men rise to their feet and rush down to the river to cleanse themselves of the blood and entrails of slaughtered pigs with which they have been smeared.[1] By this crude death and resurrection symbolism the initiates are incorporated into the mystical fellowship of the adult tribe and its gods, or ancestral spirits. Sometimes this involves a ritual combat as part of the testing of the youths,[2] and it is not improbable that originally instead of witnessing a symbolic restoration the initiates themselves had to undergo a ritual death and rebirth.

Thus, among the Kurnai they are 'laid to sleep as boys in order to be awakened as men'. That this 'magic sleep, not like ordinary sleep' is regarded as the equivalent of death is shown by the fact that their mothers and sisters mourn for them, decorating themselves with a band of clay across their faces (the customary sign of mourning), while the youths are not allowed to speak during this period of quiescence.[3] Since they chirp like their totem, the emuwren (*yiirung*), during the magic sleep suggests that they are thought to have returned to the totemic state from which they emerge as new-born members of the clan.

In the Wonghi tribe of New South Wales the youths are said to be killed by a supernatural being called Thurmulun (Daramulun) who cuts them up and then restores them to life, having knocked out a tooth.[4] This same belief survives among the uninitiated in the Central region where the Kaitish women and children are told that Twanyirika kills the boys and restores them during the initiation rites,[5] just as the Binbinga, on the west coast of the Lake of Carpentaria, affirm that the noise of the bull-roarer is made by a spirit named Katajina, eating up the novices who afterwards disgorges them as initiated men.[6] In the New World, the Omaha used to bind

---

[1] Fison, *J.R.A.I.*, XIV, 1885, pp. 20 ff.

[2] Howitt, op. cit., 333 ff., 639.

[3] op. cit., pp. 623, 625.

[4] A. L. P. Cameron. *J.R.A.I.*, XIV, 1885, pp. 357 ff.

[5] Spencer and Gillen, *Northern Tribes of Central Australia*, pp. 342 ff., 498.

[6] op. cit., pp. 366 ff., 373, 501.

the neophyte to a plank, after which one of the performers pretended to kill him and another brought him back to life.[1]

The same idea lies behind the ceremonial rebirth from the embryonic state which is a prominent feature in this type of ritual, as, for instance, in the Akikuyu custom of the mother going through the act of childbirth in pantomime before a boy is circumcised. He is then required to cry like a babe and be washed, and to live on milk for a few days.[2] In New Guinea Yabim youths after they have been circumcised live for some months in seclusion, and when they finally return to the village they keep their eyes closed and appear to be unable to speak or understand what is said to them like new-born babes.[3]

It is obvious in all these cases that initiation is a death and rebirth, brought about either through a ritual act of dying or of being born again to a new status in society. The process of regeneration is usually sacramental in the sense that it involves the communication of sacredness to the neophytes by means of a solemn meal and investiture, either with insignia, garments or other symbolic objects. Thus, in the Fijian rite, after the mimic resurrection had been enacted and the seemingly dead men had returned from bathing in the river, a cooked yam was solemnly carried into the sacred enclosure in procession, together with baked pork and a drinking-cup full of water, and carefully wrapped round with a native cloth. The end of the yam was put into the mouths of each of the novices who partook of a morsel of it; they then received the pork in the same manner, and wetted their lips with the holy water, after which their mouths were wiped with a napkin.[4] In the same area, kava, which originally was a kind of ambrosia, or drink of the gods, comparable to soma in India, is drunk during initiation into the cult of the water-sprites in order to establish a communion with the elfins which makes the initiates invulnerable.[5]

A similar significance is attached to the *churinga* in Australia, and to the medicine-bag among certain tribes, such as the Ojibway,

[1] J. G. Kohl, *Kitschi-Gami* (Bremen, 1859), I, pp. 59 ff.

[2] W. S. and K. Routledge, *With a Prehistoric People, the Akikuyu of British East Africa* (Lond., 1910), p. 152.

[3] K. Vetter, *Nachrichten über Kaiser Wilhelms-Land und den Bismark-Archipel.* (Berlin, 1897), pp. 92 ff.

[4] Fison, op. cit., pp. 20 ff.

[5] Hocart, *Kingship* (Oxford, 1927), pp. 59 ff., 134 ff.

Winnebagoes and Sioux, in North America. This ambivalent instrument which consisted in a small bag containing charms or 'medicine', thought to have such potent qualities (called *tonwan*) that no human being could withstand them, was used both to slay and to restore the candidates at the time of their initiation into secret societies. When the god of the waters prepared the first medicine-bag he tested its powers on four candidates, all of whom perished under the shock. By way of an antidote he produced little shells, the virtue of which was to restore life to those killed by the medicine-bag. When a candidate to-day is slain during the ceremonies he is revived either by a second thrust of the bag, or by means of one of these vitalizing stones which every initiated Sioux is supposed to have in his body.[1]

In the higher religions initiation is often repeated periodically as the neophyte advances through a progressive series of degrees in a mystery cult, but the principle is the same, since the purpose of the rites is a renewal of spiritual vitality through a death and resurrection drama. First a severance from the world is effected by separation rites; then a union with the divine is secured by sacramental regeneration; and lastly, a return to society is made as a 'new man' in a higher status equipped with new powers and potentialities as one begotten from the transcendent order, symbolized often by a change of name and attire appropriate to the rank achieved.

(c) *Marriage.*—The final stage is celebrated with the outward signs of victory which often include a ceremonial procession and invariably a feast with the accompaniments of nuptial revels. The licentiousness that is common on these occasions is largely the result of the close connexion in primitive society between initiation and fertility. Since these rites occur normally at the age of puberty, they constitute a preparation for sexual intercourse, and there can be little doubt that such practices as circumcision, and the corresponding operation on girls, have a practical as well as a magico-religious significance. Indeed in Australia it is believed that the mutilation increases the carnal powers of both men and women.[2] It is not surprising, therefore, that once the rites have been duly performed, this aspect of their function should be exercised without further

[1] J. Carver, *Travels through Interior Parts of N. America* (Lond., 1781), pp. 271 ff. Schoolcraft, *Indian Tribes of the United States* (Philad., 1853–6), III, p. 287, V, p. 430.

[2] H. Basedow, *The Australian Aboriginal* (Adelaide, 1925), p. 248.

delay, though in some cases the newly initiated youths are forbidden to have relations with women till their marriage.

Initiation, in short, is a preparation for marriage in the sense that it makes the boy or girl *ritually* marriageable, but the actual nuptial state has its own proper ceremonial. This may include even further proof of virility, as among the Masai, who used to require their males to have been on several man-slaying raids, before entering upon matrimonial bliss.[1] In other words, as in all rites of this nature, a person has to *fight* his way to a higher status in society, and while it is only in warrior cultures that actual man-slaying is a *sine quâ non,* in most marriage rites a ceremonial combat of some kind plays a prominent part. A good deal that goes by the name of 'marriage by capture' probably is really a survival of a contest in which the bridegroom, with or without the assistance of his kinsmen, engaged in a struggle to obtain his bride who was by no means necessarily an unwilling victim of the fray, especially in matriarchal society where she had a considerable voice in domestic matters.

Everywhere marriage is an institution regulated by custom and law 'not to be taken in hand unadvisedly, lightly, or wantonly'. Being a 'holy estate' according to the primitive conception of sacredness, it is hedged round with taboos as numerous as they are binding on the two contracting parties and their immediate associates. The supernatural danger supposed to be attached to defloration, so persistently argued by A. E. Crawley,[2] may be an exaggeration inasmuch as there is considerable prenuptial licence in many communities, but, nevertheless, marriage is a taboo-state, and it cannot be denied that many nuptial rites are directed against the imaginary dangers of defloration and the consummation of the union. To ward off evil influences and secure a 'blessing' an elaborate installation ceremonial marks the critical juncture in the upward careers of the two individuals and their families, for marriage invariably represents a rise in social status. A bachelor has no household of his own, and is debarred from many tribal privileges, so that in Melanesia and elsewhere there are seldom if ever any unmarried men except idiots, albinos and aged widowers, and any woman sexually tolerable finds a partner without difficulty.[3]

[1] A. C. Hollis, *The Masai* (Oxford, 1905), pp. 298, 302.

[2] *The Mystic Rose* (New Edition by T. Besterman, Lond., 1932), pp. 311 ff.

[3] Malinowski, *Sexual Life of Savages* (Lond., 1932), 3rd Edition, pp. 66 ff.

To promote health, wealth and fruitfulness, and expel all evil forces and forebodings, life-giving and cathartic agents are widely employed. To make the bride fertile grain, rice, fruit and nuts are thrown, and she may be required to ride on a mare when she is taken to the bridegroom's house, sometimes with a little boy sitting behind her to ensure male offspring. Fish, again, are frequently used for reproductive functions and therefore figure largely in marriage rites just as eggs are means of promoting fecundity.[1] On the negative side the dangers associated with the crisis find expression in the devices to protect the pair from supernatural evil by secluding them and imposing upon them a period of silence, the veiling of the bride, and changing her clothes and similar disguises, together with bathing and lustrations, asceticisms, circumambulations of the hearth and a mimic conflict, including the firing of guns and other noises, and the lighting of fires and torches to drive away the malevolent forces. To establish and strengthen the bond the hands of the bride and bridegroom are joined, knots are tied, rings and garments are exchanged, and sometimes blood, a meal is eaten together, while as a sign of victory they are crowned with wreaths of olive, myrtle or occasionally silver and gold. In Western Christendom this practice survives in the wreath of orange-blossoms worn by the bride, and in the Eastern Orthodox Church after the benediction the bridal pair are crowned as an integral part of the rite.[2]

In its Christian form the practice of veiling a bride became symbolical of the woman forsaking all others and keeping only to her husband, submitting to his rule over her. In ancient Rome a red veil distinguished a newly-married woman, and it was natural that a bride should also be clad in a manner that testified to her having been set apart for her office and function. Since this mode of attire suggested the obligation of constancy, it was worn by widows who made a profession of continence (*flammens virginalis*), and later it became the badge of the 'Brides of Christ' who in the Religious Life were consecrated body and soul to the service of their heavenly Bridegroom. The veil, therefore, like the crown, came to be associated with the idea of a supernatural victory in a sacred combat with 'the world, the flesh and the devil'.

[1] Westermarck, *History of Human Marriage* (Lond., 1921), vol. II, pp. 467 ff.

[2] Martène, *De Antiquis Ecclesiae Ritibus* (Antwerp, 1736), p. 609. Goar, *Euchologion* (Paris, 1647), p. 396.

(d) Death.—In the ritual centring round the final transition through physical death to the fuller and higher life of the spirit-world, the same threefold division recurs: separation, communion and installation in a new status. Throughout 'the last rites' the predominant idea is that of rebirth, only the new activities for which the deceased is being prepared, and the new status into which he is being initiated, belongs to a transcendent order of existence, though ultimately a reincarnation to a life of renewed activity in this world frequently is anticipated. Nevertheless, the passing soul has to be severed from its earthly state, strengthened and fortified for the final conflict with the powers of evil, and having prevailed, at length it is admitted to the blessed company of the victorious dead through the ritual acts performed, whatever may be its final goal. Birth, puberty and death constitute an unending cycle, in which the individual passes from one level of existence to another, and inasmuch as this eternal sequence is broken in the case of the 'unburied dead' (i.e. those who have not been duly initiated by the proper rites at the time of the dissolution), such unfortunate wandering souls are a continual source of danger and discomfort to the survivors. Therefore, every effort is made to dispose of the body in a decent manner calculated to secure rebirth and renewal beyond the grave.

To remove the death contagion and separate the corpse from his former career, elaborate purifications have to be made extending from the mortal remains of the deceased to the relatives, the house and everything with which he has come in contact during the last struggle. Death to the old life involves putting away all its taints and associations by lustrations, fumigations, clothing the body in new or clean garments, and sometimes passing it through the fire, or drying it in the sun; a practice that is closely connected with cremation and mummification and is probably part of the process of rebirth,[1] like burial in the contracted position (i.e. in that of the foetus). Similarly, the ablutions may be connected with the life-giving properties of water, while the anointing of the corpse with oil, smearing it with blood, or its surrogate red ochre, and surrounding it with shells (as in the Palaeolithic interments at Paviland, Mentone and elsewhere), can hardly be prompted by anything but a desire to impart life to the body. In ancient Egypt this mechanical

[1] cf. James, *American Anthropologist,* XXX, 1928, pp. 215 ff.

method of resuscitating the mortal remains reached its zenith in the elaborate methods of mummification whereby not only the physical integument was rendered imperishable but all the faculties were restored by magical operations.[1] Originally funeral ritual of this nature was confined to the Pharaoh and the royal family by virtue of their peculiar relationship with the gods whom they embodied, but it was subsequently extended to the rest of the community to promote the deceased to his proper status in the hereafter and safe-guard the survivors.

The mourning ceremonies are usually partly precautionary and partly initiatory. The nearest of kin (especially the widow) and the relatives who participate in the rites, and all who have come in contact with the corpse, are required to bathe or perform ablutions of some kind, undergoing fumigations, live in seclusion for a period, abstain from certain foods and from sexual intercourse, and subject themselves to strenuous ordeals, as in the other initiation ceremonies. A cathartic and protective element is certainly present in customs of this nature, but it would seem also that they are part of the process of rebirth and installation into the next life by virtue of the intimate relationship of the mourners with the deceased, so that all are actors in one and the same death and resurrection drama. Thus, at some point in the ceremonial a sacred combat is usually fought in which they have their allotted parts, as, for example, among the Sioux where a man is selected to represent the ghost, and to play against the rest with wild plum-stones marked like dice. In Ireland a fencing-match, which seems to be a degenerate form of sword-dance, was fought during the wake in the presence of the corpse, while in the Niger River wild imaginary encounters are reproduced at the death of an Ibonzo chief, performed by young men brandishing swords and cutlasses, striking their shields and singing warlike chants.

When at length 'the last enemy' has been destroyed and 'death is swallowed up in victory', then the actors celebrate the event with feasting, merrymaking and revels in which buffoonery, jesting and indulgence are conspicuous features. Irish wakes have long been a byword of debauchery and a cause of scandal, but all the world over at such times considerable licence is allowed, as at other initiation ceremonies. To the modern cultured observer this appears

---

[1] W. R. Dawson, *Journal of Egyptian Archaeology*, XIII, 1927, pp. 40 ff.

as a highly unedifying procedure, but as the concluding episode in an installation rite, in its proper context it is not as incongruous as it seems when isolated from its setting. Moreover, a deeper motive than mere eroticism lies behind the freedom of speech and action which invariably marks the end of a victorious struggle over death and the powers of evil.

Since a sacred marriage is usually the consummation of the ultimate triumph of any human or divine being who has passed through a mystic grave to newness of life, a sexual element is present in this type of ritual which finds expression in fertility symbolism, general relaxation and obscene jesting, unless, as in the higher religions, it is sublimated in mysticism and lofty sacramental concepts typifying the union of heaven and earth in a mystery cult. Thus, for instance, the Mandaeans partake of a ritual meal both at weddings and funerals. At the nuptial feast ancestors and spirits of fertility are invoked to bless the marriage, walnuts, almonds, raisins, dates, fish and salt are eaten, and raisins are squeezed into water to produce a life-giving sacramental cup representing the whole cycle of sowing, germination and fruitfulness. This ceremonial is repeated at the meal for the dead (*masiqta*) in order to enable the soul of the deceased to ascend to the 'World of Lights', and even those who died without the last rites can be regenerated by proxy. A man plays the part of the dead person, is washed, receives absolution, puts on new grave clothes, eats the sacred food and drinks the vitalizing beverage with covered hands as an elixir of immortality.[1] Such rites are clearly performed on behalf of the dead, not of the relatives, and in their essential features they conform to the ritual pattern common to all initiation ceremonies.

The mourners correspond to the inner circle of the family and the tribe at birth, puberty or marriage, and they fulfil their functions by virtue of their kinship with the deceased, so that even in the Apostolic Church it was possible for a person to be baptized for a deceased relative (1 Cor. xv. 29), thereby facilitating his resurrection, as in the case of the Mandaean proxy. It is this identification which explains the Indian practice of *Suttee* (Sanskrit, *Sati*, 'true wife'), or concremation of a faithful widow, and in many other cultures ancient and modern the wives of chiefs regard it as a privi-

[1] E. S. Drower, *The Mandaean of Iraq and Iran* (Lond., 1937), pp. 67 ff., 204 ff. *Folk-Lore*, XLVIII, 1937, pp. 231 ff.

lege to follow their lord to the grave, often arrayed as a bride adorned for her husband, that together in a more exalted state they may receive a crown that fadeth not away. The custom, however, has tended to become modified by ritual substitutions, such as the seclusion of the widow and relatives for a protracted period during which time a ban of silence is imposed. But humility rather than triumph is then the prevailing idea, so that mourners are required to wear sombre clothing and go softly till at length, when the soul they represent has won the victory, they are reinstated in society with appropriate rejoicing.

SEASONAL RITUAL

Closely connected with these *rites de passage* at critical junctures in the life of the individual from the cradle to the grave is the seasonal drama at seed-time and harvest in the wider activities of society at large. That the same general scheme should recur in the magico-religious control of the fruitfulness of the earth as in the fertility of the human race is to be expected, since to the primitive mind the maintenance of the food supply and the increase and well-being of man and beast are so intimately related. As hunting tribes resort to ceremonies of the Intichiuma type to secure the multiplication of the animals and plants on which they depend for their subsistence, so in agricultural communities the regular growth of the crops is a matter of no less concern. Consequently, at the critical seasons they call forth an emotional reaction comparable to that experienced at the turning points in the career of the individual. When the ground is prepared and the crops are sown, and later when the harvest is gathered, evil (equated with famine, disease and death) must be overcome with good, which is identified with health and plenty. To this end the struggle for existence is enacted in a ritual drama in which the beneficent and malevolent forces contend in sacred combat, and after a mimic death and resurrection of the hero-god, usually impersonated by the king or his representative, his victory is acclaimed amid universal rejoicing, frequently marked by the customary licentiousness and lack of restraints, just as the earlier conflict is the occasion of asceticisms and ordeals.

Since the fruitfulness of the earth is associated with human fertility, erotic rites are thought to have a reciprocal action on the growth of vegetation. Thus, a sacred marriage is celebrated in the fields to promote the fertility of the crops, and intercourse between the sexes is commonly resorted to to stimulate the processes of fecundity. The Pipiles of Central America, for example, practised continence for four days before the seed was sown, and on the night before the planting it was a religious duty for husband and wife to cohabit,[1] while in Java and elsewhere the sexual act is performed in the fields to fertilize the crops.[2] Frazer is probably correct in interpreting such modern customs as those of young married people rolling together down a slope on the sown fields on May Day or at Whitsuntide, and of going into the fields with bare feet at midsummer, as relics of this crude primitive rite. Therefore, it may not have been altogether without reason that the puritanical writer, Philip Stubbes, wrote in scathing terms in 1583 of 'all the young men and maides, olde men and wives', who 'against May, Whitsunday, and other times, run gadding over night to woods, groves, hils and mountains, where they spend all the night in pleasant pastimes' presided over by 'Satan prince of hel'.[3]

As the earth is regarded as a goddess fertilized by the fecundating rain descending from the sky, the union of earth and sky is represented as a sacred marriage of the supernatural powers personified and enacted by the nuptials of the king and queen, or priest and priestess, of which the marital relations of commoners and lay folk are the counterpart. Therefore, the seasonal rites follow the general ritual pattern which aims at securing the well-being of the community as well as of the individual. As the fortunes of the state are bound up with those of the human representative of the gods upon whom it depends for its continuance, the central figure is the king who is thought to control the processes of nature, fulfilling his functions in conjunction with his consort, in the role of the earth goddess.

Thus, the Annual Festival in an agricultural community represents the centre and climax of all the religious activities of the year when the king engages in a sacred combat with his spiritual foes like the gods in the creation story which is enacted as part of the drama. Having won the victory he is re-established in the throne, led forth

---

[1] Brasseur de Bourbourg, *Histoire des nations civilisées du Mexique et de l'Amérique Centrale* (Paris, 1857–9), II, p. 565.

[2] *G.B.*, pt. II ('Magic Art,' II), pp. 98 ff.

[3] *The Anatomie of Abuses*. Reprint by F. J. Furnival (1583), p. 149.

in triumph, and to ensure the fruitfulness of the earth and the multi-plication of men and beasts, he has nuptial relations with the queen.[1] This event occurs usually in spring or autumn, and while it has a wider significance than the promotion of the growth of the crops, inasmuch as the prosperity and fertility of society as a whole de-pends on it, it has a clearly defined vegetative function. Thus, it coincides with sowing and reaping, and not infrequently is con-nected with the ritual of the first-fruits and the harvest.

In addition to the death and resurrection proper, which will be examined in greater detail in the next chapter, the annual renewal often is the occasion of a drastic purification of the entire community, including the scouring of the cooking vessels in which the new crops are to be placed, the sweeping of the houses, barns and public squares, the extinction of fires (including sometimes the temple hearth), ablutions, a strict fast and purging with emetics. Through this *rite de separation* the evil of the old year is expelled and contagion removed in preparation for the consecration of the new crops and their desacralization after a solemn meal has been held in which a small portion of the first-fruits is eaten sacramentally by the king or chief and certain privileged persons. The rites are usually con-tinued for several days with appropriate dances and asceticisms, concluding with revelries, licence and lustrations.[2]

At the season of sowing a similar ritual is observed which derives its name from the Saturnalia held in ancient Rome from the 17th to the 23rd of December when originally a young and vigorous man who had personated the god of sowing and husbandry for thirty days was put to death in the guise of the dying god, and the renewal of nature thereby effected was celebrated by feasting, orgies and extravagant mirth.[3] There can be little doubt that this represents the prototype of the modern May Day and Shrovetide carnivals, Christmas mumming and Yuletide revels, and the medieval observances known as the Lord of Misrule, the Abbot of Unreason and the Boy Bishop.[4] The fatal role of the king has long

[1] S. H. Hooke, *Myth and Ritual* (Oxford, 1933), pp. 8 f. Frazer, *G.B.*, pt. VI ('Adonis'), pp. 58 f.

[2] The Creek *Busk* Festival is a typical ritual of this character. cf. F. G. Speck, *Ethnology of Yuki Indians* (Philad., 1909), pp. 86 ff.

[3] *G.B.*, pt. II, pp. 310 ff.

[4] *G.B.*, pt. IX ('The Scapegoat'), pp. 312 ff., where the evidence is given in detail. cf. James, *Christian Myth and Ritual* (Lond., 1933), pp. 293 ff.

since lost its gruesome character, and become that of a frolicsome puppet, but it seems that in the beginning he (perhaps in the person of the monarch himself) paid the supreme penalty in order to revivify nature at the turn of the year when the new crops were sown, the regenerative aspect of the sacrifice finding its customary expression in rejoicing. The lack of restraint suggests that the festival originally terminated with a sacred marriage, thereby completing the death and resurrection ritual drama.

CHAPTER IV

Myth and Ritual

We have now to consider the story enacted in affirmation of the existence of the reality set forth in ritual, regarded as the tangible expression of the hopes and fears, the longings and desires of the human spirit, and a method of exercising control over the unpredictable element in human experience. In its primary sense myth is the utterance of the rite, not abstract philosophizings concerning the ultimate ground of the universe and the essential nature of man; nor indeed fanciful explanations of how things came to be, as Andrew Lang imagined.[1] It is true, of course, that the story of creation, the origin of death and the destruction of mankind form the subject-matter of myths in most parts of the world, but not as philosophical speculations or poetic descriptions. When these themes occur they constitute the verbal part of the ritual expression of the ever-present conflict between good and evil, life and death in human society and the natural order. Thus, by the repetition of the events which according to the lore of the tribe are supposed to have happened in primeval times, supernatural influence is brought to bear on the recurrent situation as it exists at the moment. Therefore, it is out of the concrete realities of the present that mythology arises, however much the sacred story may be referred back to a remote age 'in the Alcheringa' or mythical past.

As Professor Malinowski says,

> Myth as it exists in a savage community, that is, in its living primitive form, is not merely a story told but a reality lived. It is not of the nature of fiction such as we read to-day in a novel but it is a living reality, believed to have once happened in primeval times, and continuing ever since to influence the world and human destinies. This myth is to the savage what to a fully believing Christian is the Biblical story of

[1] Lang, *Myth, Ritual and Religion* (Lond., 1899), vol. I, p. 162. cf. Frazer, *Myths of the Origin of Fire* (Lond., 1933), p. vi.

Creation, of the Fall of man, and of the Redemption by Christ's sacrifice on the Cross.[1]

It is not 'an explanation in satisfaction of a scientific interest, but a narrative resurrection of a primeval reality, told in satisfaction of deep religious wants, moral cravings, social submissions, assertions, even practical requirements'. Melanesians do not want to explain or make intelligible anything which happens in their myths. It is enough that they 'express, enhance and codify belief', and vouch for the efficiency of ritual and moral principles just as our own sacred story 'lives in our ritual, in our morality, as it governs our faith and controls our conduct'.[2]

Hocart indeed affirms that 'the myth detached from all reality can only continue to exist in a society which is itself divorced from reality, one which has such a reserve of wealth that it can afford to maintain an intelligentsia exempt from the pursuit of bare life, and free to devote all its energies to intellectual play, to poetry and to romance'. Greece in the days of Plato had attained this condition, and mythology, therefore, was no longer required 'to give bare life but to adorn it with the elegancies of fancy'.[3] In Europe to-day, on the other hand, the perplexing problems and uncertainties of our post-war world have given rise to a genuine mythology to consolidate the new totalitarian social order and express the current ways of thinking about the facts of life. Thus, the 'dictatorship of the proletariat' and the glories of the 'Aryan Nordic race' are referred back to a Golden Age when everything was lovely in the original communist or Nazi garden before capitalist or Semitic serpents perverted the scene. For the practical purposes of mythology it is of little consequence whether there ever existed in fact a godless, classless age of primitive promiscuity, or a heroic epoch when the Aryan pioneers of Nordic civilization roamed the forests of northern Europe. The historical reconstruction of myths is irrelevant for sociological purposes.

> Whatever the hidden reality of their unrecorded past may be [as Malinowski points out], myths serve to cover certain inconsistencies created by historical events, rather than to record these events exactly. The persons and beings we find in them are what they appear to be on

---

[1] *Myth in Primitive Psychology* (Lond., 1926), p. 21.
[2] op. cit., p. 23. cr. *Frazer Lectures*, Ed. W. R. Dawson (Lond., 1932), pp. 72, 81.
[3] *The Labyrinth* (Lond., 1935), p. 278.

the surface, and not symbols of hidden realities. As to any explanatory function of these myths, there is no problem which they cover, no curiosity which they satisfy, no theory which they contain.[1]

The role of the myth is to consolidate and stabilize society, and given the proper mass psychology and unquestioned loyalty to a leader or a group, invested with supernatural or quasi-divine authority, it fulfils its purposes as a cultural force and sociological charter.

In primitive society the interests of social solidarity are safe-guarded by initiation rites in which the esoteric tradition of the tribe is maintained, as we have seen, by every available psycho-logical device as potent as the means adopted to this end by the modern totalitarian state through a controlled press, broadcasting, the cinema, and appropriate educational methods. Under such conditions, be it in a savage or civilized community, there is no room for private opinion on matters of vital concern to the group, and the established order is given a supernatural sanction by time-honoured and unalterable customs and beliefs rigidly observed according to the requirements of magical procedure. If myth is the uttered rite directed primarily to practical ends, it must conform to the tradition of magic, if it is to be effective in spell, just as in its more distinctly religious guise it must confirm the established faith, and not merely satisfy curiosity. In neither aspect is it aetiological in aim. As Dr Marett says, 'it is there to cater, not for the speculative man with his "Why?", but for the practical man with "How, if not thus?"'[2]

Since the sacred story gives efficacy to the associated ritual by relating it at once to the supernatural source of its potency and the existing social order in which it is operative, it inevitably produces a static condition of which it is itself the dynamic. As a secret tradition in a closely knit community passed on from one generation to the next, or from one practitioner to another, by the most powerful aids of corporate or craft suggestion and sacred associa-tions, it is calculated to consolidate the social structure. From time to time, it is true, changing circumstances tend to demand a new traditional background, and as a result ancient customs may require reinterpretation to meet the altered situation, but the function of myth remains that of stabilizing the existing order by endowing it

[1] *Frazer Lectures*, p. 98.
[2] Marett, *Faith, Hope and Charity in Primitive Religion* (Oxford, 1932), p. 106.

with sacredness. 'It was so in Alcheringa', or its equivalent, is a transcendent reference which gives a permanent value and prestige to custom and belief, and therefore it is to the Golden Age in the past that myths tend to look for the *raisin d'être* of the present-day institutions.

While it is obvious that in the growth of civilization the emotional and critical situations which give rise to myth and ritual in one state of culture will not be identical with those in another, as is clear when the position in Melanesia or Ancient Egypt is compared with that which prevails in Russia or Germany to-day. But the fundamental principles governing the purpose of the phenomenon is the same in all cases and at all times. In those horizons in which reflective thought is operative it is concrete realities which find expression in the sacred story and its rites, and certain recurrent themes are found in association with given rituals connected with the most pressing problems of every-day life and experience; namely, birth, death and renewal, as in the royal sacred drama.

THE DIVINE KINGSHIP

At the dawn of civilization in the Ancient East a complex cultus developed around the person and function of the king as the dynamic centre of the community and the human representative and embodiment of the gods upon whom it depended for its prosperity. In Egypt, for example, the very life of the nation was wrapped up in the person of Pharaoh who has been described as 'a living epitome of all that is divine in the Nile valley', summing up in his complex personality the attributes of all the gods he embodied.[1] Primarily he was the physical son of the Sun-god, Re, whose cult at an early period in Egyptian history spread over the whole country from Heliopolis, its original home, Through his long and chequered career the solar deity assumed various forms and names, Re, Atum, Horus, Khepri (the scarab beetle), while at Thebes he was associated with Amen who from the Eighteenth Dynasty and onwards was the national god of Egypt. Even his deadly rival Osiris, the judge and ruler of the dead, eventually became solarized, and the Osirian theology was incorporated in the Heliopolitan cultus on which the kingship was based.

[1] Foucart, *E.R.E.,* vol. VII, p. 713.

About 2750 B.C. the line of Khufu, the builder of the Great Pyramid of Gizeh, was supplanted by a family of kings who assumed the title 'Son of Re'. This designation may go back to an earlier period, but in the Fifth Dynasty the Pharoahs as sons of Re erected vast temples in honour of their heavenly father who 'endowed them with life, stability and well-being like Re for ever'. In theory they alone made the offerings since it is always the king who is represented as performing the rites which secured the health and prosperity of the nation, though in practice the priests acted as their deputies except on very special occasions. As Erman says, 'the gods are no longer the gods of the Egyptian people, they are the gods of Pharaoh their son'.[1] In life and when he returned to the celestial realms at death to reign in glory with his divine father, he was the heir to the powers and qualities of the deity whose functions and attributes he symbolized in the ritual and regalia of the royal office. Therefore he was the source of vitality, so that the welfare of the king was the welfare of the state, and of the fructifying processes of nature.

To beget an heir the Sun-god in person was supposed to visit the queen in her palace, a visitation which in later times at any rate was enacted as a sacred marriage rite between the Pharaoh and his consort, who was his sister. From this incestuous union the successor to the throne was born. In his early years he was prepared for his divine vocation by a ceremonial sprinkling with waters by officiants who impersonated the gods Atum and Moreth, or Re-Harakhte (Horus) and Amen. On the day of his accession he was publicly acknowledged by the god as his son and again purified with 'the water of life which is in the sky'. This ablution was repeated every morning when at dawn the king underwent a ceremonial washing with water from the sacred pool identified with that of the primeval ocean, Nun, out of which the Sun-god was born. To unite him with Horus he was solemnly censed, and presented with balls of natron to chew to complete the re-birth. Finally, he ascended the stairs of the great window to behold the Sun-god and symbolize his rising like the morning sun out of the waters. He was then vested and given the diadem comprising the white crown of Upper Egypt and the red crown of Lower Egypt, together with the flail and the crook of sceptre.

[1] *Handbook of Egyptian Religion* (Lond., 1907), p. 52.

These 'toilet ceremonies', which would seem to be a repetition of the coronation rite and a re-enactment of the solar legend, constituted the principal part of the daily worship in the temple, performed by the priests on behalf of Pharaoh. Every morning at dawn the cult-image underwent lustration in the Heliopolitan solar temple in the same manner as the god was thought to receive ablutions in the horizon. The other episodes in the House of the Morning, viz. the censing, anointing, robing, crowning, offerings and exposition, had their counterparts in the temple liturgy. Probably the original idea, derived from the Sun-cult, was that just as the sun was purified and reborn every morning in the House beneath the horizon, so must his representative, the king, be purified and reborn every morning in the House of the Morning. Further, what had been done to the Sun-god and his son must be done to the cult-image, his visible and local embodiment. In performing this ceremony and making his gifts, the king must identify himself with Re, the lord and giver of life.[1]

But if this was the original idea, it was to some extent transformed under the influence of the Osiris myth since the god in the shrine came to be regarded as the dead Osiris requiring to be revivified each day. In his Horus manifestation, the reigning monarch took the dead god in his arms and restored him to life; then he performed his toilet, made offerings to him, and returned him to his abode. This Osirianization of the rite introduced a new mythology which had far-reaching effects on the conception of the kingship. Assuming the role of Horus in life and that of Osiris in death, Pharaoh was brought within the seasonal drama of the dying and rising god, and as for cult-purposes every divinity came to be regarded as Osiris, the king in the guise of Horus was similarly united with the pantheon as a whole, and not merely with the Sun-god.

THE OSIRIS MYTH

According to the legend in its developed form as it has been handed down by the late Greek writer Plutarch in the first century A.D.,[2] a

---

[1] Blackman, *Journal of Manchester Egyptian and Oriental Society*, 1918–19, p. 30. *Recueil de Travaux*, XXXIX, pp. 44 ff. Moret, *Le rituel du culte divin journalier en Égypte*, pp. 5 f. *The Nile and Egyptian Civilization* (Lond., 1927), pp. 392 ff.

[2] *De Iside et Osirides* in *Scripta Moralia* (Didot), tome I, 429. Eng. Trans. by Squire (Camb., 1744).

version which is substantiated in its general outline by the Pyramid Texts inscribed on the tombs to ensure a blissful eternity to the dead kings who slept therein.[1] Osiris was the offspring of an intrigue between Keb, the earth-god, and Nut, the sky-goddess (identified with Cronus and Rhea in the Greek pantheon). When Re learnt that Nut had been unfaithful to him, he put a curse on the wonder-child which was annulled by Thoth, or Hermes as the Greeks called him, who was also a lover of the goddess. The birth of Osiris was hailed with the shout that a great king had been born destined to reign on earth, reclaim the Egyptians from cannibalism and savagery, give them laws and teach them to worship the gods.

Upon growing to manhood he married his sister Isis, and travelled over the world diffusing civilization and a knowledge of agriculture. On his return he was worshipped as a deity before he was killed by his brother Set (Typhon of the Greeks). Isis thereupon went in search of his body which she recovered at Byblus on the Syrian coast. Putting it in a coffer she sailed away but eventually it was found by Set, who rent it into fourteen pieces, scattering them in different places throughout Egypt. Nothing daunted, the faithful wife sailed up and down the marches till she had collected the fragments and buried them one by one as she recovered them. So great was her lamentation and that of Nephthys (who in the Pyramid Texts is also said to have rejoiced in the love of Osiris though she was the wife of Set) that Re sent his son Anubis, the funerary physician, to mummify the remains, that the hero might be restored to life. The resuscitation was effected by Isis causing breath to enter the body by fanning it with her wings. Thereupon in the form of a hawk she hovered over her restored husband and conceived a son, Horus, who was brought up in secrecy in the Delta. When the child grew to manhood he gathered his forces and engaged in mortal combat with Set to avenge the death of his father. In the series of battles Horus lost an eye which Thoth restored to him. But after receiving it he gave it to Osiris to eat who thereby became mighty in soul. Set, however, though utterly defeated, disputed the legitimacy of his conqueror. A trial was staged before the nine gods in Heliopolis presided over by Re.

[1] Breasted, *Development of Religion and Thought in Ancient Egypt* (Lond., 1912), pp. 18 ff.

'The Two Truths heard (the case), Shu was witness. The Two Truths commanded that the thrones of Geb should revert to him (Osiris), that he should raise himself up to that which he desired . . . that he should unite those who were in Nun, and that he should bring to an end the words of Heliopolis.'[1] Thoth, the god of wisdom, pleaded the cause of Osiris and proved that he was 'true of voice' (victorious), and Horus was his son and successor. The verdict was pronounced accordingly. Set was rejected and the hero (Osiris) appointed Judge and Lord of the land of the dead.[2]

In the recently discovered papyrus Chester Beatty No. 1, the divine Heliopolitan Council, which is said to have been in session over this case for eighty years, is represented as a vacillating body unable to decide the rival claims of the contending parties (Set and Horus), and it is not until Osiris (who appears in a sinister light in this version) threatens to send 'savage-faced messengers' to draw down the Ennead to his subterranean realm, that judgement is given in favour of Horus.[3] Since in this document the Sun-god supports Set a theology is reflected in which the solar and Osirian cults are in opposition. But when every dynastic Egyptian who had not adopted the Heliopolitan worship looked to Thoth, as the champion of Horus and Osiris, to do for him what he had done for the hero of Abydos (Osiris), the royal solar priests were compelled to make terms with the death and resurrection mystery cultus. Thus, after the collapse of the central government at the end of the Sixth Dynasty, or Pyramid Age (c. 1400 B.C.), the cult of the dead ceased to be a royal prerogative, and the 'Coffin Texts' of this period bear witness to the triumph of Osiris.

With the popularization of the old royal hereafter and the Osirianization of the Pyramid Texts, the king became equated with Horus and Osiris so that in life he reigned in the capacity of the living son of the hero with whom he was identified at death. It is impossible, however, to reduce Egyptian mythology to a logical sequence of thought inasmuch as we are dealing with a complex synthesizing process which seems to reflect in some measure the ethnological history of the nation. An ingenious attempt has been made by Sethe to interpret the conflicting cults in terms of dynastic

[1] Sethe, Pyramidentexte, 316–18.

[2] Erman, Handbook of Egyptian Religion, pp. 32 f. Breasted, op. cit., pp. 24 ff.

[3] A. H. Gardiner, The Chester Beatty Papyri, No. 1, pp. 13 ff.

struggles for the mastery of the land.[1] It is not improbable that a prehistoric clan deriving its name from the falcon, or hawk, originated a line of kings whose home was the north-western Delta, and who subsequently dominated the valley of the Nile. If the head of this clan eventually became the Pharaoh, a reason is to hand for the occupant of the throne continuing to regard himself as the in- carnation and embodiment of the falcon, i.e. 'the living Horus'. But in the meantime the solar and Osirian theologies had also be- come established, and at Heliopolis the Pharaoh was made the physical son of Re. Therefore, when the Horus-kings gained pos- session they too were given a place in the sun with the result that Pharaoh was at once the living Horus and the son of Re. Further- more, the solarization of Osiris and the adoption of the hero of the underworld by the Horians, produced a further fusion of cults, so that under the influence of the Osiris myth, the relationship of the king with any god or goddess was conceived of as that of Horus with Osiris. For ritual purposes every divinity was an Osiris, while Pharaoh, or the priest who impersonated the royal officiant at the temple services, played the part of Horus.[2]

THE OSIRIAN MYSTERIES

Thus, on the first day of the ninth month, when the goddess of the granary, Ernutet, was supposed to give birth to Nepri, the corn-god, the king went in solemn procession to the temple, whence, after offerings of incense and libations had been made to the god, its image was carried forth immediately behind the king, who, in his turn, was preceded by the white bull in which was incarnate Min, the god of sexual reproduction, regarded as another form of Amen.[3] The climax of this harvest festival was reached in the ritual reaping of a sheaf of corn by Pharaoh, and since he is said to have per- formed this act 'for his father', Gardiner is probably correct in assuming that he was functioning in his Horus capacity as the son of Osiris.[4] Min in the Book of the Dead is equated with Horus

[1] Sethe, *Urgeschichte und Älteste Religion der Ägypter* (Leipzig, 1930). The confusion between Horus the Child and Horus the Elder in the myths and the Kingship has doubtless arisen in this way.

[2] Blackman, *E.R.E.,* vol. X, p. 294.

[3] Blackman, *Luxor and its Temples* (Lond., 1923), pp. 179 f. Lepsius, *Denkmaeler aus Aegypten und Aethipien* (1849–59), III, pls. 162 ff.

[4] *J.E.A.,* II, 1915, pp. 125.

'champion of his father', and Amen, the cosmic deity of Thebes (Luxor and Karnak), who was identified with the Heliopolitan Re. Therefore, when the king impersonated Horus at Koptos and walked in the procession between the sacred bull and the image of Min, he was playing a vegetation role which culminated in the symbolic cutting of the first sheaf to ensure a plentiful harvest.

Similarly, the spring festival held in honour of the death and resurrection of Osiris, celebrated all over Egypt from the 12th of the month Khoiakh for a period of eighteen days, was intimately connected with the royal control of the powers of fecundity. In the first scenes of the Ptolemaic inscription engraved on the walls of the god's temple at Dendereh, where Hathor was also worshipped, about 40 miles north of Thebes, the death of the hero is portrayed by means of a golden effigy moulded in sand, vegetable earth and barley in the form of a mummy lying in a basin. The image was watered till the 21st day of Khoiakh, and then it was taken in a boat on a mysterious voyage attended by a fleet of twenty-four vessels of papyrus, each containing the image of a deity and illuminated by 365 lights. After sunset on the 24th of the month the effigy of Osiris was swathed as a mummy and placed in a coffin of mulberry wood to be laid on a bed of seed on the 30th in a tomb-like chamber where its predecessor of the previous year had rested till it had been removed and buried in a cemetery on the 24th day.[1]

Gardiner is in no doubt that this was 'incontestably the day of the resurrection of Osiris', when 'the dead king was recalled in the tomb to a semblance of his former life'.[2] This contention is supported by the bas-reliefs on the walls of the temple where Osiris is represented as a mummy, ithyphallic and bearded, lying on a bier at which stand various deities, Anubis, Isis and Nephthys, Hathor the cow-goddess and manifestation of the Mother-goddess, and her brother Heget, together with the frog-goddess who was probably a symbol of resurrection. In the twentieth scene two hawks hover over the body and feet of Osiris, and in the twenty-second scene he is shown wearing the white crown of Upper Egypt with plumes,

---

[1] H. Brugsch, *Zeitschrift für Ägyptische Sprache und Alterumskunde*, XIX, 1881, pp. 77, 94, 99. V. Loret, *Recueil des Travaux relatifs a la Philologie et a l'Archéologié Egyptiennes et Assyriennes*, III, 1882, pp. 43 ff.; IV, 1883, pp. 21 ff.; V, 1884, pp. 85 f. E. A. Budge, *Osiris and the Egyptian Resurrection* (Lond., 1911), II, pp. 21 ff. Weigall, *Guide to the Antiquities of Upper Egypt*, pp. 45, 479 f.

[2] *J.E.A.*, II, 1915, p. 123.

holding in his hands the sceptre and flail, in process of raising himself up on his knees. Finally, in the last relief, he appears as rising up out of his chest with Isis behind him stretching out her wings, while a male bearded god holds before him the *crux ansata*, or symbol of life.[1]

The resuscitation of the dead god could hardly be more graphically depicted unless it is in the representation of the same event in the temple of Isis at Philae where stalks of wheat are shown growing from the mummy and watered by a priest from a pitcher. Below the bier the *crux ansata* is figured, and the accompanying inscription declares the body to be that of him 'who may not be named, Osiris of the mysteries, who springs from the returning waters'.[2] The use of water as a vitalizing agent is further illustrated by the numerous 'beds of Osiris' made of barley and watered during the Spring Festival to secure plentiful crops, and placed in tombs to give life to the dead. It is also significant that the Festival of Ploughing occurred in the latter part of the festival in a field known as the 'Place of Rejuvenation'.

In the temple of Seti I at Abydos, the sacred marriage of Osiris is portrayed in a bas-relief in an inner chamber of the hall of Sokar, the funerary god of Memphis. At the head of the mummy of the hero stands Isis calling her husband back to life, while over the body she is also represented as a falcon in the act of fecundation. At the feet is Horus, and a falcon protects the head of Osiris, very much as Nephthys assists Isis in the resurrection in the Denderah scenes. But in this case, the festival commemorating the raising of Osiris takes the form of a sacred marriage celebrated apparently on behalf of the king, since the inscription states, 'May Osiris Unnefer (the Good Being) give to king Menmaat-re (Set I) life and power'.[3]

That the Memphite Festival of Sokar on the 30th of Khoiakh, while the Osirian figures were still entombed, was closely associated with the kingship is further indicated by the ceremony known as the raising of the *Ded* or *Tet*-column in the city called 'House of the Soul of the Lord of *Ded*'. This object was a pillar with several cross-bars resembling a telegraph-post and regarded as having

[1] Budge, op. cit., vol. II, pp. 131 ff.

[2] Budge, vol. I, p. 58. Brugsch, *Religion und Mythologie der Alten Agypter* (Leipzig, 1885–8), p. 621.

[3] V. Lanzone, *Dizionario di Mitologia Egizia*, pl. cclxxvi. Hornblower, *Man*, 1937, p. 157.

life-giving qualities. Hence its frequent adornment with the *crux ansata* rising out of the top of it, with two arms projecting upwards to support the solar disc. Sometimes a human form was given to it, with hands holding the sceptre and flail, and the head crowned with a pair of horns and two Osirian feathers.[1] On the tomb of Kheryaf at Thebes the king himself, assisted by members of his family and a priest, is represented raising the column with ropes in the presence of the queen and her sixteen daughters who hold rattles and sistrums. Similarly, in the hall of the Osirian mysteries at Abydos, where the body of Osiris was thought to be preserved, Seti I and Isis are depicted as setting it up between them.[2] If Sethe is correct in thinking that the Memphite Festival of Sokaris commemorated the accession of Menes, the traditional deified founder of Memphis and of the centralized Egyptian state,[3] Gardiner's suggestion that the Feast of Khoiakh was considered the proper occasion for any Pharaoh to ascend the throne,[4] gives a reason for the association of the king and queen with the pillar erected at the beginning of spring. Moreover, as Sethe points out, 'the first day of the fifth month was designated the first day of the year',[5] and he also shows that the Ded-column was not exclusively associated with Osiris. It is in fact doubtless the prototype of the rites celebrated all over the world by the king and queen of the May in conjunction with May-pole,[6] and since Osiris was entombed as a mummy while this ceremony was enacted, it was probably held primarily for the benefit of his son the Horus-king to enable him to exercise his royal functions during the forthcoming year.[7]

Again, it is significant that these events appear to coincide with the periodic renewal of the throne at a rite known as the *Sed*-festival, held apparently on the first day of Spring when the flood was approaching its lowest ebb. Having erected the Ded-column, the king impersonated Osiris, wrapped in bandages like a mummy and holding in his hands the sceptre and flail. Thus arrayed he is

[1] Budge, op. cit., vol. I, p. 51.

[2] Brugsch, *Thesaurus,* V, 1891, p. 1190. M. A. Murray, *The Osireion at Abydos* (Lond., 1904), pp. 27 ff.

[3] *Untersuchungen zur Geschichte und Altertumskunde Ägyptens,* III, 1905, pp. 136 ff.

[4] *J.E.A.,* II. 1915, p. 124.

[5] op. cit., p. 134.

[6] *G.B.,* ('Magic Art', II), pp. 88 ff.; 'Adonis', II, p. 109.

[7] Hornblower, *Man,* XXXVII, November 1937, p. 173.

shown on the mace-head of the god of Narmer as seated in a shrine approached by nine steps and surrounded by fan-bearers. Near by is a scene depicting a procession headed by Upuat, the jackal-god, the 'opener of the roads' to the land of the dead, while before him is an ostrich feather called the shed-shed, on which, according to Petrie, he was supposed to ascend to heaven.[1]

This is probably the oldest religious festival of which any trace has been preserved in Egypt,[2] and while its meaning is very obscure, it gives the appearance of being a periodic renewal of the coronation ceremony. If this is correct, the Pharaoh as the potential Osiris probably underwent a ritual death in order to be resuscitated by Horus and Isis as the living king in his Horus manifestation. Hence the declaration, 'thou beginnest thy renewal, beginnest to flourish again like the infant god of the Moon, thou art young again year by year, like Nun at the beginning of the ages, thou art reborn by renewing thy festival of *Sed*'.[3] Thus the king as the centre of the social structure was ritually regenerated annually in the Osirian rites, and at stated intervals at the *Sed*-festival, in order to secure the prosperity of the community, the sacred story (i.e. the Horus-Osiris myth) investing the ceremonial drama with supernatural efficacy as 'a narrative resurrection of a primeval reality' still operative in present-day life.

The Annual Festival represented the climax of the religious activities of the year because at it was re-enacted the mythological situation upon which the religious, sociological and economic organization depended. Hence the vegetative function of the ritual reproducing the death and revival of the culture-hero who first introduced agricultural civilization in the Nile valley in order to ensure the fruitfulness of the earth and the multiplication of man and beast. Since the fertility of the crops and the cattle was bound up with the person of the king, Pharaoh in his Horus manifestation as the ever-living son of his deified father (Osiris) was the principal actor as the dynamic centre of the nation. The rites, therefore, were communal rather than individualistic in character, thereby differing from their Hellenic counterparts. Their purpose was to secure the

---

[1] Petrie, *Researches in Sinai* (Lond., 1906), p. 181. J. Capart, *Revue de l'histoire des Religions,* LIII, 1906, pp. 332 ff. *G.B.,* pt. VI, pp. 153 f.

[2] Breasted, op. cit., p. 39.

[3] Moret, *Du caractère Religieux de la royauté Pharaonique* (Paris, 1902), p. 256.

well-being of the community, not the salvation of the initiate. Behind the drama lies the primitive conception of the divine kingship, the Osiris-Horus myth symbolizing the course of the agricultural year and the renewal of the seasons, in the form recurrent in the Ancient East as exemplified in the Babylonian story of Tammuz and Ishtar or the Phoenician Adonis.

Doubtless much of the confusion and contradiction in the Egyptian story have arisen as a result of the Plutarch version having assumed its literary form in relation to the Graecized Isiac Mysteries when the original elements had undergone considerable modification and transformation. This explains, for example, the introduction of the dismemberment of the body of Osiris by Set unknown in the Pyramid Texts. That Osiris was himself a civilizing king who reigned in the Delta and was largely responsible for the introduction of agriculture, and perhaps irrigation, is by no means improbable,[1] and his association with vegetation may have been the result of his original office and function in the community. But in tradition he was essentially the dead king, and this may suggest that behind the dramatic representation of the death and resurrection of the hero lies the ancient practice of killing the ruler when his natural powers began to decline. Since the royal wives appear to have played some part in the episode,[2] it is not improbable that loss of virility was an indication of advancing years, as among the Shilluk in the upper reaches of the Nile.[3] In agricultural communities organized on the basis of the divine kingship the royal family is a class apart and traces its descent from a divine ancestor incarnate in the reigning monarch, who marries his sister, as in Egypt, to maintain the supernatural descent of his successor. He controls the weather, the growth of the crops, and the powers of reproduction so that the failure of his own generative powers would have a reciprocal effect in men, animals and plants. To prevent these calamities he is killed as soon as he betrays any symptoms of declining vitality and failing health and vigour.[4] If the practice

[1] Sethe, op. cit., 94 ff. Frazer, *G.B.*, pt. VI, pp. 20 ff. Elliot Smith, *The Evolution of the Dragon* (Manchester, 1919), pp. 29 ff.

[2] Newberry, *Report of British Association,* 1923, p. 185.

[3] C. G. Seligman, *The Cult of the Nyakang and the Divine Kingship* (Khartoum, 1911), pp. 22 ff.

[4] J. Roscoe, *The Baganda* (Lond., 1911), pp. 209 ff.

obtained in Ancient Egypt, the *Sed*-festival may very likely represent an early attempt at rejuvenescence to replace the practice of slaying the divine king after a given number of years or when he had grown old. But whether this were so or not, the rites were a reinvestiture having for their purpose the confirmation of Pharaoh in his kingdom.

In Mesopotamia the ruler of the city-states occupied a similar position, exercising his functions by divine right as the agent of the god of the country. Temples were erected and dedicated to him and offerings made to his statue. At Nippur, one of the oldest centres in the Euphrates valley, Enlil, the chief of the storm gods, was in theory the ruler of the city, governing in the person of his *pontifex maximus*. When in due course Marduk, the solar god of Babylon, succeeded to the primacy in the pantheon, he absorbed the attributes of Enlil and took Ninlil, 'the lady of the mountain', as his consort. Thus, he became 'the lord of the lands' and the controller of the seasons. As the representative particularly of the Sun-god of spring, he was associated with vegetation, and kings were regarded as his incarnation. In this capacity he constituted a later and more concrete aspect of the youthful hero, Tammuz, originally Dumu-zi, 'the faithful son', or as Langdon interprets the name, 'the son who rises goes forth'.[1]

THE TAMMUZ-ADONIS MYTH

The Babylonian sources of the myth are meagre and confused, but the cult of Tammuz is clearly the Mesopotamian version of the Egyptian Osirian drama, and that of Adonis and Attis in Western Asia, representing the seasonal decay and revival personified in a god who died and rose again from the dead, together with all that lies behind this symbolism. The Graeco-Phoenician Adonis and the Phrygian Attis are later equivalents of the Sumerian Tammuz, the lover-son of Ishtar, who like Osiris was associated with the Sun-god. Unfortunately the Babylonian sources of the myth are mainly confined to a collection of lamentations,[2] and most of our knowledge is derived from the Syrian traditions of Adonis handed down by Greek writers. It would seem, however, that it was the death of

---

[1] *Sumerian Liturgies and Psalms* (Philad., 1919), pp. 285 ff.
[2] cf. Langdon, *Semitic Mythology* (Lond., 1931), pp. 342 ff.

E

Tammuz in the midsummer flood that caused the desolation, interpreted under the figure of Ishtar wandering in barren fields and desolate sheepfolds during her sorrowful search for her lover. Similarly, the rapid renewal of life at the season of the rains was equated with his return from the underworld (Aralû) as the 're-surrected child', bringing the drought and decline in reproductive energy to an end. In the sixth month of the calendar at Lagash (September), called 'the month of the festival of Tammuz', wailings were held on his behalf, accompanied by the shrill music of flutes, when the dirges were sung apparently over an effigy of the dead god, which was washed, anointed with oil, clothed in a red robe, and censed.

> In Eanna, high and low, there is weeping,
> Wailing for the house of the Lord they raise.
> The wailing is for the plants, the first lament is 'they grow not'.
> The wailing is for the barley; the ears grow not.
> For habitations and the flocks it is; they produce not.
> For the perishing wedded ones, for perishing children it is; the dark-headed people create not.
>
> The wailing is for the great river; it brings the flood no more.
> The wailing is for the fields of men; the grain grows no more.
> The wailing is for the fish-ponds; the *dasuhur* fish spawn not.
> The wailing is for the cane-break; the fallen stalks grow not.
> The wailing is for the forests; the tamarisks grow not.
> The wailing is for the highlands; the *masgam* trees grow not.
> The wailing is for the garden store-house; honey and wine are produced not.
> The wailing is for the meadows; the bounty of the garden, the *sihlu* plants grow not.
> The wailing is for the palace; life unto distant days is not.

And all this because

> The lord shepherd of the fold lives no more,
> The husband of the heavenly queen lives no more,
> The lord of the cattle stalls lives no more.
> When he slumbers, the sheep and lambs slumber also,
> When he slumbers, the she-goats and the kids slumber also.[1]

[1] Langdon, *Tammuz and Ishtar* (Oxford, 1914), pp. 11, 14 ff.

In despair

> To the land without return Ishtar, the daughter of Sin, directed her mind,
> To the dark house, the dwelling of Irkulla.
> To the house whence those who enter do not return,
> To the road from which there is no path leading back,
> To the house in which those who enter are deprived of light,
> Where dust is their nourishment, clay their food,
> They do not see the light, they dwell in darkness,
> Clothed like a bird with feathers as a covering;
> On door and lock, dust has settled.[1]

During her sojourn in the underworld, where she was deprived of all her clothing and smitten with disease in all her members, fertility on earth ceased, and in fear lest all life should be extinguished, Ea, the god of water and patron of civilization, sent a messenger to effect her release. Tammuz was awakened from the sleep of death, and Ishtar was sprinkled with the water of life. She, in company with her lover, then returned to the upper world and the processes of fecundity again were restored.

> In Erech its brick-walls reposed; upon Erech a faithful eye he cast;
> The figs grew large; in the plains the trees thrived (?).
> There the valiant in (his) boat descended, from Hades hastened.
> The holy husband of the heavenly queen in a boat descended, from
>   Hades hastened.
> Where grass was not, there grass is eaten,
> Where water was not, water is drunk.
> Where the cattle sheds were not, cattle sheds are built.[2]

It was with 'the beautiful child Tammuz, beloved of the great goddess', that Sumerian rulers were closely related as his 'tangible manifestation'.[3] Therefore, if he was originally a divine king of Erech identified with the god Abu, as has been suggested,[4] his control of vegetation doubtless was based on the ancient belief that the king was the dynamic centre of the universe. Consequently, as in Egypt, at the Annual Festival the king played the role of the god, and the sacred story (the Tammuz-Ishtar myth) was re-enacted to

---

[1] Jastrow, *Religion of Babylonia and Assyria* (Boston, 1898), pp. 565 f.

[2] Langdon, op. cit., p. 23.

[3] Langdon, *Proceedings of the Society of Biblical Archaeology*, 1918, XL, p. 31.

[4] Langdon, *Sumerian Liturgical Texts,* Univ. of Penn., Iniv. Mus. Pub., Bab. Section, X, 2, 1917, p. 208, n. 1.

secure the well-being of the crops and the continuance of life on the earth. This death and resurrection drama was the central rite in Mesopotamia, though in different localities the hero, who of course originally was Tammuz, was known under the name of the god of the city.

THE ENUMA ELISH

Thus, for example, when Babylon became the capital and its god Marduk, the son of Ea, was elevated to the head of the pantheon, at the feast known as *Akitu*, held in the spring at the beginning of the month of Nisan,[1] the creation story, or *enuma elish* ('When above') was celebrated in a dramatic rite. This well-known epic begins with the precosmic era, when 'the heavens were not yet named' and only the primeval waters existed, whence arose the gods, Apsu, Mummu and Tiamat. A quarrel ensued and Ea overthrew his three rivals, except Tiamat who alone remained as a female monster. To avenge the death of her husband Apsu, she created a host of demons and gave them into the charge of her lover Kingu, upon whom she bestowed the 'table of destiny'. Marduk thereupon engaged in mortal combat with Timat and her monsters on the condition that he was given the 'table of destiny' as a reward of victory. Catching her in a net he slew his opponent, and cut her body in two pieces from which he made heaven and earth. Then he set the sun, moon and stars in their courses, and Ea fashioned man out of the blood of Kingu to serve the gods with sacrifice. To celebrate the victory the gods built Babylon and caused the temple Esagila to be erected in honour of Marduk.

This was the story that was re-enacted at the New Year Festival when the image of Marduk was brought in triumph to the city. Later his son Nebo arrived to rescue his father, who was imprisoned in a 'mountain'. After a fight in the town symbolizing the struggle between Marduk and Tiamat, lamentation was made by the goddess (Beltis, the wife of Marduk), who was invoked to plead with her divine spouse for the king and the prosperity of the city. On the fifth day the king himself entered the temple (Esagila), escorted by priests, where he placed his regalia before the statue of the god.

---

[1] In Erech and Ur it occurred twice in the year, 'viz. in Nisan and Tisri, i.e. spring and autumn.'

The high-priest struck him on the face and compelled him to kneel and proclaim his innocence. Finally, after he had made a confession of the errors he had committed, the priest raised him up saying, 'Be without fear. The Lord will bless thee for ever, and will destroy thine enemies before thy face.' Then his crown and sceptre were restored to him, and another blow on the cheek was given to make tears come to his eyes as an omen of the favour of Marduk, and of prosperity in the year.[1] Thus, the king resigned his office and was reinstated in it by the god whom he impersonated in order to receive for himself and his kingdom an augmentation of royal power.

At the New Year Festival a formal assembly of the gods was held at Babylon with the chief deities grouped round Marduk, as the princes stand about the king, who entered a special shrine called the Assembly Room to determine the destiny of the city during the forthcoming season. Though our knowledge of the precise details of the ritual is imperfect, it is clear that the recital and re-enactment of the creation story constituted an important element in the ceremonial, having as its purpose the regeneration of the community and the reinvigoration of the processes of Nature at their source.[2] In the evening of the fourth day of the festival the epic was recited in its entirety by the priests before the image of Marduk, but unfortunately the texts relating to the sixth and eleventh days are missing. But while we can only conjecture what was done in the Festival House on these three days, from the fact that the fight between Marduk and Tiamat was depicted on the doors of this house at Ashur,[3] it can hardly be doubted, as Gadd says, that this ritual combat took place there between the eighth and eleventh days.

It is plain, however, that Marduk was not the original hero in the great conflict between the gods of the cosmic order and the monsters of the primeval chaos. As the son of Ea he is brought into relation with Tammuz while his consort Sarpanit became Ishtar,

---

[1] Langdon, *The Babylonian Epic of Creation* (Oxford, 1923), 34–59. *Journal of Royal Asiatic Society*, 1921, pp. 67 ff. Gadd, *History and Monuments of Ur* (Lond., 1929), pp. 132 ff. *Myth and Ritual* (Oxford, 1933), pp. 47 ff. Zimmern, *Zum babylonischen Neujahrfest* (Leipzig, 1918).

[2] Zimmern, in E. Schrader's *Die Keilinschriften und das Alte Testament* (Berlin, 1902) p. 501.

[3] Gadd, *Myth and Ritual,* pp. 57 f.

and the Spring Festival was the occasion of the nuptials of the local god and goddess, enacted by the king and queen as their earthly counterparts. For example, in the inscriptions of Gudea, king of Lagash, there are numerous references to a New Year Festival of the goddess Bau (a localized form of the Mother-goddess), and of the 'wedding gifts' made by the king on this occasion, suggestive of the celebration of a sacred marriage of the goddess with Ningirsu, the patron deity of the city. This was also the case at Nippur, where Ninib and his consort Gula united to promote the fruitfulness of the year, and it seems to have been also a feature of the Annual Festival at Babylon, since a hymn refers to Marduk 'hastening to his bridal'. At a later period Nebuchadrezzar is said to have erected a connubium in connexion with the festival of the god (Marduk). That ancient kings claimed to be husbands of the Mother-goddess is indicated in a liturgy celebrating the marriage of Idin-Dagan, third king of the Dynasty of Isin, with the Mother-goddess Innini, identified with the planet Venus. In this capacity they acted as Tammuz and ruled by virtue of their relationship with Ishtar.[1] When the attributes of all the local deities were transferred to Marduk and the consorts of Ninib and Ningirsu, and other similar gods, were replaced by Sarpanitu (Beltis), the Ishtar of Babylon, the king was doubtless married to a statue of the goddess, following ancient custom.[2]

Although in the *enuma elish* there is no reference to the actual death and resurrection of Marduk, the ritual of the Annual Festival, interpreted in the light of the Tammuz-Ishtar myth which unquestionably lies behind the Creation Epic, leaves little room for doubt that this was the purpose and significance of the observance. The struggle was re-enacted to secure the release of the hero from captivity in the mountain just as the escape of Ishtar from the underworld (Aralû) was recited at the autumn festival. The forces of evil had to be conquered year by year as part of the annual renewal, and the sacred story is the warrant for the due performance of the seasonal drama.

[1] cf. Langdon, *Sumerian Grammar*, pp. 196 ff. *Tammuz and Ishtar*, pp. 27, 64. Radau, *Hilsprecht Anniversary Volume* (Leipzig, 1909), pp. 391 ff.

[2] cf. Langdon, *Tammuz and Ishtar*, p. 27.

CHAPTER V

Greece and the Mystery Religions

The worship of the Mother-goddess under various forms and symbols, which, as we have seen, was brought into relation with the dying god in Egypt and Babylonia at an early period, goes back in Europe to the Aurignacian phase of the Upper Palaeolithic in prehistoric times. As the mistress of fertility and protectress of the dead her cult extended at the dawn of civilization from Mohenjo-daro in the Indus valley, through Elam and Mesopotamia, to the Aegean, where it was the characteristic feature of the Minoan-Mycenaean substratum of Greek religion.

THE RISE OF CIVILIZATION IN THE AEGEAN

Behind the culture of Greece lay that of Crete, to which Sir Arthur Evans has given the name 'Minoan' from the legendary sea-king Minos, the first ruler of the waves. Thence it spread to the mainland and established a civilization at such centres as Mycenae in the Peloponnese, between Corinth and Nauplia. The contacts of Crete were with Egypt and Asia Minor, but it was not wholly from these two important areas that the culture was derived, since below the palace at Knossos the remains of Neolithic settlements have been found, accumulated to the depth of more than 20 feet, indicating a long period of gradual cultural growth. From the objects discovered it would seem that even in prehistoric times the island was in communication with the mainland and the rest of the Mediterranean coast from Syria to Sicily, Malta, Sardinia and North Africa, while shells from the Indian Ocean suggest a still wider intercourse.

It was not until the introduction of copper and bronze about 3000 B.C., however, that Egyptian objects, notably amulets, began to appear, and elements derived from Asia Minor became apparent in the Cyclades, which by reason of their geographical position exercised a more direct influence on the mainland of Greece. It was from these islands probably that traders landed on the coast of Argolis and settled at Tiryns and Mycenae about 2800 B.C., advancing later to Corinth. Others reached the coast of Phocis about the same time. Thus, a highly developed civilization flourished for centuries before the people known as Greeks entered the region.

If at first the mainland lagged behind the islands, the fleets of Egypt and Crete maintained commercial relations with the coast of Greece, and by the middle of the second millennium B.C. the Mycenaean Age had dawned. In a country like Greece shut in on the north and west by mountain ranges with short valleys leading in one direction to difficult passes, in the other to ports capable of harbouring small ships, intercourse must come by sea. Moreover, such an environment tends to the formation of small communities in communication with one another, but nevertheless existing as isolated units separated by mountain ridges, deep bays, and on islands, protected by natural boundaries, calculated to produce a strong independent civilization.

It was under these conditions that a composite people containing elements of the three main stocks of Europe—Nordic, Alpine, and Mediterranean—made their habitation in Greece in prehistoric and protohistoric times, and were modified by the peculiar geographical control exercised by their environment. The indigenous population was certainly not Greek, or indeed 'Aryan' at all, since the Indo-European linguistic peoples were immigrants in Southern Europe from the neighbourhood of the Caspian Sea. Exactly when they first penetrated the region is by no means easy to determine. It is now becoming apparent that the Greek language is older than has been generally assumed since the Linear B Simplified script of Knossos, recently deciphered by Ventris and Chadwick, has been shown to be an early Greek dialect identical with that current in Mycenaean Greece.[1] Professor Blegen has discovered some six hundred tablets in Linear B at Pylos[2] dated about 1200 B.C., and Professor L. R. Palmer has now contended that the Greek domina-

---

[1] Ventris and Chadwick, *Documents in Mycenaean Greek* (Camb. 1956), pp. 31 ff.

[2] Emmett Bennett, *The Pylos Tablets* (Princeton, 1951).

tion of Knossos and control of the island of Crete was from 1400–
1200 B.C. instead of 1480–1440 B.C., as generally has been supposed.
Therefore, he thinks that the Greeks entered Greece after 1600 B.C.,
and not in 1900 B.C., which has been the accepted view[1], and that
from 1400 to 1200 B.C. the civilization of Crete and the Aegean
mainland flourished side by side. Until, however, the evidence is
published in much greater detail the theory must remain *sub-
judice.*

It has long been recognized that before the Dorian invasion from
north-central Greece about 1100 B.C. an Achaean population
inhabited the Peloponnese and the southern islands, but these
brown-haired Xanthoi conquerors under their Zeus-born kings of
the Homeric tradition did not introduce the higher civilization of
Crete. They found the culture already established on the mainland
ruled over by a dark-skinned, black-haired feudal artisocracy the
contents of whose graves reveal Cretan connexions. But the fact
that they were buried in the Helladic cemetery at Mycenae in a
type of grave similar to the Minyan cists in origin suggests that they
were not true Cretans.[2]

This is further indicated by Mycenaean kings being represented
as wearing beards whereas the Minoans were usually clean-shaven,
and, unlike the Cretans, the men were clad in drawers and a sleeved
chiton. But if the Mycenaeans were not actually a migration from
Crete, they had imbibed its culture and worshipped the same
Mother-goddess as the princes of Knossos, as is shown by the
presence of the cult in the great sanctuaries of Delphi, Delos and
Eleusis. Furthermore, they had learnt the art of navigation, and they
made their influence felt along the coast of Greece, and farther
afield from Cyprus and Western Asia to Sicily and southern Italy.
Indeed, the focus of Aegean civilization passed from Crete to
Mycenae, and it was not long (*c.* 1400 B.C.) before it succeeded in
destroying the Palace-rule at Knossos.

The fall of Knossos coincides apparently with the advance of
Hellenic peoples, who spread through Greece and the islands and
later penetrated the coastlands of Asia Minor, seizing all the chief

[1] Myres, *Who Were the Greeks* (Berkeley, 1930), and footnote (1).

[2] A. J. B. Wace, 'Excavations at Mycenae' *Annual of the British School at Athens.*
1921–23, XXV, pp. 120 ff.

cities and roads, and building fortresses and dark palaces of great stones in contrast to the gypsum Cretan edifices. These mysterious folk are known to us under the name of Achaeans from the Homeric sagas, but beyond the fact that they came from the north, exactly who they were is not clear. They may have been the first 'Greeks' in Greece, but it seems probable that the bulk of the people over whom the Minoans had ruled were of composite origin, and that the 'Hellenes' never were of one blood, one language, one culture and one religion. The Achaeans may have been the ruling people in the Mycenaean Age and occupied Tiryns, Argos and Mycenae, before making roads, guarded by forts, into Arcadia, the Messeian plain and Lacedaemon. But Greek tradition ascribes the foundation of the Mycenaean states to Pelops, Cecrops, Cadmus and Danaus (i.e. to Western Asia and Egypt), and it is much more likely that this civilization drew its inspiration from Crete (with its wider contacts) in the seventeenth century B.C., prior to the consolidation of successive waves of Achaeans, Phrygians, Aeolians and Ionians as 'Hellenes'. According to Homer, Hellen, the mythical ancestor of the Greeks, was the son of Deucalion, who was the father of Dorus (Dorians), Aeolus (Aeolians, Xuthus, the father of Ion (Ionians), and Achaeus (Achaeans), and had his abode in southern Thessaly, from which centre the descendants of Hellen were supposed to have spread in the Aegean and formed the Greek-speaking states (i.e. Hellas).

It certainly seems that the Mycenaean hegemony (1400–1200) represented a mixed culture which combined to ovethrow Crete, and that the fall of Knossos marked a break in Aegean civilization coinciding with the appearance of the Achaeans. People of kindred stock (Indo-European) about this time were making their way in Asia Minor as Phrygians and Armenians; Crete was occupied by the Greek tribes and the Philistines (perhaps a Cretan tribe), like other Aegeans, by this widespread pressure from the north, were driven to harass the Syrian and Egyptian coasts. The chivalry and barbarism of this Heroic Age, which stands in such striking contrast to the peaceful Palace régime of Knossos and the Minoan culture, have been immortalized in the Homeric epic, which portrays Mycenaean Greece prior to the ravages of the Dorians (c. 1200 B.C.) who overran the land with the aid of their newly-acquired iron weapons, laying waste everything that came in their way.

THE OLYMPIAN GODS

It has been necessary to discuss in some detail the rise of Aegean civilization since it is only possible to understand the earlier phases of Greek religion in relation to their historical setting. Thus, the complex system of Hellenic polytheism was the result of the fusion of northern elements derived from the nomadic tribes settled in the pastures of Thessaly under the shadow of Mount Olympus, super-imposed on the myth and ritual of the Minoan-Mycenaean culture. The Indo-European northern tradition, as we know it from the Homeric songs sung in the courts of princes of Ionia, was essentially that of a male society; a military aristocracy with its knights and their retainers, and wandering minstrels recounting the glories of the Trojan war. The eight gods who lived on Olympus under the mon-archical rule of Zeus, the father of gods and men, and most exalted of rulers, were the heavenly counterpart of the princely warriors and their rude methods. They feasted, fought, played music; they slept, married, drank and thwarted one another like royal buccaneers.

As Dr Gilbert Murray points out, they do not claim to be Creators. Their *métier* is that of conquerors, and they behave as fighting chiefs. Zeus and his followers conquered Cronos and his allies, and 'sent them migrating beyond the horizon, heaven knows where'. Having seized the kingdom, Zeus gained the supremacy and maintained himself as the overlord, assigning to his brothers, Hades and Poseidon, portions of the land. Apollo conquered Delphi; Athena captured Athens from Poseidon; and then instead of attending to the government and developing the land, they were content to live on the revenues and blast with their thunderbolts the people who did not pay. Thus, 'the mountain gods of the old in-vading northmen were the chieftains and princes, each with his *comitatus*, or loose following of retainers and minor chieftains, who broke in upon the ordered splendours of the Aegean palaces, and still more important, on the ordered simplicity of tribal life in the pre-Hellenic villages of the mainland'.[1]

THE MOTHER-GODDESS

In short, the picture of Olympus in the Homeric poems is that of warring states with a palace surrounded by the domains of lesser

[1] *Five Stages in Greek Religion* (Oxford, 1925), pp. 66 ff.

kings as vassals whom the chief lord summons to counsels and banquets. It is true a similar political régime prevailed alike among the northern immigrants and the Mycenaeans of the south, but the characteristic feature of the Aegean substratum was the worship of the Mother-goddess who in Greece reappeared as Athena, to whose honour the Acropolis at Athens was dedicated. Since under this famous sacred rock traces of a Myceanean palace have been found, and at Mycenae a temple of Athena stood on a similar site, it is not improbable that the Minoan Mother-goddess had been adopted and made the Achaean goddess *par excellence* before the poems of Homer were composed. In name and nature like Aphrodite, the goddess of love, she is un-Hellenic, and at Corinth, with its long Mycenaean associations, occurs the cult-title of Athena ᾿Ελλωτίς (a non-Hellenic word connected with the Cretan ᾿Ελλώτια, the designation of a feast of Adriadne[1]). Indeed, it may well be that the name 'Athena' is of Mycenaean origin, and later was supplanted by the Hellenic appellative 'Hera' (the 'Noble One'). Thus, at Argolis the temple of Hera was erected on a Mycenaean site.

Similarly, in the case of Aphrodite, whose home in the Homeric poems is placed in Cyprus, her ultimate source is suggested by the shells with which she is so intimately associated; clearly a survival of the female principle of fecundity. Consequently, she has been equated with the Semitic Astarte and the Hebrew Ashtoreth, but Cyprus was the meeting-place of Aegean and Oriental cults, in both of which the worship of the Mother-goddess was deeply laid. According to Cypriote tradition, Askalon was her cradle-land whence she passed to Cyprus by way of the sea, and, as this was a Philistine city, it probably had Cretan connexions. As her functions became specialized, she assumed various guises, having affinities with the Egyptian Cow-goddess Hathor, with the Syrian Atargatis, the Palestinian Astarte, and the Babylonian Ishtar. As Apuleius recognized at the beginning of our era, the Mother-goddess has been worshipped under different names in many lands, but really she was one and the same deity in every case: 'the Phrygians called her Mother of the Gods, the Athenians Minerva (Athena), the Cyprians Venus, the Cretans Dictynna, the Sicilians Proserpine, the Eleusinians Ceres (Demeter), others Iuno, Bellena, Hecate, or

[1] Farnell, 'Cretan Influence in Greek Religion' in *Essays in Aegean Archaeology* (Oxford, 1927), p. 15.

the Goddess of Rhamnus (Nemesis), but the Egyptians called her by her right name, the queen Isis'.[1]

THE ELEUSINIAN MYSTERIES

As Demeter, the Earth or Corn Mother, her early history is more obscure, inasmuch as while the cultus at Eleusis appears to be pre-Hellenic, the name of the divinity (Demeter) betrays northern affinities. But as the Minoan goddess became Hera in Argos, so the 'Isis' or 'Ishtar' of Eleusis may have acquired a northern designation when her cult was adopted by the Indo-European section of the community. Be this as it may, it was in Mycenaean times that a self-contained state arose on the Rarian plain with Eleusis as its capital, whose 'archon' was the chief among the kings of the surrounding towns. Separated from the rest of the world by high mountains, Parnes and Cithaeron, on the east and north, by a lower range of hills (Aegaleos) on the west, and by the sea on the remaining side, so powerful did this ancient city become that eventually, with the aid of Thracian allies, it attempted to gain possession of Athens. The expedition failed, and with the rise of Athenian power under Theseus (*c.* 1200 B.C.), Eleusis lost a measure of its independence, though apparently it was not until between 650 and 600 B.C. that it was finally unified in the Athenian state.

Throughout all these changes in fortune the worship of Demeter persisted, and as her Mysteries increased in fame they gave the city an importance it would not otherwise have retained. Thus, as soon as they ceased to function in early Christian and Byzantine times, Eleusis became a small fortified town which was reduced at length to a collection of ruins on the site of the once famous sanctuary. From the meagre remains that survive it seems that the Mycenaean temple (*c.* 1500–1000 B.C.) was in the form of a dwelling-house, but its replacement by a larger 'geometric' structure, circular or apsidal at one end, or perhaps at both ends, suggests that the cult had increased in numbers since the court occupied a greater area in the new building. The shrine remained on the sloping side of the hill at the spot alleged to have been selected for its erection by the goddess herself, near the well, or Kallichoron, below the acropolis.

According to the so-called Homeric *Hymn to Demeter,* assigned

[1] *Metamorphoses,* XI (*a*), 2 ff.

to the seventh century B.C.,[1] which describes the foundation of the
cult and relates the legend in detail, when Persephone was carried
away to the underworld by Pluto as she was gathering flowers in
the meadows, her sorrowing mother, Demeter, abandoned her
home with the gods on Olympus, and clad in the mourning mantle
sought her daughter over land and sea. In her wrath at her bereave-
ment the goddess caused the fruits of the earth to wither, as in
Babylonia when Ishtar went to the underworld to seek Tammuz.
Indeed, mankind would have perished if Zeus in alarm had not
commanded Pluto to send back Persephone; a request which the
god of the dead obeyed, though he first gave his bride a pome-
granate to eat which bound her to him for one-third of the year.

In the meantime, however, Demeter had assumed the guise of
an old woman, and at length came to Eleusis, where she sat under
the shade of an olive-tree by a well called Kallichoron (καλλίχορον
Φρέαρ), so named because there the Eleusinian maidens danced
on festive occasions. When the daughters of the king, Keleos, came
to draw water she told them a fictitious story of her escape from
pirates who had carried her off from Crete and landed her at
Thorikos. Having won their confidence, she persuaded them to take
her with them to the palace, where she became nurse to their baby
brother, Demophoon. By anointing him with the ambrosia of the
gods by day and bathing him in fire at night, she endeavoured to
make him immortal. But one night the queen, Melaneira, chanced
to discover the goddess hiding the child in the fire and cried out in
alarm. Whereupon Demeter declared her identity, and called upon
the people of Eleusis to erect a temple to her honour at the well,
where she had been hospitably received by the king's daughters.
But first she revealed to the Eleusinian princes, to Triptolemus,
Eumolpus, Diocles and Keleos, the mysteries whereby she would
bestow upon her initiates a new birth to a blessed immortality.

This very ancient legend apparently occupied a place and function
in the Eleusinian festival comparable to that of the Creation epic in
the Babylonian rites and the Osiris-Horus myth in the Egyptian
seasonal drama. The temple mentioned in the Hymn appears to
have been the original Mycenaean sanctuary, and it is significant

---

[1] cf. R. Foerster, *Der Raub und die Ruckkehr der Persephone* (Stuttgart, 1874), pp.
37 ff. A. Baumeister, *Hymni Homerici* (Leipsic, 1860), p. 280. T. W. Allen and E. E.
Sikes, *The Homeric Hymns* (Lond., 1904), pp. 10 ff. *G.B.*, pt. V ('Spirits of the Corn',
I), pp. 36 ff.

that in it there is no mention of Athens. The first home of the cultus was the Eleusinian corn-land rather than the olive-clad expanse of the Athenian plain where the goddess was only a visitor. It was there on the Rarian plain that the hero Triptolemus is said to have been taught by the goddess to cultivate wheat, as Isis in Egypt instructed Osiris concerning the mysteries of agriculture.

As in Crete, the rites at first seem to have been held in the open air for the benefit of the community and not of the individual initiate, there being no evidence of a *Telesterion*, or Mystery sanctuary, contemporary with the terrace erected prior to the Athenian subjection in the geometrical period, probably shortly before the eighth century B.C.[1] There is no trace of a Mycenaean palace, or any building other than a sacred beehive tomb, in the region occupied prior to the union of Eleusis with Athens, when the communal character of the Mysteries underwent very considerable modification with the break-up of the old social order in the sixth century B.C. The peasants who migrated to the towns took with them the cultus of the fertile soil, and the youthful maiden of the meadows and the corn-fields and her sorrowing mother became the central figures in the religious life of Athens. It was at this juncture that the Telesterion was erected and a considerable part of the city set apart for the organization of the worship.

As the cult grew in popularity further elaborations became necessary, and about the middle of the century Peisistratos reconstructed the site on a grander scale with a large square hall about 180 ft. square, with steps apparently used as seats on the sides partly hewn out of the rock. Rows of columns supported the roof, and in the centre of the hall a small chamber, called 'the palace' (ἀνάχτορόν), may have existed as a sanctuary for the performance of the sacred rites. In the eastern corner there are the remains of a smaller edifice, about a quarter the size of the Telesterion, surrounded with seats and containing twenty-five columns in five rows, with a portico on the south-east side. During the Persian invasion of Attica, Eleusis shared the fate of Athens, but though the temple was destroyed it was rebuilt about its former size by Cimon in recognition of his victory over the invaders. The work, however, was not completed till after 445 B.C., when Pericles commissioned Ictinus, the architect of the Parthenon, to apply his skill to the Telesterion.

[1] cf. Noack, *Eleusis die baugeschichliche Entwicklung des Heiligtums*, 1927, pp. 11 ff.

In 311 B.C. Philo added a portico on the south-east side, and the Romans united the two naves to form the quadrangular temple now visible in the ruins. So it remained till the end of the fourth century A.D., when the goddess was dethroned and a small Christian church surrounded with Christian graves erected in the sanctuary so long sacred to the worship of Demeter.

The precise nature of the rites performed for over a thousand years in this famous shrine has been a matter of speculation since the veil was finally drawn over the Mysteries, and the early Fathers of the Church made cryptic references to the things said and done in the presence of the initiates. In the literature there is plenty of evidence concerning the external accompaniments, but what actually took place in the Telesterion is very obscure, while the excavation of the sacred precincts has done little more than to bring to light the plan of the edifice in which the mystery was performed, and to indicate that a sacred drama formed the climax of a very complex ritual.

Taking the data collectively, it would seem that it was the mystery of life through death which was enacted at Eleusis, and if the symbolism was that of the seasonal drama, behind it lay a deeper conception of the immortality of the human soul. In its original Mycenaean form doubtless it was directed to the continuation of life and fertility, as in Egypt and Crete,[1] and the subordinate part played by Pluto in the Demeter legend suggests that in its Greek guise the male partner was of secondary importance, which is not surprising in view of the prominence of the cult of the Mother-goddess in the Aegean. Usually, where a goddess is the principal figure, the mystery of birth, of life coming from life, is emphasized, whereas when a god is the hero, life issuing from death is the crux.

Of what actually took place in the Eleusinian ritual in classical times we have fairly full information up to the crucial point when the initiates arrived at the sanctuary from Athens, but from this moment onwards the evidence fails us because it was then that the secret rites began. In the Hymn the only references to the Mysteries are those announcing their institution, the drinking of the κυκεών, or gruel, and probably the fast during the preliminary ceremonies, but none of these occured in the Telesterion. The story of Demophoon refers to a domestic rite, and in later legend it is Triptolemus

---

[1] A. Evans, 'Ring of Nestor' in *Journal of Hellenic Studies,* 1925, p. 15.

who is nursed by Demeter, not the infant son of Keleos.[1] The nine days' fast, as distinct from that in the preliminary rites from dawn to sunset, may have reference to the agricultural festival known as *Thesmophoria,* celebrated by women in October in secret, rather than to the Mysteries. Indeed it is not possible to draw a distinction between the public cults of Greek cities and the Mysteries since with many of the former there were connected rites which had to be performed in secret.

Nevertheless, in its post-Athenian form, the Eleusinia had acquired an individual application in the conferment of a new birth destined to endure beyond the grave, as is shown by the later writers who refer to the worship. Thus, the orator Isocrates in the fourth century B.C. reminded the Athenians of what they owed to Demeter,[2] just as Pindar and Sophocles bore witness to the blessed state of those in the hereafter who had beheld the saving rites which would bring peace at the last.[3] Again, the Homeric Hymn declared: 'Happy is he among men upon earth who has seen these mysteries; but he who is uninitiated and who has no part in them, never has lot of like good things once he is dead, down in darkness and gloom.'[4]

The Greater Mysteries of the sixth century seem never to have been confined to women, unlike the *Thesmophoria,* and all who were able to speak and understand Greek were eligible for initiation upon application to a member of the priestly families known as the Kerykes or the Eumolpidae, who were in charge of the rites. First, however, it was necessary to pass through the Lesser Mysteries held in February at Agrae, a suburb of Athens,[5] in order to obtain a preliminary purification and consecration in preparation for the Eleusinia six months later in autumn.

This festival in the month of Boedromion (approximately September) was divided into four distinct ceremonial acts: (1) the preparation and purification of the *mystae*; (2) the procession from Athens to Eleusis; (3) the roaming about at the sea-shore; and (4) the sacred drama in the Hall of Initiation. Before entering upon this installation, the initiate went to an instructor, or μυσταγωγὸς, during the latter portion of the month, and from him received

[1] cf. Allen, Halliday, Sikes, *The Homeric Hymns* (Oxford, 1936), p. 157.
[2] *Osoer. Panegyr.,* 28.   [3] Pindar, *Fr.,* 102.   [4] *Hymn to Demeter,* 480 ff.
[5] Scholiast to Aristophanes, *Plutus,* V, 846. Clem. of Alex., *Strom,* V, 11.

instruction in the manner of performing the rites of purification and making the offerings. A fast of nine days followed in commemoration of Demeter's fast during her search for Persephone. No food might be eaten between sunrise and sunset, and then domestic birds, fish, apples, beans and pomegranates were taboo.

On the 13th of Boedromion the ceremonies proper began with the departure of the Athenian ἔφηβοι to fetch the sacred ἱερά from Eleusis. After having been conducted in solemn procession, probably on ox-wagons, with a station at the sacred Fig Tree, on their arrival at the Rheitoi, near the modern Skaramanga, the images were greeted as the actual goddesses they represented by the Athenians who had gone forth to meet them. The next day the candidates were assembled in the *Poicile* (Painted Porch) and a proclamation was made bidding all strangers and murderers and unclean persons depart before the *mystae* were led to the sea-shore (ἅλαδεμύσται) to undergo a series of lustrations in the sea, each accompanied by the pig he was to sacrifice. In the evening wine was distributed to the people in honour of the victory of Chabia at Naxon. The next two days were spent by the *mystae* in retirement, during which time the *Epidauria,* a festival of Asklepios, was celebrated.

Sacrifices for the safety of the State were offered on the 17th in the Eleusinium at Athens, and on the following night (18th) the very devout perhaps slept in the temple of Demeter, or in the temple of Asklepios, south-west of the Acropolis. Meanwhile sacred objects consisting of a bone (ἀστράγαλος), top (στρόβιλος), ball (σφαῖρα), tambourine (ῥόμβος), apples (μῆλα), mirror (ἔσαπτρον), fan, (λίκνον), and woolly fleece (πόκος), were brought from Eleusis. A procession formed in the morning of the 19th at the Eleusinium and proceeded to the Iaccheum, where the statue of 'the fair young god' Iacchus, adorned with myrtle and holding a torch, was procured and carried amid wealthy ladies in carriages and priests and people crowned with ivy and myrtle.[1]

All was now ready for the return to Eleusis along the Sacred Way which followed approximately the modern road from the Dipylon Gate and the Ceramicus, past the olive groves of Cephi-

---

[1] Iacchus, who is unknown in the Homeric Hymn, appears to have been an Athenian deity who was identified with Dionysos (Herodotus VIII, 65; Aristophanes, *Frogs*, 324 ff.; Sophocles, *Antigone*, 1119). It may have been his votaries who introduced Dionysian interpretations in the Eleusinian rites.

sus, near the Academy of Plato, to the ravine intersecting the
Aegaleos range between the hills of Corydalos and Pikilon, where
the Byzantine monastery of Daphni with its renowned mosaics
now stands on the ruins of a temple of Apollo. Stations were made
at the shrines *en route* for the performance of ritual dances and
salutations to the deities commemorated. On reaching the Rarian
plain, after crossing the salt lake of Rheitoi (now called Coumoun-
dourou) in which the priests of Eleusis alone were allowed to fish,
located just beyond Daphni at the exit of the pass, the *mystae* were
met by representatives of the ancient Eleusinian tribe of Krokonidai,
who tied fillets on one arm and one foot of each initiate. The procession then made its way to Eleusis, which was reached late in the
afternoon. At the bridge over the Eleusinian Kephisus the candidates
were greeted with shouts of delight mingled with jeers and obsceni-
ties (γεφυρισμοί), to which appropriate replies were made. At the
sanctuary the image of Iacchus and the other sacred objects were
handed over to the hierophant to be placed in the Telesterion. The
mystae were sprinkled with water from the well Kallichoron, and in
due course they were led to the sea-shore, fasting and carrying
lighted torches in their hands in imitation of Demeter's search for
Persephone, in order thereby to be brought into union with the
passion of the Mother-goddess and to be prepared for what was to
follow.

The things spoken (λεγόμενα) and the things done (δρώμενα)
within the Telesterion during the next two days, as has been explained, can only be conjectured from the scanty information
available. The *mystae*, seated on sheep-skins covering stools or the
steps along the four sides of the great hall, underwent a profound
mystic experience it would seem, from which they emerged with a
new hope and assurance of having attained salvation. Thus, Cicero,
who was himself an initiate, says that

> among the many excellent and divine gifts of Athens to the life of men,
> nothing is better than those Mysteries by which we are drawn from
> savagery to civilization. They are rightly called initiation (beginning),
> because we have thus learned the first principles of life; and have not
> only received the method of living with joy, but also of dying with
> better hope.[1]

[1] *Leg.*, II, 14.

In a passage quoted by Stobaeus from what is thought to have been a lost work of Plutarch, initiation and death correspond

> word for word, and thing for thing. At first there are wanderings and laborious circuits, and journeyings through the dark, full of misgivings where there is no consummation; then, before the very end, come terrors of every kind, shivers and trembling, sweat and amazement. After this, a wonderful light meets the wanderer; he is admitted into pure meadow lands, where are voices and dances, and the majesty of holy sounds and sacred visions. Here the newly initiated, all rites completed, is at large.[1]

Part of the ritual doubtless consisted in the re-enactment of the sacred drama of the rape of Persephone, during which the hierophant, clad in garments resembling the vestments of a deacon in the Orthodox Church, wearing long hair wreathed with myrtle and tied at the forehead with a broad fillet,[2] emerged from the Anacteron in the centre of the hall from time to time to address the *mystae* and reveal to them secret symbolic objects. If, as Frazer, Jane Harrison, Foucart and Loisy think, the evidence of the Christian writer Hippolytus is to be trusted as a safe guide to what actually occurred in the ancient Telesterion, the culmination of the Mystery was 'an ear of corn reaped in silence' ($\dot{\epsilon}\nu\sigma\iota\omega\pi\hat{\eta}$ $\tau\epsilon\theta\epsilon\rho\iota\sigma\mu\acute{\epsilon}\nu\sigma\nu$ $\sigma\tau\acute{\alpha}\chi\nu\nu$).

> This ear of corn [he says] the Athenians themselves hold to be the great and perfect light that is from that which has no form, as the hierophant himself, who is not like Attis, but who is made an eunuch by means of hemlock and has renounced all carnal generation, he, by night at Eleusis, accomplishing by the light of a great flame the great and unutterable Mysteries, says and cries in a loud voice 'Holy Brimo has borne a sacred childe, Brimos', that is, the Mighty has borne the Mighty.[3]

But since the account was derived from Gnostic sources and is obviously late, Farnell has adequate grounds for rejecting it.[4]

Nevertheless, from the general character of the ritual it seems clear that the Mystery was connected with the seasonal drama in

---

[1] Stobaeus, Ed. Meineke, vol. IV, p. 107.

[2] cf. the figure of a torch-bearer on a vase of the fifth century B.C. in the Museum at Eleusis.

[3] Hippolytus, *Refutatio omnium haeresium*, V, 8.

[4] *Cults of the Greek States* (Oxford, 1906), III, p. 183 ff.

which, as we have seen, a sacred marriage was a prominent feature.[1] It would not be surprising, therefore, if the annual autumnal celebration culminated in a symbolic union of Zeus (in the person of the hierophant) and the Mother-goddess Demeter (as represented by her priestess), Brimos (Dionysus) being the issue. But if this much be granted, it does not follow that originally Demeter was a corntotem whose divine substance was sacramentally eaten by the neophytes when they partook of a cup of κυκέων, a gruel made of water and meal, mentioned by Clement of Alexandria.[2] The password of the Mysteries may have been, as he asserts, 'I have fasted, I have drunk of the κυκέων, I have taken out of the chest, having tasted thereof (or wrought therewith)', but there is no conclusive evidence of the worship of the corn-stalk, still less of a corn-totem. Moreover, even assuming that this could be proved, it would not follow, as Jevons has asserted, that the Mystery corresponds to the annual eating of the totem on the part of worshippers of the Corn-goddess,[3] since the drinking of the κυκέων occurred as part of the preparatory rites, and not at the culmination of the initiation. Furthermore, it was confined to the *mystae*.

If anything is to be deduced from the evidence of the later Christian writers, it is that the supreme act of worship at Eleusis to which all the preliminary ceremonies were directed, consisted in beholding a sacred action, and handling certain sacred objects, not in partaking of a sacred meal. The drinking of the gruel was merely a repetition of what was done by Demeter, like the wandering by night at the sea-shore and bathing in the sea. There is no indication that the κυκέων was consecrated on an altar, or in any way connected with sacrificial ritual, while the theory that it contained the divine substance of the goddess is pure conjecture.

The purpose of the Mystery was to effect the rebirth of the initiates through a ritual death and resurrection. In this process the preliminary ceremonies were cathartic rather than sacramental or ethical in origin and action. The *mystae* were saved once and for all by the things done, seen and spoken during their admission to the cultus apart from any moral excellence or defects. Initiation was *ex opere operato*, and the most conspicuous virtue was of no avail for

[1] Noack, op. cit.

[2] Protrpt., ii, 16, 18, 21, 24.

[3] *Introduction to the History of Religion* (Lond., 1911), p. 214.

salvation unless the prescribed rites had been duly performed by and on behalf of the initiate. Therefore, as the cynic Diogenes remarked, 'the robber Pataikon because he was initiated, would fare better after death than Epaminondas', an unitiated just man; or, in the words of Plato, 'he who arrives in Hades uninitiated and without having participated in the mysteries lies in filth'. Only by slow degrees did the ethical idea of good and evil arise out of the primitive conception of a substantive pollution with quasi-physical properties removable by material agencies. Nevertheless, it is probably true that the Mysteries flourished because there was 'a brooding consciousness of failure, of the futility of human effort, of the load of human sin, the ineluctability of penalty, of gods estranged, and the need of reconciliation and purification'.[1] Consequently, in course of time, to the ritual prescriptions were added ethical notions of a pious life as a qualification of those who would walk in Persephone's meadows.

Less refined than the decorous solemnities at Eleusis were the Thracian orgies held by night on mountain tops, characterized by wild music and frantic dances in which votaries (the maenads), clad in long flowing garments with horns fixed to their heads and carrying serpents in their hands, tore in pieces a bull or calf, and devoured the flesh raw.[2] Ecstatic rites of this nature, in which probably a free use of wine was made, were scarcely likely to commend themselves to the sober and prosaic Greeks, and the worship of Dionysos, unlike that of Demeter, was essentially an alien cult.

Nevertheless, ecstasy is infectious, and at a time (i.e. the seventh and eighth centuries B.C.) when new forces and movements, political, economic and religious, were rapidly changing the outlook of the masses in Greece, and mystical ideas foreign to Homeric thought were gaining ground, the offer of salvation through ecstatic union with a mystery divinity was not without its attractions. A mysterious rapture amounting to hallucination was experienced by the frenzied votaries in their tumultuous worship, producing a state of religious ἔκστασις in which not only was the invisible divine presence dis-

---

[1] Angus, *The Mystery Religions and Christianity* (Lond., 1925), p. 206.

[2] cf. Farnell, *The Cults of the Greek States* (Oxford, 1909), vol. V, pp. 88 ff.; J. Harrison, *Prolegomena to the Study of Greek Religion* (Camb., 1922), 3rd Edition, pp. 363 ff. R. Rhode, *Psyche* (Lond., 1925), p. 256. H. J. Rose, *A Handbook of Greek Mythology* (Lond., 1928), pp. 149 ff.

cerned, but the dancers actually shared the life of the god. In other words, they became 'Sabazoi', or 'Bacchoi', i.e. spiritual beings. In this condition of divine intoxication, or hieromania (sacred madness), they were visionaries, like the Siberian Shamans, and attained mystical communion with the supernatural world. The soul left the body and found complete union with the divine, thereby rendering the worshippers ἔνθεοι, so that being possessed of the god, he spoke and acted through them. Thus freed from all limitations of time and space, they attained to the fullness of the 'beatific vision'.

Enthusiastic worship of this kind, if it made no appeal to Greeks of the Homeric tradition, awoke an unearthly longing in the hearts of the mystically-minded, and from Thrace it spread southwards and at length became established as a public cult in the State religion. As Professor Nilsson says, 'there exists in every man, however humble his station, a dormant desire to enter into communion with the divine, to feel himself lifted up from the temporal into the spiritual. This form of ecstasy found its herald in the god who, with Apollo, impressed himself most strongly upon the religious feeling of the age-Dionysos.'[1] In his cultus the initiates sought to surmount the barrier which separates man from the supernatural order and to find mystical union with the spirit world. Primitive may have been the setting of the sacred drama, and drastic the methods adopted by the devotees, but with the aid of thrilling music, giddy dances in the light of torches, phallic symbols, and a savage sacramental meal on an animal-god, the maenads unconditionally surrendered themselves body and soul to those mighty powers that transcend time and space, and the personal life of man. In these wild rites they were carried beyond reverential awe and wonder to the timeless, spaceless realm of the eternal. They took the kingdom of God by force, and having broken through all the outer defences they found salvation and satisfaction in that divine union which is the goal of all mysticism.

In such a popular outburst of religious emotion it is useless to seek for an ordered and logical mythology. Even the meaning of the name of the cult-hero is uncertain, though the first element in Dionysos appears to refer to the sky-god who was called in Phrygian Dios. For the rest we are in the realms of conjecture. His mother in

[1] M. P. Nilsson, *A History of Greek Religion* (Oxford, 1925), p. 205.

one version is said to have been Semele, a Greek modification of
Zemelo, the Phrygian earth-goddess who was loved of Zeus, and
killed by the revelation of the awful splendour of her Olympian
lover. Her unborn child was saved from the flames by his father
(Zeus), who, according to a barbarian legend, thrust him into his
own thigh, whence he was born. He was then conveyed to Hermes
to be brought up by the nymphs of Nysa, whom, as Ovid tells us,
were rewarded by the renewal of their youth. On reaching maturity
he set forth on a world tour like Osiris to teach the cultivation of
the vine, and propagate his worship. But as Osiris was opposed by
Set, so Dionysos encountered attacks from Lycurgus, a Thracian
king, from which he escaped by jumping into the sea, while Zeus
smote the enemy with blindness. Pentheus, king of Thebes, proved
to be a more serious adversary, but he was killed by his own mother
while he was concealed in a tree watching the frenzied mysteries.

There are many similar stories which take their origin probably
in the opposition the cult encountered in its earliest days, and they
all bear witness to the orgiastic nature of his worship. The Attic
legend of Icarios reveals, nevertheless, the peaceful diffusion that
occurred in some districts where the Dionysiac was welcomed.
Another saga tells of the penetration of the mystery into the interior
of Asia and India,[1] but this is probably an attempt to bolster up the
campaign of Alexander the Great in the Orient rather than a
reminiscence of the spread of the cult. Similarly, the Western influence of Dionysos belongs to a late period when he was identified
with the Liber Pater.[2]

Since Homer knows the Lycurgus myth, the cultus must have
begun to make its way in Greece by about the seventh century B.C.,
though it was not until rather later that it spread, especially among
the female population, as an epidemic of psyhcopathic religiosity.
By the end of the fifth century, however, as a vase painting shows,
Apollo, who is represented as clasping the hands of Dionysos before
the omphalos at Delphi, had stemmed the tide of frenzy by stripping
the orgies of their worst excesses.[3] The alliance modified the worship of both gods, though they were too fundamentally different

[1] Euripides, *Bacch.*, 13 ff.

[2] cf. Livy, xxxix, 8–19. G. Wissowa, *Religion und Kultus der Römer* (Munchen,
1912), pp. 298 ff.

[3] A. W. Pickard-Cambridge, *Dithyramb, Tragedy and Comedy* (Oxford, 1927),
Figs. 1, 2.

ever to merge. Prophecy by divination, as revealed by Apollo, and prophecy by inspiration, as introduced by Dionysos, were not wholly incommensurable,[1] and the union of the two methods of approach to the supernatural world was achieved at Delphi. During the three winter months the dithyramb of the Hellenized Dionysos was sung while the Thyiades roamed among the mountains in the snow with their torches and swinging thyrsi, but if the ecstatic nocturnal revels continued, and their fervour influenced even the more prosaic oracular rites, when the 'Lord of Delphi' returned in the spring, the abandonment was moderated and confined to properly elected initiates. Furthermore, when the Dionysiac spread to Athens and the centres ruled over by the Delphic Apollo, hardly any trace of the old Thracian orgiastic worship remained.

Nevertheless, the ecstatic element was never wholly eliminated, as Plutarch shows,[2] and if the urban Apolline tradition sobered the tumultuous mountain cult, the Dionysian 'enthusiasm' introduced a new conception of the 'prophecy of inspiration' in the systems in which it became incorporated, and indeed it is not too much to say that it 'planted the seed of mysticism in the very heart of Greek religion'.[3] This was accomplished by establishing *ekstasis* at Delphi, the most famous of all seats of Greek cult, for it was the Delphic oracle that was instrumental in spreading the worship of Dionysos.

The part played by the Orphics in the dissemination of Dionysian mysticism is probably less than that of Delphi, inasmuch as they never succeeded in synthesizing the two gods. Dionysos was the god *par excellence* of the Orphic religion, Orpheus, originally probably a divine king, its hero, prophet and priest being scarcely ever afforded divine worship. As Professor Guthrie has remarked, 'Orpheus was a religious founder and the religion he founded was a species of the Bacchic',[4] though he himself was very far from being a Bacchic figure. In his Thracian cradle-land, according to the tradition, he was a musician, the son of one of the Muses, and became a devoted follower of Dionysos. Being adept in the magic art he travelled far and wide with his golden lyre, Apollo's instrument, and introduced Dionysian worship wherever he went. In

[1] cf. Plato, *Phaedrus*, 244, *a–d*.
[2] *Mul. Virt.*, 13, 249 E.   [3] Rhode, *Psyche,* p. 291.
[4] *Orpheus and Greek Religion* (Lond., 1935), p. 41.

one of the later versions, his wife, the princess Euridike, was killed by a snake-bite, whereupon the distracted Orpheus penetrated the underworld in search for her, but failed in his quest because he did not fulfil the conditions imposed on him by the infernal gods. He then became a solitary, to the dismay of the women of Thrace who, in their desperation at his neglect of them, fell upon him in a Bacchic orgy and tore him in pieces, as Dionysos is said to have been rent by the Titans, and as his animal symbol was torn by his worshippers.

It is this incident in the tradition that brings the legend into relation with the story of Dionysos, but since in one variant it was by the god's command that the hero was killed, the relations between the two cults may not always have been very harmonious, if the myths reflect the historical situation. Furthermore, since the motive of the murder was neglect of the Dionysiac in favour of the worship of Apollo, it might appear that Orpheus also had Apolline affinities. He was, in short, a syncretistic figure who probably was introduced into the worship after it was an established fact. Therefore, he collected around him a number of extraneous elements and attributes, chiefly Dionysian and Apolline.

By about the sixth century B.C. a composite legend had grown out of and around the Thraco-Phrygian *omophagia,* in which Dionysos (who is called by the name of the chthonian diety Zagreus) is represented as the son of Zeus by his daughter Persephone. To him was given dominion over the earth, but the wicked Titans succeeded in getting him into their power when he had transformed himself into a bull in an endeavour to escape from them; they tore him in pieces and devoured him. Athena, however, was able to save his heart and take it to Zeus who swallowed it, as Osiris consumed the eye of Horus. He then slew the Titans with his thunderbolts, and from their ashes created the human race. Hence man is partly divine, as the Titans had eaten Zagreus, and partly evil, because he partook of their evil nature. From Zeus there sprang the 'new Dionysos', born of Semele, in whom Zagreus was restored to life.[1]

This death-and-resurrection legend represents the mythological setting of the Orphic mystery, the main purpose of which was to

[1] Orpheus, *Frags.,* 210 ff. O. Gruppe, 'Orpheus' in Roscher, *Lex. d. gr. u. röm. Mythologie* (Leipsic, 1884).

secure immortality for its initiates by the eradication of the material Titan element (i.e. their evil nature). Only by deliverance from this physical integument could the soul (the Dionysian part) go un-trammelled in search of divine union, and to secure this goal, in addition to initiation and the practice of asceticism, a cycle of births and deaths were regarded as essential. In its upward path towards freedom the soul was destined to pass through a series of bodies, both human and animal, till at length escape from the 'wheel of birth' was secured by the 'releasing grace' of Orpheus and his mysteries.

In the Orphic doctrine of metempsychosis we encounter the first attempt to introduce, in the higher religions of the West, the idea of transmigration and a moralization of the hereafter. Starting from the notion of original sin and the theory of the body as an impure prison-house of the soul, an elaborate ritual of purification arose in which salvation was sought and found in a sacramental identifica-tion with the saviour-god as a result of consecration to a higher state of life in a mystery cult. To secure immortality the evil element had to be eradicated, and although this never could be accomplished in one life, the adoption of the Orphic ascetic rule, which involved abstinence from flesh, eggs and beans, and contact with corpses and pregnant women, together with the practice of chastity, was a means to this end. But moral as well as ceremonial purity was also inculcated, and a common standard of virtue was fostered in the mystic brotherhoods by a doctrine of rewards and punishments after death. 'They who are righteous beneath the rays of the sun, when they die have a gentler lot in a fair meadow by deep-flowing Acheron. . . . But they who have worked wrong and insolence beneath the rays of the sun are led down beneath the watery plain of Cocytus into chill Tartarus.' Thus, Hades was regarded as a state of purgation and retribution in which the soul awaited its rebirth, the reincarnation being determined by the deeds performed in its former life. The wicked and uninitiated suffered physical torments consumed by thirst and hunger with vultures tearing at their liver, condemned to their ghastly fate for ever through an eternal series of rebirths.

From the gold tablets found in tombs near Sybaris, one near Rome, and one in Crete, it seems that magical amulets played their part in protecting the deceased in his perilous journey through the underworld, as in Egypt. Thus the initiate is made to declare in the fragments of a hymn—

> I am the son of Earth and Heaven. I am perishing with thirst, give me to drink of the waters of memory. I come from the pure. I have paid the penalty of unrighteousness. I have flown out of the sorrowful, weary round of life, I have entered with eager feet the ring desired. I have passed to the bosom of the mistress queen of the lower world. O happy and blessed one, thou shall be god instead of mortal.

This union with the divine nature in its completeness differed from the Indian goal, as we shall see, in that it did not involve absorption or 'cooling down'. The aim of initiation was to rid the spirit of its physical encumbrances and secure eternal blessedness in an Orphic state of bliss when at last the emancipated himself becomes βάκχος.

CHAPTER VI

Oriental Theism

As Greece was destined to be the home of an independent civilization, so India both climatically and geographically was set apart by
Nature for the development of an uninterrupted cosmic tradition
in which man was completely dominated by his environment.
Shut off by the Himalayas to the north from Assam to Afghanistan,
the only accessible means of intercourse with the rest of Asia has
been through the Khyber Pass at the south-west angle of the
openings through which the Indus and Kabul river flow into the
country. By this approach from time immemorial, peaceful traders
and settlers and conquering armies have made their way into the
fertile Indian plains from the Iranian plateau, so that in the fourth
and third millennia B.C., some 1,500 to 2,000 years before the
Aryans (or inhabitants of 'Iran') poured through the north-western
pass from the mountain plateau of Central Asia, a highly developed
culture was already established in the Indus valley.[1]

THE INDUS VALLEY CIVILIZATION

From the recent excavations at Mohenjo-daro, 25 miles south of
Larkhana in Sind, and at Harappa, in the Montgomery district of
the Punjab, it is now evident that a non-pastoral people lived in
well-planned cities with streets at right angles, running east and
west, and north and south, and houses built of fired brick, probably
with several storeys and flat roofs. The dwellings were equipped
with bath-rooms, and an elaborate drainage system with pottery
pipes communicating with the street gutter. Although there are
signs of prosperity and extensive commercial enterprise in the
earlier levels, nothing comparable to a palace or temple has come to

[1] The age of Mohenjo-daro is suggested by a seal from the Indus valley found at
Tell-Asmar in Mesopotamia, in a stratum dated about 2500 B.C., though the beginnings of the civilization are probably considerably earlier.

light, but a large public bath with eight small rooms attached, is thought to have been used for ritual ablutions, each member of a priestly order living in a cell above his bath-room, which he entered by a private stair-case.[1] As in Babylonia and Egypt, the Indus culture rested on irrigation farming. Wheat, barley and the date palm were cultivated, cotton was manufactured, gold, silver and bronze were employed for metal working, and the sheep, pig, dog, elephant, fowl, zebu, Indian buffalo and short-horned bull domesticated; but while the ox was used to draw two-wheeled carts, only in the latest layers at Mohenjo-daro are the remains of the horse and camel found, and neither animal is depicted on the seals, though models of saddles occur.

It is from the large number of finely cut seals, or amulets, that our knowledge of the religion of the civilization largely is derived, in the absence of any structure that can be identified with certainty as a temple or shrine. In addition to the bath used for ceremonial purposes, innumerable clay figurines seem to have had a magico-religious significance and probably bear witness to the existence of a fertility cult parallel to that associated with the Mother-goddess in other parts of the Ancient East. A steatite head and bust of a bearded figure clothed in a robe which is carried over the left shoulder and under the right arm, ornamented with a trefoil pattern of frequent occurrence as a sacred symbol, resembles Sumerian images of deities. This very likely represents a male god, and it has been suggested that the half-shut eyes directed to the tip of the nose may indicate a state of yogi, or contemplation, so familiar in later Hindu statues. Several clay tablets show horned male deities, while a seal depicts a goddess with horns in the midst of a *pipal* or sacred fig-tree, before which another horned deity is kneeling in obeisance. Behind stands a human-faced goat and a row of seven worshippers each wearing a sprig on the head, and a long pigtail behind. Since the Hindu Venus, Lakshmi, the consort of Vishnu, dwells in the pipal tree and is approached with offerings by women desiring male offspring, it is not improbable that the scene is connected with an ancient form of the cultus of the Mother-goddess.[2]

Scenes such as these, and the prominence of almost nude female figurines with a girdle about the loins, elaborate head-dress and

[1] Mackay, *The Indus Civilization* (Lond., 1935), p. 58.

[2] J. Marshall, *Mohenjo-daro and the Indus Civilization* (Lond., 1931), vol. I, pp. 49 ff.

collar, and occasionally ornamental cheek-cones and a long neck-lace, together with phallic emblems, including 'ring' and Baetylic stones, the linga, or conical stone, and the cult of the bull and of the snake, connect the Indus valley civilization with that of Crete and the associated cultures. Since tree spirits and female deities are seldom mentioned in Vedic mythology, and phallicism is entirely absent, these aspects of Hinduism appear to belong in origin to pre-Aryan India. In this connexion the remarkable figure of a three-faced god sitting on a stool cross-legged in *yogi* fashion, with arms outstretched and the hands resting on the knees, is of special interest. On his head are a pair of horns, and surrounding him two deer or antelopes, a rhinoceros, an elephant, a tiger and buffalo. On either arm the figure wears a number of bangles like a Mother-goddess, and between the horns a fan-shaped head-dress, as in many female figurines. But the representation is that of a male deity who seems to be a prototype of the Hindu god Shiva, 'lord of beasts' and 'prince of yogis', whatever his name may have been at this early period.

That he was mainly concerned with the promotion of fertility like Shiva is suggested by the fact that on the three seals in which similar designs occur, in each case the figure has horns and is adorned with bangles symbolic of vegetative and reproductive functions. In Hinduism Shiva has various consorts known as Kali, Uma, Parvati, Bhavani and Durga, just as Lakshmi is the wife of Vishnu. The union of god and goddess, typifying that of the sky and the earth, represents the sources of reproduction, the consort being *shakti*, a term denoting also 'power' or 'energy', which is insepar-able from the male deity and joins with him to create and sustain the phenomenal universe. The relationship, in short, is comparable to that of Isis to Osiris, so that in Hindu mythology Isis might be described as the *shakti* of Osiris inasmuch as he was powerless without his sister-spouse. Thus, as the manifestation of the ancient Mother-goddess, the female principle gave prosperity to the country and fertility to Nature as in primitive society the king's powers on behalf of the community were supposed to depend on his virility which was manifest in his ability to satisfy the sexual pas-sions of his wives. When he ceased to be able to exercise this function he was put to death in order that there might always be a vigorous occupant of the throne. Therefore, *shakti*, in the sense of vital power, is the link connecting the male and female principles in the control of the natural order, derived apparently from the Mother-goddess of Asia Minor.

Again, the occurrence of the bull on seal-amulets is suggestive of the widespread veneration of cattle in association with the worship of the Mother-goddess who, in Phoenicia, was represented as a heifer, and in Egypt was equated with Hathor (later identified with Isis), symbolized as the divine cow wearing the solar disc and two plumes between her horns. In India, while the sanctity of the cow is a characteristic feature of orthodox Hinduism, it was apparently unknown among the Indo-European population when the miscellaneous collection of epics called the *Rig-Veda* was first compiled between 1500 and 1000 B.C. in honour of the Nature deities. Thus, the first prohibition of the slaughter of the cow occurs in the Atharva-Veda, a relatively late addition of magical spells arranged by the priests (Brahmans) in liturgical form for use at the sacrifices. Prior to this cattle were freely offered to Indra and other Vedic gods, and it was only as a concession to later opinion that the cow was exempt from the altar. It would seem, therefore, that the origin of this veneration must be sought in the earlier non-Aryan culture which had established itself in northern India by 3000 B.C.

Like all other foreign influences, this culture entered from the north-west, and had affinities with the stream of civilization that extended at that time from Egypt and the Fertile Crescent to the Indus valley. While it presents certain distinct features of its own, it is clearly based upon the same fundamental ideas, discoveries and inventions as are displayed in the other centres, as is shown, for example, in the stamp seals and their designs, and beads of unusual shape, which can be linked with similar objects from Egypt, Sumer, Crete, and Greece.[1] The common centre of this widespread diffusion may have been the highland region east of the Persian Gulf where a Mongolian strain perhaps entered the stock, but it is probable that the founders of Mohenjo-daro and the adjacent sites were predominantly of Mediterranean type modified by fusion with a more primitive proto-Australoid variety of mankind. The dolicho-cephalic skulls agree with those found at Al Obeid and Kish, and pottery, beads and implements suggest, as has been

---

[1] cf. Mackay, op. cit., pp. 191 ff.; G. Childe, *The Most Ancient East* (Lond., 1934), pp. 204 ff.

pointed out, that they represent an intrusive element of common ancestry with the Sumerians. The evidence, in short, points to a cultural migration through the Mula pass to Las Bela and the Makran which developed a new type of definitely Indian civilization in its area of characterization in the Indus valley. It is to this culture that we now look for the earliest phases of some of the most fundamental elements in Hinduism, such as Shiva-worship, phallicism, and the cult of animals and trees.

Upon this non-Aryan substratum the Indo-European civilization was laid about 2000 B.C., and for 3,000 years became the predominant influence till the Moslem invasions introduced further modifications. But in this isolated continent the religious ideas of the earlier inhabitants, and their customs, persisted almost untouched by the theology of the Vedic hymns and the Brahmanas, the Upanishads and the Vedanta. Moreover, finally they surged up again and in the post-Vedic period (*c.* fifth century B.C.) profoundly modified the Aryan system. Thus, two deeply laid religious traditions existed side by side and pursued their independent developments in response to the peculiar needs and conditions of their environment, the one (after the time of the *Rig-Veda*) moving farther and farther away from theism in the direction of a pantheistic mysticism, the other deviating towards the recognition of the divine as a personal Creator and Sustainer of the world rather than as an abstract philosophical Absolute.

If the irresistible and overpowering tropical climate of India fostered the quest for release from cosmic struggle in the attainment of passionless peace, the tendency to deify the processes of Nature and to seek union with the divine by the way of devotion, were never lacking though discredited in the Upanishadic literature, and denied by the founders of Buddhism and Jainism. Actually, however, polytheism is as inveterate as philosophic pantheism from the time of the Indo-European Hymns of the Vedas to that of the great Epics, and later Hinduism represents a combination of these two movements.

VEDIC POLYTHEISM

When the Aryans entered the country from the north-west they introduced a highly developed Nature-worship of devas and

F

demons personifying the sky, storm, wind and clouds. Of the beneficent celestial 'Shining Ones' (devas) the chief was Dyaus-pitar,
the Sky-Father, who later gave place to Varuna, the god of the
'wide expanse' of sky and ocean, the ruler of the universe and lord
of the ethical law. With Varuna was associated the Sun, golden-
mouthed and golden-bosomed, variously known as Surya, Savitri,
Mitra, who daily pursued his course across the sky in his seven-
horsed chariot. His beautiful consort, Ushas, the dawn, the freshest
and youngest of all the devas, came forth from the east like a bride
adorned for her husband as she roused the world from sleep.[1] Agni,
the god of fire, burned upon the family hearth and gave cheer to
the home, summoned from heaven by the priest with his fire-sticks.
Soma, the sacred plant from which the golden sacrificial intoxicating beverage was prepared to be consumed sacramentally as the
nectar of immortality calculated to raise mankind to heaven. 'We
have drunk soma; we have become immortal; we have gone to the
light, we have found the gods.'[2] Indeed, Soma was itself a royal
god, and the sacrificer became the sacrifice so that he 'passed from
men to the gods'.[3] When the sacred plant was crushed to extract
the juice the king-god (Soma) was slain as a victim is immolated to
give life in greater abundance by uniting the worshipper with the
god who ever lives. The Soma sacrifice, in fact, was the centre and
framework of the Vedic ritual mystically united with the sun and
later with the moon, as the controller of vegetation whose waning
was explained as due to the drinking of the sacred beverage by the
gods.[4]

Of all the devas of the *Rig-Veda* Indra, the divine warrior, was
the most popular, no less than 250 hymns having been composed
in his praise. He it was who slew dragons and monsters by the help
of the soma-juice, having on one famous occasion drunk three
great lakes of it. Agni, on the other hand, who comes next to Indra
with 200 hymns at the beginning of the family-books (II–VIII),
is the divine counterpart of the priesthood, officiating at the sacrifice and acting as the messenger between the gods and men as
kinsman, friend, brother and son.[5]

[1] *Rig-Veda*, I, 113.   [2] *ibid.*, VIII, 48, 3.

[3] *Satapatha Brahmana*, ii, 5, 1, 7; i, 1, 4 ff.

[4] cf. H. D. Griswold, *Religion of the Rig-Veda* (Oxford, 1923), p. 209 ff.

[5] *Rig-Veda*, 1–36; I, 1, 9; II, 1, 9.

Behind all the gods lies *rta*, the changeless cosmic order, at once impersonal and under the guardianship of Varuna, the establisher of heaven and earth and upholder of the moral law. At first this conception was chiefly cosmical, but during the Vedic period it gained both an ethical connotation, as in the Avestan *asa*, and a sacrificial significance. Thus, Varuna was regarded as the Lord of the moral law, with Agni as Lord of the ritual order and Indra the controller of cosmic law, while the hymns addressed to each of these gods are associated with *rta* as upholders and followers of it. But as the gods change their places with startling suddenness *rta* is often employed to indicate all three meanings. Varuna is described as 'Lord of Law', and Agni is said to become Varuna when he strives for the *rta*.[1] The sacred fire is the means whereby the offerings are carried to the sky by way of *rta*, fire being the earthly counterpart of the sun, and 'Right is the Fire, Truth is yonder Sun; or rather Right is yonder Sun and Truth is this fire'.[2]

This notion of *rta* as the world order is represented as essentially righteous since morality belongs to the fundamental principle of the universe and the ritual system which sustains it. As has recently been said, 'it is clear enough that *rta* stands for moral order and is opposed to sin and unrighteousness . . . but the conception is so wide in its application that it loses correspondingly in depth'[3]. Moreover, it is mainly a ritual holiness that is sought since the violation of a law of Varuna demands the utterance of hymns and a duly appointed sacrificial offering. Agni knows the hidden part of man,[4] and he intercedes with Varuna,[5] and consumes with hottest flames 'those who regard not Varuna's commandments and the clear steadfast laws of sapient Mitra'. The same is said of Indra who punishes sin with his bolt like Zeus. Soma too grants forgiveness, as do other gods such as Mitra, Aditi, Savitri, the Sun and the Dawn. After imbibing the sacred drink, the worshipper is said to be lifted up out of the sinful state not only to fellowship with Soma but also to Aditi. 'Thou shalt be Aditi as thou hast entered within, appeaser of celestial anger.'[6] As Varuna fell into the background, and finally in post-Vedic times became merely a 'godling of the

---

[1] *Rig-Veda*, X, 8, 5.　　　　[2] *Sat. Brah.*, v, 4, 4, 10.

[3] J. McKenzie, *Hindu Ethics* (Lond., 1922), p. 8.

[4] *Rig-Veda*, VIII, 39, 6.　　　　[5] *ibid.*, IV, 1, 5.

[6] *Rig-Veda*, VIII, 48, 2.

waters', his place was taken by Indra who was 'nearer to the comprehension of the common man and appealing more to his crude instincts'.[1]

On their arrival Nature-worship was highly developed among the Aryans together with the cult of fire and the soma, and the art of composing religious lyrics to win the favour of the gods in conjunction with the offerings. The hymns preserved in the *Vedas* consist of (1) the *Rig-Veda* for the use of the hotri, or first order of priests; (2) the *Sama-Veda*, derived from the *Rig-Veda*, as the manual, or book of chants for the second order of priests, employed chiefly at the time of the soma-sacrifice; (3) the third collection, known as the *Yajur-Veda*, consists partly of formulae and partly of prose designed for use at various offerings. These were compiled somewhere between 1000 and 800 B.C., and at a later date the formulae of the *Yajur-Veda* were separated from the prose, as (a) the *Black Yajur-Veda,* a mixed and older edition, and (b) the *White Yajur-Veda,* an unmixed version. The fourth collection is the *Atharva-Veda* which probably extends over a period of several centuries. While some of these hymns were contemporary with the *Rig-Veda*, the majority of them were composed subseqent to the other Vedas, and embody current spells and magical influences which in their original form go back perhaps to prehistoric times.

THE BRAHMANAS

The term 'Veda' (i.e. 'knowledge') was applied to these texts, not in the sense of divine revelation, or philosophical search for ultimate reality, but in the belief that magical power resided in the words uttered. To them four *samhita* (collections) were added, probably between about 800 and 600 B.C., consisting of discursive theological treatises for the guidance of the priests (Brahmans) in the performance of the Vedic ritual setting forth with great elaboration the details of sacrificial procedure. The most important of these prose works is the *Satapatha Brahmana,* the 'Brahmana of a hundred paths', so called because it consists of a hundred discourses. Next to the *Rig-Veda* and the *Atharva-Veda* it is the principal production in the Vedic literature, and reveals the essential elements of the sacerdotal system. In place of Varuna and the earlier Nature-gods

[1] N. Macnicol, *Indian Theism* (Oxford, 1915), p. 15.

as the controlling deities, sacrifice became the means by which heaven and earth were maintained. Since the gods themselves depended upon this rite of cosmic efficacy, it was mightier than they, and he who controlled the rite controlled the gods, Consequently the 'mantras', or sacred texts used in sacrifice, came to have tremendous potency, since it was they who made the offering efficacious, while the Brahmans were virtually divine in status. Moreover, the ritual was not limited to securing the favour of the gods, but being potent in itself supplied a 'treasury of merit' (*ishtapurta*) from which reserves could be drawn in the next life.

This conception of *ishtapurta*[1] when brought into relation with the belief in *samsāra*, or the doctrine of migration, was destined to have far-reaching effects on Indian thought and practice. Metempsychosis, of course, is a familiar feature in the primitive notion of the soul, and there are some indications of the doctrine in the *Atharva-Veda* and the *Brahmanas*, though in the latter when man is said to be 'born into the world made by him' the reference is to rebirth in the hereafter.[2] In its specifically Indian form, however, the main idea is an endless chain of reincarnations and transmigrations on earth determined by conduct in the present existence. The treasury of merits enables a man to have a fund upon which he could draw on the other side of the grave and to which he could contribute during his earthly pilgrimage by the performance of prescribed rites.[3] Thus, in practice, good actions meant 'right sacrificing', while the idea of *karma*, though it acquired a philosophical significance as an explanation of the presence of suffering in the world, was originally action automatic and unchangeable in its operations like the processes of Nature in the physical universe. Only by its aid could men attain immortality and secure victory in their struggles with the demonic powers (asuras).

By the primal sacrifice of Prajapati, the god *par excellence* of the *Brahmanas*, the Lord of Production and personification of the creative principle, the world came into existence, created out of himself. Having made the waters, the air, the sun, the stars, the earth,

---

[1] *ishta* meaning 'sacrifice' and *purta* 'the fee paid to the priest'. These terms combined together form the idea of the merit of free or ordered acts performed on earth stored up as a heavenly substance to await the sacrificer beyond the grave.

[2] *Sat. Brah.*, 6-2-2-27. *S.B.E.*, XLI, p. 181, n. 1; cf. Hopkins, *Religions of India* (Lond., 1898), p. 175.

[3] *Sat. Brah.*, 12-9-3-12.

the animals and plants, and finally man and the gods, he renewed
his vigour by the offerings which sustain all things. This creative
process was repeated by the king in the erection of the Fire-Altar
when the creation story was recited and the emergence of the earth
from the primeval was re-enacted in the production of the fire-pan
in the midst of the altar.[1] The king, in fact, made himself divine,
and like other Vedic gods in the *Brahmanas*, was regarded as the son
of Prajapati. It would seem, therefore, that he occupied a place in
Indian society comparable to that assumed by kings in other ancient
communities, and the Brahmans shared in his divinity as human
gods by virtue of their position in society and their function in
relation to the state ritual upon which the universe and its processes
depended for their continuance.

The emanation of the world from Prajapati, however, as also in
the Vedic counterpart, from the Primal Man, or *Purusha*, contains
a pantheistic element inasmuch as he brought all things into being
out of himself: 'I will reproduce myself, I will become many'. In
the era of the *Rig-Veda* Varuna was tending to assume a pantheistic
significance since he pervaded natural phenomena and human and
animal life—a ruler of macrocosm and microcosm alike. Through
rta, the cosmic universal order, he fulfilled his operations as an
immanent dynamic process rather than as a divine personality in the
monotheistic sense. Such personality as he displays is modified by
his *rta* manifestation which controls his actions as a cosmic force
comparable to *karma*. Actually he is subject to this higher universal
law, just as *Purusha* represented a metaphysical unity as the head of
creation. Nature as a whole was regarded as an extension of the
Primal Man and the parts of the world were interpreted as the
organs of his body.[2]

In the *Satapatha Brahmana* this monistic tendency was further
developed by the universe, being equated also with Brahman
(neuter).

> It created the gods; and having created the gods, it made them ascend
> these worlds. . . . Then the Brahman itself went up to the sphere beyond.
> Having gone up to the sphere beyond it, it considered, 'How can I
> descend again into these worlds?' It then descended again by means of
> these two, Form and Name. Whatever has a name, that is name: and that

[1] *ibid.*, 1-9-2-29; VI-7-2-12.
[2] *Rig-Veda.*, 10-90 vv. 11/14.

again which has no name and which one knows by its form, this is (of a particular) form, and that is form : as far as there are Form and Name so far, indeed, extends this (universe). These indeed are the two great forces of Brahman; and verily he who knows these two great forces of Brahman becomes himself a great force.[1]

THE UPANISHADS

The notion of a universal self-existent principle as the ultimate force in the universe (*Brahman*), controlled by the sacrificial rite correctly performed, brought into relation with the breath-soul in man (*Atnam*), was the first step towards the great achievement of Indian mysticism between 700 and 500 B.C. which found expression in the Sanskrit treatises, or dialogues, known as the Upanishads. By uniting the energy which animated the human organism (*atman*) with the creative energy that sustains the universe (*brahman*), a definite break was made with the earlier ritual order. The Brahmanic dualism of a microcosm within and its co-ordinate macrocosm without was transformed into a monism by making the *Atman*,[2] the One Self, the root cause of all that is. Thus, the 'kathenotheistic' tendency of the *Vedas*, in the successive belief in single supreme gods, gave place to pantheism as the centre of interest, was shifted from the external Creator to the inner soul of man and the universe. In the equation of the *Atman* with the *Brahman* the goal of Upanishadic thought was reached, and two independent currents of speculation—the one arising from the desire to understand the true nature of man, and the other from an attempt to explain the objective world—were fused. The self and the not-self were resolved into a unity as the manifestation of the same Reality. 'That thou art, I am Brahman.'

From this synthesis the Upanishadic Absolute emerged as the all-inclusive Ultimate Reality, neither *Brahman* nor *Atman* by themselves but transcending both. The highest quest of man then became the realization of the unity of the *Atman* with the Absolute attainable by means of a process of rebirth (*samsāra*) in which the soul passes through many bodies either of men or of animals. In the *Atharva-Veda* and the *Satapatha Brahmana* there are possible

[1] *S.B.E.* (Eggling), XLIV, pp. 27 ff.

[2] *an,* 'to breathe'; *tman,* 'one's self'.

indications of the doctrine of metempsychosis, as we have seen, but instead of *Brahman* being regarded as the spoken word of the *purusha*, it was now identified with the transcendental self (*atman*) conceived as universal spirit, the one constant unity in a succession of sensations and ideas making up the multiplicity of experience. It was this essential ego which gave equilibrium and stability to the human organism, and since the principle of unity within was identical with the principle which pervades all things (*Brahman*), a mystic union with the Reality immanent in the universe was secured.

Thus from the Vedic notion of the Brahman as the vitalizing spirit which stirred within the poets as they sang their hymns, the idea of an impersonal creative principle took shape which became equated with the breath-soul in man brought into relation with the pantheistic cosmic order having a moral significance and a law of action and reaction (*karma*) to constitute a monism. But if ultimately only *Brahman Atman* exists, it is but a step to the deduction that the phenomenal world is illusion (*maya*); and in the *Svetasvatara Upanishad* this corollary was added. Thus, in addition to the problem of the nature of the universe, there was manifest in the Upanishads a desire to escape from the misery of the existence to that which is alone true and abiding. In the end it was contended all things must be absorbed in the source from which they have emanated when the cosmic cycle is complete. But before the self can return to its origin it must rid itself of every vestige of *karma*, and realize its true nature in terms of the Upanishadic equation.

Brahman, according to this line of thought, is One and Absolute.[1] He is 'the reality of realities', and all that can be said of him is 'That thou art'.[2] But in the older texts a distinction was drawn between *Brahman* as 'noumenal' and *Brahman* as 'phenomenal'. 'There are, assuredly, two forms of Brahma; the formed (*murta*) and the formless, the mortal and the immortal; the stationary and the moving, the actual (*sat*) and the (*tya*) or transcendental.'[3] Moreover, in Maitri it is declared, 'There are, assuredly, two forms of Brahma; the formed and the formless. Now that which is formed is unreal; that which is formless is real, is Brahma, is light'.[4] The lower Brahma has now become merely an appearance due to human ignorance of the fact that all is essentially One—it is an

[1] *Brih.*, 4-3-27/30.   [2] *ibid.*, 2-1-20. *Chand.*, 6-8/16.
[3] *ibid.*, 2-3-1.   [4] *Maitri*, 6-3.

illusion. The neuter Brahman, unmanifested, has became the mas-
culine Brahman, which later developed into *Īśvara*, or 'Karana
Brahman', capable of assuming a cosmic body, and not far removed
from a personal Creator inasmuch as he was identified with Rudra.[1]

Thus, while the chief emphasis in the Upanishads was upon the
Absolute, a place was found for the 'manifested' *Brahman* related
to the world as its creator and ruler, and, therefore, for the ritual
order inherited from the Vedic period. It was recognized, however,
that this was a lower level of spiritual life which did not lead to
emancipation (*moksa*) since it involved the illusion of the reality of
phenomenal existence. Consequently, until the self extricated itself
from the meshes of its own inconsistencies and earthly entanglements, it was condemned to an endless round of *samsāra*. How this
might be accomplished will be considered later, but when at length
freedom was secured, the *Atman* realized its true nature—'I am
Brahman'.

TAOISM

In China Nature was conceived to be the manifestation of the divine
in two aspects—as revealing in its order the beneficent will of God
for man, and in its disorder the manifestation of divine wrath—
bound up with the concept of *tao*, the fundamental metaphysical
principle revealed in an impersonal law governing alike man and
the natural universe. It was to this 'way' or 'method' of heaven
that Lao-tze (born *c.* 604 B.C.) gave a new significance by making
it the 'Originator and Mother of all things', 'doing everything
without apparently doing anything'.[2] Heaven never strives, he
maintained, though it continues to be creative without effort or
purpose. Pervaded by an ultimate metaphysical principle. Heaven
and Earth endure because behind the phenomenal world there is a
changeless Reality from which all becoming proceeds.

> There was something formless yet complete,
> That existed before heaven and earth;
> Without sound, without substance,
> Dependent on nothing, unchanging.
> All-pervading, unfailing.

[1] *Svetasvatara,* 3–20, 4–12.
[2] *S.B.E.,* XXXIX, 1, 1, 2, 4.

One may think of it as the mother of all things under heaven.
Its true name we do not know;
Tao is the name that we give it.
Were I forced to say to what class of things it belongs I should call it *ta* (great).
Now *ta* also means passing on,
And passing on means going Far Away,
And going away means returning.[1]

Thus just as Tao has 'this greatness' and as earth has it and as heaven has it, so may the ruler also have it. Thus 'within the realm there are four portions of greatness', the one belongs to the king. The ways of men are conditioned by those of earth. The ways of earth by those of heaven. The ways of heaven by those of Tao, and the ways of Tao by the unconditioned.[2]

Tao, then, is not a transcendent being, but a pantheistic reality immanent in sense phenomena, controlled by no higher law than itself as a spontaneous monistic principle anterior to the supreme ancestor (*Ti*). A connexion exists between the ruler and *Tao* macrocosmically in the line ruler, earth, heaven; and microcosmically so that by passing through successive stages of consciousness back to the Ultimate Unity the Way (*Tao*) may be reached which controls the multiform apparent universe.[3] This is achieved, however, in this life and not through a process of reincarnation and transmigration. The ethical ideal of Taoism is mystical union with the quietistic source of all life, and unlike Confucianism, it urges detachment from human affairs, 'acting without action', in solitude and humility of spirit. Since the Tao alone is real, the phenomenal world and all its ways and works have only a relative significance. 'All existence in the universe sprang from Being (*Tao*, as the active principle); Being itself sprang from Non-being (*Tao*, as absolute).' Ultimately all things return to the source of their origin, and while they pursue their course they can only function correctly through *Tao* in which subjective knowledge and the objective world are harmonized. Therefore, the highest virtue is to live in accordance with *Tao*, and since *Tao* effects everything by passivity, the good

[1] i.e. returning to 'what was at the beginning'.

[2] i.e. what is so in itself. *Tao-Te-Ching*, XXV, Trans. by A. Waley, *The Way and its Power* (Lond., 1934), p. 74. cf. *S.B.E.*, XXXIX, 1, 1, 2, 4.

[3] Waley, op. cit., p. 175.

life lies in mystical quietude. Consequently, 'the highest goodness is like water. Water is good for advantaging all things and does not strive. It takes the place that all men disdain. It is this that makes water so near to *Tao*'.[1] 'He who devotes himself to learning (seeks) from day to day to increase (his knowledge); he who devotes himself to the *Tao* (seeks) from day to day to diminish (his doing). He diminishes it and again diminishes it, till he arrives at doing nothing. Having arrived at this period of non-action, there is nothing which he does not do.'[2]

CONFUCIANISM

In striking contrast to this ethical ideal exalting inactivity, unassertiveness, humility and gentleness as the Way of Heaven, is the self-culture of Confucius (551–478 B.C.), who endeavoured to establish a practical philosophy to meet the needs of a generation forgetful of its duty to the State and incapable of comprehending the metaphysical significance of the teaching of his predecessor Lao-tze, whom incidentally he is said, rightly or wrongly, to have held in contempt as a baffling dreamer. Making no claim to originality of thought, he was content to return to the traditional manner of life of the national ancestors, and from the accumulated wisdom of the past preserved in the ancient records, to give a new inspiration for right living in the present and the future. With theism as such he was not concerned, and while he urged conformity to the customary rites inasmuch as they gave stability to the moral life and established order, he deprecated speculation about gods and spirits. For Confucius the impersonal T'ien (Heaven) as a pantheistic cosmic principle rather than Shang-Ti (the Supreme Ruler) or Shen (spirits) was the basic conception in which natural phenomena and human destiny were grounded. 'He who offends against Heaven has none to whom he can pray', and as deity for him was essentially the unvarying moral order, it was an impersonal conception incapable of being influenced for good or ill by supplication or coercion. The course of events being fixed, it is useless to complain against Heaven, and the whole duty of man (i.e. *li*), according to Confucian ethics, is summed up in the word 'reciprocity'—'what

[1] *Tao-Te-Ching,* chap. VIII.
[2] J. Legge, *The Religions of China* (Lond., 1882), p. 90.

you do not want done to yourself, do not do to others'. This principle of reciprocal propriety is to be applied especially in the 'five relationships' of the family and the State (relations of ruler to subject, father and son, husband and wife, elder brother and younger, friend and friend). Thus, filial piety and fraternal love are the root of benevolence, which Confucius defined as love to all men.

His aim 'was not so much the renovation of the individual as the renovation of the State; his mind and object were ethico-political, his desire the renaissance of the golden age of antiquity through a return to the virtue of primitive times'.[1] But although in the Confucian system there is very little of a specifically religious nature, it arose in an age of great intellectual activity in China characterized by conflicting philosophies concerning the fundamental nature of the universe in relation to human conduct. The Chinese being practical rather than speculative, moralization made a more ready appeal than metaphysics, but, nevertheless, the dualistic interpretation of Heaven and Earth deeply laid in the ancient religion, raised the metaphysical problem of an ultimate principle.

In the beginning all things were thought to have emerged from the interaction of two 'breaths', or forces; one warm, bright, active and animate; the other dark, cold, still and inert, known respectively as *Yang* and *Yin*. Heaven (the sky) was equated with the dynamic male *Yang* principle, and the Earth with the static *Yin* female principle. By their union, as in other primitive cosmologies, the phenomena of nature arose, the fructifying processes operated, and the seasonal rotation pursued its course. To this dualism the five elements—metal, wood, water, fire and earth—were related. In the spring wood predominates; in summer, fire; in autumn, metal; and in winter, water. These five elements had their seat respectively in the four quarters of the compass, and were ruled by five dieties, the spirits of the seasons and the four quarters.[2] It was held that these rhythmic alternating pulsations constituted creative activity as a continuous emanation, the *Yang* dividing itself into an infinite number of *shên*, or souls, the association of the male generative principle with the sky passing into an immaterial concept and

[1] Soothill, *The Three Religions of China* (Lond., 1913), pp. 31 f.

[2] J. Legge, 'Yi-king' in *S.B.E.*, XVI, 1882. Walshe, *E.R.E.*, vol. IV, pp. 140 f. De Groot, *E.R.E.*, IV, pp. 12 f. Soothill, op. cit., pp. 146, 174. A. Forke, *World Conception of the Chinese*, p. 187.

thence to spirit. Similarly, the *Yin* as the equivalent of the earth (i.e. matter) and the female receptive part of the universe, became the *ch'i*, the corporeal 'vapour', or motive-power of the senses divisible into particles, which in the human organism was the life-breath, or body-soul. Both, it was thought, were needed to maintain the proper order (*Yi*), or primordial principle governing their interaction, and with the progress of philosophical speculation, the dualism was carried into the moral sphere—virtue being produced by *Yang*, and vice by *Yin*. Thus, *Yang* was the beneficent half of the universe, and *Yin* the less favourable, so that good proceeded from the *shên* and the evil from the *ch'i*.

The *Tao*, or the 'way', in which all things are made and in which they ought to live, according to this scheme, is the ultimate category, a right understanding of this divine order being essential for harmonious existence and right conduct. To set the human will in opposition to the Way of Heaven is to court disaster. Therefore, as Confucius recognized, correct behaviour (*Li*) based on this fundamental ethical principle (i.e. right behaviour towards the whole course of Nature and the life of society) is the first duty of man. *Tao*, in fact, depends on *Li*, for harmony is only possible when life is ordered in accordance with this principle. Thus, the Stoic dictum to 'live according to Nature', was of the essence of Chinese ethics.

The idea of *Li* goes back to the original immigrants who settled on the banks of the Wei River and the Huang-ho and called themselves the 'Black-haired People', but in conjunction with that of *ch'i*, eventually in Neo-Confucianism it was resolved into a pantheistic philosophy. The founder of the movement in the Sung dynasty was Chou Tun-i (1017–1073 A.D.), who posited an ultimate principle *T'ai chi* from which the *Yang* and *Yin* proceeded in their male and female attributes, and generated the five elements in the manner described. With the advent of man the five cardinal virtues were established, and the knowledge of good and evil made ethical righteousness possible by following the way of virtue. Chu Hsi (A.D. 1130–1200) transformed this monistic scheme into a dualism of the two interacting principles *li* and *ch'i*, affirming that 'the plenum of the universe is *ch'i* and the pilot of the universe is *li*'. Always acting in conjunction as an incorporeal, immanent intelligence (*li*) and a primal, corporeal, material entity (*ch'i*), both are eternal co-equal, and as correlative as form and matter in Western thought. But if the one cannot exist without the other, *li* has the logical priority and superiority as the ethical pilot, though it was within the 'plenum' *ch'i* that *Yang* and *Yin* were brought forth through the creative activity of *li,* identified with *T'ien*. Therefore, the ultimate reality was the undifferentiated dualism *li* and *ch'i* which held sway before the material universe of *Yang* and *Yin* came into being.

This cosmology is pantheistic rather than theistic, but it can hardly correctly be described as materialistic inasmuch as the 'pilot' guiding all things is an incorporeal, immanent intelligence, though it only functions in and through the corporeal 'plenum'. Dr Bruce, in fact, maintains that Chu Hsi really taught an ethical theism, the form in which his thought found expression being conditioned by his reaction against popular anthropomorphism and transcendentalism. He accepted the God of the classics, 'whether under the title of Empyrean, or Supreme Ruler, of Heaven or God, . . . as a personal and righteous Being ruling and judging in the affairs of men; and as identical with that Law which Chu Hsi regarded as the fundamental element in the universe'.[1] But actually he interpreted T'ien in the Classics sometimes as Chu' Tsai (Ruler or Governor) and sometimes as a principle,[2] and, as Maclagan says, while 'the identification of Heaven with "li" makes the universe more than merely material, it is not unfair to say that it makes God less than personal', and that 'this less theistic interpretation is borne out by the subsequent history of orthodox Confucianism'.[3]

The State religion, on the other hand, retained its essential features as a combination of Nature worship and ancestor worship centring in the person of the divine Emperor as the Son of Heaven and religious head of the nation. The local mandarins perpetuated the veneration of Confucius, while Taosim, though it never lost its mystical outlook, in practice, like Hinduism, rapidly degenerated into polytheism, demonology and alchemy. The contemplation of the *Tao* made no more appeal to the masses than the ethical cosmic Confusian philosophy, and in order to become a popular cultus it had to develop a mythology in which Lao-tze became a Buddha, the metaphysical principle was personified as T'ai-shi the 'Great

[1] *Chu Hsi and His Masters,* pp. 316, 294.
[2] Soothill, op. cit., p. 42.
[3] Maclagan, *Chinese Religious Ideas,* pp. 107, 111 f.

Original', and the 'Yellow Emperor' (Yu-huang-shang-ti) was 'the divine, exalted, Supreme Ruler'. In the official religion of China, in addition to the imperial ancestors, a hierarchy of spirits of the soil and the grain was incorporated in the worship of Heaven and Earth, but as this was essentially a royal ritual, the people resorted to local shrines where a mixture of Taoist and Buddhist rites were performed to secure longevity, immortality and fecundity, while in their homes they made offerings to the images of the gods which they set on the shelf with the tablets of the family ancestors.

SHINTO

In Japan Chinese and Indian influences began to modify the indigenous religion early in the Christian era when writing was first introduced from the mainland which brought with it Chinese literature and Confucian and Buddhist doctrines. Since the chief literary records were not given their present form until after this process of assimilation had begun, it is not easy to arrive at an accurate estimate of the original beliefs and customs of the island-culture, but critical investigation reveals a substratum of source material indicating the general characteristics of Shinto before it was overlaid by these later ideas. The term Shinto (*shên, tao*) is the Chinese rendering of the two ideograms, *Kami no Michi*, 'the Way of the Gods' (i.e. the cultus of the indigenous deities), and first appears in the *Nihongi*, or 'Chronicles of Japan', compiled from earlier documents in A.D. 720, in which the traditional history of the land is told from the Creation to A.D. 697, covering practically the same period as the *Kojiki*, or 'Chronicles of Ancient Events', the oldest extant Japanese historical record.[1] *Kami* is the designation of a conception of the sacred comparable to the Melanesian notion of *mana*, signifying at once the deities of Heaven and Earth, the spirits of the shrines, peculiar objects (mountains and other physical features, animals and plants), and, in fact, any person or thing possessing mysterious qualities and attributes, including thunder, dragons, and echoes.[2]

[1] The *Kojiki* was completed in three volumes in A.D. 712. Probably these compilations were put together in literary form between 645 and 701 A.D., and edited in their present form early in the eighth century. The third treatise is the *Kujiki*, or 'Chronicle of Old Events', about A.D. 620, supplementing the *Nihongi*.

[2] *Motoori Norinaga, Zenshiu* (Tokyo, 1901), vol. I, pp. 150 ff. Satow, *Trans. Asiatic Society of Japan*, vol. III, pp. 42 ff.

From the oldest mythology it is clear that Shinto was a polytheistic system, the divine *kami* being potentially personal, with
spiritual emanations (*mitama*) residing in objects associated with the
shrines. According to the official estimate in A.D. 901, the pantheon
numbered no less than 3,132 deities ranging from such august
beings as *Amaterasu-Omikami* ('Heaven-shining-great-august-
Kami'), the Sun-goddess, from whom the imperial line is descended,
to divine animals, trees and plants, and household and phallic gods.
The Mikado was *akitsu-kami* ('manifest or incarnate *kami*'),
though in the *Kojiki* and *Nihongi* it was the solar ancestry that was
stressed rather than the essential deity of the emperor, as in the
later *Yengishiki* ('Institutes of the Period of Yengi', 901–23 A.D.).

The divine kingship, in fact, was the Japanese counterpart of the
Confucian theory of the State as a heavenly sanction, but whereas
in China the inviolability of the throne was dependent on the virtue
of its occupant, in Japan it rested solely on his solar descent, as in
Ancient Egypt, irrespective of ethical considerations.[1] It is this
belief that constitutes the fundamental conception of the modern
national faith, and supports the conviction that Japan ranks above
all other countries as a natural consequence of the position and
lineage of the Mikado.[2] 'The lofty self-denying enthusiastic senti-
ment of the Japanese people towards their August Ruler' arises out
of the belief that he is directly descended from *Amaterasu-Omikami*,
who instituted the State by divine decree, just as she produced the
land and gave it superiority over all other countries.[3]

Shinto cosmology, however, is of the crudest character imagin-
able, taking its rise in a very primitive nature mythology. Three
gods are said to have emerged spontaneously from primeval chaos,
Ame-no-minaka-nushi-no-kami ('The divine Lord of the very centre
of Heaven'), *Taka-mimu-subi-no-kami* ('High August Producer')
and *Kami-mimu-subi-no-kami* ('Divine August Producer'). These
were followed by a series of similar pairs till at the seventh generation, *Izana-gi* ('Male who invites') and *Izana-mi* ('Female who
invites') arose, who brought forth the islands by means of a phallus,
and then, after several futile attempts, produced the deities. In due
course the progenitor of the dynasty appeared in the person of

[1] M. Anesaki, *History of Japanese Religion* (Lond., 1930), p. 87.

[2] Satow, *Transactions of the Asiatic Society of Japan*, II, Dec. 1927, p. 197.

[3] Kato, *A Study of Shinto* (Tokyo, 1895), p. 206.

Ninigi, the grandson of *Amaterasu*, who descended to the earth with his commission from the Sun-goddess. Then follow unedifying episodes in which the storm-god, *Susa-no-wo*, behaves in a highly unseemly manner when visiting his sister, the Sun-goddess. In fact, the heavenly *Kami* are thoroughly Olympian in their conduct, fighting, quarrelling, thwarting one another, consummating marriage (or failing to be able to do so), jesting and making indecent gestures, gambling over brides, and engaging in cunning exploits. In short, they were essentially degenerate mortals surpassing man only in their possession of superior magical power, with all the desires and passions, weaknesses and limitations of the dwellers upon earth. It is therefore hardly surprising that the service of the gods was restricted to a ritual cultus devoid of any ethical significance.

With the rise of Japanese Buddhism in the sixth century (*c.* 552 A.D.) this primitive indigenous polytheism underwent considerable modification, just as the advent of Confucianism about 150 years later moulded political life and ethics by introducing a new conception of loyalty to the throne, filial piety, benevolence and justice, together with ancestor worship. Thus, Buddhism was the chief intellectual and spiritual force in the promotion of literature, art, education, philosophy, the care of the sick and a more enlightened religious outlook. As early as A.D. 625 the Buddhist school known as Sanron was established, teaching a system of transcendental idealism which denied the reality of the phenomenal world and held that the noumenal can only be defined in negative terms, as had been set forth in India by Nagarjuna, a Hindu sage of the second century A.D. Other sects followed in rapid succession, Jo-Jitsu and Hosso in 654, Kusha in 658, and in 736 the Great Vehicle or Mahayana Buddhism,[1] which was destined to capture Japan, made its first appearance with the arrival of the Kegon sect. While all these philosophical speculations were foreign to the native mind, they awakened a realization of the naïve realism of Shinto, and gradually a doctrinal assimilation of the two faiths was accomplished which in the ninth century began to produce a new type of pantheism.

The first attempt in the direction of syncretism was made by the Tendai priests who in 805 brought over from China an idealist

[1] cf. chap. VII, pp. 182 ff.

eclectic system based on the teaching of the *Saddharma Pundari-kasutra* (Japanese: *Hokkekyo*), the *Lotus of the True Law*.[1] All the Buddhas were alleged to be ultimately one absolute Reality (*ichi jitsu*) manifested in the multiform phenomena of the universe, so that all events, things and divine beings are comprehended in the ultimate unity. In this way the indigenous *kami* were given a place in *ichi jitsu* as manifest Buddhas, and Shinto polytheism became virtually a metaphysical pantheism. This process of fusion was consolidated by the pantheistic mysticism of the Shingon school, traditionally assigned to Kukai (Kobo-Daishi) in 806, which by a combination of materialism and idealism made the universe the externalized body of *Maha-Vair-ocana* (Buddha, 'Great Illuminator'). It was this dualistic system of mind and matter (*ryobu*), finding expression in a dynamic cosmic existence and ideal world of permanence, which established the syncretistic movement henceforth known as Ryobu-Shinto.[2] From the twelfth century onwards it became the dominant religion, and despite the opposition of the Pure Shinto school and the enforced separation of Buddhism and Shinto between 1868 and 1912, when the national faith was revived in its pre-Buddhist form, traces of the earlier adjustment survive even to this day, while two-thirds of the population still adhere to one of the fifty-six sects into which Buddhism is now divided in Japan.

The Confucian influence has been less strongly felt, but, nevertheless, the dualism of the Ryobu school had points of contact with the doctrine of the *Yin* and the *Yang* which had penetrated the country with other elements of Chinese thought and practice in the formative period from the fifth to the eighth centuries. Thus, the later Shintoists of the *Yui-itsu* school, who attempted to establish a philosophical approach to the original notion of *kami*, tended to postulate two cosmic principles such as the *In* and the *Yo*, 'changeless, eternal, existing from the beginning of Heaven and Earth, with neither beginning nor end'.[3] *Kami* was the original transcendent, unknowable, monistic source of the universe immanent in creation as *kokoro* (soul), and responsible for all objects, events and cosmic activity in its positive and negative aspects. From this school

---

[1] cf. Steinilber-Oberlin, *The Buddhist Sects of Japan* (Lond., 1938), pp. 74 ff.

[2] Anesaki, op. cit., pp. 125 ff.

[3] cf. Kato, *Transactions of the Japan Society of London*, XXXVIII, p. 144.

Suiga Shinto took its rise in 1618 under Confucian influence, and made Izanagi and Izanami the source of the two inseparable inter-acting forces, *suchi*, centripetal, and *kane*, centrifugal, which sustain the universe, and from which all things take their origin. The breach between Buddhism and the ruling class in the seventeenth century caused Neo-Confucianism to be widely adopted and two sects arose in opposition to the dualism of Chu-Hsi which had penetrated Japan through the Zen Buddhists in the fourteenth century. The one founded by Nakaya Toju (1608–78), called Yomei, taught that conscience (*ryochi*) is an ultimate reality em-bedded in man's original nature, while the other—*Kogakuha* ('Ancient Learning') 1622–85—maintained a monistic self-realiza-tion of the universal life in the individual manifest in benevolence and justice as the law of ultimate being.[1]

Speculations of this nature, however, were as foreign to Shinto as was Buddhism, and in the eighteenth century the time was ripe for a revival of the ancient national faith. For this renaissance the work of several scholars prepared the way. First came Keichu (1604–1701), and Kamo-no-Mabuchi (1677–1769) who concen-trated upon the ancient and neglected literature in the belief that the subsequent teaching of metaphysics and ethics was a sign of degeneracy. Nevertheless, Mabuchi was himself influenced by Lao-tze and the Taoist attitude to the natural order, a view re-pudiated by his successor Motoori Norinaga (1730–1801), who maintained the Way of the Gods as true Shinto, demanding explicit obedience to divine teaching. Finally came Hirata Atsutane (1776–1843), who threw the whole weight of his learning and zeal into the nationalistic movement in the conviction that Japan was begot-ten of Izanagi and Izanami, was the birthplace of *Amaterasu-Omikami,* and is ruled by her august descendants for ever, according to the teaching that has come down unaltered from the age of the gods.[2]

[1] Anesaki, op. cit., p. 279.
[2] cf. G. W. Knox, *The Development of Religion in Japan* (New York, 1907), p. 72.

CHAPTER VII

The Way of Salvation

THE WAY OF KNOWLEDGE

As the Confucian and Shinto emphasis on an innate goodness in man represents a definite departure from the quietism of Taoism, so in India deliverance from the misery of empirical existence was not consistently taught even in the Upanishads where, as we have seen, the doctrine of salvation by works (*karma-marga*) was taken over from the *Vedas* and the *Brahmanas*. Thus, by right actions the searcher after unqualified unity with Brahman might fit himself to proceed to the saving knowledge veiled by ignorance (*avidya*), for while emancipation was attained rather than acquired, a discipline of moral purification was an essential requirement. In this process four stages or *asramas* ('Hermitages') were defined: (1) that of the Brahman-student (*brahmachāriya*) when the *Vedas* were to be studied under the guidance of a teacher; (2) that of the householder (*grihastha*) during which a normal domestic life was lived and the sacrifices offered; (3) that of the ascetic period in the forest when the devoted lived as an anchorite (*vana-prastha*); and finally a fourth degree was added—that of *sannyāsin*, or union of equation. Hence, saving knowledge came to be attained by what is equivalent to a system of 'works', e.g. abstinence, self-control and the technique of meditation (*yoga*).[1]

A more elaborate method of the soul's ascent occurs in the doctrine of the 'five sheaths' (*kosa*)—the sheath of food, the sheath of breath, the sheath of the mind, where the individual is dependent upon instruction from a teacher, and the sheath of understanding. When these four sheaths have been stripped away the fifth and last stage is reached, the *anandamaya kosa,* in which the duality of subject and object is destroyed and complete unity is secured. 'That thou

---

[1] *Yoga* is a method of intense concentration of mind and body by the assumption of certain postures and the use of breathing exercises calculated to produce a state of mystical contemplation.

art.'[1] So long as earthly desires remain the self is bound to earth. Therefore, the seeker after salvation along the mystic paths was compelled eventually to leave home for the solitude of the forest, where as hermit he might learn the secrets of the higher life untrammelled by all fleshly desires till at length the emancipated soul could cry in triumph, 'I am Brahman'.

The essential doctrines of the Upanishads were concentrated in the Vedanta Sutras, but their brevity necessitated commentators to expound them. Of these Sankara and Ramanuja are the most prominent. Sankara (eighth century A.D.), in fact, is the greatest of the Indian scholastics, who sought to eliminate what he regarded as 'that wrong notion which is the cause of all evil and attaining thereby the knowledge of the absolute unity of the Self'.[2] Postulating a higher and a lower knowledge, he equated the former, *para vidya*, with the monism of the Upanishads, and the latter, *apara vidya*, with empirical understanding, taking his stand on the central Upanishadic Brahman-Atman equation. The universe is Brahman entire and indivisible—'there is one only without a second' (*Advaita*)—and it is only the lower knowledge that has endowed Brahman with personality (*saguna*). It is this ignorance that prevents men rising to the height of the metaphysical monistic concept.[3] The illusory self regards itself as an agent and thereby becomes subject to *samsara*. 'As long as nescience has not been abolished, the individuality of the self is not abolished, and the individual soul continues to be the sphere of good and evil.'[4] By intuitive knowledge of Brahman it can escape from *karma* and the misery of existence, attaining 'mukti', or emancipation by way of *para vidya* (higher knowledge). To this end works are of no avail, because they produce *karma* and therefore transmigration. Salvation is the result of the realization that everything except the Atman is illusion, and that this inner self is nothing less than unconditioned Reality (Brahman), 'That thou art'.

Unlike this idealistic monism, called advaitism, a dualistic solution of the problem of the universe and man was propounded by Indian thinkers and systematized by Kapila in the Sankhya philosophy, which according to native tradition goes back to the fifth

[1] *Taitt. Up.*, 2–9.   [2] *S.B.E.,* vol. XXXIV, p. 9.
[3] op. cit., pp. 23, 40, 137, 349.
[4] *S.B.E.,* vol. XXXVIII, p. 174; XXXV, p. 14.

century B.C. Though the oldest surviving treatise of this system
belongs to the fifth century A.D., there is good reason to believe
that Sankhya arose prior to the Buddhist movement, and was not
without its influence on it. It is true, however, that it flourished
chiefly in the opening centuries of our era, contemporary with
Neo-Platonism and Gnosticism in the West, which shared many of
its tenets. The metaphysical dualism consisted of two ultimate
realities, individual souls (*purushas*) and a primordial matrix
(*prakriti*), out of which existence, activity, and the material body
developed. The soul was regarded as the passive spectator of the
misery of conscious existence unaware of its spiritual character so
long as it was in bondage in a physical integument and imagined
itself to be affected by these changes in *prakriti*, till it became aware
of its true nature. The fundamental error, therefore, was this lack
of discrimination and salvation consisted not in the identity of the
Atman and Brahman, but in a knowledge of the diversity of
purusha and *prakriti*. Once the soul realized that it was merely an
onlooker and not an actor in the tragedy of existence, release of the
true self from the empirical self and its entanglements (*prakriti*)
became possible. When this was accomplished suffering was
brought to an end, rebirth ceased and the body was dissolved together with the subtle ethereal psychical mechanism and individu-
ating principle manifested in self-consciousness. The emancipated
soul continued to exist in a state of final separation from matter and
abode in eternal unconsciousness and passivity. Having freed itself
from the material basis of knowledge (*prakriti*), it returned to the
'unevolved state' out of which it emerged in the beginning, and as
an absolute monad it remained for ever pure, spiritual intelligence
without consciousness, subject without object, like a mirror in
which no image is reflected.

Since the goal of this highly complex atheistic[1] system could
only be revealed by way of the Sankhya pluralistic philosophy, it
was too intellectualistic and abstruse to make any appeal to the
popular mind in search of salvation. Nevertheless, it had a very
considerable influence on succeeding thought both within and
outside India, and it was in a Sankhya atmosphere that the two great

[1] There was no room for the idea of Brahman in this system as *purusha* occupied
the position of a pantheistic principle, while its isolation from *prakriti* rendered it
dualistic.

reformers of Hinduism were born, Vardhamana Mahavira, the founder of the Jain movement, and Guatama (Pali, Gotama), the Buddha. Setting out with a common aim, namely to break the power of *karma*, these two members of the Kshatriya, or warrior caste, differed in that the latter endeavoured to achieve the end by the entire suppression of desire, while the former found a solution of the problem in a system of abstinences. For Gautama it was existence that was evil; for Mahavira the fundamental ill was the association of the soul with a body.

THE WAY OF ASCETICISM

In enunciating the five great vows (*vrata*) and the six classes of lives, Vardhamana, who was born about 540 B.C., claimed in his first sermon to be following with perfect knowledge eternal truths revealed again and again in every one of the succeeding ages of the world. His call to the ascetic life met with a ready response, and those who adopted this path to emancipation, which was open to men and women irrespective of caste, were known as 'Jina', 'the victorious',[1] because they were thereby enabled to subdue their passions and obtain mastery over themselves. By austerities and rigid dicipline it was possible to annihilate karmic matter, and to prevent further accumulations, though logically the methods adopted involved action which of necessity produced *karma*. But 'when a man is free from passions and acts in accordance with the rules of right conduct' by 'renouncing activity he obtains inactivity, by ceasing to act he acquires no new *karma* and destroys the *karma* he had acquired before'.[2]

To attain complete inactivity and indifference the aspirants lived together in loosely organized religious orders which became divided into two rival sections of 'white robes' (*Svetambaras*) and 'sky-clad' (*Digambaras*), a name derived from the custom on the part of the latter ascetics of going about stark naked until the practice was prohibited under Moslem rule. Vardhamana was himself a monk who twelve years after his profession, at the age of forty-two, attained omniscience (*kevala*) as a result of renouncing the world, though,

[1] The word 'Jina', whence 'Jainism', is derived from the Sanskrit root *ji* 'to conquer'.

[2] *S.B.E.*, XLV, p. 167.

unlike Gautama, he is not said to have reached the goal by the discovery of a new method of salvation. Having become Mahavira he proclaimed the truths which the Jina before him had taught, and gave a fresh impetus to the older teaching by reforming it. His followers in part became members of a mendicant order, in part continued to live in the world under a rule adapted to their circumstances. The sect still survives in India as 'a theological mean between Brahmanism and Buddhism'[1] with a million and a half adherents (mainly merchants and bankers), but its influence has been confined to the land of its birth.

In opposition to the Upanishadic doctrine of the permanence of Being, the Jains maintain that only the substance of material things continues, their accidents or qualities (form) being as unstable as the shape and colour of a vessel. As the clay remains independent of the form it assumes, so matter (*pudgala*), and the atoms composing it, are eternal and subject to change and development. Distinct from material entities are *jiva*, or souls ('what lives or is animate')—the Jainist counterpart of the Atman or Purusha—which are also eternal substances infinite in number, and incapable of destruction. Their intrinsic nature is one of perfection characterized by infinite intelligence, infinite peace, infinite faith, infinite power. But while embodied in a body in the mundane state (*samsara*) these features are obscured, and they become subject to the process of reincarnation till they are finally liberated (*mukti*) from the subtle matter which is transformed into *karma*. As it is this *karma* which prevents the soul realizing its true nature, it has to be removed by the control of the senses and self-mortification. The culmination of perfect knowledge (*kevala-jnana*) is reached when all the obstacles are overcome, and the *jiva* attains omniscience and absolute apprehension without doubt or any further external aid. It is this complete dissociation from *karma* that constitutes *Nirvana* or *moksa*, in Jainism; a condition of inactivity and everlasting peace.

To reach this consummation of bliss it is necessary to be in possession of the 'Three Jewels' (right faith, right knowledge, right action). The first step towards salvation is taken when the disciple makes an act of explicit faith in the Jaina scriptures and their teaching since this opens the way to right knowledge of the meta-

[1] Hopkins, *Religions of India* (Lond., 1898), p. 283.

physics taught by Mahavira concerning the victorious struggle of the soul with *karma*. Having arrived at this stage of enlightenment, it only remains to put into practice what has been learnt and believed. This is the all-important element in the discipline, for it is by the observance of the prescribed rules of conduct that the goal is reached. The five vows consist in not injuring any living being, not uttering a lie, not stealing, abstaining from sexual intercourse and renouncing all interest in worldly affairs.

In the case of laymen they are modified as circumstances require, but more rigorous observance of the rule is encouraged periodically by the adoption of special vows, preparatory in many cases to the person becoming a monk. For the fully professed more drastic discipline is required in order that *karma* may be annihilated and every channel closed by which it might enter the soul. Having attained omniscience and escaped death the *jiva* rises until it reaches the top of the universe (*lokakasa*), and there it rests in perfect peace for ever. During the interval between enlightenment and actual liberation, known as *arahanship*, an active life may be lived without contracting *karma* because the passions have been completely neutralized and rendered inoperative. At this stage it is only a matter of awaiting the final dissolution, a process that may be hastened by self-training.

THE MIDDLE WAY

It was this method of securing the perfection and release of the soul by a rigorous asceticism which in the first instance was adopted by Gautama after he made his Great Renunciation when he was twenty-nine years of age. The early life of the founder of Buddhism is surrounded with a legendary halo, but it would seem that he was born at Kapilavastu on the Nepalese border, a hundred miles north of Benares, about 560 B.C.; though some place the date forty years later. His father probably was a landed proprietor of the kshatriya caste named Suddhodana. Exactly what led Gautama to abandon his wife and child and go forth in search of salvation it is impossible to say, but tradition ascribes it to the chance sight of a decrepit old man, a diseased person, a corpse, and a monk. But whatever may have been the cause, he renounced the world and took up his abode in the forest where, after a futile attempt to attain the goal by occult practices, he engaged in austerities and penances according to the Jain method of self-discipline till he reached the point of collapse.

As these asceticisms were of no more avail than his former cataleptic exercises, he resolved to adopt a 'middle way', or via media, after seven years of struggle. Having found that the road to Enlightenment and Emancipation lay in a different direction from that he had pursued, the supreme moment of his life came in his thirty-fifth year while seated cross-legged in the mystic posture (*padmasana*) with his face towards the east, at the foot of a *pipal* or bo-tree at Buddh Gaya, where the Mahabodhi temple now stands. Assailed by Mara and his hosts, the Lord of Death and Prince of Darkness, he overcame all the allurements and distractions of his ghostly enemies, and with one mighty resolve determined never to move from his seat till he had attained the supreme and absolute wisdom; the long-desired knowledge (*Bodhi*) came on the seventh day. In a flash the seeker of illumination (*Bodhisatta*) perceived the complete chain of causation and the method of bringing about the cessation of desire. Thus, Gautama, 'the seer', became the Buddha, 'the enlightened one' to whom the plenitude of truth had been revealed.

After enjoying the bliss of deliverance for a period, for the sake of suffering humanity he refrained from entering *Nirvana*, and returned to Benares to 'set the wheel of the Law rolling'. In the Deer Park at Isipatana he sought out the five ascetics with whom he had lived in the forests of Uruvela when he was practising his austerities, and made known to them 'the middle way'. The 'Four Noble Truths' he had discovered leading eventually 'to peace, to insight, to Higher Wisdom, to *Nibbana*'[1] consisted in (1) the universality of suffering (*Dukkha*), manifest in birth, old age, illness and death, and all the desires and cravings of physical life; (2) the cause of suffering (viz., the thirst for individual existence leading to continuous rebirth); (3) the removal of suffering and (4) the Eightfold Path leading to the removal of suffering through Right Understanding, Right Conduct, Right Resolution, Right Speech, Right Occupation, Right Effort, Right Meditation and Right Concentration.

The problem propounded in this famous discourse was the question of questions which every Indian seer sought to solve, and

---

[1] The Pali form of the Sanskrit *Nirvana*.

the solution offered really was not new. It was generally recognized that to escape the sorrowful round of ever-recurring reincarnation freedom from desire must be secured, and some way of escape found from the law of *Karma* and the illusion of empirical reality (*maya*). But although his knowledge of the ultimate problems of existence was limited and in consequence he deplored all meta-physical speculation, Gautama saw more clearly than his prede-cessors exactly where the root of the trouble lay, and in devising the Eightfold Path he opened a new way of deliverance. With Mahavira he agreed that something more than abstract 'right knowledge' was required to stop the wheel of continuous life, but for him it was *karma* and not the soul as an ego that survived death. To bring to an end the accumulation of phenomena which col-lectively makes up individual existence, belief must be given up in a real, permanent, self-contained soul. 'Without renouncing the conception of selfhood (*atmanam*), we cannot overcome sorrow and suffering.' Human personality, according to the Buddha, con-sists of five casually-conditioned elements (*skandhas*) of the life-impulse comprising the sensations and ideas pertaining to the body, the feelings of the emotional state, perception, volitions and mental faculties, and cognition. These are ever changing and capable of being dissolved at any moment in a process of 'becoming'. Thus, the ego is an organic aggregate constantly in a state of flux, never continuing in one stay, devoid of permanence or eternal reality.

On this hypothesis there is no room for an individual entity capable of realizing its identity with Brahman, for both God and the human soul, Absolute and Atman, are rigidly excluded. The elements of the self are the self, just as the parts of a chariot are the chariot. The self, in fact, is only a mere name, and the belief 'I am' is a delusion which must be laid aside since it is as transitory as the flow of water in a river, or the flame of a lamp. The recurrence of sensations and ideas gives the appearance of sameness, but actually it is only the continuity of a series of temporarily consolidated *skandhas*, or attachment groups masquerading as an 'ego'. There-fore, what transmigrates is individual *karma*, 'a stream of energy clothing itself in body after body',[1] and giving life as a resultant effect of the actions performed in a former state or states of existence. It is consequently a creative dynamic from the operations of

---

[1] K. J. Saunders, *The Heart of Buddhism*, p. 15.

which it is impossible to escape so long as the wheel of life continues to revolve. As this is set in motion by will, desire and intention, the only way to put an end to the ceaseless rotation is to break the chain of causation. Once the craving for existence (*tanha*) is overcome freedom is secured, and *karma* automatically is annihilated.

This doctrine of *anatta* (non-egoism) occupies a fundamental position in the Canon of the Pali scriptures which arose in the first century B.C. in Ceylon as a product of the oral tradition preserved by the monastic Orders. The 'Three Baskets of Tradition', or *Tripitaka*, were put into writing about 80 B.C. in the literary language known as Pali, derived probably from an original in the Magadhi dialect, some four hundred years after the death of Gautama. Of these three 'receptacles' in which the tradition is said to have been handed down, the *Sutta pitaka*, or 'Discourse Basket', is alleged to contain the utterances of the Buddha himself; the *Vinaya pitaka*, or 'Discipline Basket', the rules governing the Order of mendicant recluses; and the *Abhidhamma*, or philosophical discussions of the teaching (*dharma*).

While it is not improbable that authentic sayings and stories have been preserved in the Suttas, the critical study of this monastic literature is at present in its infancy, and until the investigation has been carried very much further it is impossible to separate the various stages in the development of thought and practice. Mrs. Rhys Davids maintains that when the monastic speculations and editorial additions are eliminated an original Sakyan period linked with the Upanishadic philosophy can be distinguished from the later accretions, commonly known as *Hinayana*, or the 'Little Vehicle'.[1] On this hypothesis it is suggested that the Buddha substituted for the notion of the empirical self as non-agent that of the man choosing by the exercise of will because 'he is man-in-becoming, not just man-in-being'.[2] He is never the same for two consecutive minutes, and there is in him no abiding principle whatever. The result of what he is or does is held 'not to be dissipated into many streams, but concentrated together in the formation of one new sentient being'.

Now granting that Gautama placed the emphasis on becoming

[1] *Hinayana* was a term of abuse employed by some of the later writers to describe what they regarded as a lower inadequate method of attaining *nirvana*.

[2] *Manual of Buddhism* (Lond., 1932), p. 139.

and only rejected the Brahmanic theory of a static divine self, it was certainly not long before Buddhism in practice became a pessimistic system of mental abstractions in which the ego was lost in a negative process of reincarnation and transformation. As the doctrine is set forth in the actual documents (and these are the only available source of information) it is difficult to discover any real continuity between 'one new sentient being' and the aggregate that preceded it. As Dahike says,

> it is no persisting something in itself that passes over; it is the individual tendency, the predispositions, the character, the consciousness, or whatever else one has a mind to call the value in potential energy represented by the I-process at its disintegration, that passes over, by immediately taking effect, striking in, imparting the new impulse to the material to which it is *uniquely attuned*—the material that appeals to it alone of all that is present, and to which it alone of all that is present answers.[1]

But if personality is eliminated in these terms, there is no very obvious connexion between one birth and the next, or any adequate reason for the transference of the *karma* of one organism to another. Conduct unquestionably determines character to a very considerable extent, and granting reincarnation the transmigration of character is a logical conclusion, but only on the assumption of an individualized identity of ego, or soul. 'The transmission of character, of personality with a person',[2] cannot be reconciled with either common sense or ethics.

The monks sought release from rebirth as the only means of escape from individual existence which is inevitably a life of suffering. In a universe where everything including the self is in a state of flux, the attainment of *Nirvana* alone could afford peace and rest. Whether or not the goal of Gautama was absolute non-existence, he counselled his followers to throw off the non-ego (i.e. the five *skandhas*) in order that the 'truth-finder' might pass in the void as a flame returns to the invisible state of fire in which it existed prior to its manifestation in the form of visible fire.[3] True, as Dr Keith points out, the Indian idea of fire is not utter annihilation,[4] but, nevertheless, the allaying of the craving for individuality is

---

[1] Dahike, *Buddhism and Science*, p. 69.

[2] Ananda Coomaraswamy, *Buddha and the Gospel of Buddhism*, p. 107.

[3] *Majjhima-Nikaya*, 1–487/8.

[4] *Philosophy of Buddhism*, p. 66.

fundamental in Buddhism, alike in the monastic Hinayana, and the more positive outlook of the 'Great Vehicle', or Mahayana. Both aim at rooting out all egoism, belief in existence and envelopment of consciousness.

To this end a system was devised to enable the *bhikkhu* (monk) to work out his own salvation as a perfected saint, or *arahan* (Sanskrit *arhat*), in this life, after a long and rigorous training through a series of rebirths till a static condition was achieved in which further progress is impossible. First, by the destruction of the delusion of self, doubt and trust in mere morality and ritual holiness, the potential *arahan* becomes a 'stream-winner', and escapes further rebirth in a state of woe. Next, by reducing to a minimum passion, hatred, ill-will and delusion he is advanced to the state of a 'once-returner', so that after returning once to this world he enters 'the Pure Abode', there to wane utterly and never to return. By the destruction of all sensual desire for existence (*asavas*) the roots of *karma* are removed and the emancipation of heart and mind which constitutes *arahanship* is realized preparatory to the trans-cendental peace of *Nirvana*.[1]

> Ah, happy saints, the Arahants! in them no craving's seen.
> The 'I' conceit is rooted up: delusions' net is burst.
> Lust-free they have attained; translucent is the heart of them.
> These god-like beings, drug-immune,[2] unspotted in the world,
> Knowing the fivefold mass, they roam the seven domains of good.
> Worthy of praise and worthy they—sons of the Wake true-born,
> The wearers of the sevenfold gem[3] in the threefold training trained.
> These mighty heroes follow on, exempt from fear and dread:
> Lords of the tenfold potency, great sages tranquillized:
> Best beings they in all the world; in them no craving's seen.
> They've won the knowledge of adepts. This compound is their last,
> That essence of the holy life that they have made their own.
> unshaken by the triple modes, set free from birth to come,
> The plane of self-control they've won, victorious in the world.
> Upwards or crossways or below—no lure is found in them.
> They sound aloud their lion's roar, 'Supreme are they that wake'.[4]

With the waning of the physical stuff of existence comes a way of escape from the limitations of personality and the change and

---

[1] *Digha Nikaya*, I, 156; III, 107, 132.　　[2] *Anasava*.

[3] i.e. the seven ways to enlightenment.　　[4] *Sanyutta*, III, 83 f.

suffering consequent upon becoming. The cessation of pain and sorrow follows naturally from the destruction of desires, and in this condition, be it that of *Arahanship* or of pari-*Nirvana*, something more than annihilation and nullity are implied to the Indian mind, as we have seen. As the earlier pantheistic system Brahman is at once the reservoir of all things and the ultimate zero (*Sunya*) regarded as the 'no-thing', the Indefinite, the 'dissolved', implying that at the source and consummation there is no continuous change through growth and decay, so in Buddhism 'no becoming' constitutes static Being as the transcendent reality of 'change no longer' beyond all empirical experience.

That the final emancipation is not annihilation is affirmed in the *Sutta of the Simile of the Snake*.

> Some ascetics and brahmins accuse me wrongly, baselessly, falsely, and groundlessly, saying that the ascetic Gotama is a nihilist, and preaches the annihilation, destruction and non-existence of an existent being. That is what I am not and do not affirm. Both previously and now I preach pain and the cessation of pain.[1]

But questioned further the Buddha is represented as refusing to commit himself lest he be compelled to deny the eternal existence of the Atman (i.e. annihilation).

> The body (with feeling, perception, aggregates, and consciousness) by which one might define a Tathagata (truth-finder) is passed away, cut off at the root, uprooted like a palm-tree, made non-existent, not liable to arise again in the future. A Tathagata released from what is called body, &c., is profound, immeasurable, hard to fathom, like the great ocean. It does not fit the case to say that he is reborn or not reborn, or not reborn and reborn or neither reborn nor not reborn.[2]

Nevertheless, if *Nirvana* is not nullity it is a negative goal, since 'becoming cool' virtually ends in 'blowing out' when temporal and spatial conditions cease for the individual. Whatever the ideal of human perfection may have meant for Guatama and his earliest followers, the impermanence of existence is fundamental in the system. The only reality is becoming, and in the absence of any abiding external transcendental reference, peace is only to be attained through the extirpation of the restless striving that constitutes the conscious life and the inevitable weary round of birth

[1] *Majjhima*, I, 139.   [2] *ibid.*, I, 489.

and death. The quest of perfection (*Arahanship*) inspires ennobling
qualities of self-discipline and almost superhuman effort, but nevertheless the conception of existence involved throughout is as
negative and pessimistic as the resultant state when the cessation or
desire has been achieved. Such a philosophy, though a recurrent
phenomenon in ages of world-weariness, can never represent the
final verdict even in the peculiar circumstances of Indian thought
and its indifference to the oncoming and receding waves of events.
Life may be a passing series of 'becomings' and 'vanishings', ever
conditioned by the empirical law of continuous change, and the
world seem as worthless as it is illusory, but after the downfall of
the Maurya dynasty (*c.* 185 B.C.) in answer to the negations of
Jainism and Buddhism, the Brahmans began to evolve a practical
way of life based on the earlier theism.

THE WAY OF DEVOTION

All theistic and devotional movements tend to be optimistic, and
the revival of the doctrine of *Bhakti*, or union between the gods and
man, introduced a new ideal of salvation which found expression
in a positive and trustful devotion towards a personal deity, and
the reality of the human soul capable of redemption by divine
grace. Out of the Vedic pantheon the Hindu Trimurti or Triad—
Brahma, Vishnu and Shiva—emerged as the threefold aspect of
deity, creative, sustaining and destructive. Brahma, like many
another All-Father, fell into the background as the Supreme Being
without a cultus so that only one temple, that in Puskara, is now
sacred to him. Always it is the more intimate saviour-god and bestower of grace who tends to overshadow the more remote Creator
unless he is brought into direct relations with mankind. Brahma was
never extricated from his earlier Upanishadic abstraction as the
metaphysical pantheistic principle. So to this day orthodox Hindus
are devotees either of Vishnu or Shiva, the heroes of the two great
Indian epics, the *Mahābhārata* and the *Rāmāyana*, and of the *Puranas*,
or legendary accounts of the creation and destruction of the world
and of the gods, together with the lore of the *Bhakti* tradition.

In this literature the doctrine of *avatars*, or incarnations of the
gods, is a prominent feature, especially in connexion with Vishnu
who is said to have come to earth in ten forms to save the world.

As the fish he saved Manu, the father of the human race, from the cosmic flood; as the tortoise he enabled the gods to rescue the fourteen precious objects for the benefit of mankind; as the boar, the man-lion and the dwarf he destroyed demons who had designs on the world, while as Parasu-Rama, the champion of Brahmanism, he exterminated the Kshatriyas. The remaining four incarnations are Rama, Krishna, Buddha and Kali, of whom Rama and Krishna, the avatars *par excellence* of modern Hindusim, are the heroes of the *Māhabhārata* and *Rāmāyana*.

The *Mahābhārata*, or 'Wars of the Great Barata Family', is a composite work dating from about the fifth century B.C. in its earliest pre-Brahmanical and pre-Buddhist sections, though it was not until some centuries later that it attained its aggregate bulk of a hundred thousand couplets. In its present recension this vast poem, which incidentally is the longest epic in the world, is double the length of the *Odyssey* and the *Iliad* combined, though the original story is only about a fifth of the whole. This has undergone considerable revision at the hands of the Brahmans for their own particular sectarian purposes. No attempt has been made to subject the compilation to critical analysis, and there is considerable difference of opinion concerning the suggested dating of its component parts.

At the time of its composition the Aryan-speaking peoples were settled in the Kurukshetra on the banks of the Ganges where in the capital, Hastināpura, the old blind King Dhritarashtra lived with his hundred sons the Kauravas, and his five nephews, the Pāndavas, who were eventually banished, through the jealousy of Duryodāna, the eldest of the Kauravas, and his cousins. They made their way to the court of the king of the Panchālas, whose daughter Draupadi became the polyandrous wife of the five brothers. Their cousin, Yadava, Prince Krishna, the 'Blessed One', became their adviser, and a period of great prosperity ensued till Yudhishthira lost everything to the wicked Duryodāna at a game of dice. For twelve years the Pāndavas were forced to live in the forest. A civil war broke out between the cousins in which tribes from distant parts of India (e.g. Bengal and the Punjab) took a share. For eighteen days the battle raged and at the end only the Pāndavas, Arjuna and his charioteer, Krishna, survived. Yudhishthira was installed as king of Hastināpura, but the five brothers gave up their royal state, and retired to the forest where two years later they immolated themselves and so gained Indra's heaven in Mount Meru.

In this composite poem the *Bhagavad-Gītā,* or 'Song of the Blessed One', was incorporated early in the Christian era, in which Krishna is idealized as an *avatar* of Vishnu in the capacity of the charioteer of Arjuna who was perplexed about the civil war. 'Is warfare righteous?' 'Is it lawful to kill?' 'Is the war of life worth waging?' These are some of the questions raised in this great philosophical poem which has come to be regarded as the New Testament of Hinduism; an eternal Gospel having a message for every century. As such it is one of the most important of the Sanskrit writings, and while the date of its composition is uncertain, the genuine *Gītā* may perhaps have arisen before the orthodox philosophic systems were expounded in Sutras.[1] But in this case, it is probable that additions were made during the first two hundred years of the Christian era, theistic doctrines being incorporated in the original Upanishadic version. The Sankhya cosmology is retained, but Krishna is identified with the sovereignty of the Soul of the universe (Brahman) as the source of all things and yet independent of time. The universal self is at war with his five senses and his sins, a struggle symbolized in terms of the great eighteen-day battle in the Mahābhārata epic.

Like the medieval mystery play, the *Bhagavad-Gītā* is the story of Everyman told in the poetic narrative in which it is embedded. Thus the Song opens with the blind king Dhritarashtra, 'the Holder of the World', conversing with Sankaya, who represents the 'Inner Eye' seeing and describing to his master all things near and far. 'Tell me now, Sankaya, O thou of supersensual vision, in the field of life, the field of religion', asked Dhritarashtra, 'how fare they, my hundred sons, marshalled against the five children of my brother Pandu?' Arjuna, the hero of the *Gītā,* acts as the mouthpiece of the Pāndavas, who symbolize the five senses opposing the hundred errors of Everyman. It is he who questions his charioteer, Krishna, as the incarnation of Vishnu, concerning the ethics of warfare, and the discussion resolves itself into a defence of active resistance to evil.

The problem raised by the battle of Kurukshetra was not merely

[1] E. J. Thomas, *Song of the Lord* (Lond., 1931), p. 12. R. Garbe, *Die Bhagavadgita* (Leipzig, 1905), Introd. and p. 64. Telang, *S.B.E.,* VIII, pp. 7 ff., 25.

that of non-violence and passive resistance, but of a bloody conflict between kinsmen, sons and fathers, uncles and nephews, cousins and friends. To Krishna, however, Arjuna's hesitation to engage in such a carnage and allow the sons of Dhritarashtra to work their evil will unopposed seemed to be an exhibition of unmanliness and lack of courage. Therefore, he proceeded to put an end to his scruples by showing that he is merely fulfilling his caste duty. Arjuna must remember that he belongs to the warrior-caste of Kshatriyas, and consequently it is a matter of honour to fulfil his obligations as a soldier and knight. 'Yield not therefore to this faint-heartedness but do thy duty (*dharma*), perform the settled functions of thy great calling, unmindful of results. Let thy mind and reason be solely and wholly applied to thy duty on the field of battle. Stand up, O Parantapa, and fight!'

Translated into spiritual terms, the poem teaches salvation by works and the need of divine grace to enable the soul to attain supreme bliss symbolized by the union of Krishna and Vishnu. By the surrender of the heart the soul is redeemed, and in words that have a genuine ring of the Christian Gospel, the great poem concludes with a lofty appeal: 'give thy mind to me, be devoted to me, sacrifice for me, honour me. Thus shalt thou come to me: truly do I promise it unto thee for thou art dear to me. Forsake all other duties and precepts and come unto me; I will liberate thee from sin; therefore be of good cheer' (xviii, 64 f.).

Both in theory and practice the religion of the *Gitā* is a way of salvation by divine grace, however much Vedantic pantheism may have entered into its theology and metaphysic. Krishna is God incarnated as the God-man, and the Eternal Self of man called Narayana. Arjuna is Nara-Narayana, the temporal Self of God, or Man-god. Within every soul Nara and Narayana, Man-god and God-man, resides, and the dialogue discusses in its several aspects this dual conception in relation to the temporal and eternal issues. Despite the inconsistencies of a work that has passed through many hands and been subjected to several conflicting influences, unquestionably it sets forth in a mythological and pantheistic setting, a doctrine of grace in theistic terms. Vishnu, the all-permeating, having shed his ancient Vedic characteristic, has become the eternal sole-Brahman, and as the Isvara, he is the form of the personal unique Deity-ego, rather than a pantheistic impersonal Absolute.

Similarly, Narayana is the eternal, inexpressible, changeless true and only God, while Krishna is the human embodiment of Vishnu. Psychologically, therefore, the trend of thought was in a monotheistic direction, and devotionally spiritual experience found a gospel of the grace of God in the sublime story of Vishnu-Krishna as the supreme personal deity in human aspect through whom was given the offer of salvation as an act of divine grace, though he was also equated with the pantheistic Absolute.

The *Bhagavad-Gītā*, in fact, represents an attempt to combine into one system all the current ways by which salvation could be obtained, and, therefore, notwithstanding the beauty of its language, it is too comprehensive to be consistent. This doubtless partly accounts for its widespread appeal since the orthodox Brahman, the Vedantist, the Yogin and the theist equally find their own sentiments and theologies expressed therein. Works, faith, knowledge, are each and all given their place in this gospel, together with the doctrine of *Bhakti*, which maintains the duties of caste above all other obligations.

Second in importance to Krishna is the *avatar* of Rama, recorded in the *Rāmāyana* ('Adventures of Rama'), which is assigned to the poet Valmiki (*c.* 400 B.C.), though the first and seventh books are unquestionably much later additions.[1] In this epic the exile of Rama, the eldest son of king Dasaratha of Ayodhya, the capital of Kosala, or Oudh, is described. For fourteen years he lived in the forest with Sita, his wife, and his brother Lakshmana, as a result of the jealousy of his stepmother. There he encountered demons and engaged in acts of gallantry, till he was enticed away by Ravana, the demon king, by means of a magic deer. In his absence Sita was abducted and carried off to Lanka (Ceylon), till she was rescued by the aid of the monkey clan. Ravana was slain and the purity of Sita was attested by an ordeal of fire. In the later books Rama becomes the seventh incarnation of Vishnu, who voluntarily underwent suffering and privation in order to give strength and grace to struggling humanity instead of being the supreme example of morality, loyalty and filial piety, with Sita as the personification of the dutiful wife, as in the earlier portions of the epic.

The philosophical interpretation of the *Bhakti* way of salvation was undertaken by Ramanuja in southern India in the last quarter

[1] A. A. Macdonell, *A History of Sanskrit Literature* (Lond., 1900), p. 309.

of the twelfth century A.D. (1175–1250) with the purpose of vindicating the ultimate oneness of man with God (Vishnu), regarded as the Supreme Creator, without denying the reality of the individual soul and the external world. In this qualified monism God is the Ultimate Reality, all-powerful, all-pervading and all-merciful, but within this divine unity are distinct elements of plurality so that both souls and matter exist eternally in Him without losing their separate and independent identity, the soul always having a conscious existence apart from God. In His earthly manifestation the Deity dwells in images, in partial and complete incarnations, and within man, perceptible by the supernatural visions of the yogi. Salvation is secured by *bhakti*, interpreted as complete trust in divine grace bestowed through the loving kindness of God apart from human merit, and demanding the surrender of the heart and will. Penance, sacrifice, almsgiving and performance of pilgrimages are enjoined as integral elements in the practice of *bhakti* as a continuous process of meditation leading to an intuitive perception of God, which is the highest spiritual experience realizable on earth. After death the released soul is accompanied in its passage to heaven where it enjoys eternal bliss in perfect communion with Vishnu, free from the fear of rebirth. Thus, it was the school of Ramanuja, as Dr Barnett points out, 'that blended in full harmony the voices of reason and devotion, by worshipping a Supreme Being of infinitely blessed qualities, both in His Heaven and as revealed to the soul of man in incarnate experience'.[1] In the next century it split into two opposed divisions on the question of 'justification', the southern section, like the Calvinists in Western Europe, maintaining the doctrine of irresistible grace as against the northern advocacy of co-operative grace and the need of works. Something more than the passive surrender of a kitten carried in the mouth of its mother is required, it was argued by the latter school, but both sections agreed that salvation is the gift of God through grace, and, therefore, they completed the doctrine of *bhakti* foreshadowed in the *Bhavagad-Gitā* and the *Rāmāyana*.

Under the influence of the devotional movement in Hinduism the theory of *avatars* was adopted by Mahayana Buddhism in the second century A.D. when the historical teacher of the way of release became an incarnation of the Adi Buddha, 'the self-created

[1] L. D. Barnett, *The Heart of Hinduism* (Lond., 1909), p. 42.

Father of the universe', animated above all things by the spirit of compassion. While it is admitted that he urged his followers to seek deliverance from rebirth, the Mahayanist teachers affirmed that he did this only because the world was not yet ready for the fuller revelation of the gospel of grace bestowed through the exalted beings known as *Bodhisattvas,* who having reached the enlightenment of a complete Buddha declined to enter *Nirvana* in order to devote themselves to the compassionate work of obtaining the release of others. It was this doctrine which led to the schism between the southern 'Little Vehicle' (Hinayana) with its negative monastic and ethical tradition, and the more positive and mystical 'Great Vehicle' (Mahayana), after the Council at Kashmir in the reign of Kanishka, who is thought to have lived from about A.D. 120 to 162, though the date is in dispute.

In the northern school Gautama was no longer regarded as an *arahan,* but one of many deified *bodhisattvas* to whom prayers and offerings were made as the supreme object of veneration among his followers. He did not himself enter *Nirvana* at all, it was claimed, but as a heavenly being took upon himself the form of a man in order to spread throughout the world the knowledge of salvation. In some form of existence he has always lived in the world in every age, and in the *Saddharma Pundarika,* or 'Lotus of the True Law', while the personal Buddha is represented as the supreme object of worship, he is also identified with the eternal Absolute, surrounded by thousands of gods and Buddhas and *Bodhisattvas,* having their abodes in particular at the ten points of space (the four quarters, the intermediate quarters, the zenith and nadir) as ancient gods under new names.

There is probably some truth in the Mahayanist claim that its doctrines are not new, and that the Hinayanist tradition supports this contention. Even in the lifetime of Gautama there may have been a tendency among the disciples to look upon their Master as more than human, and to endow him with quasi-divine attributes by virtue of his superhuman knowledge. In point of fact if he was an idealist and dreamer, as a practical, reasonable and unsentimental thinker he has few if any rivals in the history of the world, and for his followers when he passed out of the stage of *Bodhisattva,* at the time of his Great Illumination, he became *Buddha,* the Enlightened in a sense of being omniscient, which henceforth became an essential element in the arahanship. Therefore, the beatified teacher was already on his way to becoming a divine Founder of a redemption religion. His birthplace and the bo-tree under which he reached his goal were centres of pilgrimage, and those who died *en route* were rewarded by a blessed rebirth in heavenly realms distinct from *Nirvana*. Over his relics shrines were erected to which a cultus became attached. Around his birth and the principal incidents in his career legends grew up in which the entire universe and a complete pantheon were actors in the drama of salvation. In the Pali post-canonical works he is described as *devâtideva* (the *deva* above *deva*) and in the series of conversations between the Indo-Greek king Milinda (Menander) and the Buddhist teacher, called the *Milindapanha* ('Questions of Milinda'), composed about 80 B.C., while the exalted state of the emancipated *arahan* is maintained, *Nirvana* is portrayed as a city in which the pure in heart live a communal life as social beings rather than as isolated forest hermits. Moreover, the architect of the Dhamma-city has become 'peerless, unequalled, incomparable, admirable beyond all measure by weight or calculation'. From being the Elder Brother of mankind, the Buddha is now in process of transformation into the divine all-compassionate saviour of the human race, pre-existent and sinless, supernaturally conceived and miraculously born.

The change in outlook, however, though in part a natural development of the veneration of Gautama as the Buddha, was also an attempt to interpret Buddhism in terms of the *avatar* theories of devotional Hinduism, the *Lotus*, for example, being a product of the same period as the *Gitā*. It was also due to the new influences—Greek, Christian, Zoroastrian and Central Asian—that were making themselves felt in north-western India at the beginning of our era. Thus, when Buddhism became the religion of the foreign invaders from the northern steppes, its founder became a saviour-god comparable to Krishna and Rama. In this form it spread across the Himalayas to China where in the fourth century A.D. it established itself, and, as we have seen, passed thence by way of Korea to Japan as a salvation religion.

Fundamentally tolerant, Buddhism found a responsive ally in Shinto, and under the patronage of the Prince Regent Shōtoku (572–621), the new religion gradually penetrated Japanese civilization till at length it became the dominant influence. In the process

of adjustment it was the Mahayana doctrine of salvation that prevailed, and while the Hinayana sects—Kusha, Jo-Jitsu, and Sanron—
played their part, they became extinct because in a virile environment nihility and vacuity did not meet a fundamental need. Rather
men turned to Jôdo and Shin-shu, the sects of the Pure Land,
wherein grace was to be found through faith in the meritorious
work of the Amida Buddha ('Infinite Light'). Instead of self-
discipline, or the attainment of transcendental knowledge leading
to *Nirvana*, illumination was secured by *Tarikikyo*, or the 'strength
of another'. Amida in his loving compassion desires to save all
creatures from suffering and ignorance, and since 'the way of the
wise' is beyond the reach of the simple, and the world had become
too degenerate to understand great truths, Honen (Genku), the
founder of the Jôdo sect in A.D. 1175, revealed that deliverance
could be obtained merely by the incessant repetition of the sacred
name of the all-compassionate, *Namu Amida Butsu!* ('Hail, Amida
Buddha!'). To perform this pious exercise ten times with sincerity
sufficed to secure rebirth in the Pure Land after death, because in
the sacred name resides the Absolute whose grace alone can bestow
the free gift of salvation.

> The faith that Buddha, invoked by us, will welcome us in his Paradise
> [declared Honen], form our certitude of our coming salvation. Our only
> practice consists in repeating the holy name with confidence. All that
> we can teach proceeds from our absolute faith in the will of Buddha to
> make us to be reborn in Paradise. Those of you who are scholars, and
> who have studied the words of Shaka, must consider themselves as
> ignorant. We are all equal by the effect of our common faith, and of our
> confidence in the grace of Amida-Buddha. In common with those who
> know nothing of doctrines, and taking no account of the methods of
> wise men, let us put all our heart into the practice which consists in
> uttering the name Amida-Buddha. [For] none shall fail to be in his Land
> of Purity after having called, with complete desire, on Amida.[1]

Of the three methods of salvation in sectarian Buddhism, *Shodo-
men* (self-help), *jadomen* (the help of another), and *dhyana* (meditation), justification by faith represents the most influential movement
because it brought the saving grace of Amida Buddha within the

[1] Coates and Ishizuka, *Honen the Buddhist Saint* (Kyota, 1925), pp. 403 ff. Anesakim,
'Honen, the Pietist Saint', *Transactions of Third International Congress of the History of
Religions* (Oxford, 1908), vol. I. pp. 125 f. E. Steinilber-Oberlin, *The Buddhist Sects
of Japan* (Lond., 1938), p. 192.

reach of every man irrespective of social status and intellectual equipment. To escape from suffering and attain the supreme goal, the intervention of the all-compassionate effected what no human effort or merit could hope to secure. The personal equation was not wholly eliminated since the recitation of the Nemhutsu was only efficacious when it proceeded from a sincere and believing heart, but it did not insist on a new vision of life and the world (*satori*) as in the *dhyana*, or Zen method. Nevertheless, it was neither the moral discipline of the Zen school nor the subjective idealism of Hosso, Tendai and Kegon, but the doctrine of a personal saviour and a Western Paradise, attained through faith and the operation of divine grace, that was the main inspiration in the Far East under the influence of Mahayana Buddhism.

CHAPTER VIII

Monotheism

As early as the period of the *Rig-Veda* (*c.* 1500 B.C.) the Indian mind began to seek a unifying principle in the multiplicity of gods thought to control and pervade all cosmic manifestations from the heavenly bodies to man as macrocosm and microcosm alike, so that Varuna became the one dominant power. But, as we have seen, behind all the gods lay *Rta*, the dynamic universal order, and neither Varuna nor Indra were personal transcendent deities creating and sustaining the universe from without. Indeed the Vedic poets indiscriminately assigned all the divine attributes and functions to any god they happened to be magnifying in a particular hymn—a practice described by Max Müller as 'Kathenotheism'—though Varuna was regarded as the upholder of the moral law, as the guardian of *rta* in its ethical aspect. Nevertheless, all the Vedic gods were subordinate to the one immanent pre-existent cosmic order which was ultimately the source of all change and activity in phenomena.

MONISM AND MONOTHEISM

The search for a unifying principle in such a system could but lead to monism as distinct from monotheism, though the deeply laid idea of divine plurality also found expression in a kathenotheistic or henotheistic tendency. When *rta* gave place to *karma* the same impersonal self-active cosmic order was maintained by the law of action and reaction, while even in *Bhakti* mysticism, though the supremacy of one God was maintained, neither Vishnu nor Shiva was ever regarded as a universal deity in a monotheistic sense. Both were derived from the Vedic polytheistic pantheon, and Vishnu was believed to be subject to the process of reincarnation in so far as he descended to earth in the various forms which included animals as well as human avatars. Similarly, in the later Buddhism, while the supreme Buddha was eternal, and in such sects as the Tendai equated with the Absolute, in former lives he took the form of a tortoise, a deer, a parrot, a wood-pecker and a crow; all these incarnations being on the same level as the human manifestations. Cosmic rebirth, in short, has been a fundamental theme in Indian cosmology, and in consequence inevitably the gods have been dependent on the impersonal law governing the process. Therefore, no supreme being has been the originating source of all phenomena since the entire universe has been regarded as the product of the inviolable law of cause and effect manifest in action and reaction in which gods, men and nature equally participate.

The same pantheistic mysticism obtained in the conception of the Tao as the ultimate monistic principle of the universe. Being anterior to Shang-ti it took the place of a Supreme Being, but while in this sense it was transcendental it was immanent in all phenomena, and controlled heaven as well as earth. Again, the Confucian notion of T'ien was equally devoid of personality, and if it was monarchian in tendency, the dualistic cosmology and the deeply laid practice of ancestor worship prevented it from developing towards mono-theism. Moreover, the imperial cult of Shang-ti limited to the emperor the approach to the Supreme Ruler.

ZOROASTRIANISM

In Iran, on the other hand, at a very early period a serious attempt was made to establish a universal monotheistic religion with an outlook transcending the limitations of race and culture inspired by the belief in one Deity, Ahura Mazda ('Wise Lord, or Lord of Wisdom'), 'Creator, radiant, glorious, greatest and best, most beautiful, most firm, wisest, most perfect, the most bounteous Spirit!'[1] Although the date and personality of the founder of Zoro-astrianism are obscure, not later than 660 B.C., and possibly as early as 1000 B.C. (or even 1400 B.C.), Zarathustra,[2] as he is styled in the *Avesta*, became the recipient of a divine revelation to reform the faith of Eastern Iran and induce the tribes to practise agriculture

[1] *S.B.E.*, XXX, p. 195 f.

[2] Zarathustra is rendered Zoroaster from the Latin variant 'Zoroastres', deriving its origin from a similar Greek spelling.

instead of pursuing a restless and aggressive pastoral life. The original religion was a form of Vedic polytheism, and, according to Herodotus, the Persians sacrificed to 'Sun, Moon, Earth, Fire, Water and Winds from the beginning,' to which 'they have learned in addition from the Assyrians and Arabians, to sacrifice to Urania'.[1] In the Mitanni region, in the north-west, the names of Mithra, Indra and Varuna occur on an inscription of about 1400 B.C., and Ahura Mazda (i.e. Ormuzd in its Parsi form) was probably a derivative of the Aryan Asura which may be identified with Varuna. It is this deity who in the *Gathas*, which represent the oldest parts of the *Avesta*, or sacred scriptures of Zoroastrianism, is revealed as a transcendent monotheistic Being, ethical in his nature and requirements, the embodiment of truth and righteousness, and the bestower of all good. Since the exaltation of Ahura Mazda to the foremost place in the pantheon probably goes back to a time before the days of the prophet, it would seem that Varuna, as the guardian of morality in Vedic India, in Iran was already on the way to becoming the ethical god *par excellence*. But it remained for Zoroaster to transform all the other devas and asuras into either divine attributes, or to reduce them to the level of subordinate immaterial spirits, angelic and diabolical, without image or anthropomorphic form.

Over against Ahura Mazda, however, stands a twin-spirit, the 'Lie', the hostile source of evil.

> Between these two [says the Gathas], the wise one chose aught, and the foolish one not so. And when these twain spirits came together in the beginning, they established Life and Not-Life, and that at the last, the Worst Existence shall be the followers of the Lie, but the Best Thought to him that follows Right. Of these twain Spirits he that followed the Lie chose the worst things; the holiest Spirit chose the Right, he that clothes him with the massy heavens as a garment.[2]

From such a statement as this it might seem that Zoroastrianism was a dualism rather than a monotheism, but it is by no means clear how far the later Mazdaean doctrine of Ahriman (Angra Mainyu) as the Devil was maintained by the Prophet. In the *Gāthas* the enemies of Ahura Mazda are the daevas and Druj (the Lie)—the earlier Vedic-Iranian gods—and while the mention of 'Twin-

[1] *Herod*, I, 13.   [2] *Yasna*, XXX, 3–5.

Spirits' suggests the idea of two eternal and co-equal principles of good and evil contending for the mastery of the world, the name 'Angra Mainyu' occurs only once in the *Gāthas* as the designation of the Supreme hostile spirit (Ahriman).[1] Moreover, good is assumed to be ultimately destined to prevail, and the final destinies of man are in the hands of Ahura Mazda who is lord of all spirits.[2] But as this really makes him responsible for evil, it raises the funda-mental ethical problem of monotheism and opens the way for a dualistic solution.

MAZDAEAN DUALISM

Whatever may have been the actual teaching of Zoroaster, the Twin-spirits of the *Gāthas* were interpreted in the subsequent Mazdaeism in terms of two independent hostile principles—Ormuzd (Ahura Mazda, i.e. Spenta Mainyu) and Ahriman (Angra Mainyu), equated with light and darkness, as in the Babylonian contest between Marduk and Tiamat, whence the mythological setting was derived. The universe therefore becomes the scene of the age-long struggle between good and evil personified in the figures of the two divine antagonists assisted by their respective supernatural allies of lesser spirits and demons. While the mono-theistic background was preserved inasmuch as Ormuzd is repre-sented as the final victor, the ancient gods were restored in the marshalling of the forces. Mithra, the eye of Mazda, in his capacity of the god of light gave victory to the beneficent armies by his sacrifice of the primeval bull, the first creature created by Ormuzd, and thus gave life to mankind. This Vedic solar deity took over the ethical attributes of Ahura Mazda, and in the syncretistic mystery cult known as Mithraism that arose out of his worship, he had a profound influence on the Roman Empire at the beginning of the Christian era.

Actually he seems to have played no part in the religion of Zoroaster, who doubtless regarded him merely as one of the daevas to be excluded from the pure monotheistic faith he sought to establish. Since 'the ox and the sun' are said to be the 'worst thing to behold with the eyes',[3] the sacrifice of the bull may have been one of the 'abominations' tabooed to his followers. Therefore, it is

---

[1] *Yasna*, XLV, 2.   [2] *Yasna*, XIX.   [3] *Yasna*, XXXII, 10.

probably not until after the time of the Prophet that contact with
Zoroastrianism introduced an ethical element into his worship and
gave it a place in the revelation of Ahura Mazda.[1] He then became
the guardian of truth and good faith, and protector of the poor and
the oppressed. Being unconquered in the struggle with darkness,
as the heavenly light he gave victory to kings and the helper of
mankind in the destruction of evil. By the immolation of the primeval bull he liberated life and became the guide and mediator of
souls in quest of immortality. To his initiates he secured ascent
through seven spheres to the supreme heaven, where full communion in the beatific vision was attained prior to the ultimate
defeat of the Spirit of Darkness and the rejuvenation of the universe
in a reign of eternal bliss.[2]

In the development of Mithraism elements were borrowed from
Babylonian astrology in addition to those derived from Persian
sources, but it was its Zoroastrian background that gave the mystery
its ethical inheritance and enabled it to set a high moral standard
before its initiates. Nevertheless, it was essentially a solar cultus in
origin, and while Mithras is declared to be the heavenly light as
distinct from the sun, the incorporation of Vedic polytheism,
Iranian dualism and Babylonian mythology prevented it from
rising to the monotheistic height of the worship of the Aton
instituted in Egypt by Amenhotep IV (Akhnaton).

SOLAR MONOTHEISM IN EGYPT

As Professor Breasted has remarked, 'the all-enveloping glory and
power of the Egyptian sun is the most insistent fact in the Nile
Valley',[3] and it is therefore not surprising that solar worship
dominated religion and thought from the earliest times. The original
home of the cult, as we have seen, was Heliopolis to the north-east
of Cairo, where Re reigned supreme and spread his influence over
the whole country so that Pharaoh exercised his royal functions as
his physical son, and every god was in some way identified with
him. Moreover, he himself assumed various forms. At Edfu he
appeared as a falcon (Horus) taking his daily flight across the sky,

[1] *Mihir Yasht*, X, 1, 7. J. Darmesteter, *S.B.E.*, XXIII (1883).
[2] Cumont, *Mystères de Mithra* (Paris, 1913).
[3] *Religion and Thought in Ancient Egypt*, p. 9.

so that the sun-disc with the extended wings of a hawk surmounting an anthropomorphic figure having the head of a falcon became one of the most familiar symbols in Egypt. Thus equated with the ancient solar god Horus (as distinct from the son of Osiris), he was called Re-Harakhte, Re-Horus of the Horizon. At Heliopolis he was represented as an old man tottering down to the west, while in the east he rose as the sacred beetle, Khepra, full of vigour, and self-created as the scarab.[1]

In the beginning the Sun-god alone existed, having taken his origin as Atum in the primeval watery deep, Nun. According to a stele in the British Museum[2] he was created by Ptah, the divine artificer, who first came into being as a thought conceived in his heart, and then proceeded to the gods, men and the universe, including the cult-image. But in addition to this Memphite tradition, the Sun-god as Atum was also affirmed to have appeared out of a lotus flower, or at Heliopolis as a Phoenix. Having emerged in these various ways, he begat Shu, the god of the air, and his wife Tefnut, the goddess of moisture. Of these two were born Geb the Earth-god, and Nut the Sky-goddess, whose offspring were Osiris and Set, and Isis and Nephthys. Thus, the Great Ennead of Heliopolis were descended from Re-Atum-Khepra, and during the Old Kingdom the Sun-god retained his position as the head of the pantheon, the supreme ruler of the celestial realms, and the father of Pharaoh on earth. Furthermore, as the dispenser of justice and upholder of truth (Maāt) he acquired an ethical significance.

In the Middle Kingdom Osiris usurped the function of the judge of the dead, but the scene in the Hall of the Double Truth never lost its solar origin and character, and in the Eighteenth Dynasty (*c.* 1580–1321 B.C.) the worship was restored by the Theban rulers of the New Kingdom who equated Amon, the god of Thebes, with Re as the supreme deity of Egypt. To him the victories of Thutmose III, the Napoleon of Egyptian history and probably the Pharaoh of the Oppression of Israel, and his successor Amenhotep II, were ascribed, and as the Empire was extended to Palestine, Syria and the Euphrates, westwards to the islands of the Aegean, and in the south to the fourth cataract of the Nile, the dominion of the Sun-god assumed a universal character. Thus, Amon-Re became

[1] A living beetle was thought to emerge from dung by spontaneous generation.
[2] No. 498.

an imperial deity exercising his jurisdiction over many lands and receiving worship in resplendent temples in many strange cities from Canaan to Nubia. He was the 'sole lord, taking captive all lands every day, as one beholding them that walk therein'. Moreover, as Atum he was 'the creator of mankind, who distinguished their nature and made their life: who made the colours (of men) different, one from another'.

Nevertheless, despite this imperialistic monotheistic tendency, Amon-Re remained a composite deity with a complex polytheistic heritage so that as soon as Amenhotep IV succeeded to the throne about 1375 B.C. as the devotee of the Sun-god, a struggle ensued between the royal house and the Amon priesthood, whose adherence to solar theology was nominal. Furthermore, in the previous reign (Amenhotep III) the Sun-god was frequently described as the Aton, an ancient name for the physical sun and associated particularly with the disc from which he shone upon the world. The king's palace at Thebes and his royal barge were named 'Aton-Gleams', and the divine offerings known as 'Aton offerings'. Therefore, a cult of Aton was already established before the ardent and youthful son of Amenhotep III became co-regent with his aged father and introduced his far-reaching reforms.

Hitherto, however, Amon-Re was unchallenged as the state-god *par excellence*, but the new Pharaoh promptly set to work to eliminate the entire pantheon, leaving the solar Aton *exclusively* in possession throughout the Empire. Had he been content, like the Heliopolitan priesthood in the Fourth Dynasty, to raise the Sun-god (Aton) to the place of supremacy his movement would have caused no surprise. Instead he was determined to establish a genuine monotheism inasmuch as he would tolerate the worship of no other deity. To this end he closed all the temples, cast forth the priests and erased the names of the gods from the monuments as thoroughly as Somerset and Cromwell obliterated the signs and symbols of medieval Catholicism during the Reformation period. Having changed his name from Amenhotep ('Amen is satisfied') to Akhnaton ('Profitable to Aton'), he removed his palace from Thebes with its Amonite associations—a veritable 'Babylon' to the ardent Atonist—to Tell el-Amarna, where he erected a new capital known as Akhetaton ('The Horizon of Aton') as the centre of the new faith. A similar city was founded in Nubia and another in Syria, whence the pure light of the heavenly disc might shine throughout the Empire.

For the remaining eleven years of his life the heretic king and his wife, Nefertiti, devoted themselves to religious exercises in the temples dedicated in honour of the Aton, where no cultus-image was permitted, and the singing of remarkable monotheistic hymns in praise of the Sun-god was the principal act of worship, together with the presentation of food and drink offerings, of perfumes and flowers, censings and libations, instead of the former toilet-ceremonies. A male and female choir was in attendance during the rites in which the queen equally with the king had her part, for the worship was essentially a royal cult. Pharaoh was still the earthly embodiment of the Sun-god, and as such the dispenser of good fortune, the giver of life and length of days, though the texts are curiously silent about the hereafter, which in the earlier Solar and Osirian theologies was so conspicuous a feature.

The new religion in all probability was mainly the creation of Akhnaton himself, though it is possible, as Budge has suggested, that it owed something to the influences introduced from Mitanni by his mother Tii, and his wife, Nefertiti, both of whom, together with his grandmother (the queen of Thutmose IV), are thought to have come from this region north of the Euphrates.[1] If this conjecture could be substantiated, it might be possible to connect the movement with the corresponding monotheistic tendencies in Vedic-Iranian thought, though the Aton does not actually bear any real resemblance to Mithra, Varuna or Indra. It seems to be primarily a product of Egyptian solar theology differentiated from all that had gone before and all that followed this short-lived interlude in a definitely polytheistic tradition by the amazing heights of spirituality attained in the hymns, which were apparently written by Akhnaton himself.

The simplicity and beauty of the young king's faith appears in the following exaltation of the universal splendour and power of Aton, taken from the tomb-chapels at El-Amarna:[2]

[1] Budge, *Tutankhamen, Amenism, Atenism and Egyptian Monotheism* (Lond., 1923), pp. 21, 113.

[2] Davies, *Rock-Tombs of El-Amarna* (Lond., 1903–8), VI, pl. xxvii, xxix. Erman, *Literature of the Ancient Egyptians* (Lond., 1927), p. 289.

Beautiful is thine appearing in the horizon of heaven, thou living sun,
    the first who lived!
Thou risest in the eastern horizon, and
Thou fillest every land with thy beauty.
Thou art beautiful and great and glistenest, and art high above every
    land;
Thy rays, they encompass the lands, so far as all that thou hast created.
Thou art Re, and thou reachest unto their end and subduest them for
    thy dear son.
Though thou art far away, yet are thy rays upon earth;
Thou art before their face . . . thy going.

This *Hymn to the Sun* goes on to describe how the earth is in
darkness like the dead when Aton sets in the western horizon, but
as soon as he rises 'the Two Lands (Egypt) are in daily festivity'.
Men resume their labours and 'all cattle rest upon their pasturage,
the trees and the plants flourish, the birds flutter in their marshes',
and 'the sheep dance upon their feet' (cf. Ps. civ. 20–3). His work
as the 'Creator of the germ in woman' and the source of all life,
is next extolled, and his loving care for all his creatures. 'How mani-
fold are thy works! They are hidden from before us. O sole God
whose powers no other possesseth. Thou didst create the earth
according to thy heart while thou wast alone.' Moreover, even in
'foreign countries, Syria and Kush', as well as 'the land of Egypt',
'thou settest every man in his place, thou suppliest their necessities'.
But the dominion of Aton is not confined to the earth since it was
he who made 'the Nile in the Nether World', and the 'Nile in the
sky'. 'O how excellent are thy designs, O Lord of eternity!'

Finally, the hymn concludes with a revelation to the king showing
that despite these lofty sentiments, Akhnaton was still thinking in
terms of the Egyptian conception of the royal office.

> Thou art in my heart,
> There is no other that knoweth thee
> Save thy son Akhnaton.
> Thou hast made him wise
> In thy designs and in thy might.

While the general level of thought was in advance of the current
henotheistic ideas, the Cairo hymn to Amon, probably written in

the reign of Amenhotep II (1447–1420 B.C.) is **not** far removed, as the following section shows:

> He who made herbage for the cattle
> And the fruit tree for men.
> He who made that whereon live the fish in the river,
> And the birds which inhabit the firmament.
> He who giveth bread to him that is in the egg, and sustaineth the son of the worm.
> He who made whereon the gnats live,
> The worms and the flies likewise.
> He who maketh that which the mice in their holes need,
> And sustaineth the birds (?) on every tree.[1]

Akhnaton would seem to have derived his inspiration from this passage, but, nevertheless, he developed a conception of monotheism which is genuinely unique in Egypt. By substituting the solar disc with emanating rays for the anthropomorphic and theriomorphic symbols of deity, he spiritualized the concept, the only vestige of anthropomorphism being the human hands in which the rays ended. Aton, in fact, was a new god, and beside him 'there was no other'. As the solar disc was one alone, without counterpart or equal, so Aton reigned alone.[2]

The monotheistic movement, however, was in advance of its time, and being the work almost exclusively of one man who was admittedly a genius, it died with him. As a ruler Akhnaton was weak and disinterested in imperial affairs, and his one great achievement in the sphere of religion made little or no appeal to the common people of the fourteenth century B.C. The dispossessed Amonite priesthood was antagonized, and the country was full of dissatisfied soldiers. Therefore, in the confusion and disturbance that arose after his death Atonism came to an inglorious end and the nation speedily returned to its former gods with the accession of his son-in-law, Tutankhaton, in 1350. The new king took up his abode in Thebes and changed his name to Tutankhamen as a devotee of Amon-Re. Thus faded into oblivion in Egypt the vision of the one God.

[1] Erman, *The Literature of the Ancient Egyptians*, p. 286.
[2] Budge, op. cit., p. 79.

HEBREW MONOTHEISM

Very different were the history and fortunes of monotheism in the outlying province of Palestine where during the reigns of Amenhotep III and Akhnaton, as is shown by the Tell el-Amarna tablets written about 1380 B.C., the vassal kings were being hard pressed by a group of confederated invaders called Habiru (ideographically—S A.GAZ), who, in alliance with the Hittites, were making serious inroads. Egyptian rule in Canaan began to decline in the opening years of the fourteenth century B.C., and, according to the Amarna letters, no army of Pharaoh had visited the country for fifty years. That the Hebrew tribes from the ˙desert seized the opportunity afforded by the general unrest in the district to strike a blow for supremacy in Palestine is shown alike by the Biblical narratives and the cuneiform records inscribed on the clay tablets found in the capital of Akhnaton, which include appeals for help addressed to the king by the oppressed Palestinian chiefs. But the heretic ruler was too engrossed in his religious reformation to give thought to such mundane affairs, just as his father in his latter years had found bull-fights and lion hunts more to his taste than the serious business of the Empire. Therefore, having weakened the power of the vassal Canaanite chiefs, Egypt was content to leave them to their fate. Thus, there is some ground for seeing a hidden allusion to Egypt in the phrase attributed to Yahweh in the Book of Joshua, 'I sent the hornet before you which drave them (the Canaanites) out'.[1]

Be this as it may, there can be little doubt that the invasion of Palestine from the south and east by the Israelite Hebrews under Joshua and other tribal leaders was inspired by a religious conviction which goes back to the days of Moses, who consolidated the tribes as a national entity in the conviction what they were a people under the special care and protection of a pastoral deity worshipped under the name of Yahweh. How far Moses was the creator of this belief it is difficult to determine, but it would seem that Yahweh was a god familiar to the Semites over a considerable area. Thus, the Biblical JHWH, transliterated in the English version of the Hebrew scriptures as 'Jehovah' through a misreading in the thirteenth century A.D. of the consonants with the vowels of 'adonai' (lord)—the word substituted by the Jews for the divine name— occurs in various forms in ancient Semitic inscriptions. In cuneiform

[1] Garstang, *Joshua, Judges* (Lond., 1931), p. 258. cf. Joshua xxiv. 12.

documents and the tablets recently discovered at Ras Shamra on the Syrian coast (*c.* 1500–1300 B.C.),[1] *Ya, Yo, Yau, Yami* (or *Yawe*) are syllables compounded with personal names, sometimes connected with gods, and in Minaean inscriptions from South Arabia, thought by many scholars to belong to the fifteenth century B.C., the divine name is *Yah.*

While it is not possible to arrive at any definite conclusions concerning the precise meaning and significance of these terms, it is not improbable that before the time of Moses a god called Yahweh, or some parallel form of the word, was known among the nomadic pastoral tribes of Arabia and the surrounding district from Syria to Babylonia. Indeed it is difficult to believe that Moses could have succeeded in his mission unless he went to his captive kinsmen in the name of a god who was already established among them. Thus, he is said to have declared that the 'god of their fathers' had appeared to him and sent him to them.[2]

If, however, he interpreted his numinous experience at the 'burning bush' during the period of his exile in Midian in terms of a revelation from a god who was more than a Kenite deity, and no stranger to the Hebrews, he must have given a new significance to his power and attributes. As Andrew Lang demonstrated in his pioneer volume, *The Making of Religion,* in 1898, the existence of remote, ethical, beneficent Supreme Beings is widely recognized among people in a primitive state of culture. Thus, for instance, in Australia Atnatu, the All-Father of the Kaitish tribe, stands apart from all the lesser spirits, totems, and ancestors since he is said to have made himself and given himself his name before he ascended to the sky in a period prior to the *Alcheringa,* when the ancestors roamed the earth.[3] Similarly, Daramulun, the High God of the Yuin coastal tribes, is supposed to have lived long ago on the earth when the ground was bare and only animals, birds and reptiles existed. It was he who made the trees to grow, gave the people their laws and their magic, and presided over the initiation ceremonies. When a man dies he meets his spirit and takes care of it,

---

[1] The Ras Shamra tablets represent an ancient type of Hebrew or Canaanite language written in a cuneiform alphabet.

[2] Exod. iii. 13.

[3] Spencer and Gillen, *Northern Tribes of Central Australia* (Lond., 1904), pp. 488 ff.

giving it a place in his abode in the sky.[1] Or, again, for the Kamilaroi Baiame, the tribal All-Father, is the equivalent of the *Alcheringa* among the Arunta. He lived in the 'Dream Time' and changed birds and beasts into men and women, made human beings of clay or stone, taught them everything, and left laws for their guidance before he returned to the sky. In matters of custom and belief he is the ultimate authority, so that 'because Baiame says so' is the equivalent in this district of the Arunta 'it was so in the *Alcheringa*'.[2]

As Dr Wilhelm Schmidt has shown by his laborious and exhaustive researches, this type of High God is of almost universal occurrence in primitive society,[3] and inasmuch as these Supreme Beings are thought to have existed before death came into the world, it cannot be maintained, as Herbert Spencer following the Greek philosopher Euhemeros (330–260 B.C.) imagined, that the idea of God arose in ancestor-worship.[4] The 'ghost-theory' breaks down when it encounters self-existent Creators independent of culture heroes and other otiose divinities, who live a life of their own in the sky remote from human affairs. On the other hand, if such deities cannot be explained as deified rulers or ghosts carried to the highest power, neither can they be equated with the Hebrew conception of monotheism, as Dr Schmidt endeavours to prove.

Thus, to affirm that a tribal All-Father was prior to the advent of death does not suggest a realization of time which admits of eternity as a corollary, any more than to assert that he is able 'to go anywhere and do anything', as is alleged of Daramulun,[5] means that he is omnipotent or omniscient, except in the very limited sense in which the terms might be applied to a powerful medicine-man. Similarly, his creative functions are limited by the fact that for the primitive mind problems of causation have little or no meaning beyond the powers exercised by rain-makers. Therefore, to say with Schmidt that the primitive religious beliefs that found expression in High Gods 'arose from the profoundest depths of a conviction of the person of the Supreme Being as the Universal

---

[1] Howitt, *Native Tribes of South-East Australia* (Lond., 1904), pp. 494 ff.

[2] L. Parker, *The Euahlayi Tribe* (Lond., 1905), pp. 5 ff.

[3] *Ursprung der Gottesidee* (Munster, 1926–35). *High Gods in North America* (Oxford, 1933). *The Origin and Growth of Religion* (Lond., 1931), pp. 172 ff.

[4] *Principles of Sociology* (Lond., 1885), 3rd Edition, vol. I, pp. 286 ff., 385 ff., 411.

[5] Howitt, op. cit., p. 543.

Cause'[1] is to lose sight of the fact that such a concept was as foreign to its outlook alike in the matter of personality and causation as is the scholastic and metaphysical concept of creation *ex nihilo*, to which this exponent frequently refers as an attribute of the original 'revelation'. Finally, the control of conduct and tribal custom exercised by these beings hardly rises above the maintenance of ritual holiness without regard to ethical considerations. Therefore, even granting the tribal All-Father belief was the special possession of a hypothetical first race of men, or 'archaic culture substratum', as Schmidt supposes, now represented by Pygmies, Andamanese, Fuegians and Australians, we are no nearer the origin of genuine ethical monotheism at the threshold of religion in a conception of a '*hochstes Wesen*', or Supreme Being regarded as a First Cause with theological attributes.[2]

In every community, it would seem, there are always a few people to whom religion in its loftier aspects makes a ready appeal, and and since the High God in all states of culture stands head and shoulders above the more intimate spirits, totems and ancestors, the concept probably represents the climax of religious experience, evaluated within the limits of the mentality in which it occurs. But the very loftiness of the All-Father tends to render him unapproachable and liable to pass into obscurity in the background. That the belief arose spontaneously as 'a purposive functioning of an inherent type of thought and emotion'[3] rather than as the result of speculation about the universe, is suggested by the fact that when man began to work out philosophical schemes he was led to animistic, polytheistic and pantheistic theorizings, as in Vedic India, Greece and Egypt.

So far as the evidence available can be taken as a guide, it seems that while there are no adequate grounds for the assumption that monotheism was the primeval religion of mankind, a universal monotheistic tendency is probably more fundamental than any final product of an evolutionary system, being the emotional evaluation of the *mysterium tremendum* in the intuitive realization of a Power awful and mysterious as the transcendent ground of the visible order, though not to the exclusion of other lesser supernatural

[1] Schmidt, *Origins and Growth of Religion*, p. 150.

[2] cf. Schmidt, *Ursprung der Gottesidee,* IV, p. 492.

[3] Radin, *Monotheism among Primitive Peoples* (Lond., 1924), p. 67.

beings in their respective spheres. Akhnaton, so far as we know, represents the first pure monotheist in the history of religion, if by this term is understood the recognition of one God to the exclusion of any and every other divine being. But from time immemorial, doubtless, the All-Father belief has prevailed everywhere.

Among the Hebrews, Moses apparently was the genius who first succeeded in giving Yahweh a peculiar place in the allegiance of the nation as the result of the theophany in Midian. But it was not until long after the days of Moses and the wanderings that Israel came to a knowledge of one, universal, transcendent, ethical ruler of the entire universe and guide of historical events in accordance with his eternal purposes. This post-exilic achievement in the sixth century B.C. which gave Judaism the distinction of framing the loftiest religion in the Ancient World, had behind it a protracted period of monolatrous development during which a small minority of deeply religious men and women, by virtue of their spiritual experience, was able to foster a monotheistic tradition in the nation as a whole. Unlike Akhnaton and Zoroaster, these leaders did not reach a conception of the one and only God of the universe, since they merely asserted that Yawheh was the god of Israel to the exclusion of all other tribal deities. Nevertheless, he was jealous of his own preserves,[1] and forbade any rival in Israel. Moreover, he was more than a localized desert deity inasmuch as he still claimed the allegiance of his people when they established themselves in Palestine in very different surroundings as an agricultural community.

At the original theophany he manifested himself apparently in a numinous experience as a mountain-god revealing his power in volcanic eruption and seismic disturbances.[2] The Holy Mount was almost certainly Horeb and not Sinai of later tradition,[3] and there like any other primitive High God he spoke in the thunder.[4] But he differed from the typical tribal All-Father in not being remote and disinterested in human affairs. On the contrary, he was at once brought into the most intimate covenant relationship with

[1] Deut. vi. 14.

[2] cf. Exod. xix. 18, Deut. iv. 11 f., Ps. lxviii. 7. 8, Judges v. 4 f., 1 Kings xix. 8–14.

[3] Oesterley and Robinson, *Hebrew Religion* (Lond., 1930), pp. 106 ff. Phythian-Adams, *The Call of Israel* (Oxford, 1934), pp. 131 ff.

[4] All-Fathers are usually associated with thunder through the bull-roarer.

the Hebrew clans, thereby welding them into a theocratic nation. This consolidation was essentially the work of Moses.

The conquest of Palestine presented a new situation since a change of territory normally involved a change of gods, as in the case of Ruth the Moabitess who, when she decided to throw in her lot with Naomi, made her own the god as well as the people of her mother-in-law.[1] Or, again, Naaman who in his anxiety to worship the god of Israel in his Syrian home, took with him on his return from his visit to Elijah two loads of Palestinian soil.[2] Therefore, when the Hebrew settled in Canaan it would have been in accordance with the accepted custom of the age for them to conform to the religious allegiances of the land of their adoption where an animistic and polytheistic vegetation cultus was established. The mono-Yahwists, however, strenuously opposed the adoption of the local divinities and their worship, and in the face of considerable opposition maintained the desert tradition. Hence the struggle with 'Baalism' in the early days of the monarchy, illustrated by such incidents as the contest on Mount Carmel.[3]

As a reaction against this syncretistic movement, the Rechabites and Nazarites adhered strictly to the customs of the nomadic life, regarding all agricultural culture as tainted.[4] As Yahweh was the god of the desert his worship was only secure, as it seemed to them, so long as the inheritance of Israel from its Aramaean ancestry was preserved in all its completeness. This was the conviction of the men who kept alive the monotheistic tradition from the time of the settlement to the collapse of the northern kingdom in 721 B.C., and in Judah, after the Josiah Reformation in 621, it led to the maintenance of the central sanctuary at Jerusalem as the only place of legitimate worship. But the abolition of the local shrines (high places) with their vegetation associations proved to be insufficient, and it was not until after the discipline of the Exile had done its work that the nation as a whole was weaned away permanently from its contaminated cultus, and the tradition of Moses, Elijah and the literary prophets of the eighth and seventh centuries finally and completely established.

[1] Ruth i. 16.   [2] 2 Kings v. 17.

[3] 1 Kings xviii, 21 ff. It is not without significance that the challenge between Yahweh and the Phoenician fertility god Melkart on Carmel appears to turn on a rain-making ceremony.

[4] 2 Kings x. 15 f., Jer. xxxv. 6–10, Amos ii. 12.

In the light of the accumulating evidence it now appears that the
religion of Yahweh before the Exile was much more syncretistic
than was previously imagined. Thus, the temples to Astarte and
Yahweh erected side by side on the Israelite wall at Mizpah in the
ninth century B.C. show that the two cults existed simultaneously,
while the Aramaic papyri discovered at Yeb, or Elephantine, in
1907 and 1908 reveal that in the fifth century female consorts were
assigned to Yahweh in this Jewish military colony in Upper Egypt.
It was doubtless this cultus that in the previous century called forth
the denunciations of Jeremiah, who declared that in Israel there
were as many gods as there were cities.[1] The fall of Jerusalem in
586 B.C. was an epoch-making event because subsequently it
necessitated the re-establishment of the nation at a time when a
fundamental change in outlook was occurring all over the civilized
world from the Mediterranean to China. In these changes Palestine,
Judah and Jerusalem were inevitably involved, and while they
constituted geographically only a very small and insignificant
region, the new religious movement was destined to have a widespread influence on the progress of civilization as a whole.

Amos before the fall of Samaria had emphasized the essential
righteousness of Yahweh, just as Hosea had proclaimed his long-
suffering and never-failing love, and Isaiah in the southern kingdom
had insisted on his essential holiness. But it remained for Ezekiel
and the Deutero-Isaiah among the captives in Babylonia to reveal
the conception of one creative and sustaining omniscient and
omnipotent Will behind all phenomena and historical events,
controlling the earthquake, smiting His enemies and determining
the destinies of nations, notably of His chosen people Israel. These
Jewish ethical monotheists, unlike the Vedic Indians and the Greek
philosophers, never speculated concerning the ultimate principle in
or ground of the universe. For them the rise and fall of nations
became a revelation of the divine will and purpose of the Lord of
all the earth. Through a conception of the moral order and a common good they were led to a monotheistic interpretation of
history. Their conviction was not so much that Yahweh was the
only God but that He alone was worthy of worship, or even of
recognition. They made no pretence at scholarship, and they were
distinguished from their fellows only in respect of their religious

[1] Jer. ii. 28.

experience and spiritual insight.[1] They were, in short, men to whom monotheism was calculated to make an overwhelming appeal, and call forth in them a realization of divine self-disclosure and a sense of vocation to a sacred cause in the community.

The utterances of each individual Hebrew prophet from the eighth century and onwards bear a stamp of originality, of opposition to contemporary thought, of a word of God forcing itself to find expression through the human instrument. Under their influence the monotheistic tendency and tradition were fostered and developed in Israel as in no other country in the ancient world. The All-Father of the desert in the person of the God of Sinai was permanently rescued from oblivion, and while the nation even after the Exile occasionally lapsed into syncretistic worship, yet,[2] contrary to Egypt after the Akhnaton reformation or post-Zoroastrian Persia, the main light shone more powerfully and purely as time went on, until at length all shadows of polytheistic deities and dualistic divinities were fled away, together with those of orgiastic fertility cults of the Mother-goddess and the animistic worship of sticks and stones. If this was not fully accomplished till well into the second century B.C., by the time that the last book of the Old Testament was admitted into the Canon, the Jews had reached a stage of religious develop-ment that justified the Psalmist's assertion: 'Yahweh hath not dealt so with any nation, neither has the heathen knowledge of his laws.'

ISLAM

Throughout its chequered career Judaism has maintained con-sistently the prophetic doctrine of ethical monotheism, and belief in the unity of God has equally been the battle-cry of Islam, pro-claimed daily from the minarets of its countless mosques in the familiar phrase, 'There is no God but Allah (God) and Moham-med is his prophet'. This was the foundation principle of the revelations the founder claimed to have received to restore the 'religion of Abraham' (Ibrahim of the Qur'an) at a time when the indigenous Semitic polytheism and animism in Arabia had been overlaid successively by Jewish, Abyssinian, Persian and, in the north, Byzantine Christian influences. He was not alone among

[1] Amos vii. 14.   [2] Macc. i. 13.

his countrymen in the sixth century A.D. in being profoundly dissatisfied with the religious situation, and several of his contemporaries in Mecca, Medina and Taif were by conviction monotheists. But it remained for Mohammed to raise Allah (Al Ilāh), probably a Meccan High God, to the position of 'Deity' to the exclusion of all minor divinities.

At the end of a retreat on Mount Hera, at the age of forty (*c.* A.D. 610), the angel Gabriel is said to have appeared to him and commanded him to 'Recite in the name of thy God who created man of a clot of blood'.[1] Thereupon he returned to Mecca and consulted his trusted friends who confirmed him in the belief that he had been called to become the prophet of his people and to make known the revelation of the one absolute Creator and Judge of the world. For twelve years he continued to have visions, but apart from his wife, Khadijah, his adopted son, Zaid ibn Harithah, his cousin, Ali, and Abu Bekr, his successor, a son of his faithful disciple Abu Quhāfah, he made few converts among his townsmen, who resented his attacks on the gods, and distrusted his intentions. Gradually, however, he collected a small band of followers, but his increasing success only led to more determined persecution by the Meccan leaders. In 622 he was compelled to flee for his life with Abu Bekr, and take refuge in a cave where he narrowly escaped capture. He then made his way to Medina (Yathrib) in northern Arabia, and succeeded in establishing the rule of Allah in the city with himself as dictator and warrior prophet. Henceforth his career was one of almost unbroken success, and just before his death in 632 Mecca capitulated.

At first he sought alliance with the Jews and Christians in defence of monotheism, but when his advances were rejected, bitter hostility ensued which has lingered through the ages. He never ceased to claim, however, that his revelation confirmed the Biblical record though his own knowledge of the Jewish and Christian Scriptures, and that of his successors as revealed in the contents of the Qur'an, was hopelessly confused. Abraham, Moses and Jesus are all regarded as prophets, and Israel is admitted to be the chosen people. The Founder of Christianity is alleged to have declared, 'Verily, I am the apostle of God to you, verifying the law that was before me, and giving you glad tidings of an apostle who shall come after me,

[1] Qur'an; Sura, 96, 1 f.

whose name shall be Ahmed.'[1] But as the Old Testament was known to him chiefly through Rabbinic Midrash and the apocalyptic writings, so the Gospel narratives came from apocryphal and heretical sources. He accepted the Virgin Birth, the Resurrection and the Ascension of Christ, and in later times the mystical movement in Islam, known as Sufiism, owed its inspiration largely to the Christian hermits of the desert, though it was also influenced by Gnostic theosophy, Hindu monism and Neo-Platonism, and in practice became a spiritualistic pantheism.

The doctrine of the Incarnation and the Trinity, however, appeared to Islam in the light of polytheism, and, therefore, an offence to the rigid monotheism which was the pre-eminent and consistent message of Mohammed and his followers. The idea of God is essentially that of the Hebrew prophets though lacking the ethical and spiritual content of the Jewish revelation. Allah is transcendent and omnipotent, all-powerful, all-knowing, all-willing, but he is not fundamentally righteous, and such morality as is enjoined is based on an appeal through fear. Love is restricted to those who do good, follow the prophet, believe and act rightly, and fight for the faith. As the word suggests, Islam is 'submission' to the sovereign will of Allah, and the way of salvation is obedience to His inscrutable will as revealed in the Qur'an dictated to Mohammed, as it is held, from an original code, 'the Mother of the Book', preserved in heaven.[2] The system, therefore, is legalistic, and in practice consists of the 'five pillars'—repetition of the *Kalimah* ('There is no God but Allah and Mohammed is His prophet'), and the performance of divine worship five times daily after the prescribed ablutions; the observance of the fast in the month of Ramadan; almsgiving, and making the pilgrimage to Mecca at least once during a lifetime when the sacred mosque must be circumambulated. Thus, Islam is little more than a belief in the absolute sovereign Ruler of the world who is merciful and compassionate to believers but whose demands hardly exceed those of ritual holiness.

[1] Sura, 61, 6. cf. Rodwell's Translation, p. 405 f.

[2] The theory of verbal inspiration is rigidly maintained by the Sunnis (orthodox) in the form that the actual words of the Qur'an are the literal utterances of Allah to His prophet, but the Mutazilite school hold that the teaching is eternal; the Arabic expression of it is mediated through Mohammed, a view that is regarded as definitely heretical.

CHAPTER IX

Sin and Atonement

ISLAM

The legalistic outlook of Islam arising from its doctrine of the supreme sovereignty of Allah has determined the Qur'anic idea of sin as opposition to divine commands and decrees. According to Moslem theology, to fail to perform the prescribed duties denotes a wrong attitude to God and false pride which may lead to a man becoming irreligious and even to his degenerating into polytheism and atheism. But sinfulness is acquired and not inherited. 'I declare not myself innocent: for the self habitually urges to evil, except in so far as my Lord hath compassion; verily my Lord is forgiving, compassionate.'[1] No method of atonement is offered or required by way of redemption. As Gardner says,

> all through the Qur'an the message is that while repentance must be sincere, it is a very easy matter, while forgiveness is a question scarcely worth troubling about, so simple is its attainment. Muhammad nowhere displays anguish of heart and contrition in the sight of a pure and holy God, and therefore does not demand that others should experience that of which he himself had no knowledge.[2]

Thus, it is affirmed in a late addition to the Qur'an that after 'an indecency or wrong against themselves' has been committed, all that is required by the offender is to 'remember Allah and ask forgiveness for their sins—and who forgiveth sins but Allah?—and do not persist in what they have done, when they know better. The recompense of such is forgiveness from their Lord and gardens through which the rivers flow, in which to abide.'[3] The reward of Paradise is, in fact, a bribe for well doing rather than the ultimate end of a life lived in a Godward direction steadily advancing in

[1] Sura xii. 53.
[2] W. R. W. Gardner, *The Qur'anic Doctrine of Sin* (Lond., 1914), p. 40.
[3] Sura iii. 128 f.

holiness as 'a light that shineth more and more unto the perfect day'. Nevertheless, repentance does imply sorrow for sin, purpose of amendment and restitution of the wrongs committed, though the actual offences are frequently ritual faults and neglect of arbitrary divine commands. For example, adultery, drunkenness, usury, perjury, theft, and murder are coupled with breaking the fast of Ramadan and neglect of Friday prayers, as 'great sins' (*kabira*), all and any of which can be removed by ablutions, almsgiving and similar meritorious actions. Moreover, the Deity is regarded as saving whom He will independent of any moral condition on the part of the believer. Some He guides into the right path, but this doctrine of predestination does not involve any idea of regeneration, and it is significant that in the Moslem version of the Garden of Eden story, the fall of Adam is not thought to have given the human race a bias towards evil, as in Augustinian theology.[1] On the contrary, it was beneficial since it drove man out of paradise to people the world,[2] and the only impediment experienced by 'fallen humanity' in consequence is a desire to sin, which can be overcome by explicit obedience to the commands of the Qur'an.

ZOROASTRIANISM

This Islamic doctrine of 'submission' is ethically on a rather lower plane than the Zoroastrian conception of sin as a refusal of the human will to conform to the 'Good Thought' of Ahura Mazda. By the endowment of intelligence man can 'frame his confession'[3] and determine his own destiny by following either the Right or the Lie. Unlike Oriental pantheism, evil is not regarded as an illusion of phenomenal and temporal existence which dissolves away when life is seen *sub specie aeternitatis,* or the moral order merely an impersonal unconscious process controlling alike gods, men and nature till the 'wheel of the law' ceases its wearisome revolutions in the attainment of *Nirvana*. In the Avesta evil proceeds from an external source (Angra Mainyu, or the demonic daevas) independent of the good God, but despite this dualism which in

[1] Sura ii. 33 ff.

[2] Sells, *Faith of Islam* (Lond., 1907), p. 245.

[3] Yasna xxxi. 11.

later Mazdaean theology, as we have seen, becomes clearly defined, the moral law is revealed by Ahura Mazda.

So far from seeking a way of escape from existence as synonymous with suffering and rebirth, life is represented as a gigantic struggle between good and evil, and man as working out his own salvation by persevering in well doing and following the good thoughts, the good words and the good deeds shown by the prophet who was sent to deliver humanity from the Lie. In this way he acquires merit which is transferred to his heavenly account and will render him solvent in the Day of Judgement, when he appears before Mithra (truth), Rashnu (justice) and Sraosha (obedience). If he can show a credit balance of merits, and thereby atone for his evil deeds,[1] he will have a safe passage across the Chinvat Bridge to the heaven (Garō demāna) of Ahura Mazda. Conversely, if his evil works predominate he is consigned to hell for ever, but if the good and evil balance equally he goes to an intermediate state (*Hamēstakāns*) till the Last Judgement. Thus, the soul's eternal condition is determined by its conduct on earth in relation to the moral law of Ahura Mazda.

Each man works out his own salvation, but under divine guidance and supported by the aid of angelic hosts,[2] though the actual sins from which he must keep himself unspotted are of a very varied character. Some are definitely ethical in principle, as, for example, sexual immorality, cruelty to animals and acts of violence, but most of them are of a ritual nature and include such acts as not disposing of nail parings, killing an otter or land-frogs, and giving food too hot to a dog, while no expiation is possible for burning or burying a corpse, eating human or dog flesh and unnatural vice. Therefore, despite the ethical trend of Avestan thought, it had only partially emancipated itself from its primitive background, and in Mazdaism ethical monotheism rapidly deteriorated into animistic polytheism when sin was supposed to produce demons.

EGYPT

In Egypt the Akhnaton revival made no attempt to deal with the question of sin and its removal, the worshipper of the one God

---

[1] Demerits are counterbalanced by a surplus of merits, though only in this sense can an evil deed be undone.

[2] Moulton, *Early Zoroastrianism* (Lond., 1913), pp. 164 ff.

manifest in the solar disc being content merely to pray for health and strength and provision for life in the conviction that then he would be 'safe from that which would terrify' him.[1] In the normal polytheistic religion, immortality in the Pyramid Texts (which originally only applied to the king) was secured without reference to ethical considerations, and the efficacy of potent spells and funerary rites always remained of primary importance in the Egyptian doctrine of the future life. But if physical purity aided by magical devices constituted the chief passport to the solar paradise, the weighing of the heart before Osiris in the Hall of the Double Truth after death was not without its influence on the practice of virtue.

If, as Breasted says, 'the requirements of the great judge in the hereafter were not incompatible with the grossest sensuality', both in this life and beyond the grave,

> nevertheless that was a momentous step which regarded felicity after death as in any measure dependent upon the ethical quality of the dead man's earthly life; and it must have been a deep, abiding moral consciousness which made even the divine Pharaoh, who was above the mandates of earthly government, amenable to the celestial judge and subject to moral requirements.[2]

But it was the king alone who was the personification of righteousness in a peculiar and unique sense as the earthly incarnation of the Sun-god, and the living manifestation of Horus. Moreover, if originally salvation was confined to the reigning monarch by virtue of his divine character and attributes, he was the effective mediator between the gods and man, and his eternal welfare was a matter of vital importance and public concern to the entire community.

After the VIth Dynasty, when every dead man became identified with Osiris, salvation took over a more individualistic form. It was not enough to concentrate upon the eternal blessedness of Pharaoh. Henceforth it was the aim and earnest endeavour of rulers and commoners alike to be 'righteous' and 'justified' at the Great Assize when the soul would be weighed in the balance by Anubis and judgement passed by Osiris, in whose final triumph over his accusing enemies frail mortals hoped to share, aided by powerful charms, spells, and funeral rites.

[1] Budge, *Tutankhamen, Amenism, and Egyptian Monotheism* (Lond., 1923), p. 115.
[2] *Development of Religion and Thought in Ancient Egypt* (Lond., 1912), p. 177.

H

In *The Book of the Dead* (chapter 125) the deceased is made to state the forty-two sins he has committed, some of which, such as deceitfulness, violence, immorality, injustice, avarice, and disobedience to parents, have an ethical significance. On the funerary inscriptions of the Feudal Age the virtues of the dead are set forth showing a sense of moral responsibility in the hereafter, while in certain hymns of the XIXth Dynasty, after the Akhnaton movement had spent its force and the nation had returned to polytheism, a penitential note is heard, as in the prayer addressed to Amon-Re, 'punish me not for my many sins. I am a witless man. All day long I follow my mouth like an ox after fodder, as at eventide'.[1]

BABYLONIA

Similarly, in most of the Babylonian penitential psalms and ritual texts, ethical concepts and ritual holiness are intermingled. Thus, the lofty prayer to Ishtar to 'dissolve sin and iniquity', concludes with a rubric concerning ceremonial lustrations and sacrificial offerings,[2] showing that Babylonian thought was really moving within the sphere of ritual holiness. Nothing could sound more sublime than the prayer:

Turn thou into good the sin which I have done;
May the wind carry away the error which I have committed!
Strip off my many evil deeds as a garment!
My god, my sins are seven times seven; forgive my sins!
My goddess, my sins are seven times seven; forgive my sins![3]

Yet the sins bewailed were for the most part ritual errors, often committed unwittingly, and the general outlook was that of the primitive conception of propitiation.

The same is true of the public lamentation ritual which from early times appears to have formed a part of the official cult on occasions of calamity. Thus, in the Sumerian texts and their Babylonian translations, the land is represented as being in a taboo-condition in consequence of which the gods have forsaken the cities and

[1] Erman, *The Literature of the Ancient Egyptians* (Lond., 1927), p. 307. Erman, *Sitzungsberichte d. Berliner Akademie d. Wissenschaften*, XLIX, 1911, pp. 1102 f.

[2] L. W. King, *The Seven Tablets of Creation* (Lond., 1902), I, pp. 233-7.

[3] Zimmern, *Bab. Busspsalmen*, IV, pp. 100-6. Langdon, *Babylonian Penitential Psalms*, pp. 43 ff.

brought disaster upon mankind. To restore their beneficence a fast is demanded together with elaborate purificatory ceremonies and appropriate magical lamentations.[1] The king is usually the speaker and by uttering laments in his official capacity he efficaciously voices the complaint of the entire people. It was upon these royal public incantations that the priestly and private psalms, hymns, dirges, litanies and confessions were modelled, and having been originally compiled for the use of the king as the chief and all-embracing penitent, they could easily be adapted to individual use. But whether public or private, there is no real sense of ethical sin and righteousness. Seldom are moral faults enumerated, and often the suppliant is quite at a loss to know why a calamity has fallen upon him, since he declares he has not neglected any of the ritual commands, failed to observe the appointed feasts, or despised the images of the gods. The daily cry of the penitent was the pathetic protest, 'I know not the sin which I have done; I know not the error which I have committed.' Somehow he had 'missed the mark', and brought down upon himself the wrath of tyrannical deities ever on the alert for the slightest infringement of the ritual order.[2]

Believing themselves to be surrounded by a hierarchy of evil spirits of various kinds and shapes, the Babylonians developed an elaborate propitiatory system of ritual atonement in which light, fire and water figured prominently. From the potency of water the 'curse of Eridu', or *síptu* (i.e. the curse of expiation) derived its efficacy till the spoken *síptu* became the all-important spell and the rite a series of exorcisms. Originally it was the life-giving water itself that drove forth the malevolent influences and so freed the person from evil contagion by absorbing it into itself. The act of expelling evil was called *kuppuru*, a term which raises a host of philological difficulties, but which probably signifies to 'blot out' or 'wash away'; the equivalent of the Hebrew *kapper*, 'to cover'.[3] Therefore, it conveyed the notion of a mechanical act of atonement in order to remove or carry away a taint from a defiled person or object.

[1] Jastrow, *Aspects of Religious Belief and Practice in Babylonia and Assyria* (New York, 1911), pp. 319 ff.

[2] Langdon, *Babylonian Penitential Psalms* (Oxford Edition of Cuneiform Texts, Paris, 1927), pp. 40, 41, 42–7.

[3] Zimmern, *Zeitschrift für Assyriologie,* XXVIII, p. 76. Gray, *Sacrifice in the Old Testament* (Oxford, 1925), pp. 69 ff.

Closely associated with this conception of purging evil is the kindred ritual of expiation by means of a scapegoat. As running water carries away impurity so an animal or human being may be employed as a sin-remover, as in the ceremonial of the Hebrew Day of Atonement. In Babylonia there is no definite evidence of the practice, though it is widespread among people in a primitive state of culture both in ancient and modern times, as, for instance, in North America where the Iroquois held a festival in the opening months of the year at which two white dogs without blemish were strangled and hung up near the door of the Council-house. A number of men were then selected to collect the sins of the tribe and concentrate them within themselves. The dogs were taken down and the guilt of the community was conveyed to them by a man who had had all the iniquity transfused into him. Laden with the sins of the people, the carcasses were placed in a pile of wood and burnt.[1]

A rite of this nature may lie behind the Sumerian ritual-text which describes an 'incantation by means of the horned wild goat'. Ea, the water-god, commands his son Marduk to take a scapegoat to the king bound by a curse, and place its head against his head as an act of atonement so that 'his poisonous tabu into his mouth may be cast'.

> May the king be pure, may he be clean.
> He who knows not the curse by which he is cursed,
> From his body may he chase it away.
> May the demon of his device stand aside.[2]

ISRAEL

On the reverse the scapegoat is said to have been 'unto the plain let loose' like the goat drawn by lot 'for Azazel' in the Hebrew annual purification at the 'going out of the year' about the time of the autumnal equinox. In the Sumerian text the atonement appears to have been for the king who communicates the sins to the scapegoat, but as in primitive society the life and prosperity of the nation were bound up with the health and vigour of the ruler, the Jewish observance may represent a later stage in the development of the rite when the high priest and his assistants made atonement for 'the

---

[1] Bauchamp, *American Antiquary*, vii, pp. 236 ff.

[2] Langdon, *Expository Times*, XXIV, 1912, pp. 11 ff.

holy sanctuary, the tent of meeting and for the altar, for the priests and for all the people of the assembly' by first censing the adytum of the temple and then sprinkling the sanctuary with the blood of a goat. After these cathartic rites had been performed, a second goat was taken, which in the preliminary stage of the ceremonies had been selected 'for Azazel'. Upon this animal the high priest laid his hands, confessing over it 'all the iniquities of the children of Israel and all their transgressions, even all their sins'. It was then led to the wilderness laden with the evil of the nation to carry its burden to the sin-receiver.[1]

The identification of Azazel is complicated by the fact that the Hebrew spelling has been deliberately changed to conceal the supernatural being to whom the name originally referred. But whether it be regarded as one of the dreaded *se'irim* who in the form of goat-demons were thought to haunt waste places, to whom sacrifices were offered in post-exilic times in Judaism,[2] or an evil genius not unfriendly to man who supplied the scapegoat to remove the danger of the *se'irim*,[3] in either case he was a personal being directly associated with the *elohim*. Now it was these *elohim* who were thought to be responsible for introducing evil into the world,[4] and, therefore, whether Azazel was a satyr or a leader of the 'fallen angels', he was intimately concerned with the absorption of evil through the scapegoat who bore away the sins of the people to a 'solitary land'[5] wherein the demons made their habitation. The part played by the goat was merely that of a carrier like the living bird in the purification of a leper,[6] and it was not until very much later that he was regarded as a sacrificial victim thrown over a precipice as an act of atonement.[7]

Although the observance has every appearance of representing the climax of the new religious movement instituted by Ezekiel in Babylonia and his priestly successors after the return from the Exile, the conception of sin is that of a ritual uncleanness which can be removed by substances such as blood charged with magico-religious potency, or driven forth by means of a scapegoat. It was apparently unknown either to Ezekiel or Zechariah, who regulated the

[1] Lev. xvi.   [2] Lev. xvii. 7.
[3] cf. Cheyne, *Zeitschrift für die Alttestamentliche Wissenschaft*, XV, 1895, p. 153 ff.
[4] Gen. vi. Enoch vi. 7, viii. 1, ix. 6, x. 4.
[5] Lev. xvi. 21 f.   [6] Lev. xiv. 7.   [7] *Yoma*, vi.

offerings and fasts in commemoration of national disasters without reference to it,[1] and Nehemiah, while he mentions a joyous feast on the first day of the seventh month, and the subsequent celebration of the Feast of Tabernacles,[2] is silent about the Levitical annual day of expiation, though he records a general fast on the 24th day. It may be, as Dr Kennett suggested, that it became 'the annual commemoration of the solemn act of penitence with which the Jewish community under Nehemiah inaugurated a new phase of religion at Jerusalem',[3] but in any case it incorporated primitive ideas and rites possibly derived from Babylonia.

Thus, in the fifth century B.C. the conception of sin and atonement in Israel was not very far removed from that which obtained elsewhere in the Ancient East. Expiation was mainly a mechanical process consisting of wiping away material uncleanness, though the fact that the goat was loaded with *all* the sins of the nation[4] may indicate that something more was involved than impaired ceremonial holiness. Moreover, the observance presupposes that the daily sacrifices did not suffice in themselves, and in later Judaism the Rabbinic penitential theory maintained that the more 'grievous' offences committed with 'a high hand' required expiation through the Day of Atonement ritual which to be efficacious must be performed with sincerity of heart and true repentance.[5] It is forbidden in the Mishna to say, 'I will sin and the Day of Atonement will effect atonement' . . . 'for transgressions that are between a man and his fellow the Day of Atonement does not atone, until the man appease his fellow'.[6]

Behind both the Levitical and Rabbinic doctrine lay the prophetic movement which placed the emphasis on the ethical conception of repentance, and in the main was in reaction against the sacrificial approach. Thus, Amos who had been brought up in the pastoral culture of Tekoa in isolation from the agricultural community, appears to have denied the divine origin of the institution, and refused to admit that it was part of the desert tradition. 'Did ye bring unto me sacrifices and offerings in the wilderness forty years, O house of Israel?' he asked,[7] while Hosea, his successor from the north, declared, 'I desire mercy and not sacrifice; and the know-

---

[1] Ezek. xlv. 18 ff. Zech. viii. 19.　　　　[2] Neh. vii. 73–viii.
[3] *Old Testament Essays* (Camb., 1928), p. 109.
[4] Lev. xvi. 34.　　　[5] *Yoma*, viii, 9.　　　[6] *Yoma*, ix.　　　[7] Amos v. 25.

ledge of God more than burnt offerings.'[1] Isaiah in the southern kingdom of Judah condemned even the sacrificial worship of the Temple. 'To what purpose is the multitude of your sacrifices unto me? saith the Lord: I am full of burnt offerings of rams, and the fat of fed beasts; and I delight not in the blood of bullocks, or of lambs, or of he-goats.'[2]

Jeremiah, in the strenuous days before the fall of the capital, fell back on an intense individualism in which sacrifice had no place. Each man must suffer for his own sins and each must be saved by his own righteousness. 'I spake not unto your fathers, nor commanded them, in the day that I brought them out of the land of Egypt, concerning burnt offerings or sacrifices. But this thing commanded I them saying, Obey my voice and I will be your God.'[3] The new covenant that Yahweh will make with them when the approaching desolation of the nation shall have worked its reforming purpose will be purely ethical, for then He will put His laws 'in their inward parts' and write it 'in their heart'. Then 'they shall teach no more every man his neighbour and every man his brother, saying, Know the Lord: for they shall all know me, from the least of them unto the greatest of them, saith the Lord: for I will forgive their iniquity, and their sin will I remember no more.'[4]

Reformers, however, are always liable to be reactionary and iconoclastic in their endeavours to sweep away abuses, and the zeal of the pre-exilic prophets went farther than the restored nation was prepared to go in the rejection of its deeply laid sacrificial covenant with its God. But the protest was not unheeded, and Ezekiel, the priest-prophet of the Exile, was as insistent as his predecessors on the need for a radical change of heart and ethical outlook when the Temple should be restored and worship re-established in the beauty of holiness.[5] While he condemned the former abuses[6] he looked forward to the time when the abominations should have been overcome and the backsliding people again offer an acceptable service in the sanctuary of Zion. The exile was for him a process of regeneration to bring about an internal spiritual change both in the individual and the nation. The new ritual order modelled on its heavenly counterpart[7] would include expiatory

[1] Hos. vi. 6.   [2] Isa. i. 11.   [3] Jer. vii. 22 f.   [4] Jer. xxxi. 33 f.
[5] Ezek. xxxvi. 26, xx. 40–4, xxxvii. 26 ff.
[6] viii. 5–18, xxii. 2–6.   [7] xl–xlviii.

sacrifices and a ceremonial law, but the ethical righteousness of Yahweh demanded above all things righteous conduct, though not to the exclusion of objective worship. Henceforth the sacrificial system in Judaism was invested with a spiritual content, and non-moral holiness no longer sufficed, though the actual setting of the ceremonial, as in the case of the Day of Atonement observances, was definitely primitive and carried over many of the earlier ideas. But the ethical teaching of Ezekiel and the Deutero-Isaiah gave a new significance to the Deity which inevitably reacted on the work of Ezra and his successors in the restoration of the religious organization of the post-exilic community.

The ancient symbolism of the blood as the life remained,[1] but instead of being outpoured in the 'sin-offering' (*ḥaṭṭōth*) to revivify and augment the power of the god, or drive forth the forces of evil, it became a compensation for injury and a symbol of an inward cleansing by true repentance, 'the sacrifices of God are a broken spirit'.[2] The outward oblation was conditioned by the spirit of penitence and contrition on the part of the offerer.[3] The 'peace-offering' (*shelem*) again, which in pre-exilic times was a sacred meal,[4] developed into the votive offering (*Nedar*), the free-will offering (*Nedabah*), and the thank-offering (*Todah*), or sacrifice of atoning efficacy offered in a thankful spirit.[5] Thus, the ceremonial banquet was on its way to acquiring a eucharistic meaning independent of propitiation.

In post-exilic Israel the notion of appeasing an angry god by sacrificial gifts, though not unknown in a former age among the Hebrews,[6] was transformed into that of expiation by 'covering' sin or 'compensating' for evil. The manipulation of the blood of the victim was directed to this end. In its crudest interpretation in the Old Testament, the blood is said to make atonement 'by reason of the nephesh', or soul-substance, contained therein,[7] as evil was removed in Babylonia by the 'waters of life', or carried away by a scapegoat. The vitalizing agent is poured out to cleanse and regenerate the persons or objects concerned, and this is the most

[1] Lev. xvii. 11. cf. iii. 2, 7, 13, vii. 1, 2, 7, viii. 14 f., ix. 2–4, 8 f. 12, 16, 18.

[2] Ps. li. 16 f.　　　　　　　　　　[3] Ps. iv. 5. Eccleus. xxxiv. 18 f., xlv. 16.

[4] 1 Sam. xi. 15, 2 Sam. vi. 17 f.　　[5] Lev. iii.

[6] 1 Sam. xxvi. 19. 2 Sam. xxiv. 25. Gen. viii. 21.

[7] Lev. xvii. 11. Dt. xii. 23.

fundamental principle in the institution of sacrifice throughout its long and complex history—the giving of life to promote and preserve life and remove impurity.[1] The slaying of the victim is only incidental as a means of liberating the life contained in the blood, and, therefore, the ritual centres not in the killing but in the disposition of the vital essence. The victim may be regarded as substitutionary in the sense that it gives its life-blood to revivify the god or regenerate the sinner, or, as in the case of Achan, the breaking of a taboo may require the extermination of the offender and all his belongings[2] in order to remove the taint from the entire community.

An infinitely loftier conception of redemptive suffering occurs in the so-called Servant Saga embedded in the later portion of the Book of Isaiah.[3] In these poems of uncertain date there emerges a vision of a mighty deliverance through the faithful discharge of a vocation of suffering. The Servant of Yahweh is represented as receiving a commission not only to raise up the tribes of Jacob and restore the preserved of Israel, but also to be a light to the Gentiles that salvation may be unto the ends of the earth. This mission is said to have been accomplished through much suffering. 'I gave my back to the smiters and my cheeks to them that plucked off the hair; I hid not my face from shame and spitting.'[4] Notwithstanding his innocence, 'it pleased Yahweh to bruise him', and put him to grief in order that his soul might be 'an offering for sin'. He was led as a lamb to the slaughter that he might make an act of vicarious atonement—'He shall see the travail of his soul and shall be satisfied: by his knowledge shall my righteous servant justify many: and he shall bear their iniquities.'[5]

Here is set forth a doctrine of representative suffering which transcends the Levitical conception of atonement and the later Rabbinical teaching. The Servant bears the sins of the people vicariously, though as Dr Bennett has pointed out, no explanation is given why sinners should be forgiven because an innocent man had suffered.[6] Nevertheless, it was recognized that sin must be

---

[1] cf. James, *Origins of Sacrifice* (Lond., 1933), pp. 256 ff. Hicks, *The Fullness of Sacrifice* (Lond., 1930), pp. 177 ff.

[2] Jos. vii. 16–26.

[3] Isa. xliii. 1–4, xlix. 1–6, l. 4–9, lii. 13–liii. 12.

[4] Isa. l. 6.   [5] Isa. liii. 10 ff.

[6] *The Religion of the Post-Exilic Prophets* (Lond., 1907), p. 327.

atoned for, and the sufferings of the righteous Servant are compared to the guilt-offering (*āshām*).[1] Something had to be done to
remove the consequences of sin, and one of the functions of the
Servant was to restore the captivity of the exiles and to renew their
prosperity.[2] But it was the deeper problem of vicarious atonement
that lay behind the conception of the Suffering Servant, and it was
this which became the fundamental doctrine of Christianity.

The idea of a suffering Messiah was foreign to Judaism, and to
suppose that any human being could atone for sins by a self-
offering was repugnant to the Jewish mind. Resort was made,
therefore, to animals without blemish and the punctilious observance of the Law, together with repentance, prayer, almsgiving, and
fasting, as the only available means of securing divine favour.[3]
With the destruction of the Temple in A.D. 70 the 'broken heart'
was declared to take the place of the sin-offering,[4] while he who
studied the precepts concerning the daily oblation[5] was regarded
as having offered sacrifice.[6] In the '*Amidah* the Jew still prays that
the sacrificial system may be restored, and in the meantime that
'the prayers of our lips may be accounted, accepted and esteemed
before Thee, as if we had offered the daily sacrifices at its appointed
time, and had been represented by our delegation'.[7]

CHRISTIANITY

In addition to this legalistic attitude, in the years immediately
preceding the Christian era the Messianic movement had made
considerable progress in Judaism during and after the Maccabaean
Revolt. But while the apocalyptic speculations, coloured to some
extent by Mazdaean influences, looked for the coming of a New
Age and the setting up of the divine rule on earth as the result of a
gigantic cosmic intervention, the Servant prophecies were not
brought into relation with this eschatology till they were given a
new prominence and interpretation by the mission of the Baptist
and his greater successor. In later Jewish thought while suffering

[1] Isa. liii. 10, 5, 8.   [2] Isa. xlix. 5 ff.
[3] *Yoma*, 23a.   [4] *Pes*, 158b.
[5] Exod. xxix. 38–42. Num. xxviii. 1–8.   [6] *Pes*, 60b.
[7] M. Gaster, *The Prayer Book and Order of Service* of Spanish and Portuguese Jews
(Lond., 1901), i, p. 11.

led men to repentance and was a means of expiation, the Messiah was regarded as the reigning king, and nowhere in the Rabbinical literature is he represented as the sin-bearer.[1] Jesus, on the other hand, appears to have fastened on the Servant conception as the basis of His Messiahship and come to regard His sufferings and death as essential for the establishment of His kingdom.

It is of course contended by many New Testament scholars that this aspect of the Gospel narratives represents the subsequent reflections of the Church on the person and work of Christ,[2] and the authenticity of the Sayings attributed to Jesus is a problem of such extreme complexity that it would be futile to attempt to discuss it within the limits of a volume of this character.[3] But whatever view is taken of the historical situation regarding the actual words put into the mouth of the Founder of Christianity, we are left in no doubt concerning the evaluation put upon Him by His followers within a very few years of His withdrawal from their midst. For them He was the victorious Messianic King and Saviour of mankind, the Suffering Servant whom God had raised from the dead and exalted to the right hand of the majesty on high, whence very shortly He would return in power and glory to gather together His elect and establish His kingdom. Moreover, prior to the destruction of Jerusalem in A.D. 70, it seems that this new movement appeared in the light of a dangerous heresy to the Jews calculated to destroy the Temple and have far-reaching effects on Judaism.[4] The persecution that broke out as a result of these fears scattered the sect throughout the surrounding region, and by about A.D. 40 congregations of Christians existed outside Palestine in such cities as Damascus and Antioch.

With the accession of St Paul, who had been brought up in the cosmopolitan environment of Tarsus in the province of Cilicia in Asia Minor,[5] and trained in a Rabbinical school at Jerusalem, not only was the missionary activity intensified but the theology was

---

[1] H. L. Strack-Billerbeck *Kommentar zum Neuen Testament aus Talmud und Midrasch*, II, pp. 273–92.

[2] cf. Bousset, *Kyrios Christos* (Göttingen, 1921), pp. 69 ff. F. C. Burkitt, *Christian Beginnings* (Lond., 1924), pp. 35 ff. Rawlinson, *The New Testament Doctrine of the Christ* (Lond., 1926), pp. 238 ff.

[3] For an investigation of the Passion-sayings, cf. V. Taylor, *Jesus and His Sacrifice* (Lond., 1937), pp. 88 ff., 125 ff., 192 ff.

[4] Acts vi. 14.   [5] Acts xxii. 3 f.

systematized as a redemptive religion. For him after his conversion on the road to Damascus, Judaism was a dead end because what it failed to do the crucified Messiah accomplished, so that to be in Christ was to be a new creature. The old covenant, he affirmed, had given place to the Gospel of the grace of God mediated through the risen and glorified Saviour which had already ushered in the new life of the apocalyptic 'Age to Come'. Those who had been buried with Christ in a symbolic 'baptism unto death' were also 'raised with Him through faith in the working of God who raised him from the dead'.[1] Henceforth the conditions under which they lived differed from those which constituted their former existence inasmuch as they had been freed from the law of sin and death and animated by a new life-principle enabling them to walk, not after the flesh, but after the Spirit.[2] In other words, for the apostle embracing Christianity meant passing out of the 'present age' with all its evil and entering the life of the Age to Come, wherein the Levitical law was no longer operative and the power of sin was destroyed by the victory of the triumphant Messianic Saviour, now exalted as the heavenly Christ.[3]

This mystery interpretation of the death of Jesus permanently separated the new sect from its Jewish moorings, for clearly there was no point of contact between such a theology and the current conceptions of either legalistic or apocalyptic Judaism since it amounted to a complete repudiation of the Jewish Law (Torah) which, according to the Rabbis, was invariable except by God and must endure till the Messianic era arose.[4] Thus, the seeds of disruption detected by the Jewish leaders in the original mission of Jesus came to fruition in the work of St Paul which completed the schism. Starting from a dualistic view of human nature, the apostle formulated a theory of two warring elements within the individual symbolized by flesh and spirit, and the 'two Adams'. It was from the bondage of evil that Christ had delivered man by His death and resurrection. He 'gave himself for our sins that he might deliver us out of this present evil world, according to the will of our God and Father'.[5] What the 'works of the Law' failed to accomplish in those who were 'Jews by nature', the 'Gospel of the grace of God

---

[1] Col. ii. 12. Rom. vi. 3 f.   [2] Rom. viii. 4. 2 Cor. v. 17.
[3] cf. S. H. Hooke, *The Age of Transition* (Lond., 1937), vol. I, p. 246.
[4] *Lev. R.,* xiii. 3, *Shemini.*   [5] Gal. i. 4.

through faith in Jesus Christ' achieved by giving a new kind of life. 'I died unto the Law that I might live unto God', and 'yet no longer I, but Christ liveth in me'.[1] This for him was 'the power of God unto salvation to every one that believeth'.[2]

The divine agent in the salvation of the soul he regarded as 'spirit' ($\pi\nu\epsilon\hat{\upsilon}\mu\alpha$) rather than 'grace', which in some passages he identified with Christ.[3] It is from the pneumatic gift that the cardinal virtues proceed—'love, joy, peace, long-suffering, kindness, goodness, faithfulness, meekness, temperance'[4]—not as reward for good works, as in the Law, but as a sanctifying influence bestowed by divine beneficence to complete man's redemption and spiritual regeneration. This new life of forgiveness in his theology constitutes a 'state of grace' because the 'justified' as 'spirit-possessed' enjoy divine 'favour' in a relationship of sonship with God.

To pass from the hampering conditions of the 'present age' to the glorious liberty of the sons of God in the 'age to come', was so tremendous a privilege that it could be explained in no other way, he thought, than as an act of divine election, so unmerited as to be outside human ingenuity. Consequently he concluded that man is justified, not by any efforts of his own devising, but by predestined grace. 'For whom he foreknew he also foreordained to be conformed to the image of his Son that he might be the firstborn among many brethren; and whom he foreordained them he also called, and whom he called them he also justified; and whom he justified, them he also glorified.'[5] Indeed he did not hesitate to describe the Deity under the figure of a Potter fashioning 'vessels of mercy' and 'vessels of wrath', who had 'mercy on whom he wills, and whom he wills he hardens',[6] though the language seems to suggest that while God could act in this arbitrary manner if He wished, actually He does not emulate the potter.[7]

This reaction to the problem of sin and redemption was doubtless the outcome of the psychological experience on the Damascus road, as the instantaneous conversion of St Augustine in the Milanese garden and of Luther on the Scala Santa was largely responsible for their 'twice-born' theology. A sudden awareness of the awful majesty and unapproachable holiness of God produces a sense of

[1] Gal. ii. 15-20. [2] Rom. i. 16.
[3] 2 Cor. xiii. 17. Rom. viii. 10 f. [4] Gal. v. 22. Rom. xiv. 17.
[5] Rom. viii. 29 f. [6] Rom. ix. 18, 23 f. [7] Rom. ix. 22.

utter unworthiness and exceeding sinfulness such as the prophet Isaiah experienced when he cried, 'Woe is me! for I am undone; because I am a man of unclean lips, and I dwell in the midst of a people of unclean lips.' But the *mysterium tremendum*, as Otto has pointed out, is also the *mysterium fascinans*, drawing men towards it in mystical communion to make it somehow their own.[1] It is this sense of self-abasement and allurement in the presence of the all-holy, of human nothingness and divine ability, that lies behind the doctrine of election and predestination based on the idea of God as the sole Cause of all reality and being, and all existence, purpose and function as divinely ordained according to an eternal predetermined plan. Grace, as Tertullian maintained, becomes an impersonal sanctifying force neutralizing the corruption of human nature, without the aid of which man is unable to do or think anything that is good. Therefore, he depends solely on God's saving purpose for salvation, and the divine predetermined will cannot be thwarted even by human unwillingness.

In opposition to Pelagius, who denied original sin and made grace an inclination of the will to good, St Augustine maintained that by the Fall Adam lost the power to will the good, and passed on to his descendants a corrupt nature as a *massa peccati* through 'seminal identity' with the primeval ancestor, from which deliverance could be secured only by justifying grace bestowed unconditionally and gratuitously on those whom God wills to save.[2] This doctrine of irresistible grace represents the extreme form of the Pauline conception of election, and if the Western Church did not give it its imprimatur, Augustinianism had a profound influence on the subsequent attitude to the problem of redemption both in Catholicism and Protestantism.

Closely connected with the question of salvation by grace is that of the manner in which the death of Christ restored divine favour. The fact of the Atonement was not questioned by any section of Christian opinion, but its interpretation has been a matter of controversy and speculation all through the ages. St Paul having made death the penalty for sin inherited from Adam, and the sacrifice of Christ the perfect offering which rendered justification possible inasmuch as it was a vicarious victory won on man's

[1] *The Idea of the Holy,* p. 31 ff., 35.

[2] *Enchiridion,* 99. cf. *Ep.* cxciv. 6, 8.

behalf,[1] the way was opened for a forensic evaluation of the mystery of redemption. Thus, as early as the second century, Irenaeus introduced the notion of the human race having been ransomed from the power of Satan, and this theory was further developed in the succeeding centuries, notably by Origen and Augustine, till Anselm substituted the word 'satisfaction' for 'ransom', and laid the emphasis on the vindication of Gods' honour instead of on a compact with the Devil.[2] By the willing surrender in perfect obedience to the incarnate life, all debts of sinful humanity were more than paid and the surplus merits placed to the account of the redeemed.

Against this penal hypothesis Abélard denied any necessity for a satisfaction for sin. The life and death of Christ were merely the supreme exhibition of the love of God and this in itself is sufficient to call forth loving trust in return, and induce the sinner to adopt the way of righteousness.[3] But, as St. Bernard contended, this interpretation seemed to be a denial of the 'sacrament of redemption', and the medieval Church, while it accepted the Abélardian rejection of the absolute necessity of a full satisfaction for sin, adopted Anselm's view of satisfaction as the basis of the doctrine of the Atonement. Thus, St Thomas Aquinas maintained that the restoration of fallen humanity was a work of divine grace and benevolence, and could have been achieved without the sacrifice of the Cross, but since God so chose to redeem mankind, nothing less than the method selected in His inscrutable wisdom could suffice as satisfaction for the offence against His honour.[4]

The Reformation brought a return to the cruder form of the penal theory and a new soteriology in which man's own part in his salvation was minimized in a doctrine of justification by faith carrying with it a forensic imputation of Christ's righteousness to believing sinners. The death on the Cross came in effect to be regarded, not only as redemptive, but also as an achievement

[1] I Cor. vi. 20, vii. 25. 2 Cor. v. 19, 21. Rom. iii. 24, viii. 1, 17, 32 ff. Gal. ii. 17, iii. 15 ff., iv. 4 f. Actually, however, St. Paul merely affirmed that the sacrifice of Christ availed on behalf of man's forgiveness by initiating a new dispensation of grace, the change being wrought not in God but in man, and God's dealing with the redeemed race in response to this offer of salvation.

[2] *Cur Deus Homo* (Lond., 1889), pp. 8 ff., 100 ff.

[3] R. S. Franks, *The Atonement* (Oxford, 1934), p. 2. H. Rashdall, *The Idea of the Atonement in Christian Theology* (Lond., 1920), pp. 437 ff.

[4] *Summa Theol.*, III, xlvi–xlix. cf. H. N. Oxenham, *The Catholic Doctrine of the Atonement* (Lond., 1869), pp. 85 ff.

accomplished 'in our stead' rather than 'on our behalf'. With it came a return to the Augustinian doctrine of justification and predestination in an even more absolute scheme of election. As Dr N. P. Williams says,

> all through the medieval period, within the bosom of the most imposing ecclesiastical system which the world has ever known, Augustine the predestinarian mystic was silently contending with Augustine the hier-arch, and the Reformation in the sixteenth century was in great measure the posthumous rebellion of Augustine against Augustine.[1]

From the predestinarian Augustine the Protestant leaders derived their contempt for unregenerated human nature, and their complete reliance on divine grace in the salvation of the soul. In interpreting justification in terms of justice and the imputation of Christ's merits, unlike Augustine however, they departed entirely from the institutional tradition of Christendom in the matter of the visible Church as a grace-bearing body. Redemption was a wholly un-merited gift of the Holy Spirit bestowed by virtue of the promise vouchsafed through Christ to the elect, made known through the foolishness of preaching. The Holy Spirit alone could bring men to Christ and Christ to man, it was contended, and salvation could only be appropriated by faith regarded as the free gift of God.

The function of the human will in the acceptance of the offer of salvation became a matter of acute controversy among the followers of Luther, while the Calvinistic sects were in dispute concerning Election and the Fall, Calvin and the Supra-lapsarians maintaining that the elect were predetermined irrespective of the Eden tragedy, whereas the Infra-lapsarians made the Fall the cause of perdition. Arminius, the leader of the latter school, placed the emphasis on grace as the beginning of the redemptive process, and so made the Atonement efficacious for all mankind irrespective of predestination. This was anathema to the Calvinists, and the expulsion of the Ar-minians from the Reformed Church of Holland in 1618 diffused the movement over Northern Europe, and played no small part in determining the theological outlook in England in the seventeenth and eighteenth centuries, notably in Methodism and among the Caroline divines.

---

[1] *The Ideas of the Fall and of Original Sin* (Lond., 1927), p. 321.

Meanwhile on the Continent the Counter-Reformation had met the challenge of Luther on its own ground, and in the protracted sessions of the Council of Trent (1545–64) the Augustinian doctrines as defined by Aquinas were affirmed, the reality of free-will safeguarded and the universality of Christ's redemption maintained. In reply to the Protestant attack on the Church and the Sacraments, the Council anathematized those who denied the efficacy of sacramental grace conferred *ex opere operato* as an integral element in salvation and justification, but no attempt was made to reconcile grace and the freedom of the will, a problem that gave rise to a heated controversy between the Jesuits and Dominicans. The condemnation of the Jansenists as the upholders of the doctrine of human depravity and irresistible grace, marks the formal declaration of the Holy See against the more extreme expression of Augustinianism.

Modern theological scholarship has necessarily undergone a profound change in outlook on the problem of sin and forgiveness in the light of present-day evolutionary thought. But while it is no longer possible to maintain a doctrine of the Fall based on the Genesis cosmology, sin as a breach of or failure to adhere to the sanctions recognized as the approved standard of social and religious conduct on the part alike of the individual and of society as a whole is a universal phenomenon in human history. The Pauline-Augustinian interpretation of the Eden story is only one of many attempts to explain the origin of evil in terms of ethical monotheism. Actually no reference to the Adam theory of original sin occurs in the canonical scriptures of the Old Testament, or in the Gospels.

The Jewish Rabbis saw in 'the evil imagination' the hand of Yahweh because the conflict between the good and evil *yetser* developed character.[1] Like the modern psychologist they realized that desires which cannot be satisfied lawfully may be diverted into other channels and by reassociation and redirection may be rendered not only harmless but also effective in the attainment of higher ends and ideals. But inasmuch as the Rabbinical theory appeared to make God ultimately responsible for sin even though He utilized it for beneficent purposes, later Judaism upon further reflection on the problem, sought an alternative explanation first

---

[1] Ecclus. xv. 11–17. cf. Ps. cxxx. 3, cxl. 2, li. 5.

in the very primitive story of the apostate angels, or *Nephilim*, preserved in Genesis vi and elaborated in the book of Enoch[1] and other
apocalyptic writings. As this hypothesis failed to account for the
continuance of evil after the flood, the transgression of Adam and
Eve was called in aid, although actually the idea of original sin
is not inherent in the story.[2] St Paul having adopted this theory as
the basis of his doctrine of the two Adams, redemption in Christian
theology came to be regarded in the light of the restoration of a
fallen race to a new state of grace through the atoning sacrifice of
Christ, though, as we have seen, the Church affirmed that the
conflict between good and evil is independent of the Fall. Only
man's original spiritual endowment of supernatural grace which
otherwise would have enabled him to triumph in the struggle was
lost by the initial catastrophe.

Apart, however, from speculations about origins, which are
singularly absent in the Synoptic Gospels, the Augustinian psychology is more fundamental than that of Pelagius, which failed to
realize how deeply laid in human nature is the conviction of sin
and the reality of suffering. It is this essential problem in all its
complexity that has led to the diverse interpretations throughout
the ages in every state of culture from the most rudimentary to the
most advanced. Pelagianism with its easy-going optimism gave
no answer to the ultimate question, just as the Abélardian theory of
the Atonement failed to supply the satisfaction for sin which the
storm-tossed soul requires. If Jesus said nothing about the origin of
evil

> in all that He said and taught [as Dr. Vincent Taylor points out], there
> is nothing to suggest that His object in dying was to confront men with
> the untiring love of God that through penitence and contrition they
> should be brought to trust and love Him in return. It is even doubtful if
> He thought of these things; they are the beliefs we read into the mind of
> Jesus seen with the eyes of the imagination, not the Jesus of history. . . .
> The thoughts of Jesus in relation to the Cross are 'objective' in the older
> sense in which this term was used in the theories of the Atonement;
> that is to say, it is a principle cardinal to His thinking that, as the Son of
> Man, He fulfils a ministry for men before God.[3]

[1] Enoch ix. 6, x. 7, 8, lxix. 9, 10.
[2] cf. N. P. Williams, op. cit., pp. 3–91.
[3] *Jesus and His Sacrifice* (Lond., 1937), pp. 302 f.

If Christianity was not able to supply a completely satisfactory philosophical and theological explanation of the problem of evil, it succeeded where most of its rivals failed because it brought transcendent Deity into a vital relationship with man, and made incarnate God at once a partaker of human suffering and the conqueror of sin by removing its causes.

CHAPTER X

Sacrifice and Sacrament

Theological discussion and popular misconceptions regarding the Christian doctrine of the Atonement have been determined hitherto very largely by the later Jewish sacrificial ideas connected with the notion of propitiation. Actually, however, there is no reason to think that Jesus Himself to any great extent was influenced by the worship of the Temple in arriving at His own evaluation of the Messianic role since apparently it was principally from the Suffering Servant prophecies that He derived His inspiration, though it is true He seems to have associated the outpouring of His life's blood with the covenant offering,[1] and to have connected His death with the Paschal symbolism. But in neither case is the Hebrew ritual propitiatory in the sense of appeasing the wrath of an offended god by a sacrificial gift on the principle of a life for a life.

Sacrifice was an established institution in the Ancient East when it was systematized in Israel along the line set forth in the Old Testament narratives in their present form, but, as we have seen in the case of the Day of Atonement observances, behind the ritual lay a long and complicated development. Unquestionably many primitive ideas lingered on in association with the various rites, and when Moses is said to have ratified the Covenant with burnt-offerings and peace-offerings,[2] he was regarded as acting in accordance with established custom, whether or not the action really can be attributed to him in the far-distant days of the wanderings in the desert. But the sprinkling of the blood of the victim on the altar and on the people does not involve the notion of substitutionary propitiation.

THE BLOOD COVENANT

Since the blood derives its efficacy in ritual from the primitive belief that it constitutes the animating principle of a living organism,

[1] Saint Mark xiv. 24.　　　　[2] Exod. xxiv. 1-11.

its outpouring establishes a vital alliance between those united in a blood-bond. Consequently, it was a potent agent in consolidating tribal relationships and effecting intercommunion between the human and the sacred order. Thus, as we have seen, in Australia, the men of the Undiaro kangaroo totem repair to a rocky ledge thought to be haunted by the spirits of ancestral kangaroos and open veins in their arms to allow the blood to stream over a stone representing the spot where a celebrated kangaroo went down into the earth in the *Alcheringa*, apparently to increase the species by a renewal of life and consolidate the alliance with their sacred ally.[1] Finally, the bond of union is further strengthened by a sacramental meal on the flesh of the totem killed and eaten ceremonially.

It is not to be supposed, as Robertson Smith urged, that sacrifice arose in an act of communion with a theanthropic animal at once god and kinsman,[2] or that a totemic organization lay behind the Hebrew rites. It is very doubtful indeed whether totemism ever existed among the Semites, but if it did occur it was at a period so remote from the time when Hebrew tradition was organized that it had long since ceased to be operative. Moreover, as it does not represent a universal phase in primitive society,[3] it can hardly have been the originating cause of sacrifice everywhere, though as a secondary development in the social organization of certain hunting people, it is illustrative of the bond-covenant which in more advanced cultures found expression in the institution of sacrifice.

From time immemorial, as Tylor maintained,[4] simple 'gifts' in kind may have been made to propitiate angry and malevolent gods and spirits, but as a ritual institution sacrifice belongs essentially to a later stage in human society when the community was organized on a theocratic basis with certain individuals, notably the divine king, set part to exercise representative functions in relation to the gods upon whom the human group and the processes of nature depended for their well-being. To establish and maintain a bond of union with the benevolent powers, and so to enable them to perform their beneficent offices on earth, as well as to meet the forces of death and destruction by a fresh outpouring of vital potency to

[1] Spencer and Gillen, *Native Tribes of Central Australia*, pp. 195 ff., 199 ff., 206 ff.
[2] *Religion of the Semites* (Lond., 1927), pp. 245 f., 226.
[3] cf. chap. I, pp. 46 ff.
[4] *Primitive Culture*, II, p. 375.

'cover' or purge away sin, appropriate offerings were made at critical junctures, and at the special seasons of the agricultural year. The blood being the life constituted the universal and indispensable constituent of sacrifice, except, as in the higher thought of Greece,[1] where the vegetation offering was introduced as a substitute, and then the bloodless oblation was still regarded as having life-giving qualities. Normally, however, as the story of Cain and Abel suggests the blood rite was thought to be the more efficacious, and certainly the Hebrews were no exception to the rule, since the firstlings of the flocks and herds were more acceptable to Yahweh than the first-fruits of the ground.[2] Thus, not only was the Covenant ratified in blood, but the redemption of the firstborn in Israel[3] was probably a survival of a grim practice that obtained in earlier times before an animal replaced the human victim.

HUMAN SACRIFICE

The widespread custom of killing the divine king when he showed signs of diminishing virility,[4] was doubtless largely responsible for the development of human sacrifice in agricultural communities since it led to the substitution of captives and other commoners for the royal victim who gave their lives to augment the powers of the gods that the processes of nature night be maintained. But the practice was not confined to this aspect of the vegetation cultus. Thus, for example, the presence of bodies of children in the foundations of buildings in Palestine and elsewhere reveals that oblations of this character were made to strengthen the walls of houses and cities,[5] as well as to revivify gods and divine kings, and renew vegetation at its source, while we need go no further than the pages of the Old Testament to be reminded that children were passed through the fire to Moloch (i.e. the king) in the valley of Hinnom prior to the Josiah reformation in 621 B.C.[6] From the same source comes the familiar story of the vow of Jephthah and its execution,[7] and if that of the offering of Isaac is in the form of an eighth-century prophetic Midrash, the view that the incident is recorded to show

[1] Porphyry, *De Abstinentia*, II, 56.   [2] Gen. iv. 1–5.
[3] Exod. xiii. 13, 15.   [4] cf. chap. IV. pp. 112 f.
[5] Joshua vi. 26. 1 Kings xvi. 34.   [6] 2 Kings xxiii. 10.
[7] Judges xi. 30 ff.

that human sacrifice was repugnant to Yahweh is groundless. In ancient times doubtless the injunction in the 'Book of the Covenant' (Exod. xx. 22–xxiii. 33)—'the firstborn of thy sons shalt thou give unto me'—was literally enforced, as is suggested by the annual commemoration of that terrible night when the angel of Yahweh set forth on his bloody campaign against the Egyptians.[1]

THE PASSOVER

The origins of the Paschal ritual are wrapped in obscurity, but as Frazer says, 'the one thing that looms clear through the haze of this weird tradition is the memory of a great massacre of firstborn'.[2] If it were a ritual offering on behalf of the king, it falls in line with widespread custom since it appears to have been part of a New Year Festival (in the month of Abib or Nisan) when the renewal of the vigour and vitality of the king had to be made, to secure the prosperity of the land. The firstborn, on this hypothesis, were slain in the first instance as a substitution for the royal victim, but in Israel the divine kingship had undergone considerable modification, and was confined apparently to the southern kingdom and the Davidic cultus. Consequently, in the comparatively late Priestly tradition of the Passover, only a few traces of the earlier observances have survived. Moreover, when it was restored in the reign of Josiah,[3] it seems that the feast had not been kept with the proper rites since the time of the judges. By then a ritually perfect lamb or kid had replaced the firstborn sons of the Hebrews, killed at the full moon at the vernal equinox. The animal victim was eaten during the night with bitter herbs and unleavened bread. The blood was smeared on the door-posts and the lintel, and the inmates were confined to the house till the morning. For seven days the festival continued, during which time unleavened bread was eaten.

The coincidence of the event with the Spring Festival is suggestive of a fertility motive as is the lunar reference. Thus the cult of the Mother-goddess and the life-giving powers of women were identified with the moon. It was under this guise that Diana gave

---

[1] Exod. xii. Deut. xvi. 1–8.
[2] *G.B.*, Pt. IV ('Dying God'), p. 176.
[3] II Kings xxiii. 21 ff.

abundance to the harvest and bestowed offspring on childless women,[1] while in the Aztec calendrical rites the heart of a human victim was offered to the moon in February at midnight to promote fertility, and on the following day a feast was held on his flesh.[2]

Doubtless in the Paschal rite the flesh was eaten raw in the beginning as otherwise the prohibition in Exodus xii. 8, 9, would be meaningless[3]; the purpose of the meal being that of imbibing sacramentally the inherent vitality of the victim, as in the Arabic camel sacrifice in the fifth century A.D. described by Nilus. Like the Thraco-Phrygian worshippers of Zagreus who consumed the raw flesh of bulls and calves,[4] the Arabs appear to have drunk the warm blood of the camel victim before 'hacking off pieces of the quivering flesh and devouring them raw with such haste, that in the short interval between the rise of the day star which marked the hour for the service to begin, and the disappearance of its rays before the rising sun, the entire camel, body and bones, skin, blood, and entrails, is wholly devoured'.[5] In this way the life of the sacred victim, which originally was itself divine, was absorbed by all who shared in the ceremony, and the common bond between them re-established and confirmed. The sprinkling of the blood on the lintel and door-posts was a later addition to the Passover narrative, derived from the practice of smearing houses with blood to repel demons.[6] This would be regarded as an efficacious barrier against 'the destroyer' when the story was formulated, but the rite does not appear to have anything to do with the feast as such. It is not clear whether it was to be a sign to the Israelites or to the 'angel',[7] and in either case, if the blood was poured on the altar prior to the feast it could hardly have been also smeared on the door-posts.[8]

A more important and significant addition to the rite of the firstborn (*Pesach*) is the *Maṣṣôth*, or Feast of Unleavened Bread,[9]

---

[1] Catullus, XXXIV, 9–20. Cicero, *De natura deorum*, II, 26, 28 f.
[2] J. de Acosta, *The Natural and Moral History of the Indies* (Lond., 1880), II, 348 f.
[3] Robertson Smith, *Religion of the Semites*, p. 345.
[4] Firmicus Maternus, *De err. prof. rel.*, VI, p. 16 (Ziegler).
[5] *Religion of Semites*, p. 338.
[6] Curtiss, *Primitive Semitic Religion To-day* (Chicago, 1902), pp. 226 ff.
[7] Exod. xii. 13, 23, 27, xi. 4.
[8] Oesterley, *Sacrifices in Ancient Israel* (Lond., 1937), p. 101.
[9] Exod. xii. 15 ff.

which belongs essentially to the agricultural community as an offering of the first-fruits. The mention of a second Passover in Numbers ix. 6–12 reflects the unsettled relations which the pastoral *Pesach* originally bore to the agricultural harvest festival, the two apparently not being at first simultaneous.[1] Both, however, were celebrated at the vernal equinox at the time of the barley harvest,[2] when in Babylonia on the seventh of Nisan the Annual Festival in honour of Shamash, the Sun-god, was held in Sippar. In this connexion it is significant that Psalm lxxx., with its references to Yahweh 'shining forth' from between the Cherubim, occurs in the Jewish liturgy at this feast,[3] suggesting that solar ideas may have lingered on in Judaism long after the ritual had lost its original meaning, as in so many other instances. But the predominant theme was the offering of the first-fruits, symbolized by the waving of the sheaf of barley ('*omer*) before Yahweh on the second day (Nisan 16th) to promote the fertility of the crops during the forthcoming season, just as seven weeks later at the end of barley-harvest and the beginning of wheat-harvest, two 'wave-loaves' baked with leaven[4] were offered at the Feast of Weeks (*Shābu'oth*).

Taken collectively this ceremonial shows that the Hebrew agricultural festivals were typical vegetation rituals directed towards the renewal of the crops. The taboo on leaven and the extreme care taken to remove every possible trace of it as the sun set on the 13th of Nisan,[5] represent the expulsion element characteristic of first-fruit observances in preparation for the offering and solemn sacramental eating of the new crops.[6] In the case of the Passover in its composite form as *Pesach* and *Maṣṣôth* combined, the Paschal meal became a sacrificial feast upon the animal victim, but in the process of transforming the rite into an aetiological myth to commemorate the Exodus, the Hebrew annual spring festival has lost its original significances and only a few traces of the earlier customs and beliefs survive. But though greatly modified they are sufficient to indicate the nature of the event as a seasonal sacrificial and

---

[1] Hirsch, *Jewish Encylopaedia,* IX, 554 *b.*

[2] Exod. xii. 15 ff., Lev. xxiii. 10. Deut. xvi. 9.

[3] Thackeray, *The Septuagint and Jewish Worship* (Lond., 1921), pp. 40 ff. Oesterley, *Myth and Ritual,* pp. 115 f.

[4] Lev. xxiii. 17.   [5] Exod. xxiii. 18, *Pes.* I, 1.

[6] J. R. Swanton, *43rd B.B.A.E.* (Wash., 1911), pp. 113 ff. C. MacCauley, *5th R.B.A.E.* (1887), pp. 522 ff. F. G. Speck, *Ethnol. of Yuki Indians* (Philad., 1909), pp. 86 f.

sacramental ritual to promote the prosperity of the community and its crops during the ensuing year, in which a propitiatory element played only a very secondary and unimportant part, as in any other Annual Festivals in the Ancient East.

THE EUCHARIST

In post-exilic Judaism the Passover remained primarily a communion-sacrifice, though in two passages in the Talmudic literature the blood of the Paschal lamb is spoken of as 'covenant blood'.[1] Jeremias thinks that Jesus put this interpretation on Zechariah ix. 11 at the close of His ministry,[2] and, therefore, regarded 'His death as an atoning death which establishes the new and eternal communion of a humanity cleansed from sin with its God—the communion of the kingdom of God'.[3] But the institution of the Eucharist is a problem which presents peculiar difficulties, and it is by no means clear whether it was the actual Paschal meal as the Synoptists assert, that Christ and the disciples partook of on the night before He suffered,[4] or, as the Fourth Evanglist appears to suggest, a special gathering before the feast.[5] Against the Synoptic view is the difficulty of reconciling the events described in connexion with the trials and crucifixion, especially the bearing of arms,[6] with the Jewish observance of the Feast Day. A rebellious teacher might have been executed on a festival,[7] but the priests and people presumably would have been too much occupied at this season with their Paschal duties to conduct a public trial amid popular demonstrations. Moreover, although the Synoptic tradition places the Supper on the night of the Passover, it records the warning of the Sanhedrin against taking action during the festival—'not on the Feast-day, lest there be a riot'[8]—it is possible to read into Luke xxii. 15, 16 an unfulfilled desire on the part of Jesus to partake of the Passover.[9] It is also remarkable that no mention is made of the

[1] Targum, Zech. ix. 11; Mekh, Exod. xii. 6.

[2] Saint Mark, xxx. 5.

[3] *Die Abendmahlsworte Jesu* (Göttingen, 1935), p. 82.

[4] Mark xiv. 25. Luke xxii. 13. Mat. xxvi. 18.

[5] Saint John xviii. 28, xix. 14.

[6] Mark xiv. 47.   [7] *San,* xi. 3.

[8] Mark xiv. 2, Mat. xxvi. 5.

[9] Oesterley, *The Jewish Background of the Christian Liturgy* (Oxford, 1925), p. 181.

Paschal victim, or the liturgical narrative of the Passover, in either the Marcan or the Matthaean accounts of the meal, while the word used for the bread (ἄρτος) suggests that it was unleavened (*matsoth*; *azyme*). Again, instead of the four cups prescribed for the Paschal meal, only one cup was passed round among the apostolic company.

But if there are cogent reasons for dissociating the Eucharist from the Passover,[1] it is by no means easy to determine the precise nature of the gathering. Some form of *Kiddûsh*, or quasi-religious meal held on the eves of Sabbaths and Feasts, is suggested,[2] but in ordinary circumstances there would have been no such 'sanctification' on the Thursday night, since the *Kiddûsh* immediately precedes the actual celebration of the day.[3] The feria, or week-day, rite consists simply of a blessing appropriate to the meal, varying according to the viands. Therefore, despite the criticism of Jeremias,[4] Leitzmann[5] and Otto[6] may be correct in assuming that the Last Supper was a *Ḥaburah*, or gathering of groups of friends, which took the form of a Passover-Kiddûsh, having been put forward a day in view of the approaching crisis. Realizing that the blow might fall at any moment, and having a particular desire to eat, or rather to anticipate, this Passover with His disciples before He suffered,[7] Jesus may have gathered them together on the Thursday evening for a *Ḥaburah*, as doubtless He had been wont to assemble them from time to time during His ministry to discuss at a meal the Messianic mission.[8]

The stories of a miraculous feeding of a great multitude appear to be connected with ritual gatherings of this nature. That the Early Church attached considerable importance to these traditions is clear since they are the only miracles recorded in all four Gospels. Indeed, there is no other incident before the Passion, except the

[1] For the opposite view see Dalman, *Jesus-Joshua* (Leipzig, 1922), pp. 86 ff. Chwolson, *Das Letzte Passamahl Christi* (Leipzig, 1918), p. 11. Jeremias, *Die Abendmahlsworte Jesu*, pp. 8–13.

[2] cf. G. H. Box, *Journal of Theological Studies*, III, pp. 359 ff. X, pp. 106 f. Oesterley, op. cit., pp. 159 ff. G. Dix, *The Shape of the Liturgy*, 1945 pp. 50 ff.

[3] Burkitt, *Journal of Theological Studies*, XVII, p. 294.

[4] Jeremias, op. cit., p. 30 ff.

[5] *Messe und Herrenmahl* (Bonn, 1926), p. 210.

[6] *Reich Gottes und Menschensohn*, pp. 234 ff.

[7] Saint Luke, xxii. 15.

[8] Schweitzer, *Quest of the Historical Jesus* (Lond., 1910), p. 374. Otto, op. cit., p. 241.

work of the Baptist, which is mentioned by all the Evangelists. St Paul before the Synoptic narratives were put together, had connected the Eucharist with the 'spiritual food' which sustained Israel in the desert, where the feedings are said to have occurred, and a reference to the manna forms the transition from the Feeding Story to the Eucharistic discourse of John vi. If these 'feedings' were anticipatory of the coming Messianic banquet, the sacramental interpretation is near at hand; and the whole setting of the miracles is indicative of a mystical significance. Thus, emphasis is laid on Jesus first giving thanks (John vi. 23), and the five loaves are called ἄρτος in the singular, as in 1 Cor. x. 16 f., xi. 27. The disciples are rebuked for their hardness of heart because 'they understood not concerning the loaves',[1] and judgment is passed on the crowd for following Jesus, not because they saw σημεῖα but because they 'ate of the loaves and were filled'. As St Paul condemned the sordid excesses at the Corinthian Supper,[2] so the Fourth Evangelist contrasts the barley loaves with the 'true bread', Jesus. 'Labour not for the mat which perisheth, but for the meat which abideth into eternal life.'[3] It is the deeper significance of the ritual meal that matters, for 'the flesh profiteth nothing'; the ῥήματα of the Logos made flesh are spirit and life.

It would seem, then, that the origin of the Eucharist must be sought in whatever lies behind the Feeding Stories, reaching its climax in the Upper Room on the eve of the Crucifixion and there brought into conjunction with the Passover. All the accounts agree that it was during the Supper that the rite was instituted, though however the meal is understood there were certain departures from the normal order of the Jewish observance, probably because it was a gathering hurriedly assembled to meet an urgent situation. But the Paschal associations remained and gave a special significance to what was said and done.

The essential elements in a *Kiddûsh* were the 'blessings' over the food and drink according to prescribed formulae: 'Blessed art thou, O Lord our God, King of the universe, who createst the fruit of the vine'; 'Blessed art thou, O Lord our God, king of the universe, who bringest forth bread from the earth.'[4] After the benediction over the wine, the sanctification of the day followed. Two loaves

---

[1] Saint Mark vi. 52.   [2] 1 Cor. xi. 20 f.   [3] Saint John vi. 26 f.
[4] *Tosephta Berakhoth*, vi, 24. cf. Singer, *Daily Prayer Book*, p. 124.

symbolized the double portion of manna, one of which was cut in pieces and distributed to the guests, and the other was reserved for the next day. *Before* the meal began, the head of the family chanted the praises of a virtuous wife[1] and those assembled joined in singing songs on this theme. A solemn washing of hands preceded or followed the blessing of the wine according to the particular rite observed, and on the eve of Sabbath two benedictions over the cup were prescribed, though the Rabbinic schools of Hillel and Shammai disputed the order in which they should be used.[2]

If the Eucharist was instituted at a ceremony of this character, either the meal did not begin with bread and wine, and Jesus blessed the elements when they came; or, if the meal began with the blessings of the bread and wine, the duplication of the blessings point to an innovation implying that the previous blessings, *Kiddûsh* or otherwise, were invalid, and they were repeated because henceforth they were to have a new significance. The reason for the *Kiddûsh* of every festival and Sabbath is its historical reference. On Sabbath the remembrance of the Creation and Exodus both occur because of the differing explanations in the two recensions of the Fourth Commandment,[3] and, if the words 'do this as my memorial'[4] were uttered during the Supper, they were singularly appropriate to the occasion.[5] By identifying the cup with the blood of the covenant, Jesus made the Eucharist a new *Kiddûsh*, introducing a new division of time, Jewish chronology being divided into two parts: from the Creation to the Exodus, and the Exodus onwards. As Leitzmann says, in offering Himself like the Paschal lamb at the last of the solemn banquets with His disciples, Christ in effect said, 'I am the sacrificial victim whose blood is poured out for you—that is, for the believing folk—to seal a new Covenant with God, and whose blood is slain for you.'[6]

Therefore, if the meal was not the actual Passover itself, it had a

[1] Prov., xxxi, 10–31.

[2] *Ber*, viii, 1. *Pesahim*, x, 2.

[3] Exod. xx. 10. Deut. v. 15.

[4] 1 Cor. xi. 24 f. These words in the *textus receptus* of Saint Luke xxii. 14–16 are omitted in several important manuscripts. cf. Westcott and Hort, *The New Testament in the Original Greek* (Camb., 1881), appendix, pp. 63 f. Introduction, p. 175.

[5] The author is indebted to Mr Loewe for a good deal of this information concerning Jewish practice in relation to the *Kiddush*.

[6] *Messe und Herrenmahl*, p. 221.

very real Paschal significance, and it was certainly so understood by the first generation of Christians. The Snyoptic narratives, as we have seen, identify the two events and bring them both into conjunction with the death of Jesus, as in some sense the offering of the blood of the new covenant, be it that of the Paschal lamb or the Mosaic institution.[1] For St Paul Christ was the Paschal Lamb on whom the faithful feed as the true Passover.[2] As the old covenant had been sealed in blood, so the Eucharistic wine was none other than the blood of Christ in which He sealed the new covenant comparable to the Paschal memorial before Yahweh of the deliverance from Egypt.[3] 'The cup of blessing which we bless, is it not a communion of the blood of Christ? The bread which we break, is it not a communion of the body of Christ?'[4] Moreover, 'as often as ye eat this bread and drink this cup ye proclaim the Lord's death till he come'.[5] From these words it can be argued that the sacramental and sacrificial aspects of the rite were united in the mind of St Paul who interpreted the Eucharist as a divinely appointed *koinonis*, the common participation in the blood and body of Christ and an *anamnesis* of His atoning death re-enacting the covenant offering as the drama of redemption till the *parousia*, the goal of the *opus redemptionis*. Thus fortified and sustained, the believer lives the life of the age to come, as in St John vi. 53 f.

SACRAMENTS AND THE MYSTERY RELIGIONS

This mystery interpretation of the Eucharist would seem to be a natural consequence of his doctrine of the initial sacrament of the Christian Church since he regarded baptism as a burial with Christ unto death and a rising again to newness of life, so that henceforth death has no more dominion over the initiate who lives under conditions entirely different from those which constituted his former existence. Having been freed once and for all from the law of sin, and animated by a new life-principle, he walks not after the

---

[1] Saint Mark xiv. 24.

[2] I Cor. v. 7.　　　　　　[3] I Cor. x. 1–5.

[4] x. 16. 'Communion' can be rendered as 'participation' or 'fellowship'.

[5] ix. 26. In what sense the apostle used the word 'proclaim' is a matter of acute theological controversy, but later it was certainly understood as a mystery of sacrificial representation.

flesh but after the spirit as a new creature.[1] But, nevertheless, his sacramental outlook differed from that of the pagan Mysteries in several important respects. So far as we know, initiates in these cults were neither baptized into the name of the saviour-god or goddess, nor were they the recipients of a pneumatic gift as a result of the ritual of lustration. For St Paul incorporation into the person of Christ through the operation of the divine Πνεῦμα was the central feature of the redemptive process.[2] Moreover, the new-born Christian initiate passed from death unto life by a mystical experience rather than through a magical rite, and having attained as a new creation to the measure of the stature of the fullness of Christ, he became a member of a spiritual order. Union with Christ for St Paul, in short, was a personal mystical relationship by a conscious act of self-renouncing trust involving death to the old life and a rising again in newness of life and status in Christ, in whom the initiate was 'sealed with the Holy Spirit of promise'. Thus, the *unio mystica* replaced the experience of deification which characterized the pagan Mystery cults. Baptism was merely the *rite de passage* through which entrance was gained to the higher spiritual life of the age to come with all its possibilities for growth in Christ-likeness till finally when the mortal body had put on immortality and death was swallowed up in victory, the glorified soul attained the Beatific vision.[3]

In this sacramental process, however, ritual holiness does not suffice, as is clearly demonstrated by the unmeasured terms in which the scandals of the Corinthian Eucharistic observance are condemned. Communion being nothing less than a reception of the body and blood of Christ, to eat and drink unworthily, it is contended, is to become guilty of rather than reconciled through the offering of the Cross.[4] Therefore, as the fruits of a worthy participation are revealed both in this life and that of the world to come, so the consequences of unworthy reception bring physical ills—'for this cause many among you are weak and sickly and not a few sleep'.[5] But normally in a Mystery cult initiation was an end in itself irrespective of any ethical considerations, whereas in Pauline

[1] Rom. vi. 3–5, viii. 4. 2 Cor. v. 17. Col. ii. 12.

[2] Gal. iii. 27. Rom. vi. 3. 1 Cor. xii. 12 f. Acts i. 15. Rev. iii. 4, xi. 13.

[3] 1 Cor. xv. 51 ff.   [4] 1 Cor. xi. 27.   [5] 1 Cor. xi. 30.

theology the fruits of the spirit are regarded as evidence of new life in Christ.

(*a*) *The Eleusinia.*—At Eleusis the new birth was effected by a long series of purificatory ceremonies preliminary to the revelation of the hidden secret of Demeter in the Hall of Initiation. While we are still very uncertain about what was revealed at the supreme moment in the sacred drama, there is no ground for the assumption that a mystic sacramental communion constituted the climax of the ritual. Whatever the drinking of the κυκέων may have signified, it was clearly not the central mystery of the cult, and it is very doubtful whether in itself it had any sacramental significance at all. So far as we know at no point in the protracted ceremonial did the initiate receive the divine substance of the goddess, or enter sacrificially into her passion.

It is possible that the admonition to the priest to 'cut up and minister the cake, and distribute the liquid to the votaries', recorded in the fragmentary inscription of the Kabeiroi mysteries from Tomi on the Black Sea,[1] indicates a sacramental element in the Samothracian cult; but the restoration is conjectural and from the few fragments we possess it is impossible to determine what was done or implied at the meal. Taken as it stands, the inscription merely records the practice of communal meals in this society which may or may not have been sacramental in character.

(*b*) *The Dionysiac.*—In the orgiastic Thraco-Phrygian worship of Dionysos, the *omophagia*, as we have seen, may have been a means of entering into communion with the god as in the Arab camel rite, and there are indications that the devouring of live bulls at certain feasts of Dionysos was familiar to the Athenians in the fifth century B.C.[2] Again, according to Euripides, the initiated votary in Crete became one with his divinity after he had fulfilled 'the solemn rite of the banquet of raw flesh',[3] and this rite is connected with Orphism by the Christian Fathers.[4] Now, it is doubtless a fact that the Dionysos whose story and whose rites were given such a prominent place in Orphic belief and practice was the Dionysos of Crete[5] with whom was associated this very primitive form of

---

[1] Dieterich, *Eine Mithrasliturgie* (Leipzig, 1903), p. 106. Farnell, *E.R.E.,* VII, p. 631.
[2] Reinach, *Cultes, Mythes et Religions* (Paris, 1906), vol. II. pp. 95 ff.
[3] *Frag.*, 472, Nauck.
[4] Clem. of Alex., *Protrept.,* II, 12, 17. Firm. Mat., *De err. prof. rel.*, p. 84.
[5] cf. Guthrie, *Orpheus and Greek Religion* (Lond., 1935), pp. 110 ff.

chthonian ritual to secure communion with the god. Moreover, from the time of Homer onwards, Thracian orgiastic bull worship had gained very considerable popularity in Greece despite its unhellenic character, and the sacramental eating of the bull was familiar in the time of Aristophanes.[1] That the Dionysiac had been absorbed by the ancient Cretan culture as it was incorporated in Orophism is beyond question, and it would not be surprising if the orgies, being a characteristic feature of the worship, also found a place in the Orphic mysteries. But in becoming a mystical movement based on the story of the Titans' crime, which was introduced into the myth, the wilder rites would naturally be repellent, and as the Jews made the drinking of sacrificial blood taboo, so the Orphics placed a ban on killing and eating animals to eliminate the *omophagia* from the Dionysian worship they had inherited.

Therefore, long before the beginning of the Christian era, the ancient sacramental orgy had ceased to be part of the process of becoming *bakchos*, and in its place purity of life was sought by abstention from certain actions, some of which had a moral significance and others had not. Initiation, regarded as a quasi-magical operation, was thought to be an essential qualification for blessedness hereafter and release from the weary round of reincarnation, but in the mythological setting of the Orphic mystery, if the dying and resurrected Dionysos was the means of salvation from inherited impurity, there is no conception of self-offering attached to his death, or of a rising again to newness of life in the spiritual sense as a condition of faithful membership of the *thiasoi* (brotherhoods).

(c) *The Attis-Cybele Cult.*—In the worship of the Phrygian Mother-goddess Cybele and her consort Attis, Hellenized at an early period, initiation to a blessed immortality was secured by anointing the body of the novice with a mixture of mud and bran.[2] At some point in the ritual, according to Firmicus Maternus and Clement of Alexandria, the neophyte ate out of the timbrel and drank from the cymbal, and went down into the bridal-chamber (παστός).[3] Our informants, however, do not explain the precise significance of these rites, and while it is true that Attis in the Liturgy is called the 'cornstalk', to affirm that the sacred meal from

[1] *Frogs*, 357. *Clouds*, 985. A. B. Cook, *Zeus* (Camb., 1914), vol. I, p. 715, n. 6.

[2] Demosthenes, *De Corona*, XVIII, 259.

[3] Firm. Mat., *De err. prof. rel.*, XVIII, 1. Clem. of Alex., *Protrept.*, II, 13.

I

the drum and the cymbal was a sacramental communion of cereals or fruits, with bread eaten by the votary 'as the very substance or body of his (Attis') divinity', is pure conjecture on the part of Farnell.[1] It has yet to be proved that Attis was 'the mystic bread in a sense in which Demeter is never found to have been'. More plausible is the suggestion of Hepding that in some cases there was an actual burial as part of the resurrection ceremonial, the initiate rising from the grave with the divinity to a new life.[2] This, as we have seen, is a widespread custom in initiation rites, and the journey to the bridal-chamber commemorating the death of Attis would naturally suggest the rebirth of the *mystae* from the cave-sanctuary of the Mother-goddess.[3]

(d) *The Magna Mater in Rome*.—In the cult of the Magna Mater from Pessinus, which was introduced in Rome in 205 B.C. at a critical juncture in the Hannibalic war, the people found escape from the formalism and remoteness of the State religion, and the story of Attis was celebrated in the poem by Catullus.[4] But no Roman citizen was allowed to become a mutilated priest (*gallus*) of the Goddess, hold any office in the cult, or walk in the processions, while the Bacchanalia was such a scandalous procedure that it was suppressed altogether.[5] To Romanize the alien worship, the goddess was given a place in the precincts of Victoria, an official sacrifice was offered by the praetor, and games (*ludi*) were celebrated in her honour. In the time of Claudius it was fully naturalized and henceforth the *archigallus* was a Roman citizen, but he was not a eunuch. In this reign, or perhaps later in the second century A.D.,[6] the drama was enacted in a series of festivals occupying six days beginning on March 15th, with 'the entrance of the reed' carried in procession by cannophori ('reed-bearers') and the sacrifice of a steer of six years in commemoration of the finding of Attis by Cybele in the Phrygian reeds. On 22nd of March 'the tree' was brought to the Palatine temple of the sacred pine in honour of the tree under which Attis mutilated himself; and then, after a day of fasting on the 24th, the self-mutilation and death of the hero

[1] *Hibbert Journal*, XI, 1904, p. 317.

[2] *Attis, Seine Mythen und sein Kult.* (Giessen, 1903), pp. 196 ff.

[3] W. Scott, *Proceedings, Society of Historical Theology* (Oxford, 1917–18), p. 56.

[4] *Cat.*, lxiii.   [5] Livy, xxxix.

[6] cf. Wissowa, *Religion und Kultus der Römer* (Munchen, 1902), p. 322.

(*Sanguis*) were celebrated, the neophytes performing their own castration amid general lamentation.[1] In the evening the resurrection of Attis was announced, and the next day, known as *Hilaria*, was observed with feasting and rejoicing. Finally, on the 27th, the festival terminated with the washing (*lavatio*) of the goddess.[2]

(*e*) *The Taurobolium.*—It was in association with the worship of Cybele that one of the most striking sacramental rites in the Roman Empire occurred, though there is no conclusive evidence that it was originally connected with the mystery. Cumont contends that the baptism of blood known as the *Taurobolium* made its way into Italy in the second century A.D. from Cappadocia where it had been part of the worship of the Eastern Artemis Tauropolis.[3] This view is maintained by Dill,[4] but it is rejected by Hepding,[5] who regards it as a Phrygian rite. But whatever may have been its original home, it had acquired a definitely sacramental significance in the third and fourth centuries A.D., when the Attis initiate who had been drenched with the blood of a bull slain on a perforated platform above a pit in which the recipient stood, was regarded as having been baptized *in aeternum renatus*.[6] Actually the earliest inscriptions give no indication of its meaning, except that it was done on behalf of the Empire and the Emperor. It is only in the later references that the individual is said to have been 'reborn for twenty years' and finally 'reborn for ever'. A ram was sometimes substituted for the bull, and this *criobolium* is thought by Showerman to have been a sacrament of later institution introduced in order to bring the Attis myth into greater prominence, whereas the *taurobolium* had a long sacrificial history behind it.[7]

(*f*) *Osiris-Serapis Cult.*—Of all the Hellenized Oriental mysteries in the Empire at the beginning of the Christian era, the chief was the cult of Serapis, the Greek form of Osorapis of Memphis, the dead Apis bull which became an Osiris after death. Although he

---

[1] Later this was modified by the *archigallus* cutting his arms as a ritual substitution for the actual operation.

[2] C. Bailey, *Phases in the Religion of Ancient Rome* (Oxford, 1932), p. 198.

[3] *Revue d'Histoire et de littérature religiuses,* VI, No. 2, 1901. *Les Religions Orientales* (Paris, 1909), pp. 332 ff.

[4] *Roman Society from Nero to Marcus Aurelius* (Lond., 1904), p. 556.

[5] *Attis*, p. 201.

[6] Dill, op. cit., p. 547, n. 4. *Corpus Inscript. Latin.,* VI, 510; VIII, 8203.

[7] *The Great Mother of the Gods* (Madison, 1901), pp. 280 ff.

was worshipped earlier at Memphis and known to the Greeks before the Ptolemaic period, it was Ptolemy I, acting on the advice of Manetho, who established the cult in Alexandria in Greek form. Thence it spread rapidly, taking with it Isis, Horus, and Anubis as anthropomorphic figures easily rendered in Greek style. Thus, the worship of Serapis, Isis, and Horus reached Rome and became one of the leading cults in the West till the Serapeum of Alexandria was destroyed in A.D. 385. The Isis-Horus myth was celebrated in Rome before that of Attis, the lamentation in commemoration of the search for the dismembered body of Osiris occurring on the last days of October, followed on the opening days of November by rejoicing at the discovery and restoration of the scattered limbs, and his subsequent trial, acquittal and installation as judge and king of the dead. This annual drama was celebrated, not merely for the benefit of those in process of initiation, as in most Mysteries, but as a public festival, though the rites had a special significance for the devotees.

In the eleventh book of the *Metamorphoses,* written under Marcus Aurelius, Apuleius gives a full account of the initiation of an Isis novice, and makes known through Lucius, the hero of the romance, the profounder aspects of the mystery for the devout in the second century A.D. In a vision of the goddess Lucius was promised 'thrice blessedness' vouchsafed by her to him who 'by the innocence and constancy of his former life has won so noble an inheritance from heaven, that he should be reborn and forthwith devoted to the service of the sacred rites'. Moreover, 'when thou shalt have run the course of thy life and passed to the underworld, there too in the lower hemisphere thou shalt see me shining amid the darkness of Acheron and reigning in the secret recesses of Styx, and thyself dwelling in the Elysian Fields shalt constantly adore me as thy protector'. In due course he was taken to the inner chamber of the temple on the night of his initiation, where, by the aid of the sacred drama and occult methods, he was brought face to face with the gods to receive mystic revelations and witness rites which he was not permitted to divulge. He declared, however, that he had 'approached the borderland of death' and set his foot 'on the threshold of Proserpine (Persephone)', returning to earth after being borne through all the 'elements' (realms of nature). At midnight he saw the sun gleaming with bright light and came into the presence of the gods below and the gods above and adored. The next morning he appeared before the people in the gorgeous array of an initiate, with twelve stoles, a coloured garment of linen, and a precious scarf on his back, all decorated with animal designs. In his right hand he carried a burning torch, and on his head he wore a crown of palm leaves. Thus adorned he was revealed for the admiration of the crowd. But before his 'voluntary death and hope of salvation' was complete, he had to undergo a further initiation at the end of the year into the mysteries of Osiris-Serapis, and shortly afterwards, in order to become a member of the college of *pastophori,* and devote himself to the service of the goddess all the days of his life in the priesthood, a third installation was required.[1]

From this account, which undoubtedly is based on an inner knowledge of the rites, a sacramental drama with an elaborate death and resurrection ritual appears to have constituted the means by which the regeneration to newness of life and status was effected in union with the passion of Isis and the restoration of Osiris.[2] Unlike the Cybele Mystery, the Isiac emphasized the subduing of the flesh as a means of obtaining clearer spiritual perceptions, not infrequently to the despair of husbands whose wives were devotees of the goddess. At first doubtless the abstinences from sexual intercourse, wine, flesh and even bread, and the repeated ablutions before taking part in the rites, were designed to rid the worshipper of ritual impurity, but they acquired a more ethical content in course of time. Thus, Lucius before his initiation declared that he had abstained from 'profane and evil foods that he might more rightly approach the secret mysteries of this, the purest of religions'.[3] And those who were invited to 'sup at the couch of the Lord Serapis'[4] in the Serapeum found behind all the outward purifications and ceremonial observances a deeper meaning which enabled them to gain renewal and strength from the goddess in this life and in the world to come everlasting bliss through the immortal glory of Osiris.

As Osiris was lord of the dead, Isis was the protector and patroness

---

[1] *Metam.,* xi, 3, 23 f., 26, 30.

[2] Since Lucius received a vision of the sun at midnight and was arrayed in sacramental garments in the likeness of the Sun-god, with whom he was identified before entering into the full service of the goddess, it seems that the cultus contained a solar element.

[3] *Metam,.* xi, 21.

[4] *The Oxyrhynchus Papyri,* Nos. 110, 523.

of the living, summing up the attributes of the Mother of the Gods in other lands and cults—Demeter, Athena, Venus, Cybele—but purified of their orgiastic elements. Like the Virgin Mother who eventually was to dethrone her, she was 'the goddess of many names'; the 'queen of the sky', 'mother of the stars', first-born of all the ages, parent of Nature, patroness of sailing and of mariners, and *Marter Dolorosa,* giving comfort and consolation to mourners and those in distress. Lastly in the *Metamorphoses,* she is called several times 'the saviour of the human race'. Therefore, her mysteries met the needs of initiates in life and death as no other cult had done in the pagan world, though they failed ultimately because, like the Phrygian and Eleusinian religions, they could not free themselves from their mythological matrix. Behind the cult lay the long history of Egyptian polytheism, and while it spread rapidly and gained an ever-increasing importance in the first centuries of the Christian era, despite the ethical element in its sacramentalism, it could never cut itself off from its ancestry.

(*g*) *Mithraism.*—The same is true of Mithraism, the last serious rival of Christianity in the Graeco-Roman world, which, as has been explained, was an Indo-Iranian solar cult in origin.[1] By the time it reached Europe, however, at the beginning of our era, the hero had become detached from his Persian setting and acquired the status of a mystery divinity with ethical attributes and a sacramental cultus. As the unconquered warrior (*sol invictus*) who never grew old or lost his vigour, Mithras unquestionably was an inspiring figure calculated to stir the devotion of soldiers in particular who flocked into the sect to find strength to fight victoriously not only on the field of battle but also against their own passions and temptations, and when the earthly struggle ceased, to be assured of a blessed immortality.[2] From the inscriptions and monuments in Mithraea, such as the sanctuary recently discovered at Dura-Europos on the Euphrates, the highly syncretistic character of the worship is apparent, elements having been borrowed from Vedic polytheism, Zoroastrianism, Mazdaism, Greek mythology and Babylonian astrology. But the central feature of the ritual was the slaying of the bull as depicted in the great bas-relief of Heddernheim, and similar monuments.

[1] cf. pp. 189 ff.
[2] Pseudo-Dionysus, *Areop. Ep.,* vii, 2.

In its completion this *tauroctonus* represents the young god in
Persian costume with peaked cap kneeling on the bull and plung-
ing his dagger into his neck. A dog springs up on its hind legs
towards the wound, a serpent licks up the blood, a raven sits near
by, serpents occupy the foreground, and two youths in Persian
attire stand on either side with torches in their hands. From the tail
of the dying bull springs the germinating corn, and the blood gives
life to the vine, the fruit of which was used in the cultus for the wine
of the sacramental banquet with the Sun-god. In one scene Mithras
stands beside the slain animal holding a drinking-horn in his left
hand, receiving a bunch of grapes from Ahura Mazda.

In contrast to the other Graeco-Oriental Mystery divinities, the
Persian saviour-god did not himself pass through death to life,
though by his sacrificial act he was a life-giver.[1] Consequently, as
Miss Weston has pointed out, there is a marked difference between
Attic and Mithraic initiations: 'the Attis initiate dies, is possibly
buried, and revives with his god: the Mithra initiate rises direct to
the celestial sphere, where he is met and welcomed by his god.'[2]
Having ascended through the seven spheres to the supreme heaven,
he attains full communion in the beatific vision and celestial banquet, of which perhaps the sacramental communion of bread,
water, and possibly wine, administered to the votary on his admission to the higher degrees of the Mystery, was a counterpart.[3]

But the sacrifice of the bull may have been a substitute for the
offering of the royal victim, and, in any case, the fact that Mithras
is frequently associated in art with Attis, and the *Taurobolium* was
borrowed from the Cybele cult,[4] suggests that a death and resurrection regeneration was not wholly alien to Mithraism. Repeated
ablutions were prescribed to neophytes to wash away guilt, as in
the Isis cult, but after the first three initiations had been passed,
honey poured on the hands and placed on the tongue was substituted for water as a preservative against sin. It was only in the higher
stages probably that participation in the sacramental meal as a re-
enactment of the heavenly banquet was permitted. This was a
survival of the Vedic Soma-ritual (and its Persian counterpart, the

[1] cf. pp. 128 ff.

[2] *From Ritual to Romance* (Camb., 1922), pp. 157 ff.

[3] Dieterich, *Eine Mithrasliturgie* (Leipzig, 1903). Cumont, *Mystères de Mithra*
(Bruxelles, 1896–9).

[4] cf. p. 264.

Haoma) in which a sacred intoxicating plant depicted as growing on the tree of heaven, was regarded as the king-god.[1] Originally Mithras, like the Soma and Dionysos, was the giver of the drink-offering and himself was the sacrificer, which no doubt explains his connexion with the vine, just as the association of Soma with Agni and the Sun is in accordance with his solar attributes.

> From this mystical banquet in Mithraism, and especially from the im-bibing of the sacred wine, supernatural effects were expected. The intoxicating liquor gave not only vigour of body and material prosperity but wisdom of mind; it communicated to the neophyte the power to combat the malignant spirits, and what is more, conferred upon him, as upon his god, a glorious immortality.[2]

The similarity between this banquet and the Christian Eucharist did not escape the notice of the early Fathers of the Church, but[3] nevertheless, however much the two faiths may have reacted on one another and even influenced the cultus of each, Mithras re-mained one of a triad of divinities, Mίθρα τριπλάσιος, a god of heavenly light, the dispenser of the *hvareno*, or nimbus, which shed its radiance on kings and consecrated their powers. The popularity of the Mystery, in fact, was largely due to imperial patronage, and after the reign of Commodus (A.D. 180–93) Emperors began to assume the surname *Invictus* which hitherto had been reserved exclusively for Mithras. But it unquestionably met a spiritual need inasmuch as it offered salvation in terms of a dualistic struggle with the powers of darkness and evil. Nevertheless, when it came into open conflict with Christianity it fell because the Church was able to meet its adversary on the sure ground of historical fact. All that Mithraism, and the other pagan Mysteries, offered in the search for a renewal of life and strength in this world and the next it supplied but, like the Hebrew prophets, in place of fantastic mythologies it based its claim on the possession of the divine secret of history revealed in all its fullness in the sacrificial death and resurrection of the God-man Who laid down His life in perfect surrender to a great and noble ideal, pursued with singleness of aim and stead-fastness of purpose. This raised the central mystery of Christianity

---

[1] cf. p. 146.

[2] Cumont, *Mystères de Mithra* (Eng. Trans., Lond., 1903), p. 160.

[3] Justin, *Apol.*, i, 86; Tertullian, *de Praescr. Haer.*, 40.

to the ethical plane and removed it from the ancient seasonal drama with its polytheistic background. Since it was in the higher order of reality that Christ was claimed to have conquered, a renewal of spiritual life and regeneration of outlook were offered to His initiates to a degree unknown and unattainable in any rival system. Therefore, Christianity ultimately prevailed because it provided a different gift of life from that bestowed in the pagan cults.

CHAPTER XI

Worship and Prayer

The Eucharist, regarded as the extension of the Incarnation and the perpetual memorial of the Passion of Christ, at a very early period became the central and most characteristic act of Christian worship, with which was coupled what is called in the Ignatian Letters 'the sacrifice of prayer'. 'Whosoever cometh not to fellowship stands apart from the altar or the sanctuary, the holy place where the assemblage of God's people offers up the sacrifice of prayer, and particularly that of the eucharist.'[1] It was of the essence of the Atonement that the offering of the Cross demanded a personal and corporate response from man. To be efficacious it was felt that its merits must be appropriated sacramentally and sacrificially by the Church as a society and by every individual member of the body corporate. As Dr Vincent Taylor says,

> man is not saved by appropriating the merits of another; he has no peace by substituting the sacrifice of another for his own. The sacrificial principle provides release from this dilemma. It does this because it reminds us that the sacrifice is more than the offering, that it is not complete apart from the worshipper on whose attitude and spirit its ethical value depends.[2]

Worship, in short, is 'the response of the creature to the Eternal'[3] arising out of a sense of absolute dependence on the transcendent order, in whatever terms this may be conceived at different cultural levels. The Holy, as we have seen, is at once awe-inspiring and fascinating, and it is in the religious reaction to the numinous that the fundamental conceptions of worship are found. In this undifferentiated emotion of fear and hope, dread and trust, the human soul surrenders itself to a supernatural source of strength individually and

[1] *Ad. Eph.*, 5. *Magn.*, 7. *Trall.*, 7. *Philad.*, 4. *Smyrn.*, 6 f. cf. Acts ii. 44, 47.

[2] *Jesus and His Sacrifice*, p. 298.

[3] E. Underhill, *Worship* (Lond., 1937), p. 3.

corporately in veneration and abasement as in the presence of an 'otherness' which it can only dimly comprehend, but which it feels transcends it and yet is not so wholly outside its reach as to be unresponsive to its urgent and inmost needs. Therefore, worship, unlike magic, being an expression of complete dependence, or 'creatureliness', has prayer, as distinct from spell, as its natural corollary, however involuntary and inarticulate the cry may be in its earliest and most rudimentary utterance.

SPELL AND PRAYER

To increase the food supply or call down refreshing showers on the kindly fruits of the earth, rites of a quasi-magical character are called in aid in primitive society, but even so when they are directed to an external supernatural agent, be he god or spirit, they become in the nature of an enacted prayer, accompanied sometimes by appropriate exclamations, ejaculations and gestures. The spontaneous cry and gesture-language that issue from the numinous experience of reverential wonder and the sense of dependence on a beneficent Providence as the Highest Good, belong to a different category from the charm and the spell, inasmuch as the appeal is not to the magical virtue as an essential human possession inherent in the rite and the associated formula, but to a transcendent order of reality external to man. Prayer is a means to an end; spell, on the other hand, is an end in itself. Both arise out of intense emotional situations, and operate in the sphere of the supernatural, but while the former is an aspect or outcome of worship—a free, unpremeditated, informal outpouring of the heart be the cry never so inarticulate—the latter is a practical circumscribed technique carefully guarded by strict adherence to procedure in word and act.

The language of prayer is as impromptu as its utterance is unrestricted, a free creation of the moment on the part of the worshipper and interceder, though not to the exclusion of more stereotyped forms and repetitions on specific occasions. The words used in magic are chosen with the greatest care and precision, and any slip of the tongue may break the spell and render the rite null and void, just as being a human possession it is only a properly qualified practitioner who can utter the formulae and perform the actions with any hope of success. The language of magic, in fact, is often archaic and unintelligible, the potency lying in the actual sounds rather than their meaningfulness. Finally, if prayer in its most rudimentary form like magic is generally directed to specific ends, it is not confined to practical requirements. In it can be discerned the germ of what in higher religious experience becomes gratitude, thanksgiving, praise and adoration.

Thus, for example, on the ninth day of the annual Thanksgiving Ceremony of the Lenape-Delawares in North America, the high-priest prayed as follows:

> I am thankful, O thou Great Spirit, that we have been spared to live until now to purify with cedar smoke this our House, because that has always been the rule in the ancient world since the beginning of creation. When any one thinks of his children, how fortunate it is to see them enjoy good health! And this is the cause of a feeling of happiness, when we consider how greatly we are blessed by the benevolence of our father, the Great Spirit. And we can also feel the great strength of him, our Grandfather. First, to whom we give pleasure when we purify him and take care of him, and when we feed him with this cedar. All of this together we offer in esteem to him, our Grandfather, because he has compassion, when he sees how pitifully we behave while we are pleading with all the mannitto above, as they were created, and with all those here on earth. Give us everything, our father, that we ask of you, Great Spirit, even the Creator.[1]

Similarly, 'when certain natives of Eastern Central Africa, after they have prayed for a successful hunting expedition, return home laden with venison, and ivory, they know that they are indebted to "their old relative" for their good fortune, and give him a thank-offering'.[2] But while first-fruit rituals are frequently in the nature of an honorarium in grateful recognition of the beneficence of Providence, they are primarily directed to practical ends as life-giving ceremonies, and the eucharistic conception in primitive cult is seldom prominent. Moreover, it is only in the higher religions that ethical notions of self-sacrifice and the oblation of the contrite heart are to be found.

Gratitude in the lower cultures consists in the humble acknowledgement of dependence upon the bountiful powers for favours, sustenance and preservation—life and health, rain and sunshine,

---

[1] Speck, *Publications of the Pennsylvanian Historical Commission* (Harrisburg, 1931), vol. II, p. 75.

[2] Westermarck, *Origin and Development of Moral Ideas*, II, p. 615.

good harvests and successful hunting, food and fertility—in short, for all the blessings of this life. Indeed, all through the ages, and in every phase of religious development, man has tended to approach his Maker primarily for benefits of a utilitarian kind, for protection from evil, and as a very present help in time of trouble, rather than in terms of the loftier spiritual aspirations of saint and sage. Therefore petition, supplication, and propitiation occupy a more conspicuous place in the history of prayer and worship than thanksgiving and adoration.

It is this practical aspect of ritual invocation that causes worship in practice to degenerate into a quasi-magical control of impersonal supernatural forces, and prayer to become virtually spell, when the success or failure of a rite is made dependent upon procedure and the result secured by 'vain repetitions' of prescribed utterances. If this is more apparent in primitive cult, it is by no means unknown in the higher religions, from Hinduism to Christianity. The fact that veneration finds expression in cultus and prayer in gesture and rite, makes the outward and visible signs always liable so to overshadow the inward and spiritual strivings of the soul till the exercise becomes a mechanical process more closely allied to magic than to religion. This applies equally to prayer and sacrament and the entire technique of worship. Given the correct 'intention' the performance of the rite suffices and is calculated to bring about the desired results, viz. the benefits sought. Since the god to whom the action is directed knows the thoughts and needs of the worshipper he (the god) can be safely left to fulfil his part of the contract. Therefore, all that is required is the faithful and correct ritual invocation by a person qualified to perform the rite or make the petition. The way is thus prepared for prayer to become spell when, as in Brahmanic Hinduism, a *mantra*, or hymn, gave efficacy to the sacrificial rite, so that any mistake in the correct pronunciation of the sacred words annihilated the sacrifice and endangered the life and health of the priest because 'speech leads the sacrifice to the gods'.[1]

ANCIENT ROME

Similarly, in ancient Rome, every effort was made to obtain the correct recitation of the formulae of prayer or incantation (*carmen*)

[1] Sat. Brah., I, 4, 4, 2.

on the ground that verbal accuracy was essential to the validity of
the rite. As a safeguard against mistakes the words were preserved
in books and in the course of time the language became so archaic
that it was scarcely intelligible to the priests themselves[1] and the
worshipper repeated the traditional formulae as they were said by
the officiant. But notwithstanding these precautions, Plutarch
affirms that 'in later ages one and the same sacrifice was performed
thirty times over because of the occurrence of some defect or
mistake or accident in the service—such was the Roman reverence
and caution in religious matters'.[2]

This is hardly surprising since besides the exact wording of the
carmen the god, Lares or Manes addressed had to be given his or
her correct titles, however numerous they may have been, and
every detail observed with absolute precision concerning the number of times the repetitions were to be made, the tone of voice in
which they were sung, and the position occupied by the priest
during the incantation. Thus, the verses of the *Carmen Saliare* were
each chanted three times as the leaping of Mars danced in threefold
measure,[3] and Horace in invoking Ilithyia (Diana) to protect
mothers adds 'whether you prefer to be addressed as Luana or
Genitalis',[4] just as Lucius in the *Metamorphoses* is careful to make his
petition to the Queen of Heaven as Ceres, Venus, the sister of
Phoebus, Proserpina, or 'by whatever name, with whatever rite, in
whatever appearance it is right to invoke thee'.[5]

But, although the *carmen* was little removed from magic and was
frequently in the nature of a command, in the ancient prayers
handed down by Cato in the *Farm Almanack* the language of petition
(subjunctive or imperative) is used. For example, at the lustration
of a field the prescribed formula was as follows:

> Father Mars, I pray and beseech thee that thou mayest be propitious and
> of good will to me, to my house, to my dependents; and for this reason
> I have ordered the offering of pig, sheep, and ox to be led round my field,
> my land, and my farm, that thou mightest prevent, ward off and avert
> diseases, visible and invisible, barrenness and waste, accidents and bad
> weather; that thou wouldest suffer the crops and fruits of the earth, the
> vines and shrubs to wax great and prosper, that thou wouldest preserve

[1] Quintilian, *Inst. Or.*, i, 6, 40.   [2] *Coriol.*, 25.
[3] Warde Fowler, *The Religious Experience of the Roman People* (Lond., 1911), p. 187.
[4] *Carmen Saeculare*, 13–16.   [5] xi, 2.

the shepherds and their flocks in safety and give prosperity and health
to me and my house and household; for all these causes, for the lustration
and purification of my farm, land and field, as I have said, be enriched
(*macte esto*) by the sacrifice of this offering of sucking pig, lamb and calf.[1]

Here unquestionably Warde Fowler is correct in seeing 'the language of prayer, not of compulsion or even of bargaining',[2] and
the same is equally true of the other supplications in the *Farm
Almanack*.[3] The *suovetaurilia,* or sacrifice of pig, sheep, and ox, when
the fields had been circumambulated three times at the *lustratio,* is
more than a magical rite, being an offering to the god with prayer
to Mars, beseeching him to be 'propitious and of good will' to the
worshipper and his household. In a primitive agricultural community requests for ethical and moral virtues could hardly be
expected since as Cicero remarks, 'men call Jupiter greatest and
best because he makes us not just or temperate or wise, but sound
and healthy and rich and wealthy'.[4]

For the Roman the relationship between the gods and man was
legal and precisely measured in terms of contracts. Hence the
prayer known as the *Votum,* or vow, wherein the worshipper under-
took to make an offering when a particular request had been granted, as distinct from the *devotio,* or payment made in advance to
ensure the bestowal of the benefit. From simple requests in private
domestic life accompanied by a promise of a just and equitable
recompense to the god addressed,[5] a State cultus developed in which
the nation bound itself to the gods in formal legal contracts.[6] But
in its earlier form the *votum* was a prayer comparable to that of
Jacob at Bethel rather than the formal legal bargain of later times
when the State cult was systematized. Behind it may lie coercive
magic, but when we first encounter the practice in ancient Roman
religion it is, as Dr Bailey says, 'really a religious and not a legal
act, and its nearest parallel is the free-will thank-offering made
without any previous vow by a worshipper who has received a
blessing'.[7]

[1] Cato, *De Re Rustica,* p. 141. Warde Fowler, op. cit., p. 129.

[2] op. cit., p. 189.   [3] cf. pp. 127 f., 130, 134.

[4] *de Nat. Deor.,* iii, 36, 87.

[5] cf. De Marchi, *Il culto privato,* pp. 271–8. Warde Fowler, op. cit., pp. 201 f.
Wissowa, *Rel. und Kultus,* ii, 381 f. Horace, *Sat.,* ii, 3, 288–92. Virgil, *Aen.,* v, 235–8.

[6] Livy, xxii, 10, 2.

[7] C. Bailey, *Phases in the Religion of Ancient Rome* (Oxford, 1932), p. 95.

Our knowledge of Roman religion before it was influenced by the
Greeks and the Etruscans is dependent for the most part on fragmentary calendars dating from the early Empire, such as the *Farm
Almanack,* but the general character of the festivals and cultus
reveals a lack of imagination and a severely practical outlook directed
to the soil and the homestead in striking contrast to the spontaneity
and spirituality of Hellenic belief and practice. Thus, the worship
of the more temperamental Greeks, instead of being rooted in the
earth and confined to the house and the family, was raised to the
heights of Olympus where Zeus and his retinue reflected the
splendour of an Ionic prince surrounded by his captains.

The aim of the Hellenic epic poet was primarily artistic, and he
treated religion with a freedom and freshness foreign to the prosaic
and orderly Roman mentality, devoid of the philosophical reflection which characterized later Athenian thought. The Homeric
gods were anthropomorphic creations of poetic imagination,
superhuman in their beauty and power, but in other respects
singularly like mortals, so that gods and men belonged to one
common society in which obligations were binding on both sides.
Man, however, was dependent on these divine heroes, and sought
to secure their favour by offerings and meritorious actions. 'Hear
me, lord of the silver bow, who reignest supreme', said Chryses to
Apollo, 'if ever I built (or adorned) a temple pleasing to thee, or if
ever I have burnt to thee the fat flesh of the thighs of bulls or goats,
then grant this my petition (or desire).'[1]

Again, Hesiod, the later less imaginative son of the soil, made
material prosperity the sole purpose of worship.

> According to thy ability offer sacrifice to the immortal gods with thy
> person pure and undefiled, and burn the goodly thigh-pieces; again
> propitiate them with libations and with sacrifices, both when thou liest
> down and when the sacred light comes, that they may have a heart and
> mind kindly disposed towards thee; that thus thou mayest buy the
> land of others and not another thine.[2]

Nevertheless, Hesiodic poetry shows that by the seventh century
B.C. the Greeks were beginning to recognize that justice was a
divine attribute and the basis of a right relationship between man

---

[1] *Iliad,* i, 37–42.   [2] *Works and Days,* 336 ff.

and man, and man and the gods, though ethical values had not attained sufficient power to serve as a motive of prayer and worship. The invocation of Chryses was an entreaty for vengeance—'with thy shafts avenge on the Achaean host thy servant's tears'—and in the nature of a bargain—'if ever I built a temple pleasing to thee' then 'grant this my petition'. Similarly, Nestor prayed to Athene, 'be gracious, O queen, and give me fair fame—for myself and my children and gracious wife; and I in turn will sacrifice to thee a heifer'.[1] But Diomedes, on the other hand, appealed to the love shown him by the goddess rather than to his own merits or any contract. 'Unconquered daughter of Zeus, Aegis-armed! If ever me, propitious, or my sire thou hast in furious fight helped heretofore, now show thy love for me.'[2]

The absence of any real sense of ethical holiness makes the prayer of the contrite heart foreign to Greek mentality, but the philosophers recognized that since only goodness proceeds from God, it is proper only to ask of Him that which is good. 'Some pray for gold and some for limitless land,' says Pindar, but 'mine be it with the favour of my townsmen to hide my limbs in earth, praising what is worthy of praise and sowing rebuke on sinners'.[3] The Socrates of Xenophon 'prayed to the gods simply that they would give him good things, believing that the gods know best what sort of things are good. As for those who prayed for gold or silver or a tyranny or such like, he believed that was just as if they prayed for gambling, or battle or any thing else the issue of which is uncertain.'[4] Into his mouth Plato puts the loftiest of all Hellenic prayers, when in reference to Alcibiades he is made to say, 'he seems to have been a wise poet who seeing, as I believe, his friends were foolish men, praying for or doing such things which it was good for them to do, offered a prayer in behalf of them all to this effect: "King Zeus, give what is good even without request; but keep far from us evil, though we ask for it".'[5] Or again, in the *Phaedrus,* the moral ideal is sought: 'Beloved Pan and all ye other gods here, grant that I may become inwardly beautiful (καλῷ γενέσθαι τἄνδοθεν), and grant that whatever outward possessions I have may be friendly to that which is within.'[6]

[1] *Iliad*, vii, 115.   [2] *Iliad*, v, 115–17 (Cowper).
[3] *Nem.*, viii, 36 ff.   [4] Xenophon, *Mem.*, i, 3, 2.
[5] *Alcibiades*, II, 143 A.   [6] *Phaedrus*, 279 B.

Such utterances as these, when Greek thought was at its height, represent the nearest approach to a comprehensive moralization of religious experience in the ancient world outside Israel. The highest good for man is likeness to God; that is the fullest participation in the ideas of the Good which are in the Absolute finding expression in ethical righteousness. In Egypt, on the other hand, despite the emergence of the moral sense in relation to the hereafter,[1] official worship centred in securing the favour of the gods for Pharaoh. The offerings were made in order that in return for services rendered the 'duration of heaven'—health, stability, abundance, and victory—might be bestowed on the king as the source of the nation's well-being. In magical formulae and adorations requests are absent, and such an exclamation as 'Come unto me, Amon-Re, open for me the gates of heaven, throw open for me the gates of earth', appears to refer to the ritual on behalf of the god rather than to a human cry for succour.[2] There is scarcely any evidence of a sense of dependence on divine aid until the latter part of the New Kingdom, the purpose of the rites being to secure control over the gods, and bend them to the will of man by magical means, as Isis gained power over Re when she discovered his secret name.

After the short-lived monotheistic movement in the days of Akhnaton, at the end of the XVIIIth Dynasty, we encounter for the first time prayer as a genuine revelation of inner personal experience, an expression of individual communion with God. It was then that the worshipper turned to his god for protection and sustenance, and prayed with a 'desiring heart'[3]

> O Amon, thou herdsman bringing forth the herds in the morning, leading the suffering to pasture; as the herdman leads the herd (to) pasture, so dost thou. O Amon, lead the suffering to food, for Amon is a herdsman, herding him that leans upon him. . . . O Amon-Re, I love thee and I have filled my heart with thee. . . . Thou wilt rescue me out of the mouth of men in the day when they speak lies; for the Lord of Truth, he liveth in truth.[4]

[1] cf. chap. IX, p. 209.

[2] A. Moret, *Le Rituel du culte divin journalier en Egypte* (Paris, 1902), p. 81.

[3] *Papyrus Sallies*, i, 8, 5–7. Erman, *Hnadbook of Egyptian Religion, p.* 34.

[4] Breasted, *Religion and Thought in Ancient Egypt*, p. 355.

But this age of personal piety was as transitory as the monotheism of the heretic king, and it was rapidly followed by a period of decadence from which Egypt never recovered.

BABYLONIA

In Babylonia incantations of a magical character to appease the gods were of frequent occurrence on occasions of public and private misfortune, and were accompanied by confessions of guilt, expiatory sacrifices and atonement ceremonies. These lamentations occupied an intermediate position between the official and the extra-official cult, and if originally they formed no part of the worship of the temples, as Langdon contends,[1] they were subsequently incorporated into the public services. The daily Babylonian liturgies and Assyrian offices were derived from the Sumerian forms, whereas the private prayers and magic rituals were largely from Semitic sources. Thus, the Babylonians in the private purificatory cultus usually employed Semitic prayers known as 'prayers of the lifting up of the hands', which though they arose out of the curse in the Sumerian incantations, reveal an ethical content. 'My heart is distressed and my soul faileth. I cry unto thee, O Lord in the pure heavens. Faithfully look upon me, hear my supplication.' 'May my sin be undone, my frivolity forgotten. May the good genius, the good spirit walk beside me. May evil mouth and tongue stand aside. Before thee I will walk and sing thy praise.'[2]

If demons were the cause of misfortunes they could only act by permission of the gods. Just as earlier their onslaughts could be averted by spells, so when they came under divine control confession and contrition restored the beneficence of the offended deity who thereupon sent 'the good genius' to walk beside the repentant sinner, and made 'evil mouth and tongue stand aside'. Therefore, hymns in praise of the gods find a place in the incantations in which prayers and exorcisms are inextricably blended. These composite texts and rituals which collectively constitute the public temple cultus, only gradually acquired an individualistic character, and intercessions, at first almost entirely absent in the Sumerian liturgies, were added as recessional epilogues (*er-sem-ma*, i.e. 'a song sung to the flute').

[1] *Sumerian and Babylonian Psalms* (Paris, 1909).
[2] King, *Babylonian Magic and Sorcery* (Lond., 1896), No. 6, 60–2, 31–4.

O heart, repent, repent; O heart, repose, repose.
O heart of Enlil repent, repent.
O heart of Anu repent, repent.

.   .   .   .   .   .

O heart of the lord repose, let be spoken unto thee.
Unto thy city hasten in glory like the sun.
Unto Nippur hasten in glory like the sun.

They city of Nippur be rebuilt.
Thy temple Ekur in Nippur be rebuilt.

.   .   .   .   .   .

>May one utter petition unto thee.
>May one utter intercession unto thee.
>O heart be reconciled, O heart repose.[1]

Before 2000 B.C. these texts were used by the Semites in the
original Sumerian, and even after they had been translated, the
earlier language continued to be employed in the public liturgies
and in the more personal penitential litanies (*er-sag-tug-mal,*
'weeping that appeases the heart') recited between the priest and
choir. This tended to restrict liturgical worship to the educated and
ruling section of the community and to drive the masses to the
magical cults where incantation could be uttered in Semitic. In
some of these unofficial private prayers there is an ethical element,
but the Babylonians never really got beyond an impersonal conception of justice uninspired by love for the gods or man. Thus, in
a long hymn to Shamash as the enforcer of morality, the god is
addressed in the following coldly abstract terms:

O Shamash, out of thy net no sinner escapes,
From thy sling no evil-doer is saved;
Far-flung is thy net for the doers of wickedness.
Against him who lifts up his eyes towards his neighbour's wife
Thy weapons go forth, and there is none to save;
When he stands before the judge, his father helps him not;
Against the word of the judge his brothers may not stand.
In a brazen trap is he caught unawares.
Thou destroyest the horn of him who plans wrong;
Of him who abets the sinner, the ground vanishes from under his feet.

[1] Langdon, *Sumerian Liturgical Texts from Nippur* (Philad., 1917), cf. Zimmern,
Sumerische-Kultlieder aus altbabylonischer Zeit. (Leipzig, 1912–13), No. 12.

Thou causest the unjust judge to see fetters;
Him who takes a bribe perverts justice, thou dost punish.
He who takes no bribe, who befriends the poor,
Is acceptable unto Shamash; he will live long.
The prudent judge who utters righteous judgements
Makes ready for himself a palace; a dwelling for princes is his dwelling.[1]

As in the penitential psalms and atonement rituals,[2] the suppliant
is aware that the sinner cannot hope to escape out of the net of the
gods whether the errors into which he has fallen have been committed wittingly or unwittingly, but if such prayers are clearly
removed from spell, they are confined to material benefits, e.g.
prosperity, length of days, as the reward of the utterance of righteous judgements. 'Lamentation, mourning, and woe' constituted
the characteristic feature of Sumerian and Babylonian worship
which originated from a desire to pacify the gods whose anger
manifested itself in calamity and all the ills to which flesh is heir.

BUDDHISM

In Oriental mysticism, on the other hand, there is no room for
prayer and worship in the absence of any personal attribute of
Deity or dependence on a transcendent order of Reality. It is mani-
festly useless to appeal to an impersonal law which nothing can
violate. Therefore, the only way to escape the evils of life is to seek
release from *karma*, and meditation, having as its aim absorption in
the ultimate metaphysical unity of the Absolute, takes the place
occupied by prayer and worship in the theistic religions. Self-
abnegation alone remains in the quest of self-perfection. Consequently, Gautama and his earliest disciples repudiated all notion of
external superhuman guidance through rite or prayer. 'Live as they
who have the self for a lamp, the self for a refuge, *dhamma* for a
lamp, *dhamma* for a refuge, with none other.'[3] Dhamma in Early
Buddhism alone was the supreme guide, corresponding to Brahman
in the Upanishads, and only through the identification of the self
with this ruling principle could perfection be secured. But when the
original non-theistic Dhamma was transformed into *dhamma kaya*
by making the founder the embodiment of universal truth, merit

[1] Ungnad,, *Die Religion der Babylonier und Assyrer,* pp. 187 ff.
[2] cf. chap. IX, pp. 210 f.   [3] *Digha Nikaya,* II, 100.

and grace were sought by the Mahayanists through prayers of supplication and offerings of adoration to the all-merciful Saviour of mankind. Admiration readily passes into devotion (*bhakti*), and when this was directed to a particular individual in process of deification, prayer and worship inevitably follow. In Buddhism this transition was facilitated by the practice of *pranidhāna*, or the fulfilment of vows through the assistance of the Buddha. A fixed intention to attain to the ideal passes almost imperceptibly into a prayer for grace to accomplish the end sought, once a universal source of truth is concentrated in one or more personalities with superhuman attributes and powers. Therefore, the discipline of *bodhisattva* was accompanied by vows addressed to a certain Buddha who guaranteed their fulfilment if they were accepted and faithfully carried into effect in the dedicated life.

This conception of prayer and worship arises out of the essential unity of the human soul and the ultimate cosmic principle which for the Mahayanists had become transcendent Deity. But even in northern Buddhism God has never been *wholly* external to man any more than in Hinduism *bhakti* means devotion to a single god. In the background of all the Oriental mystical systems is the reciprocal participation in a fundamental unity of spiritual nature, and however theistic they may become, a pantheistic identity of essence in all phenomena, animate and inanimate, constitutes the ultimate principle. Thus, in *The Lotus of the Perfect Truth*, as in the Buddhist sects of Japan, the 'absolute nature of Buddha' permeates all things in some form producing 'mutual participation' or interdependence of all existences, worship being the elevation of the self to Buddhahood rather than the abasement of the soul before its Creator. For Nichiren, the Japanese exponent of *The Lotus* (A.D. 1222–82), adoration was the means of realizing the truth of mutual participation in every one's life, and the repetition of the wisdom of *The Lotus* crystalized in formulae the prayer calculated to awaken in the self true enlightenment as revealed by Buddha.[1]

Even the simple invocation of Amida-Buddha 'with a sincere heart', or faith in his redemptive power, is a form of adoration calculated according to the Jodo sect to bring mankind within the natural activity of Amida, the essence of all things and the infinite light penetrating all regions of the universe and knowing no limit

[1] Anesaki, *Nichiren, the Buddhist Prophet* (Camb., Mass., 1916).

in time or space. He is not a transcendent external deity, but a qualitative identification of the external notion of space and time with that force which is continually working for salvation. The repetition of the sacred name is an act of faith in redemptive grace to secure release from suffering reduced to the simplest form possible in order to place salvation within the reach of every one who is convinced of the mercy of Buddha. In practice doubtless the devotion frequently becomes a mechanical repetition of a formula, but in theory at least it must be the expression of a sincere conviction of the compassion of Amida, who, according to the Sukhavati Sutras on which the sect has been founded, declared, 'if I arrive at Buddhahood I will not take to myself complete enlightenment unless all living beings in the universe who sincerely believe in me and desire to be born in my land shall be born there, though but ten times they direct their devotion to me'. It is not a request for material benefits since Buddhism regards the affairs and destinies of this life as unalterable and inevitable. Only in the hereafter does faith receive its reward, and the invocation of the name of Amida is an act of gratitude for salvation already granted, and the spiritual peace and enlightenment thereby enjoyed in the ascent towards the Pure Land.

CONFUCIANISM

In Confucian ethics, on the other hand, prayer had no place. For Confucius God being essentially the moral order, unvarying and impersonal, while the destinies of states and individuals were ordained by Heaven, they were as unalterable as in Buddhism, determined strictly by conduct. Therefore, 'he who offends against Heaven has none to whom he can pray'. The process of self-culture was independent of any spiritual aid and intervention, and no objective value was attached to the traditional rites and ancestor-worship, which were countenanced merely as an integral part of the ancient heritage of the State. It was the absence of this transcendental element in the doctrine of the founder that facilitated the introduction of Mahayana Buddhism in China and Japan, under the influence of which a temple cultus developed when Confucianism became a national religion in the true sense of the term, with objective worship on specified occasions. It was not until after the Buddhist invasion that images of Confucius and his disciples began to appear, subsequently replaced by wooden tablets as the symbol of the sage, now raised to divine rank. Before the tablet altars came to be erected with candles and an incense-burner, for the purpose of making offerings to the spirit of Confucius which was thought to inhabit the tablet as soon as the sacred music began, in order to take part in the rite. In the opening hymn he is thus addressed:

> Mighty art thou, O Confucius,
> Preserver of the future, endowed with foreknowledge,
> Compeer to God our father, and of Earth our mother,
> Teacher of the myriad ages,
> Auspicious fulfilment of the skein on the lin (a fabulous animal)
> Thy voice has a music of metal and silk,
> By thy aid the sun and moon run their courses,
> And the stability is preserved.[1]

This, however, is as extraneous to the original ethical system as is Amidism to Early Buddhism.

ZOROASTRIANISM

In Persia, on the other hand, the Zoroastrian movement seems to mark a definite departure from Oriental mysticism. The prophet claimed to have been the recipient of a special revelation from Ahura Mazda—'As the Holy One I recognize thee, O Mazda Ahura' was his repeated assertion, but there is no indication of any ecstatic or quietistic state of soul, or of self-abnegation. It was rather the prophetic attitude and outlook that constituted the communion between Zoroaster and Ahura. 'With outspread hands in petition for that help, O Mazda, first of all things will I pray for the works of the Holy Spirit.'[2] But not to the exclusion of temporal affairs. 'May Mazda Ahura by his dominion bring us to work, for prospering our beasts and our men, so that we may through Right have familiarity with Good thought.'

In place of animal sacrifice and the Haoma offering, according to the Gathas, Ahura Mazda was to be worshipped with praise, but in what outward form, if any, is not explained.

[1] H. A. Giles, *Confucianism and its Rivals* (Lond., 1918), p. 186.

With Zarathustra [says Söderblom], action is the issue of religion. Songs and hymns of praise are to be offered to Ahura and the other celestial beings. It may be even that the Gathas were composed for the regular divine worship. But the most acceptable kind of worship consists in the care of the pastures and the management of the cattle. Cult and ritual play but a slight part in the religion of the Gathas. Good Thoughts, Good Words, and Good Deeds, form a trinity common to religion in India and Iran. But while the Veda religion deems this to refer to the rites of worship, in the Gathas this trinity of Thought, Word, and Deed refers to the pious man's active life.[1]

But when this short-lived reform had spent its force a return was made to animal sacrifice and the Haoma offering, and in the Late Avestan period the elaborate system of Mazdaean cultus speedily developed. Each day of the month had its appointed devotions to its particular divinity, with prayers assigned to the five divisions of the day (*gāhs*), while special festivals were held in honour of Ahura Mazda at the appropriate seasons. The liturgy consisted mainly of extracts from the Avesta in the form of ritual invocations for the living and the dead, though requests for material benefits are less conspicuous in the earlier than in the later texts when the desire for ethical and mental enlightenment had waned. But Zoroastrianism has always been a religion of practical morality having as its purpose the regeneration of the world. 'All prosperous states in being which have been enjoyed in the past, which men are now enjoying, and which shall be known in the future, do thou grant (me) these in thy love. Cause (our) bodily and personal life to be blest with salvation.'[2] But notwithstanding the profound impression which the prophet made on Iranian thought and practice, so that animal sacrifice does not constitute a normal part of modern Parsi worship, the rapid return to the earlier beliefs of traditional Iranian religion rendered whatever contribution he may have made to devotional monotheism of little permanent value, whereas the Hebrew prophets succeeded in establishing in Judaism the conception of the universal rule of Yahweh.

JUDAISM

The concentration of worship at Jerusalem after the Josiah reformation in 621 B.C. gave a new significance to the Temple and the

[1] *The Living God* (Oxford, 1931), pp. 207 f.   [2] *Yasna*, xxxiii, 10.

sacrificial system if it represents an alliance in the southern kingdom between the prophetic and priestly parties. It is unfortunate that the date and origin of Deuteronomy are still matters of dispute among Old Testament scholars,[1] and until these questions are settled it is not possible to arrive at a correct estimate of the pre-exilic sacrificial cultus in relation to the prophetic movement. But whether the Deuteronomic religion took shape at Jerusalem before the Exile or at Bethel in the exilic period, the legislation of the priestly school was not systematized until after the return of the remnant from Babylonia in the series of migrations that occurred subsequent to the decree of Cyrus in 538. It was then that the work of restoring the Temple was begun in 520 B.C., during the reign of Darius, and completed four years later (516), despite the opposition of the conservative party and the Samaritan schism.

With the establishment of the sacrificial system, the Aaronic succession and the Sabbath observance, a new order of worship was brought into being freed from the earlier abuses by the drastic purging of the Exile. The work of the prophets and of Ezekiel in their insistence on ethical righteousness as the first requirement of Yahweh had borne fruit, and the nation as a whole never again relapsed into its former practices, however much it may have failed to maintain the highest ideals of objective worship and true holiness. The Temple became 'the house of prayer for all people'[2] hallowed by a continual stream of sacrificial offerings and oblations referred back to the days of Moses, David, and Solomon, liturgical prayers and psalms, music and stately processions which were certainly not devoid of spiritual meaning and appeal. This is revealed in the Psalter which gives expression to the religious consciousness of the post-exilic community in the form of liturgical prayers appointed for use in the Temple worship at the festivals and on other occasions in conjunction with the rites. Many of the psalms, of course, like the cultus, are pre-exilic in origin, reflecting the thought of the prophetic movement, and in their new liturgical setting they invested the ritual with an ethical content by emphasizing the moral teaching of the earlier literature.[3]

Coupled with the Psalter was a deeper affection for the Law

---

[1] cf. R. H. Kennett, *Deuteronomy and the Decalogue* (Lond., 1905), *Old Testament Essays* (Camb., 1928).

[2] Isa. lvi. 7.   [3] Ps. lxxxiv, cxxxviii. 2.

(*Torah*) fostered by the Pharisees and Sadducees and the institution of the synagogue consequent upon the movement initiated by the school of Ezra, though it was not until after the Maccabaean revolt that this aspect of later Judaism became a dominant feature. Of the two parties the Sadducees were clerical conservatives and the Pharisees (probably the descendants of the *Hasidim*) were the lay liberals, and while both were equally concerned with the maintenance of the Torah and the sacrificial system, under Pharisaic influence the synagogue was established on a democratic basis in contrast to the priestly and aristocratic constitution of the Temple. Gradually, during the last two centuries of its existence, the synagogue system permeated the sacerdotal cultus, so that the daily morning offering was interrupted by a confession made by the penitent sinner, the singing of songs and psalms by the Levites, the recitation of the *Shema* (Deut., vi. 4 ff., xi. 13 ff.), and the Decalogue, and at the close of the rite the priestly benedictions known as *tephillah* ('prayer'). On the Day of Atonement the blessing over the Torah was to be recited 'as in the synagogue',[1] and the Pharisees translated the lectionary into the vernacular. Indeed it was they who formulated the liturgy as it has been handed on throughout the ages in Judaism to this day.

With the destruction of the Temple in A.D. 70, the synagogue and its cultus naturally took its place as the only surviving place of Jewish worship, as it had already become for the Diaspora who were cut off from Jerusalem by the fact of their dispersion in the Graeco-Roman world and beyond. The fall of the capital, however, brought the two systems into closer relationship. Such elements of the Temple worship as could be incorporated were introduced into the synagogue services, Hebrew became the official language for the prayers, with the exception of a few Aramaic survivals (*Qaddish*), but in place of the former sacrifices, the appropriate lessons, psalms, hymns, and prayer could only be substituted as efficacious memorials of the actual offerings till the hope of Israel be fulfilled.

CHRISTIANITY

On the Jewish liturgy that of the Christian Church was modelled.

[1] *Tos. Y.K.*, iv. 18.

Christ Himself taught in the synagogue and in the Temple courts, and apparently took part in the great festivals at Jerusalem, as did the apostles and the first generation of their followers. In fact, the Eucharist is the only specific act of Christian corporate worship recorded in the Apostolic Church together with the closely associated *agape*, or 'love feast', both of which appear to have grown out of Jewish communal meals.[1] The earliest accounts of these gatherings on the first day of the week follow the synagogue pattern up to the dismissal of the catechumens, since the service was composed of the reading of lections from 'the memoirs of the apostles, or the writings of the prophets', and an instruction on these Scriptures followed by prayers. The Eucharist began with 'the prayer of the faithful', after which came the kiss of peace, the oblation of bread and wine, and the giving of Communion to those present (the deacon carrying the Consecrated Elements to the sick), thanksgiving and almsgiving.[2] Until the emancipation of the Church by the Edict of Milan in A.D. 313, beyond this weekly act of corporate worship little was attempted in the matter of daily prayer at fixed times and places, though the anniversaries of martyrdoms were commemorated in the catacombs and elsewhere, and vigils, or 'night-watches', observed.

In the fourth century when churches began to be built and pagan temples transformed into Christian places of assembly, liturgical worship was organized on a more elaborate scale according to the instructions preserved in the Church Orders, such as the *Apostolic Constitutions* (c. A.D. 375), the *Apostolic Canons,* the *Testament of our Lord* (360–80), based largely on the *Apostolic Tradition of Hippolytus.* Moreover, service-books began to appear, containing collections of prayers for various occasions, of which the earliest extant is the *Sacramentary of Sarapion,* Bishop of Thmuis (c. 350) in the Nile Delta. This private compilation, which was discovered on Mount Athos in 1894, gives the main structure of the liturgy in broad outline, and covers roughly the ground of the seventh and eighth books of the *Apostolic Constitutions* of a quarter of a century later, though the contents are not arranged in a systematic order with rubrication, beyond the titles of the prayers for the Eucharist

[1] cf. chap. X, p. 236 f.

[2] Justin Martyr, *Apol.,* i, 6, 65. Ignatius, *Ad Eph.,* 5; *Magn.,* 7; *Trall.,* 7; *Philad.,* 4; *Smyrn.,* 6 f. Didache, ix, 5. Iren., iv, 18. Origen, *Cels.,* viii, 57.

(19–30, 1–6), Baptism and Confirmation (7–11, 15, 16), Ordination (12–14), Benediction of oils, bread and water (17), and Burial of the Dead (18).

While this Sacramentary cannot be regarded as a service-book in the more authoritative sense of a carefully compiled liturgy for general use in a given area, it is the most complete liturgical document prior to the seventh century, when the manuscripts of the Western Liturgies begin to make their appearance. From it, taken in conjunction with the 'Orders' mentioned above, it is possible to reconstruct the general scheme of public worship at the end of the fourth century.[1] The office opened normally with prayers, lessons, litanies and psalms, during which the sacred ministers went to the altar, the elements were carried in by a priest, the sanctuary was censed by the bishop, and the congregation by a priest. For the reading of the Gospel the people stood and the book was censed by the deacon. The sermon, or homily, followed, after which the catechumens and penitents were dismissed with a blessing from the bishop. The Liturgy of the Faithful then began with a deacon's litany, a prayer and the kiss of peace. After the *lavabo* and the oblation of the elements (Offertory), the *Anaphora* opened with the Eucharistic or Consecration Prayers introduced by the salutation and *Sursum Corda,* said by the bishop vested in white vestments, surrounded by the priests, who assisted in the manual acts (i.e. the Fraction of the Host and Commixture of a particle of It with the consecrated Wine). Communion was given first to the clergy and then to the laity in the following order: widows, virgins, the newly baptized and children, and finally the rest of the congregation. The service ended with the thanksgiving and prayer of dismissal said by the bishop.

In East and West alike this general scheme obtained and has been maintained throughout the subsequent history of the Church. Eastern liturgies have been more elaborate, particularly in the matter of the preparation of the elements, the solemn Entrance with the book of the Gospels and the sacred vessels, and the ceremonies connected with the Fraction and Commixture. These developments reached their climax by the eighth century, and subsequently only

---

[1] Brightman, *Liturgies Eastern and Western* (Oxford, 1896), pp. 3 ff., 189 ff., 510 f. *Apostolic Constitutions,* ii, 57, viii. 5–14. *Ethiopic Church Order.* Maclean and Cooper, *Testament of our Lord,* 19, 23. Gibson, *Syriac Didascalia,* xii. W. Riedel and Crum, *Canon of Athanasius of Alex.,* 5, 7, 13, 25, 39.

a few variations have occurred.[1] Throughout the dominant note of mystery has been maintained, the action culminating in the *epiklesis,* or invocation of the Holy Spirit upon the elements, as the method of consecration.

In the West the tendency has been in the direction of simplification and an increasing emphasis on the sacrificial aspect of the rite. In Rome Oriental liturgies survived till after the end of the third century, when the new order began to appear which was destined to permeate the whole of Western Christendom. The Greek Great Intercession became two separate unchanging prayers, and consecration by the recitation of the Words of Institution instead of the *epiklesis* dislocated the Canon, and modified the *epiklesis* almost beyond recognition. From this Canon the liturgy developed so that the history of the Mass in the West is the history of the gradual predominance of the Roman rite and the influence of the non-Roman types upon it. Of these latter, the less formal and more verbose Gallican variety, which continued to prevail in France till the ninth century when Charlemagne abolished it in favour of the Roman rite, in modified form survived only in the Mozarabic rite at Toledo (and on occasions in the Capilla de San Salvador in the Old Cathedral at Salamanca), and the Ambrosian rite at Milan, where it has approximated to the Roman pattern. All other Western liturgies, including the local uses in England (Sarum, Bangor, Hereford and York), and the post-Reformation rite in the English Prayer Book of 1549, and its subsequent revisions in 1552 and 1662,[2] are Roman in structure, while in the Latin Church, despite the alterations in the sixteenth century, the essential features of the medieval rite have been preserved.

The chief note of the Roman rite has always been its austere simplicity compared with its florid Eastern counterparts, and the absence of an Ikonostasis, or solid screen separating the sanctuary from the nave of the church, has made the Eucharistic offering the sacred drama in which all the faithful have an active and visible part in word and deed. The virtual elimination of the *epiklesis* and

[1] cf. H. Holloway, *A Study of the Byzantine Liturgy,* p. 182. F. Gavin, *Liturgy and Worship* (Lond., 1932), pp. 122 ff. B. J. Kidd, *The Churches of Eastern Christendom from A.D.* 451 (Lond., 1927), pp. 70 ff.

[2] In this connexion it is of interest to notice that in the revision of the English Prayer Book in 1927–8, a return was made to a more Eastern type of rite with the reintroduction of the *Epiklesis* as the mode of consecration after the words of institution.

the introduction of the Elevation of the Elements at the Consecration, symbolizing the Godward offering, have had the effect of bringing into greater prominence the priestly sacrificial action,[1] while the innovation of Low Mass, which has never been adopted in the East, has tended in the same direction and militated against the earlier notion of a corporate act of worship and oblation. To correct these tendencies a Liturgical Movement, associated particularly with the Benedictines, is now active in the West seeking to concentrate attention on the liturgy as the centre of corporate devotion as the common prayer of the Church. A freer use of the vernacular is urged to this end and the private devotions of the laity are brought into direct relation with the worship of the altar as the offering of the whole Church in heaven and on earth.

At the Reformation those who repudiated Catholicism decentralized Eucharistic worship completely and substituted for an organized liturgical rite preaching, hymn singing and extempore prayer. Even the ancient practice of the daily recitation of the Divine Office, consisting mainly of psalms and prayers said at the Canonical Hours (Mattins, Lauds, Prime, Tierce, Sext, None, Vespers and Compline), was abandoned. In the Church of England, however, the Catholic framework was retained, and the medieval offices were amalgamated as Morning and Evening Prayer (Mattins and Evensong). These became the central services till, under the influence of the Oxford Movement in the last century, Eucharistic worship was gradually restored to its former position. In Germany Luther attempted a reform of the Latin Mass in 1523, but having repudiated all 'that signifies oblation' his '*Formula Missae*' was robbed of the essential element in the traditional rite, and the same is true of the other Protestant service-books which subsequently appeared in Cologne, Strassburg, Geneva, and Zürich. They one and all took their departure from the Latin Mass and placed the emphasis on Communion through a memorial meal to the exclusion of the sacrificial Godward approach of the earlier rite, though in Sweden the actual medieval liturgy continued in use for a time till it was ousted by the *Church Order* of Laurentius Petri in 1571, and the later revisions in 1614 and 1811, which embodied the spirit of the Swedish reformation. In England Methodism widely adopted and adapted the Anglican Prayer Book to its particular devotional

---

[1] Hebert, *Liturgy and Society*, p. 82.

and sacramental requirements, but generally speaking English
Nonconformity until recently discarded altogether liturgical worship in favour of hymnody, extempore prayer, and the reading and
expounding of the Scriptures, with occasional administration of the
Lord's Supper independent of any specific rite in the traditional
meaning of the term. Thus, while Eastern Christendom has placed
in the foreground the idea of the Mystery-drama of adoration and
glorification and the Western Church that of sacrifice, Protestantism has returned to a subjective type of devotional experience
associated with a prophetic ministry in which sacrificial worship,
the sacred drama and liturgical prayer have no essential place.

ISLAM

Similarly in Islam, although daily public and private prayers at
appointed hours have always been a primary religious duty,
worship has never found expression in a sacrificial cultus. At first
verses of the Qur'an were recited in secret owing to the hostility
of the Meccans, and this exercise, known as the *salat*, was performed
facing Jerusalem till the prophet quarrelled with the Jews when, in
the second year after his arrival at Medina (*c.* A.D. 624), he received
a revelation to turn towards Mecca.[1] In a portico adjoining his house
he and his followers assembled for their daily ejaculations, which
in due course were systematized both as regards the manner and
times of recitation and the preliminary formulae and ablutions. In
addition to the *salat* said just before sunrise, at the close of the day
and during the night, one a few minutes after noon (the Jewish
minhāh) and a fifth between the middle of the day and nightfall,
were prescribed, though how far all were of obligation was a matter
of dispute. Ultimately the five-fold scheme was adopted together
with certain voluntary acts of devotion (*rak'ahs*), regarded as
meritorious, and a prescribed mode of ceremonial procedure.

At the appointed hour, which was fixed so as not to coincide
exactly with the times observed by the Arabs before their acceptance of Islam, the call to prayer is ordered to be sounded by the
muezzin from the minarets of every mosque in a set form of words
(*adhān*): 'God is Great (four times), I confess that there is no God
but Allah (twice); I confess that Mohammed is the Apostle of

[1] Qur'an, II, 136-45.

Allah (twice); come to prayer; come to do good (twice); God is great (twice); there is no God but Allah.' At this cry, wherever he may be, the Moslem is required to wash his face from the top of the forehead to the chin and from ear to ear, his feet up to the ankles, his hands and arms up to the elbows, and to rub with his wet hand a fourth part of the head.[1] He then spreads his prayer-carpet and facing Mecca repeats the passages from the Qur'an, making the prostrations and uttering the *takbir* (ejaculation of God's greatness) at stated intervals. Finally, at the conclusion of the *rak'ahs* he says, 'O God! have mercy on Mohammed and on his descendants, as Thou didst have mercy on Abraham and on his descendants. Thou art to be praised and Thou art great.'

In the mosque the *imam* leads the public devotions, not as a priest, but merely as the conductor in order to ensure the simultaneous repetition of the words and the performance of the actions. All face the niche (*mihrab*) in the rear wall indicating the direction of Mecca, but beyond assuming common postures and saying the same words, there is no attempt at liturgical worship. The mosque is essentially a place of corporate prayer devoid of altar, sanctuary, shrines or objects of worship and veneration of any kind. The *mihrab* is 'the heart of the house of worship'.[2] To the left stands the *minbar* (pulpit) on steps with a portal and a canopy resembling a ciborium over the platform. On the opposite side in the forepart of the portico is another platform on which the *muezzin* stands for the Friday *salat*, when all the men of the city are required by Moslem law to assemble at the principal mosque for the special noonday prayers preceded by a sermon. During the month of Ramadan, when the annual fast is observed, twenty *rak'ahs* are said after the evening *salat* which, though not of obligation, are considered to be a pious act carrying merit.

This daily routine of worship unquestionably has developed a strong sense of corporate religious solidarity and fostered a continuous life of prayer, however much it may have encouraged formality and the mechanical repetition of formulae in a language (Arabic) often imperfectly understood. To neglect the *salat* is to become an unbeliever, and the individual prayer (*du'a*) as well as

[1] The teeth should also be cleaned, the mouth and nostrils rinsed three times, the space between the fingers and toes rubbed with the wet hand, and the beard combed with the fingers, the correct order being maintained throughout the ablutions.

[2] *Encyclopaedia of Islam*, III, 485.

K

the prayer of public worship is secondary to this prayer of obligation which is the first service demanded of the faithful by Allah, being nothing less than the confession of faith. Therefore, it has to be performed with appropriate attention to detail and the utmost solemnity and decorum. If the exercise lacks mystical devotion, it cultivates personal religion, and makes God and the spiritual world ever-present realities in the routine of daily life.

CHAPTER XII

Immortality

PALAEOLITHIC CEREMONIAL INTERMENTS

No study of the history of religion is complete without an examination of the problem that has exercised the mind and imagination of man for at least two hundred thousand years since *Homo Neanderthalensis* first answered in the affirmative the question of questions, 'If a man die shall he live again?' From the Palaeolithic caves of Western Europe to the Parsi towers of silence and our Christian churchyards and cemeteries, an unbroken chain of evidence exists bearing witness to the universal conviction that human effort and achievement does not end with the grave. It was this belief that led the brutish-looking Mousterians to lay to rest a youth about sixteen years of age with such care and ceremony in a cliff cave near the village of Le Moustier in the Dordogne, the type-station of this phase of Palaeolithic culture. The body was placed in the attitude of sleep, with the knees drawn up in the contracted position and the right forearm under the head. A bed of flint flakes formed his pillow, and close by the hand was a splendid *coup-de-poing* implement 17 cm. in length. Other flints characteristic of the period were discovered in the grave, together with the bones of the wild ox, charred and split; doubtless the remains of a funeral feast.[1]

Moreover, this is not an isolated instance of ceremonial interment in the mid-Palaeolithic. Thus, similar burials have been found at La Chapelle-aux-Saints in the department of Corrèze where, 3 metres from the entrance of a cave near the village, a middle-aged Neanderthal male skeleton lay on its back, the head to the west, and wedged in position with stones. The right arm was bent up and turned to the right. Fragments of bones of a large cow were deposited above the head, and flints, quartz, ochre and broken bones

---

[1] Klaatsch and Hauser, *Arch. für Anthrop.*, XXXV, 1909, p. 287.

were arranged round the body.[1] A third example occurred in the Dordogne at La Farrassie. Here four Neanderthal skeletons were concealed in a rock shelter in a Mousterian stratum beneath flat stones, special care having been taken to protect the skull and arms. When it was first discovered this body lay on its back with the lower limbs bent to the right, and the left arm lying along the side, the right raised up and bent. In the same deposit were the remains of two children with Mousterian implements and fragments of the bones of bison, reindeer, and horse, evidently, again, the remnants of a funeral feast.[2] At Krapina near Zagreb in Croatia charred bones and a Neanderthal skull with cuts on the cranium have been explained by Gorjanovic-Kramberger, who discovered them, in terms of cannibalism,[3] but there is no conclusive confirmatory evidence of this practice in Palaeolithic times.

If there is much that is conjectural in the interpretation of these ceremonial interments, Professor Macalister is on sure ground when he affirms that

> the lowly Mousterian Man, degenerate though he may have been, was conscious of something more than merely animal within him; already he had begun to look forward to a life beyond the grave—a life like that to which he was accustomed, for he could conceive of none other, where he would need food and clothing, and the instruments for procuring them. As his comrades passed, each in his turn into the silent land, he laid beside their bodies such things as he imagined would minister to their necessities in the mysterious other world.[4]

It has been suggested that the limbs were flexed to prevent the return of the departed to disturb the living, while others have urged that the contracted posture was adopted in imitation of the attitude of the foetus to secure new birth beyond the grave. In later times such meanings were attached to this method of disposal on occasions, but it is doubtful whether *Homo Neanderthalensis* had sufficient anatomical knowledge to enable him to think in terms of pre-natal symbolism, while the grave equipment is indicative of care and solicitude rather than of fear as the motive.

[1] A. and J. Bouyssonie and L. Gardon, *L'Anthropologie*, XIX, 1908, p. 513. M. Boule, *Annales de Paléontologie*, VI, 1911, pp. 111–72.

[2] L. Capitan and D. Peyrony, *L'Anthropologie*, XXI, 1910, p. 372.

[3] *Mittheilungen der Anthropologischen Gesellschaft in Wien*, XXXII, 1902, p. 189; XXXIV, 1904, p. 187.

[4] *A Text-book of European Archaeology* (Camb., 1921), p. 343.

In the Upper Palaeolithic the earliest ancestors of *Homo sapiens* in Western Europe were not content merely to protect their dead and provide them with food and implements. To secure their restoration to life in the hereafter they appear to have painted the bones red, as at Paviland,[1] or surrounded the body with ochre as the surrogate of blood, the vitalizing agent *par excellence*, together with shells, widely employed as fertility charms.[2] In the Grottes des Enfants at Grimaldi, near Mentone, for instance, most of the skeletons were covered with multitudes of shells, and in the highest stratum the remains of two children (from whom the site has derived its name) rested on a shroud composed of nearly a thousand sea-shells.[3] At La Grotte du Cavillon, in the same series, the body of a man of Cro-Magnon type lying in the contracted position had over two hundred pierced shells about his head, while a collar of Nassa shells adorned the neck of a boy's skeleton at Barma Grande.[4] In the original Cro-Magnon burial at Les Eyzies three hundred pierced marine shells, chiefly of the *littorina* species, were found beside the skeletons,[5] and at Laugerie-Basse, a neighbouring site, cowries were arranged in pairs upon the body.[6]

At this early stage in the development of the cult of the dead there was probably no notion of the soul as a separate and separable entity in the form of an *anima*, as in the later animistic hypothesis. The distinction between a life-principle, or soul-substance, associated with the body and its organs and secretions, and a phantom, or second-self connected with dreams, trances and visionary experiences, presupposes conceptual thinking in terms of personality and philosophical reflection, which, as has been explained, are hardly likely to have arisen under Palaeolithic conditions when man was mainly occupied with practical questions based upon observation rather than with mystical interpretations. As a hunter he had been led to associate the heart with the centre of vitality, as the cave-paintings reveal, and life and death were facts of everyday

---

[1] Sollas, *J.R.A.I.*, XLIII, 1913, pp. 325 ff.

[2] J. W. Jackson, *Shells as Evidence of the Migrations of Culture* (Manchester, 1917), pp. 138 ff.

[3] R. Verneau, *Les Grottes de Grimaldi* (Monaco, 1906), II, pl. ii. Boule and Verneau, *L'Anthropologie*, XVII, pp. 257–320.

[4] A. J. Evans, *J.A.I.*, XXII, 1892–3, pp. 287 ff.

[5] Lartet and Christy, *Reliquiae Aquitaniae* (Lond., 1875), pp. 62 ff.

[6] *Comptes-Rendus de l'Accademie des Sciences*, LXXIV, 1872, pp. 1060 ff.

experience. The obvious inference to be drawn from a dead body is that something of vital importance has left it, and no hunter could fail to realize that loss of blood produced loss of vitality, faintness and death. It would not require much speculation, therefore, to connect the blood with the life, or vital essence, the restoration of which by the aid of ochre, for example, was calculated to revivify the corpse.

PRIMITIVE CONCEPTION OF IMMORTALITY

Such ideas as these, together with an undefined belief in human survival which may not have involved the notion of a land of the dead and certainly not that of eternal existence, represent in all probability the extent to which Palaeolithic Man formulated a doctrine of immortality. The next life was a continuation of earthly existence, but on a new and different plane of being, so that it became possible to do things not done before, or in a new manner, the hereafter often being regarded as a kind of 'looking-glass world' where the normal order is reversed. But food and drink, weapons and warmth are still required. Death for the primitive mind is accidental, an unnatural intrusion in the normal sequence of events due to violence, witchcraft or some malicious magical operation. Sickness and disease are consequently curable by appropriate treatment unless more powerful magic counteracts the beneficent functions of the medicine-man, when the patient inevitably succumbs. It follows, therefore, if life and health are the norm in human existence, that immortality is an inherent possession, so that, as Frazer says,

> a life after death is not a matter of speculation or conjecture, of hope and fear; it is a practical certainty which the individual as little dreams of doubting as he doubts the reality of his conscious existence. He assumes it without inquiry and acts upon it without hesitation, as if it were one of the best-ascertained truths within the limits of human experience.[1]

When he attempts to codify his belief in terms of myths it is the origin of death and the recurrent cycle of life that finds a place in the sacred story of the tribe to express its conviction that the human race is inherently immortal. Thus, man is represented as having

[1] *The Belief in Immortality* (Lond., 1913), vol. I, p. 468.

been created eternally young until he lost the secret of perpetual youth through some accidental event or wile which prevented his changing his skin periodically like the serpents, crabs, lizards and other animals who rejuvenate themselves, as it is supposed, by this means.[1]

The futility of the alleged cause of the initial disaster[2] is comparable to the factors in actual experience which are responsible for the termination of life prematurely. 'In the midst of life we are in death', and to none is this fact more apparent than to the native living under precarious conditions in a hostile environment, natural and super-natural. In addition to the abundant accidental causes of death awaiting him at every turn, the prevalence of sorcery makes existence a risky business. To meet this complex situation he expresses his hopes and fears in a concrete myth and ritual not so much to explain what happened in the past as to deal with the emergencies of the present, and to seek rejuvenation hereafter. What was lost by a trivial incident cannot lie outside the wit of man to regain, and however much the approach of death may be feared, the conviction that it is an intensive element in a recurrent cycle of life gives fortitude and confidence in ultimate victory.

Thus, when an individual dies he is believed to be still alive because life is the normal condition of existence, but, nevertheless, clearly something has happened in the dissolution of the body which demands explanation. At first the facts and inferences may have sufficed for practical purposes, but in course of time animistic interpretations arose to account for 'the life as able to go away and leave the body insensible or dead', and the phantom, or second self, as appearing to people at a distance from it. It may have been, as Tylor suggested, that 'by combining the life and the phantom as parts of the body, and therefore as belonging to one another, the conception of an *anima*, or "ghost-soul", arose as a separable vital principle with a form of its own'.[3]

The association of soul-substance with particular seats of vitality doubtless paved the way for the division of the human organism into the duality, body and soul, and, therefore, provided a basis for Tylorian animism, especially as these ideas took shape in conjunction with the belief in human survival. The provision of the dead

[1] Frazer, *Folk-Lore in the Old Testament* (Lond., 1918), vol. I, pp. 66 ff.

[2] Gen. iii. 3.

[3] *Primitive Culture,* vol. I, pp. 428 ff.

with food and drink and weapons, and the fact that despite the use of vitalizing agents (ochre, shells, incense, &c.) the corpse remained immobile, probably suggested the existence of a spiritual entity which comes into existence at death, namely the ghost.

The distinction between the vital force which animates nature impersonally and assumes a more personal manifestation in man, capable of leaving the body in sleep and sickness, and the ghost that separates permanently at death is brought out by the Dutch ethnologists in Indonesia. Thus, Warneck explains that

> man has two souls, one of which, the bodily soul, pertains to him during his life-time. The other soul, the shadow soul, emerges only when the man dies. The soul of the living man is conceived of as a kind of life-stuff (*seelstoff*), indestructible and animating alternatively this man or that. Among peoples of lower grade the soul-stuff is conceived imper-sonally as a vital power which, at the death of its present possessor, passes over to something else, man, animal or plant. Higher-developed peoples conceive the soul as a refined body, to some extent an *alter ego*, a kind of man within the man. But it is so independent and incalculable a thing that it may at any moment leave him for a longer or shorter period, as, for example, in dreams, when it is frightened, or when it thinks itself insulted. The well-being of the man depends upon its moods. It can be nourished, strengthened and augmented; it can also be weakened, diminished, and enticed away.[1]

Persistent illness frequently is attributed to a failure to recover the missing soul and unless a medicine-man, or shaman, succeeds in restoring it to its owner, death ensues. After permanently quitting the body it may hover around its old haunts for a while, sometimes inhabiting the grave or its immediate vicinity to partake of the offerings of food and drink placed at the tomb for its benefit, and warm itself at the fires kept burning there. The Feast of the Dead at a stated interval after the funeral is usually regarded as the oc-casion of the final departure of the ghost to its ultimate destination, and the practice of secondary burial, when the bones have been exposed or buried for a season, is probably a variation of the same belief. The mourning ceremonies are then terminated as their object in enabling the soul to reach its goal has been attained.

Conversely, when the return of the dead is feared, elaborate

---

[1] cf. Chapman, *American Anthropologist*, New Series, 1921, pp. 298 f. See also .H. Hutton, *A Primitive Philosophy of Life* (Oxford, 1938).

precautions are taken to prevent the ghost finding its way back to
its former abode. Hence the destruction of the house and property
of the deceased, shifting the camp, binding the corpse, burial at the
cross-roads, beating drums, creating unpleasant odours, and similar
devices calculated to scare off the unwelcome visitor. Rites of this
character are common in the case of persons dying a violent death,
such as warriors slain in battle and suicides, women passing away in
childbirth, those who die away from home with no relatives to
perform the funerary rites.[1] But while fear is often the dominant
motive in certain aspects of the cult of the dead, it is frequently
mingled with love and regard, and arises more from dread of the
mysterious than a deep-seated antagonism to the departed, unless
the spirit is known to be revengeful on account of the manner of
its death.

The method adopted in disposing of the mortal remains may
indicate the direction and character of the next life, as, for example,
when a cave used as a burial chamber is thought to be the entrance
of the underworld.[2] When the Isles of the Blest are situated across
the sea, or along a river, the corpse is usually put in a canoe and set
adrift, the destination sometimes being the ancestral home of the
tribe. The widespread custom of placing the dead in trees, or on
platforms or canoes lodged among the branches, seems to be connected in Borneo with the notion that men are derived from and
return to trees,[3] and generally, like cremation, raised burial is the
more honourable mode of disposal. Therefore, it is reserved for the
ruling classes where it is not a universal practice.[4]

MUMMIFICATION

In Ancient Egypt, on the other hand, where the cult of the dead
reached its zenith, the idea of a life beyond the grave was centred
in the preservation of the mortal remains of the Pharaoh in the
tomb. The fact that bodies buried in the sand were naturally desiccated and so continued little changed in appearance after death

[1] Frazer, *The Fear of the Dead in Primitive Religion* (Lond., 1933–6), vols. I–III.

[2] *28th B., B.A.E.* (Wash., 1904), p. 251. Brasseur de Bourbourg, *Histoire des Nations
civilisées du Mexico*, III (Paris, 1859), p. 21.

[3] A. C. Kruijt, *Het Animisme in den Indischen Archip.*, 1906, p. 373.

[4] Radin, *37th R. B.A.E.* (Wash., 1923), pp. 140 ff.

doubtless strengthened if it did not actually give rise to this notion of human survival.[1] Furthermore, the adoption of large and airy brick-lined tombs, which at once destroyed natural desiccation, led at an early period (i.e. not later than the IInd Dynasty) to attempts at mummification by bandaging and the use of preservative agents to prevent corruption. By the Vth Dynasty the internal organs had begun to be removed and the cavity filled with resin and linen. The wrappings were soaked with resin, the body was moulded into shape, and the features were depicted by means of paint.[2] But it was not until the New Kingdom in the XVIIIth to the XXth Dynasties, that the art was perfected. First the brain was extracted and then all the internal organs were removed except the heart as the seat of life, and possibly the kidneys. The corpse was next soaked in a salt-bath for several weeks to remove the fatty substances and enable the epidermis to be peeled off except from the head, fingers and toes. The viscera was embalmed separately and placed in canopic jars with stoppers carved in likeness of the four sons of Horus. When the body was taken out of the bath it was desiccated in the sun or over a slow fire, and then resin mixed with natron or salt and animal fat were applied to the surface. Linen wads dipped in the mixture were packed into the body-cavity, cranium and nostrils prior to the solemn process of bandaging and the insertion of appropriate amulets, which included a model of the eye of Horus, and the heart-scarab in green stone, or the *crux ansata*, to restore life to the heart and prevent it witnessing against the owner at the time of judgement. The entire process occupied seventy days.[3]

In the next two Dynasties (XXI and XXII) various devices were employed for making the reconstruction more life-like, and the mummy was painted with red ochre, artificial eyes were inserted and the cheeks rouged. After this period the art began to decline, and although the practice survived into the Christian era, evisceration ceased, preservation being secured merely by packing the body in common salt.[4] But throughout the long and complex history of mummification the motive was the same—the preser-

[1] Elliot Smith, *Proceedings Royal Phil. Society of Glasgow*, 1910. *Essays and Studies Presented to William Ridgeway* (Camb., 1913), pp. 9 ff.

[2] Eliot Smith, 'Egyptian Mummies', *J.E.A.*, I, 1914, p. 192.

[3] W. R. Dawson, 'Making a Mummy', *J.E.A.*, XIII, 1927, pp. 40-9.

[4] W. R. Dawson, *Proc. Soc. of Medicine*, XX, 1927, pt. vi.

vation of the body to life immortal either in the tomb or in some
distant realm. Hence the ceremony known as 'Opening the Mouth'
held at the conclusion of the mechanical operations.

First the mummy was sprinkled with holy water and censed, and
the lips touched with various sacred emblems as the principal priest
proclaimed, 'I open thy mouth with the Great Magician where-
with the mouth of every god is opened'. Another priest, impersonating Horus, completed the transformation of the dead man
into a living soul (*ba*), as the eye of Horus had resuscitated Osiris.
Furthermore, to render the deceased in the hereafter invulnerable
and irresistible, as well as immortal, he was offered bread and beer.
Finally, to enable him to leave the tomb and enjoy the delights of
the idealized after-life, as depicted on the walls of the necropolis,
he was equipped with a roll of papyrus (the *Book of the Dead*)
containing magical texts written in hieroglyphic script.

Originally, it would seem, the Egyptians thought that the dead
lived in or at the tomb, and, therefore, they made adequate provision
for their comfort and sustenance in the cemeteries. But side by side
with this belief there developed the notion of the underworld ruled
by Osiris and the celestial realms of Re, subsequently fused into one
theology. Similarly, the idea of the soul was as complex and contradictory as the conception of personality. With a man was born a
guardian, or *ka,* which resided in his body during the whole of his
life, except when it went on a journey during sleep. It gave all the
attributes of life to the individual, but the actual personality consisted of the visible body and the invisible intelligence (*khu*), which
was situated in the heart (*ab*) or abdomen. At death the *ka* guided
the fortunes of the individual in the hereafter, and appears to
have preceded the deceased to the abode of Osiris or Re since in
the Pyramid Texts a man is said to go 'to his ka to the sky'.[1] Thus,
it was separated from its *protégé* by more than the mere distance to
the cemetery, playing the part of a guardian angel rather than an
integral element of his personality. Moreover, the *ka* was at first
confined to kings, and only gradually became a universal possession.

The breath, as distinct from the intelligence, was the vital essence,
and after the XIIth Dynasty the two were symbolized by the *ba*,
or human-headed bird with human arms, hovering over the

[1] Breasted, *Religion and Thought in Ancient Egypt,* pp. 52 ff.

mummy, extending to its nostrils in one hand the figure of a swelling sail, the hieroglyph for wind or breath, and in the other the *crux ansata*. As the disembodied soul, or ghost, which came into existence for the first time at death, the *ba* was represented as flying down the tomb-shaft to the mummy in the chamber below, and wandering about the cemetery. It was in order to transform the deceased into a *ba* that the 'Opening of the Mouth' ceremonies were performed, for only when the missing parts were restored to the physical body could it become a living entity again in the hereafter, just as the mummy of Osiris was revivified by the eye of Horus. The process of mummification, therefore, was the solemn act by which the dead man was made into a living soul (*ba*) after the technical skill of the embalmers had rendered the body imperishable, and the ritual acts of the priests had reconstituted the mental faculties, and supplied the magical devices to enable the resuscitated individual to leave the tomb and enter upon his new life beyond the grave. To assist him in any laborious tasks he might be called upon to perform in the Elysian Fields, wooden or blue-glazed statuettes of men, known as Ushabti, were provided from the time of the Middle Kingdom, equipped with hoe and basket to take his place in the cultivation of the soil and the transportation of sand from the east to the west in the Nether World.[1] In the tomb of Seti I, the second Pharaoh of the XIXth Dynasty, over seven hundred Ushabti figures were found, showing the extent to which this principle of magical equipment had developed in the luxurious days of the Empire.

Distinct from these figures were the portrait statues placed in the tomb as an image of the deceased in stone or wood in order to provide a recognizable habitation for the disembodied soul should the mummy perish or be destroyed.[2] Since the first requisite in their production was the perpetuation of the likeness of the actual person represented, physical deformities were often displayed, and like the mummy they had to be reanimated by means of an 'Opening of the Mouth' ritual, to transform them into a living organism. Therefore, they were more than soul-receptacles, and were treated as the deceased himself. The sculptor was called *s'nh*, 'he who makes to live', and it was the duty of the king to perform the reanimation

[1] *Book of the Dead,* chap. VI.

[2] Although they are often designated '*Ka* statues', they are nowhere described as such in the Pyramid Texts, nor do they seem to have fulfilled this function, being associated with the *ba* rather than the *ka*.

ceremony of the portrait of his father. At the top of the tomb-shaft a hut, or *serdab*, containing a statue was erected at which offerings were made.

Nevertheless, the transference of the immortal element to a *simulacrum* of the deceased other than the actual mummy doubtless tended to dissociate the soul from the body. In Egypt the continuation of life beyond the grave was always bound up with the imperishability of the mortal remains, or their surrogate, but elsewhere the body, or its image, often became merely the vehicle of freeing the soul from its fetters. In California, for example, the Diegueño made an effigy of eagle feathers, matting and cloth, supposed to contain the soul of the deceased, and bearing some likeness to him. For a week funeral rites were held in conjunction with it, and then it was burnt to set free the soul.[1] A further stage in this process is illustrated in the Tyrian version of the legend of Herakles where the hero is made to ascend to the heavens in the smoke of his own pyre, the body acting as a vehicle for the conveyance of the immortal element to its celestial home.[2]

THE GREEK CONCEPTION OF IMMORTALITY

(*a*) *Homeric.*—In Greece the primitive conceptions of the animating principle became the *psyche*, originally a 'breath of air', or thin vapour, breathed out in the last breath of a dying person. But the soul as a double of man, though it might be a shadowy image independent of the body, was often represented in material form as an animal, such as a snake or a bird flying out of the mouth. In classical design it combined anthropomorphic features with wings and the lightness of air, the practice of cremation giving a more ethereal aspect to the conception.

The *psyche* in the Homeric poems had nothing to do with the conscious life before the dissolution of the living organism, and as the ghost identified with the expiring breath, it is merely a shade and nothing more. The souls of the murderered suitors followed Hermes into Hades squeaking like bats, recalling the notion of the bird-like appearance of the soul, while the 'impotent heads of the dead', as Homer calls them, are described as witless and feeble things

[1] *Contrib. to Mus. of Amer. Indians,* Heye Foundation, X, 1919, pp. 5, 9 ff.
[2] Sophocles, *Trachiniae,* 1191 ff. Diodorus Siculus, IV, 38.

comparable to the unfortunate inhabitants of the Babylonian 'Land of No-Return', or the Hebrew Sheol. 'Speak not soothingly to me of death, glorious Odysseus. For so I might live on earth, I would rather be the servant of another, of a poor man who had little substance, than to be lord over all the dead.'[1] So spake the shade of Achilles to Odysseus, just as in Babylonia when Gilgamesh asked his former companion Enki-du, then in the underworld, to relate the law of the land he had seen, he replied, 'I cannot tell thee, my friend, I cannot tell thee. If I were to tell thee the law of the earth which I have experienced, you would sit down and weep the whole day.'[2] The same uninspiring doctrine of the hereafter prevailed among the Hebrews at the time of the Exile, when the dead were regarded as lying huddled together in a subterranean region of darkness, covered with dust, conscious but inactive and silent.[3] 'The small and the great' were there without distinction, the righteous and the wicked, for Sheol was 'the house appointed for all living'.[4]

In Greece until the middle of the fifth century B.C., 'the writing on the graves is entirely silent concerning posthumous existence. The dead person speaks only of this life, his city, his family, clan or children, and often of his own achievement, with pride or with love.'[5] Nevertheless, as the pre-exilic Sheol doctrine replaced an earlier belief in a conscious existence beyond the grave among the Hebrews involving food offerings in the shaft-tombs and rock-cut chambers of Palestine, together with funerary rites mentioned and often condemned in the Old Testament,[6] so in Homer we find references to a developed cult of the dead. As Rhode has pointed out, the elaborate offerings at the obsequies of Patroklos are 'inexplicable if the soul immediately upon its dissolution flutters away insensible, helpless and powerless, and therefore incapable of enjoying the offerings made to it'.[7] The whole narrative clearly presupposes that the *psyche* can be strengthened and refreshed in

---

[1] *Od.*, xi, 488 ff.

[2] cf. chap. IV, pp. 114 f. for Babylonian conception of the Land of No-Return.

[3] Job x. 22. Ps. xxii. 15, xxx. 9, xxxi. 17, xlix. 19, cxv. 17. Isa. xlvii. 5.

[4] Job xxx. 23. cf. iii. 13–19, xiv. 12–14.

[5] Farnell, *Greek Hero Cults and Ideas of Immortality* (Oxford, 1921), p. 397.

[6] cf. Deut. xxvi. 14. Lev. xix. 27 f., xxi. 1–5. Isa. xv. 2, xx. 12. 2 Sam. iii. 31. Gen. xxxvii. 34.

[7] *Psyche* (Lond., 1925), p. 13.

the hereafter by the dutiful sacrifices of the survivors on earth, and it was only under the influence of the Olympian religion that Hades was transformed into a *cul-de-sac* peopled by inert shades, with a Tartarus reserved for the punishment of those heroes who had been guilty of offences against the gods, and Isles of the Blest in the Western Sea for the reward of divine descendants, such as Achilles, Herakles and Menelaus.

(b) *The Mysteries*.—Equally foreign to the Olympian distinction between immortals and mortals whereby a permanent gulf was fixed between the gods and men, was the Mystery conception which in the sixth century B.C. introduced a new attitude to the life of the world to come. If in the Homeric period the gods had been held capable of raising mortals to their own realm, that is to say, to immortality, the human and divine orders were regarded as absolutely divided in place and nature so that any attempt on the part of man to enter into direct relationship with the gods was calculated to bring upon him the vengeance of heaven.[1] The Mysteries, on the other hand, provided, as we have seen, a means of attaining such union by the identification of the worshipper with the cult-deity through wild music, orgiastic dances and Bacchic frenzy, or in the more restrained rites at Eleusis, in undergoing a mystical death and resurrection during the process of initiation. However it was secured, the blessed life hereafter resulted from communion with the deity on earth and sharing in his or her life and experiences. Those who had confessed the faith of Demeter and Persephone, associated themselves with their sorrow and joy, and assisted at the sacred drama in the Telesterion, were set apart from the rest of mankind and redeemed from shadowy existence in the subterranean regions of darkness and gloom, and destined to enjoy for ever the delights of walking in Persephone's meadows.

But attractive as was this new hope of salvation and eternal life, and dignified the procedures, the cult failed to give any ethical significance to the idea of immortality, as Diogenes was not slow to recognize. For the Eleusianian initiate the future was secure. By virtue of his purification and regeneration he had already attained the higher life which eventually would lead to the flowery fields and streams of living waters, beneath trees laden with delicious fruits which awaited him beyond the grave. There in the golden sunshine,

[1] Rhode, op. cit., pp. 253 f.

shaded with thickets of myrtle and cooled by gentle breezes, he would hold pleasant and enlightened converse with his fellow-initiates, singing and feasting, and listening to sublime strains from the Elysian choir. In short, a veritable terrestrial paradise differing in place rather than in kind from the cloudless serenity of Olympus, and the Homeric Isles of the Blest.

It remained for Orphism to introduce a moral content into the doctrine of the hereafter by making the soul's lot in Hades conditioned by its former life on earth.[1] The daily struggle between good and evil found its counterpart in the myth, and the Orphic initiate in his endeavours to escape from his 'Titanic' nature, felt that he received grace and strength which enabled him to engage successfully in the conflict between two superhuman principles. But he also realized that a fundamental change of heart was essential if the curse of the Titan was to be overcome permanently, and the soul be transformed into the true image of Dionysos. Consequently, he underwent a protracted system of discipline to cleanse his soul from original sin, believing that while this life was too short to accomplish the task, the progress he made would be carried over into the next phase of existence when he was reborn after an interval in paradise. Gradually the vicious circle of transmigration and reincarnation would be broken and the soul attain rest and enlightenment at length in Dionysos through the sanctifying grace of Orpheus. Thus, released from its bondage it would return once more to the gods and take its place among them.

(c) *The Platonic Conception.*—The Ionian monists, on the other hand, although they were contemporaries of the Orphics, had a very different outlook and with the exception of Heraclitus, they were not concerned with the deeper human problems. The Pythagoreans, who regarded the soul as a 'blend' (κρᾶσις) of the elements composing the body, adopted the theory of transmigration and practised asceticism as a factor in purification. Anaxagoras first introduced the conception of νοῦς, or reasoning thought, as the source of motion, bringing cosmos out of chaos, and having kinship with the Supreme Mind of the world. Thus, in the sphere of intellect, he affirmed a relationship between the human and the divine analogous to that postulated by the Orphics in the ethical order. The scientific philosophers and the humanistic Sophists of the fifth

[1] cf. chap. V, p. 139.

century B.C. were thorough-going materialists, but Socrates realized that the soul is man's real self, his personality, which should be kept pure from the body in this life because it is the seat of virtue and knowledge. Indeed he went about doing nothing else but urging his fellow-citizens, young and old alike, to care for their souls rather than their bodies.[1]

For the first time it was realized that within man, as an integral part of himself and not as an intrusive element from without, there was something called the *psyche* which was capable of attaining wisdom, and this is merely another name for virtue, goodness, and righteousness. No one had ever put this interpretation on the 'breath of life' before, and if Socrates combined the Orphic doctrine of purification with the scientific view of the soul as the waking consciousness, he gave a significance to the term comparable to our conception of 'spirit'. Hitherto in the fifth century it had been used almost exclusively by the Athenian writers in the traditional sense of the escaping life-breath of a dying man about to become the 'ghost', and occasionally for the seat of the emotions.[2] But for Socrates normal consciousness was the true self which was capable of striving after 'wisdom', and by its essential nature of surviving the dissolution of the body to which it gives life. Because vitality is an indispensable condition of its existence it must be imperishable and therefore immortal. So when the body dies the soul withdraws to some other sphere of action.

It was seemingly this method of approach to the theory of the soul and the doctrine of immortality that Plato developed though it is not easy to arrange his conclusions in chronological order, or to determine precisely how many of the statements are his own, and how much he owed to his master. He is clearly convinced, however, that the soul in all respects is superior to the body, and in this life it 'makes each one of us to be what we are'.[3] It is of divine origin and functions in thought to correlate pure knowledge with the phenomenal world apprehended by sensation. In its intrinsic nature it is indestructible.

> because that which is ever in motion is immortal; but that which moves another and is moved by another, in ceasing to move ceases to live. Only

[1] *Apol.*, 29d, 4 ff.; 30a, 7 ff.
[2] J. Burnet, *Essays and Addresses* (Lond., 1929), pp. 151 ff.
[3] *Laws*, 959.

the self-moving, since it never leaves itself, never ceases to move; but this is also the source and beginning of motion to all that moves besides. The beginning, however, is unbegotten, for everything that is begotten must have a beginning, yet the beginning is not begotten of anything; for if the beginning were begotten, it must be indestructible. Thus that which moves itself must be the beginning of motion; and this can be neither destroyed nor begotten. But since that which is moved by itself has been seen to be immortal, he who says that this self-motion is the essence and the very idea of the soul, will not be put to shame.[1]

It might be objected, however, that as in this life the 'motions' of the soul are quiescent in sleep or trance, so in death they cease to operate altogether.

With the Orphics Plato agreed that the soul is distinct from the body as a 'separable entity' derived from the Supreme God. Its purpose is to correlate absolute reality, apprehended by pure knowledge, with the phenomenal world, apprehended by sensation and in will to bring the body into harmonious relation with the idea of the Good. It is not clear whether he believed in the survival of individuality after death though he adopted the Orphic doctrine of retributive justice extending to the hereafter. Successive lives of the soul were based on the supposition that a lifetime is insufficient for purification by philosophy to accomplish its task of setting free the individual from the body altogether to return to the heavenly sphere whence he came. For the majority this deliverance involved a cycle of ten thousand years, and even for the philosopher, guileless and true though he be, not less than three thousand years. But the philosophic soul, released at death, is freed from all carnal appetite, and will not again pass to another body.[2]

The cycle of birth in successive lives was never elaborated by Plato as in the Oriental doctrine of *karma* in terms of either pantheistic monism or pluralism, though if all souls are one in origin, derived from the divine principle itself, and if the soul's activity is essentially moral, transmigration is a natural corollary unless release from the body can be secured in this life to enable it to embark upon a purely spiritual career hereafter.[3] Plato, however,

---

[1] *Phaedrus*, 245 f. cf. *Laws*, 893–6.

[2] *Timaeus*, 42. *Phaedrus*, 248–9. *Phaedo*, 63 ff., 81 ff.

[3] The Oriental attitude to the problem has been discussed at some length in chapters VI and VII.

was a dualist inasmuch as he believed that soul and body belonged to two different worlds. Thus, in the theory of Ideas in the macrocosm the phenomenal world is set over against the ideal world, in the microcosm man's material body is contrasted with the immortal soul. Since divine communion can never be attained fully while physical conditions remain, the emancipation of the reason (i.e. the soul) is essential to the complete mystical apprehension of pure Truth and Being: hence personal immortality. But in the process of securing eternal life Deity plays no part. Certain qualities are of themselves inherently immortal and therefore have survival value. The soul that cultivates these attributes becomes indestructible by its own unaided efforts.

For Aristotle the soul is 'the first actuality of a natural body' and the life of pure reason is the highest human activity. But while on this hypothesis the active reason is the immortal part of the soul, the notion of impersonal reason does not carry with it any implications of a personal survival after the dissolution of the body.[1] Certainly he did not credit the eternal soul with memory as this faculty he assigned to the passive part of the intellect which is perishable. Neither could it have individuality or conscious life apart from the body.[2] Pre-existence he denied, and though he accepted the facts of personality and moral responsibility, he regarded parentage as the cause of succession in offspring thereby cutting across reincarnation and transmigration. The Aristotelian conception of the function of the Active Reason as coming from without and supervening upon an animal body, became the 'rational soul' of patristic and scholastic theology, created *ex nihilo* by God.

JEWISH IDEA OF IMMORTALITY

In Christianity, however, several streams of thought and practice met, and if in the Gentile world these were largely conditioned by Platonic and Aristotelian ideas, in its cradleland a very different approach to the problem of the soul and the after-life was adopted. The former negative Sheol doctrine gave place in post-exilic Judaism to a belief in a future resurrection of the righteous in a reanimated body, The relationship between Yahweh and His

[1] *De Anima*, 415, 23 ff.; 429, 10 ff.; 430, 22 ff.
[2] op. cit., 430, 22 ff.

people, as represented by the Hebrew prophets, was too intimate and enduring to be terminated by death, and, therefore, although the Sadducees persistently rejected all innovations and Pharisaic speculations, gradually a new conception of immortality found expression deriving its inspiration from the lofty universalism of the Deutero-Isaiah and the prophecies respecting the Messianic Kingdom. As the belief in the omnipotence and omnipresence of God developed, it was found impossible to confine His jurisdiction to this world. With the fuller apprehension of the ethical nature of Deity, and the recognition of the apparent triumph of the wicked in this life, it was realized that even those who made their bed in Sheol could not escape the supreme Lord of creation.[1] Consequently, devout Jews became convinced that beyond the grave they would be guided and upheld by Yahweh and eventually received by Him in glory.

Thus, from a belief in ethical monotheism the hope of personal immortality arose as a natural corollary.

> The specifically religious desire of Immortality [says Baron von Hugel] begins not with Immortality, but with God. The religious soul does not seek, find, or assume its own immortality; and thereupon seek, find, or assume God. But it seeks, finds, experiences, and loves God; and because of God, and of this, its very real though still imperfect, intercourse with God—because of these experiences which lie right within the noblest joys, fears, hopes, necessities, certainties which emerge within any and every field of its life here below—it finds, rather than seeks, Immortality of a certain kind.[2]

It was in this way that the post-exilic community came to a knowledge of an individual relationship with the Lord of all the earth that transcended even death itself, and to look forward to a time when God's world of moral order should be established in a new heaven and a new earth wherein righteousness prevailed.[3] Nothing short of the fullness of the entire earth could be His inheritance, and sooner or later the divine kingdom must be established and death abolished.[4] But this implied that the faithful Israelite would pass eternity in the restored kingdom on earth and

---

[1] Ps. xvi. 10, lxxxvi. 13, cxxxix. 7–12. Job xix. 21–7, cf. xiv. 13–15.

[2] *Essays and Addresses on the Philosophy of Religion*, 1st Series (Lond., 1928), p. 197.

[3] cf. Oesterley, *Immortality and the Unseen World* (Lond., 1921), pp. 208 ff.

[4] Isa. xxiv.–xxvii., esp. xxv. 7, 8, xxvi. 11–21.

not in Sheol, while those who had already crossed the veil would return with joy and be reinstated in their physical bodies. Thus, by the second century B.C., when the apocalyptic literature was beginning to take shape in the strenuous days of persecution under Antiochus Epiphanes (175–163 B.C.) and the subsequent Maccabaean bid for freedom (167), it was definitely asserted that 'the dead shall arise: the inhabitants of the dust shall awake and shout for joy'.[1] The earlier prophecies concerning the restoration of the nation[2] had a special significance, and prepared the way for the conception of a general resurrection when 'many of them that sleep in the dust of the earth shall awake, some to everlasting life and some to shame and everlasting contempt'.[3]

If the mission of the Suffering Servant was to make many righteous,[4] unfaithful Israelites were to be destroyed in the valley of Hinnom outside Jerusalem[5]—doubtless the sources of the conception of Gehenna as a place of torment—it was but a step to the inference that rewards the punishments will be meted out at the final scene when 'the judgement is set and the books are opened'. Thus, Sheol, from being a non-ethical abode of inactivity, was transformed into a place in which penalties, remedial or eternal, were to be meted out at the world-judgement.[6] The next life then became divided into four stages, two for the righteous and two for the wicked,[7] and after the Judgement an age of bliss would be established on earth, as a kind of Messianic kingdom, while the wicked would be punished in an 'accursed valley', or, in the case of those in the second division, destined to remain in Sheol for ever.[8]

The apocalyptic eschatology betrays some traces of Persian influences, but, nevertheless, the doctrine of the Last Things and the conception of immortality in the two systems proceed from very different theological premises. According to Zoroastrian thought, the whole creation is moving towards a 'renovation of the world' at the 'consummation' when 'Right shall smite the Lie'.[9] This

---

[1] Isa. xxvi. 19 (a passage belonging to the Greek period).

[2] Isa. liii. Hos. vi. 1 f. Ezek. xxxvii.

[3] Dan. xii. 2. 2 Macc. vii. 9.

[4] Isa. liii. 11.   [5] Isa. lxvi. 24.   [6] Enoch i.–xxxvi., esp. xxii.

[7] Rev. vi. 9 f.   [8] Enoch v. 7 f., x. 17, 19, 21, xxvi. I, xxvii.

[9] *Yasna*, xliii, 12; xlviii, 1.

represents the final triumph of Ahura Mazda and the victory of good over evil. A General Judgement will then take place when a flood of molten metal will be poured out and the wicked will be consumed.[1] The victory of the world of Ahura over that of the Daevas will be secured by the preponderance of good works over evil at the Last Day, and though the Gathic texts are by no means clear concerning the renovated world, it would seem that the merits of the *Ashavan* (men of the Right) were being faithfully recorded day by day against the final account. Then 'they that get them good name shall be partakers in the promised reward in the fair abode of Good Thought, of Mazda, and of Right'.[2] But while this goal will be reached through the intervention of future deliverers,[3] each man may make his contribution and thus be among the company of saviours (*saoshyants*).[4]

Zoroaster, in all probability, was the first to teach quite un-hesitatingly a double judgement with a final consummation,[5] based on a right choice in the earthly struggle. It is those who 'make for themselves a good name' who are to receive the promised reward as against the pain and torment awaiting the followers of the Lie. This notion is far removed from the Egyptian weighing of the heart in the Hall of the Double Truth, or the Orphic-Eleusinian hope of eternal life by initiation. Even Plato and the Oriental mystics in their conception of retributive justice could never get away from the idea of an immortal soul seeking release from a hindering mortal body. The Jews never reached the position where the destiny of the individual was independent of that of the nation as a whole, and if Persian eschatological beliefs were current in Palestine prior to the Greek period, as seems probable, the attitude to the hereafter was by no means identical in the two cultures.

The conquests of Alexander, however, broke down all the barriers separating the nations, and the process of Hellenization made rapid progress in Jewry before the Maccabaean revolt.[6] This reached its climax among the Diaspora in Alexandria, the chief intellectual centre in the ancient world after 300 B.C., whence Greek culture was radiated in all directions in educated circles.

[1] li, 9; xxx, 8.   [2] xxx, 10.   [3] xxxiv, 13; xlvi, 8; xlviii, 9, 12; liii, 2.

[4] xxx, 9; li, 21, cf. Moulton, *Early Zoroastrianism* (Lond., 1913), pp. 158 ff.

[5] cf. Söderblom, *The Living God* (Oxford, 1933), p. 218.

[6] 2 Macc. iv. 11–15.

Here Hellenic and Semitic thought intermingled as may be seen in the Wisdom of Solomon addressed to Alexandrian Jews about the beginning of the Christian era, and in the writings of Philo (20 B.C.–A.D. 50). In this literature the doctrine of immortality is set forth in Platonic terms particularly by Philo who makes man intermediate between the mortal and the immortal nature, sharing in each; mortal as to his body and immortal as to his intellect. The 'breath of life' (πνοὴ ζωῆς) breathed into Adam becomes a πνεῦμα-soul, along Stoic lines, for which Philo finally substitutes 'intellect' (διάνοια), like a true Platonist. On the other hand, in the Wisdom of Solomon 'soul' and 'mind' are synonymous,[1] though here again the body is regarded as an 'earthly tabernacle' comparable to the Platonic prison-house (σῶμα σῆμα).

But though the Judaeo-Alexandrian philosophy prepared the way for the Christology of the Fourth Gospel and the subsequent Neo-Platonic movement in its pagan and Christian aspects, it made very little permanent impression on the Jewish mind, which was fundamentally unphilosophical in outlook. Men like Aristeas, Aristobulus and the master-thinker Philo, represent the confluence of the two great streams of thought, Jewish and Hellenic, destined to meet ultimately in one theological system deriving its inspiration from a new conception of resurrection in this life. The apocalyptists had established a crude conception of the reanimation of the flesh in a materialistic hereafter brought about by divine intervention, while Platonism had no place for either God or the body in the immortality of personality, however godlike the soul might be in its essential nature. It was left for Christianity to integrate in one whole the notion of eternal life as a divine gift evaluated in ethical terms of quality but involving the full personal life, body and spirit.

THE CHRISTIAN CONCEPTION OF IMMORTALITY

Jesus Himself assumed the existence of a future life without advancing any arguments in support of the contention, or throwing any new light on the problem by His teaching, as His words have been recorded. But throughout His career He was primarily concerned with actions, and according to the New Testament, the conviction that in Him the Messianic hope had its fulfilment, led Him to assert

[1] ix. 15.

that 'there be some standing here which shall not taste of death, till they see the Son of Man coming in His kingdom'.[1] Within the existing generation the rule of God would be set up[2] and with the consummation both corporate and personal salvation would be secured. Eternal life is a present reality, regarded from the Christian standpoint, because it constitutes an integral element in the union of the soul with the living God which cannot be severed by the dissolution of the physical organism. It is also an inevitable consequence of membership of the Kingdom that transcends all temporal and spacial limitations, the citizenship of which is in heaven. 'For here we have no continuing city, but we seek one to come.'[3] The Christian hope of immortality, therefore, is both individual and corporate, present and future. It is grounded in the relationship of man to God under existing conditions of time and space which finds its completion in the transcendent order, sealed by the actual resurrection of Christ.

Because He had established 'a new and living way' to the life of the age to come here and now, His followers were conscious of 'the power of an endless life' in the spiritual experience which was theirs. Throughout the New Testament the antithesis of 'life' and 'death' is recurrent because 'to be carnally minded is death, but to be spiritually minded is life and peace'. Therefore, where Christ reigns 'the body is dead because of sin but the spirit is life because of righteousness'.[4] In this state of salvation 'though our outward man perish, the inward man is renewed day by day'.[5] And St Paul contends that he dies daily in order that by 'crucifying the flesh with the passions and lusts thereof' he may walk in the Spirit.[6] Thus, for the Apostle, the death and resurrection of Christ were the means whereby he was enabled to realize eternal life as an ever-present spiritual experience and to look forward with confidence to the consummation beyond the grave as an accomplished fact.

From Judaism he had inherited the belief in the dualism of 'the flesh' (σάρξ) and 'the spirits' (πνεῦμα) as constituting the personality, but the sharp distinction he draws between the carnally minded and the spiritually minded is suggestive of Hellenic influence even though he does not adopt the Orphic-Platonic doctrine

[1] Matt. xvi. 28.   [2] Matt. xxiv. 34.   [3] Heb. xiii. 14.
[4] Rom. viii. 6, 10.   [5] 2 Cor. iv. 16.   [6] Gal. v. 24 f.

of the flesh as inherently evil.[1] The νοῦς (mind) is equivalent to πνεῦμα, but his subtle distinction between the ψύχη as the animating principle and the πνεῦμα as the higher spiritual life enables him to develop a doctrine of the resurrection of the body as distinct from the immortality of the soul. It is not the νοῦς as a divine principle of pure intelligence that survives the dissolution and becomes absorbed into the ultimate mind, as the Platonists believed, nor the resuscitation of the mortal remains, as the apocalyptic school supposed. There is both a 'spiritual body' (σῶμα πνευματικόν) and a 'natural body' (σῶμα ψυχικόν), according to the Pauline contention, for in the hereafter the soul must be clothed with a body 'not made with hands, eternal in the heavens'.[2] 'Flesh and blood cannot inherit the kingdom of God', but even so in this life the spiritual resurrection of the Christian is an accomplished fact.[3] Already the body has been made an 'instrument of righteousness' having become subservient to the interests of the spirit. Therefore, when the present order vanishes at the Second Coming of Christ (which St Paul regarded as imminent) we shall be changed so that we too may become incorruptible.[4] Then death will be swallowed up in victory, and the body will become spiritual. The body that will be 'raised', however, will be identical with that which was 'sown', for it is the entire personality that has been redeemed. A disembodied state will not suffice because human personality is neither wholly corporeal nor solely spiritual. Consequently, beyond the grave it must continue to function in an incorruptible celestial body.

In the subsequent Johannine writings the emphasis was still placed on eternal life as a present experience,[5] but in the Apocalypse the eschatological scheme introduced the notion of a millennium on earth and the creation of a New Jerusalem after the Parousia as the consummation of the righteous.[6] Therefore, at the beginning of the

[1] Rom. vii. 7–25. St Paul refuses to admit that the body is evil since it is the 'temple of the Holy Spirit' capable of being made 'a living sacrifice, holy, acceptable to God' (I Cor. vi. 19. Rom. xii. 1). If the flesh, as distinct from the body, is a lower element in human nature, it is neutral rather than inherently sinful.

[2] I Cor. xv. 44. 2 Cor. v. 1–10.

[3] Rom. vi. 5–8. Col. iii. 1.

[4] I Cor. xv. 24 ff., 51 ff. Rom. viii. 11.

[5] John xvii. 3. I John iii. 14, v. 11 f.

[6] Rev. xx. 1–3, xxi, 1, 5, 10–21.

second century of our era there were conflicting ideas concerning the future state, derived partly from Judaism and partly from Greek sources. As the new Faith was systematized in a Gentile environment, Platonic ideas asserted themselves again, re-interpreted in terms of the death and resurrection of Christ as the cardinal doctrine of Christianity. Clement, Origen and the Alexandrian Fathers (A.D. 150–254) generally regarded the soul as incorporeal, pre-existent and eternal. The pure in heart alone could attain to the Beatific Vision, so that the imperfect, who constitute the majority of mankind, though finally freed from eternal punishment, could never see God face to face.[1] In explaining the apocalyptic idea of the destruction of the earth at the Last Day, Origen fell back on the Stoic prediction of a conflagration (ἐκπύρωσις), and maintained that in every man's body there is a 'seminal logos', or principle of renovation and individuation, which ultimately re-creates a new body in the new world-order. But this theory viewed in the light of the posthumous appearances of Samuel, Moses, and Elijah in their terrestrial forms, encountered difficulties, as did the attempt to establish which part of personality is located in the 'seminal logos'.

The Alexandrian effort to reconcile the conflicting opinion of later Greek thought with the Judaeo-Christian theology of the soul and the future life met with little success till the confusion was in a great measure cleared by the adoption of a modified Neo-Platonism on the part of St Augustine (340–430). Realizing that the inner life is *sui generis*, he identified the soul with the vivifying agent identical with the memory, intellect, and will, of which the will is the highest function. As a Platonist he denied that the soul is corporeal or material, or capable of spatial extension. As pure intelligence it has perfect knowledge of its own nature and is the source of knowledge of abstractions. Without it the body is dead, but equally the soul is inseparable from the body, whereby Augustine departed from Platonism. For him immortality involved the survival of human personality as a whole.[2] After death the soul continued in an ethereal disembodied state, unextended or occupying an extended space, and there suffered punishment for the sin committed

---

[1] Origen, *In Num.*, xxi, 1; xxvii, 2–4; *In Math. Comm. Sec.*, 39.

[2] *De Immortalitate Animas*, 387. *De Quantitate Animae*, 387 f. *De Anima et eius Origine*, 420.

in life. At the general ressurection the righteous would be clothed
with spiritual bodies in which they would enter eternal bliss, while
the wicked would suffer the pain of hell in bodies suited to their
fiery environment.

With the growth of Aristotelianism in the Middle Ages, the
Augustinian anthropology was combined with Aristotle's conception of the soul in the Scholastic attempt to produce an ecclesiastical
metaphysic true alike to the Greek and Hebrew-Christian traditions.
Man, as St Thomas regarded him, represents the connecting link
between the two realms of 'form' and 'matter', united as a microcosm. Together they make up the material thing; apart they are
nothing but abstractions. Applied to human personality, if the soul
is individuated by matter, then in its survival after death it will
have no individuality at all. This would lead to the denial of immortality on the Thomist theory of the relation of the soul to the
body were it not that St Thomas maintained the Aristotelian
hypothesis of body and soul together constituting one human being
in the manner of matter and form. The soul is man's form, and
form is that which gives substantiality to a body, unifying and
determining it. But in a human personality the form is intelligent
and rational, endowed with the power of reflection, and intrinsically
independent of the body although extrinsically dependent on the
instrumentality of the organism. The form, therefore, has so far
freed itself in this case from the matter it determines as neither to
grow nor to decay with it. Hence its immortality.[1] Yet the fact
remains that a self-conscious being does in great measure make
himself, and at the same time is made to some extent by his parents
and ancestors. The doctrine of a special creation of a ready-made
rational soul, therefore, is not without its difficulties.

THE ISLAMIC HEREAFTER

St Thomas Aquinas, however, while he made Aristotelianism the
basis of a Christian philosophy, and returned to Neo-Platonic
mysticism in his eschatological scheme, also incorporated Arabic
as well as Jewish thought in his system. As his model he used the
'Grand Commentary' of the Moslem philosopher Averroes,
though he controverted the theory that the Active Intellect and the

[1] *Summa Theol.,* I, q. 4, 12. *Contra Gentiles,* II, 80.

Passive Intellect are separate from the individual soul and are identical in all men; a view which destroys human personality so far as rational thought is concerned, and renders immortality at most a question only to be settled by revelation, as Averroes affirmed. Actually beyond maintaining the soul's continued existence after death, the Qur'an has very little to say on the abstract question, attention being concentrated on rewards and punishments in the hereafter, determined by the balance struck between the debit and credit side of the account. Sinful conduct will be weighed against virtuous deeds,[1] and on the result will depend the time spent in hell. 'No one is there of you who shall not go down into it (hell) this is a settled decree with thy Lord. Then will he deliver those who had the fear of God, and the wicked (i.e. infidels) will he leave in it on their knees.'[2] Unbelief is the sin of sins, and the principle of judgement is primarily concerned with the acceptance of Mohammed and his message rather than with ethical behaviour. 'Whoso shall have done the things that are right, whether male or female, and *is a believer,* these shall enter paradise; good things unreckoned shall they enjoy there.'[3] Moreover, good works bring their reward beyond their merits, while evil is punished only as it deserves.[4]

The joys awaiting the justified in paradise are of a purely mundane character. Their dwelling will be 'mid gardens and delights, and rejoicing in what their Lord hath given them, and that from the pain of hell-fire hath their Lord preserved them'. They will 'eat and drink with healthy enjoyment', recline on couches, and marry 'damsels with large eyes'. 'Therein shall they pass to one another the cup which shall engender no light discourse, no motive of sin.'[5] Thus, the goal is merely an idealized earthly life as in the Egyptian Fields of Aalu, involving luxurious living and unrestricted carnal indulgence.

In contrast to this primitive Qur'anic attitude to immortality, the mystic movement known as Sufism developed in a pantheistic direction, though under the influence of Al-Ghazali (d. A.D. 1111) it retained the personality of God. In man is a divine spirit which makes him restless till he finds union with his Maker because both share the same essential volition. Consequently, will is more

[1] Sura, XXV–LXX.   [2] XIX.   [3] XL–XLIII.
[4] XXVII, LXXXIV.   [5] LII, 17/23.

fundamental than thought, and the domain in which man's spirit
rules is his own inner life. The material world of the body is the
sphere of absolute necessity. In that realm God's omnipotent will
is all in all, but in the domain of the sensuous and psychical, man
has a relative freedom. The true end of man in this realm is so to
use that freedom that he can find the way to union with God.[1]
Intellectual belief and external obedience are secondary to ecstatic
surrender which, according to this ethical mysticism, is the highest
state of the soul, when the mind becomes closed to everything but
God. The soul is a substance distinct from the body, an immaterial
psychic principle of divine origin and nature, beside which the
physical integument is of inferior worth. The *unio mystica* is the
means by which it returns to its source in the Supreme Essence,
aided by pious exercises and asceticisms; but the Beatific Vision is
attained not as a reward of merit but by the gift of Allah.

This essentially religious movement was profoundly influenced
by the impact of Neo-Platonic philosophy on Moslem thought,
though it also owed something to Christian asceticism, Gnosticism
and Hindu pantheism. Ghazali opposed the belief that the personality of the enraptured mystic can be annihilated to the point of
absorption in that of God, thereby safeguarding himself against the
absolute pantheism of his predecessor, Mansur al-Hallaj (d. A.D.
822). But the pantheistic tendency was so inherent in Sufism that
monism became the characteristic feature of mysticism in Islam, as
formulated by Al'Arabi (d. 1240), Jalal al-din Rumi (d. 1273) and
Hafiz (d. 1389). Henceforth the quest of immortality became sub-
sidiary to the necessity of a metaphysical realization of the illusive-
ness of individual existence of the sole reality of the One Real.
To relate the Allah of the Qur'an with this pantheistic One Being,
man and the phenomenal world—everything else in fact except
Allah—they identified with Not-being which reflects Being like a
mirror. Since man is endowed with the spark of Real Being, he is
Contingent Being (a kind of Being which is and is not, as Plato
would say) so long as he remains in his present probationary state,
subject to laws and creeds to restrain his evil tendencies.[2] But the
end of man is to return to that from which he emerged.

[1] D. B. Macdonald, *Muslim Theology* (Lond., 1903), pp. 231 ff.
[2] E. H. Whinfield, *The Gulshan-i-Raz* (Lond., 1880), pp. vii, 14 f.

When waves of thought arise from the Ocean of Wisdom,
They assume the forms of sound and speech.
These forms of speech are born and die again,
These waves cast themselves back into the Ocean.
Form is born of that which is without form,
And goes again, for 'Verily to Him do we return'.[1]

Thus, Sufi mysticism tends to pantheism, and Al-Ghazali accused the philosophers of denying resurrection altogether. Averroes denied the charge, affirming that 'that which will be resuscitated will be a representation of what is seen in this world; it will not be that very thing *in essentia*. For what has perished cannot be born again, except in so far as it is individualized; and existence can be bestowed only on the semblance of what has perished in its identity.' Quoting the traditionist Ibn'Abbas, 'there is of the other world nothing but names in this world', he concluded that this 'proves that the future existence has a kind of generation more elevated than that of actual existence, and constitutes a more excellent order than the order of this world'.[2] But he admitted that on philosophic grounds he was unable to establish the doctrine of individual immortality. Though he held the belief as a religious tenet, in the eyes of St Thomas and the Scholastics Averroism was as incompatible with Christian teaching as it was with orthodox Moslem theology. Nevertheless, if the Arabian commentator was thought to have perverted the Peripatetic tradition, he was always treated with courtesy and respect by both Aquinas and Dante, and his influence in Europe continued till the beginning of the scientific renaissance in the seventeenth century when thought was concentrated on natural processes in time and space.

[1] Whinfield, *Masnavi-i-Ma'navi* (Lond., 1887), p. 24.

[2] *Tahafut alTahafut* (Caior, A.H. 1303). Renan, *Averroes el l'Averroisme* (Paris, 1896), pp. 158 ff.

CHAPTER XIII

Conclusion

From the evidence brought under review in the foregoing chapters it would seem that religion is a world-wide phenomenon recurrent in every known phase of culture, and revealing remarkable homogeneity in given areas of dispersal. Thus, in food-gathering communities a particular type of cultus occurs the purpose of which is primarily the control of the necessities of life by supernatural agencies, conceived in terms of magic or of religion, or, as frequently happens, a combination of the two techniques. While strata in the history of human institutions cannot be assumed comparable to those exhibited by the geological record of the earth, it is nevertheless true that in primitive states of culture, and therefore by analogy in prehistoric society, magic plays a very important part in the elaborate system of food-providing processes. Religious rites readily become spells when directed to such matters as fertility and the fortunes of the chase, or the river, but side by side with these operations is the belief in a beneficent Providence external to man and outside his direct control by coercive measures. There is also a spirit-world regarded as a transcendent order; the abode of gods, ancestors, spirits and culture-heroes, to which the dead return when they 'shuffle off this mortal coil'. It is this spiritual reality, the existence of which is affirmed in myth and ritual, that man seeks to control, and by which in turn he is controlled.

In every cultural horizon and religious sytem there exist a sacred tradition and ritual organization which determine conduct and maintain a correct relationship with the powers of the unseen world. So closely is this technique interwoven with the structure of society that it becomes virtually the dynamic and unifying principle, fulfilling a vital cultural function. A primitive community is a group in which all the members, living or dead, are bound together by spiritual bonds and trace their descent from a common ancestor. Enshrined in this closely knit organization is the esoteric tradition

which at initiation is passed on from one generation to the next by
the most powerful aids of corporate suggestion and supernatural
sanctions, calculated to maintain intact the social structure. The
sacred lore of the tribe is not a fanciful tale told in explanation of
natural phenomena and inexplicable events, but a method of
expressing certain ways of thinking and feeling about the facts of
life and of regulating human actions. Things are as they are because
the powers that be have so decreed in the beginning, and man's
behaviour is prescribed accordingly both in relation to Providence
and to the society of which he is an integral part. But the mythological setting and its ritual representation may vary as new revelations
of reality become explicit and receive tribal sanction. Thus, the
ancient rites and beliefs are given a new significance and made to
fulfil a new function.

Man being essentially a living soul, he seeks to invest his culture
with a spiritual dynamic which provides the energy necessary for
sustained effort. As Professor Christopher Dawson says, 'every
religion embodies an attitude to life and a conception of reality, and
any change in these brings with it a change in the whole character of
the culture, as we see in the case of the transformation of ancient
civilization by Christianity, or in the transformation of the society
of pagan Arabia by Islam'.[1]

The function of religion, regarded as a sanction, is to stabilize
the existing order by endowing the accepted social tradition with
sacredness. 'It was so in the Alcheringa' is a transcendent reference
among the native tribes of Central Australia, which gives permanent
value and prestige to custom and belief by referring them back to
a higher supernatural reality of initial events. The struggle for
existence demands co-ordination of purpose and activities, and
religious sanctions supply the necessary dynamic. The conditions
of life make adherence to explicit faith in tradition essential to the
continuance of the group, but this inevitably tends to produce a
static order. Nevertheless, religion by its appeal to the supernatural
as an intervening creative force, and being rooted in the necessities
of life, has constantly introduced a new vision of reality, and so far
from being an 'opiate for the people' has constantly been bringing
forth out of its treasure things new and old.

Nor is it true to say that religion has been 'otherworldly' in the

[1] *The Age of the Gods* (Lond., 1928), p. xx.

sense of concentrating attention on a heavenly citizenship to the exclusion of present-day needs. On the contrary, as we have seen repeatedly throughout this study, the main interest and purpose of the discipline have been the maintenance of society, the well-being of mankind and the continuance of the natural order as they exist here and now. Even in the case of Oriental pantheism with its life-negation, the doctrine of metempsychosis has exercised a restraining influence on human conduct in daily life. Thus, the *karma* hypothesis, however much it may work against progress, makes this world the sphere of activity for good or ill till release can be secured. Moreover, progress is not merely the sum-total of products of civilization. It may be the process through which civilization is obtained, but all change certainly is not progressive. There can be no conception of progress without ideals, which are standards set up towards which humanity travels. But having established its ideals the great test is whether there is sufficient ability to approximate to them, and to bring a new vision of reality into line with that which has preceded it. Sometimes cultural advance has been in a steady upward direction, but very frequently it has come about as an 'emergence', something genuinely novel arising out of that which has gone before, ushering in a new era or cultural horizon, as in the case of the discovery of fire, agriculture, the domestication of animals, the use of metals, or of steam and machinery.

In the earlier phases of this process religion has played a determining part inasmuch as it has not only held society together but it has supplied the supernatural apparatus essential to enable the innovators to break through the barriers of taboo and custom to introduce new ideas and ways of life. The 'fire-dragon' had to be tamed and brought under control by some ritual device before it could be serviceable to man, just as fertility in nature and fecundity in the animal and human world were subject to ritual processes at the dawn of civilization. Without accepting Jevons' theory of the totemic origin of the cultivation of crops and the domestication of animals, it is nevertheless beyond reasonable doubt that religion played an essential part in the transition from food-gathering to food-producing. So the corn-sheaf was regarded as the Corn-Mother blessing with her divine presence the harvest-home, and the rhythm of the seasons was equated with the mysterious cycle of life renewed through death in a sacred drama.

L

The twin beliefs in Providence and Immortality as the fundamental affirmations of religion throughout the ages, found expression in a new Nature-worship and Mystery cultus when man became dependent upon the soil and the seasons for his subsistence. His methods of food production were of the simplest kind and his economic security was at the mercy of the sun, the wind and the rain. Small wonder then if a universalized Providence became departmentalized into a polytheistic pantheon guiding the destinies of the forces with which the life of man was so intimately connected in his precarious earthly environment, and when his terrestrial struggles were accomplished receiving him at the last in a paradise fashioned idealistically after the pattern of his most cherished hopes in this world. Thus was awakened a keener sense of dependence on a transcendent order of reality external to himself, beneficent and providential.

In Egypt the sun and the Nile, on whose combined action the fertility of the land depends, were the two primary divine sources of life and increase here and hereafter. Around the figures of the Egyptian Re and Osiris, of the Sumerian Ishtar and Tammuz, of the Greek Zeus and Demeter, a dual cultus arose directed on the one hand to the fruitfulness of the soil and on the other to the attainment of a blissful eternity. This will to live, manifesting itself in a life-giving and a life-getting ceremonial, centres in Egypt in the king and his functions in securing the prosperity of the nation as its divine head. In this capacity the sovereign was a consolidating supernatural force inasmuch as he ruled as the incarnation of the god or gods whom he personified, and the royal mystery drama differed from the later Hellenic rites in being communal rather than personal in its purpose. The king renewed his reign to ensure the prosperity of the whole country, while individuals sought union with Demeter, Dionysos, Orpheus or Isis in order to secure for themselves salvation and a happy hereafter.

So far from immortality being a royal prerogative, as was originally the case in Egypt, every Hellenic initiate was assured of a resurrection after death into the abodes of the blessed, irrespective of rank or sex. The Mysteries recruited their adherents from all classes, from princes to slaves, their exclusiveness being confined to the esoteric cultus which constituted the means whereby the gift of eternal life was bestowed. If behind this movement is the primitive custom of killing the ageing king on behalf of the community at large, this crude sociological practice became in the Graeco-Oriental societies a spiritual experience whereby individual salvation was obtained through the grace of a divinity who had suffered and died, and whose resurrection held out to his devotees the promise of victory over death and attainment of divine felicity. This conception of personal immortality as a secret vouchsafed to members of a particular sect produced a new type of social cohesion, and *esprit de corps,* characteristic, for example, of the Orphic *Thiasoi.*

The Eleusinian worship being more catholic in its appeal and membership, failed to produce the same intensive cultus as the rigidly sectarian Orphism. Initiation sufficed to secure all the benefits of the Eleusinian way of life whereas in Orphism faith without works did not suffice. The fortunes of the soul beyond the grave were conditioned by moral character and ethical conduct. Indeed redemption came to be thought of in terms of release from a hindering body and a corrupt world; a search for unity with the divine regarded as a pantheistic essence of the universe. As the king was deified as a result of his coronation, so the human soul as the goal of initiation became the All, losing and dissolving its nature in the Absolute, rather than finding its eternal home in an idealized paradise.

Since Orphism grew out of the wild ecstatic Dionysian frenzies which had as their aim a barbaric form of primitive mysticism, it is not surprising that the cultus in its later developments differed so markedly from the Eleusinian Mystery tradition with its Mycenaean background and Asiatic contacts with the Great Mother and the death and resurrection of her divine son or lover. Dionysos, like Demeter and Ishtar, was connected with the fertility of the earth and of the harvest, but the Thraco-Phrygian ritual was one of exaltation and self-abandonment in which the worshipper sought to become possessed by a super-human divine being, losing himself in the object of his adoration. It was this 'becoming god' which later, when the wilder elements of the rites were sobered under Hellenic influence, developed into a pantheistic mysticism, moralized in terms of Orphic dualism. Henceforth salvation was to be sought and found not in an Eleusinian paradise but in a casting off of the 'old man' with all its impurity inherited from the Titans, and absorption of the divine element eternally in Dionysos. 'Happy and Blessed One, thou shalt be God instead of mortal.'

This transition from a ritual to a moral order represents the most profound cultural movement in the middle of the first millennium B.C., and if it came to fruition on its more negative side in India, it was equally apparent in Zoroastrian dualism and prophetic Judaism, to say nothing of Confucian, Platonic, and Aristotelian ethics. Even prior to this golden age of creative religion there were in every community visionaries who acquired, as it was supposed, supernatural knowledge either through ecstasy or trance, or by means of dreams and visions. When the possession of occult powers is regarded as an essential condition in the determination of the mind and will of the gods or spirits, only those who have a right disposition can hope to find a vocation as a shaman or medicine-man.

Thus, in Israel the 'prophetic movement' associated with the Nebi'im, or 'sons of the prophets', centred in groups of esctatic mystics connected with particular sanctuaries, such as Gibeah, Ramah, Bethel, Gilgal, and Jericho, who worked themselves into a frenzy by the aid of the timbrel, pipe, harp and psaltery, in order to attain unity with the deity.[1] In this condition a spokesman of the company would utter a prophetic oracle,[2] and so contagious was the ecstasy that it rapidly spread among the onlookers.[3] While under the influence of the inspiring power the prophet's own personality was in abeyance so that he became 'another man',[4] or god-possessed like a divine king. In this way he was able to be the medium of divine communication.

Psychologically the phenomena presupposes a deeply religious disposition and spiritual insight, a strong personality and a passionate nature on the part of the ecstatic. It was often coupled with divination, the Hebrew *kôhén*, or seer, corresponding to the Babylonian *barû*, or sooth-sayer, whose duty it was to divine the will of the gods by the inspection of the liver, as the seat of the soul-substance of the sheep offered in sacrifice. Since the victim was in vital union with the god to whom it was dedicated, the future could be determined by reading the divine mind as reflected in the centre of its vital essence. Therefore, this class of diviner studied the liver and the gall-bladder with great care to detect signs which might give a clue to forthcoming events; a custom which led to every part of

---

[1] 1 Sam. x. 5 ff.   [2] 1 Kings xxii. 11 f.
[3] 1 Sam. x. 10; xix. 20-4   [4] 1 Sam. x. 6.

the organ being noted and interpreted with the minutest care.[1] In the Old Testament the liver is twice mentioned in connexion with divination,[2] but it was the Ark of the Covenant which is represented as the principal means by which the will of Yahweh could be ascertained, coupled with the 'ephod' and the 'urim and thummin'.

It is unfortunate that we are still in doubt concerning the nature of these sacred objects. According to tradition the ark was a chest overlaid with gold containing, as the Deuteronomist imagined, the tables of stone on which the Law was said to have been inscribed.[3] But this is a late interpretation of what seems to have been originally an oracular instrument charged with the personality of Yahweh so that it was regarded as his earthly abode.[4] Reichel's suggestion that it was a portable throne symbolizing the invisible presence of the god, accepted by Dibelius and Gunkel[5] and supported by certain documentary evidence,[6] raises philological difficulties.[7] That it was some sort of coffer, resembling the sarcophagus of Osiris,[8] and carried in procession on occasions, but normally a 'miniature temple' housing the spirit of the deity when the sacred lots were cast, makes it comparable in function to the 'ephod' and fits in with its use.[9] But whatever was its precise form, it featured in connexion with oracular divination and the early phases of the prophetic movement.

The classical epoch of Hebrew prophecy, however, introduced an entirely different and new approach to Yahweh through the instrumentality of inspired human speech rather than esctasy or oracular methods.

The step forward which Amos, Hosea and Isaiah took (as Edouard Meyer pointed out) denotes one of the most momentous changes in the history of mankind. The all-subduing force of conscience, or, more exactly, of the conscience of a single individual in opposition to the whole surrounding

[1] Jastrow, *Religious Belief in Babylonia and Assyria* (New York, 1911), pp. 150 ff.

[2] Lam. ii. 11. Prov. vii. 23. cf. Tobit vi. 4–16, viii. 2. Ezek. xxi. 21.

[3] Deut. x. 1–5. cf. Exod. xxv. 10 ff.

[4] Num. x. 35 f. 1 Sam. iv. 5–8. 2 Sam. vi.

[5] Dibelius, 'Die Lade Jahves', VIII, in *Forschungen zur Religion und Literatur*, Gottingen, 1906.

[6] 1 Sam. iii. 10 f. Ps. xxiv. Jer. iii. 16 f.

[7] Bude, *Theologische Studien und Kritiken*, 1906, pp. 489 ff.

[8] R. Hartmann, 'Zelt und Lade' in *Zeitschrift für die Alttestamentliche Wissenchaft* Giessen, 1917–18.

[9] W. R. Arnold, *Ephod and the Ark* (Harvard Press, 1917).

world, came into action and made itself felt for the first time. The consequences of the struggle fought out in the eighth and seventh century B.C. within the small area of Palestine are still felt throughout the whole range of our civilization.[1]

This remarkable movement was initiated by uneducated laymen distinguished from the rest of their fellow-countrymen only by their religious experience and spiritual insight. Thus, Amos, the earliest of the new prophets, expressly denied kinship with the professional *Nebi'im*, or ecstatic seers,[2] having received his call independently in 760 B.C. in the wilds of Tekoa during a raging storm while he was pursuing his ordinary life as a herdsman and pruner of sycamore figs. Nevertheless, though they felt themselves to be the mouthpiece of a revelation quite different from that hitherto revealed either by the 'sons of the prophets' or through 'ephod' or 'urim', they were essentially visionaries. Like the ecstatics they felt themselves 'full of god', speaking that they did know, and testifying that they had heard and seen. It was the character of the message rather than the manner of its reception that constituted the new departure, the words of each of these spiritual giants being stamped with genuine originality and opposition to contemporary thought. They themselves seem to have been conscious of the contrast between their own feelings and ideas on the one hand, and of the purpose and mind of God Who constrained them on the other.[3] Thus, they gave utterance to what they believed to be the word of Yahweh forcing itself to find expression through them, having been invaded by His spirit. Consequently, they prefaced their prophecies with the formula, 'Thus saith Yahweh', or 'The Word of Yahweh'.

Not content with verbal utterance, they frequently resorted to symbolic actions to make known their message, as, for example, when Jeremiah broke a pitcher at the gate of Jerusalem to foretell the destruction of the city,[4] and Hosea married a zonah in the service of Astarte to demonstrate, by his never-failing love for a Temple harlot, the long-suffering patience of Yahweh for the nation he had betrothed to himself.[5] This was a daring figure for a

---

[1] E. Meyer, *Kleine Schriften zur Geschichtstheorie und zur wirtschaftlichen und politschen Geschichte des Altertums* (Halle, Niemeyer, 1910), p. 213.

[2] Amos vii. 14.

[3] Amos vii. 2 ff. Isa. vi. 5 ff., viii. 11, xxii. 4 ff., xxxvii. 1.

[4] Jer. xix.   [5] Hos. i. 2.

prophet to use in view of its intimate associations with the fertility
cultus of the sacred marriage, but it brought out a conception of
ethical union with God based on love which became fundamental
in later Judaism and Christianity.[1] The real genius of the Hebrew
prophets is seen in this power of spiritual penetration and discern-
ment rather than of any predictions of the future. By their words
and actions they interpreted the events taking place around them,
and the circumstances of their own lives in relation to their deeper
significance, however repellent they might be to themselves and to
their hearers. Thus, to announce the approaching doom of their
nation was a severe test of their own faith and that of the people to
whom the message was addressed, since Israel was thought to be the
Chosen People of God. Such a reversal of all preconceived ideas
could only be accepted and proclaimed by men permeated with a
sense of vocation, giving utterance intuitively to a 'word of God'
forcing itself to find expression through them, whether the people
will hear or whether they will forbear.

In times of crisis such as the days of the Assyrian or Chaldean
menace, there was frequently a conflict between those who advo-
cated opposed policies, as, for example, in the case of the four
hundred prophets of Yahweh who gave an affirmative answer to
Ahab before the battle of Ramoth-Gilead, and the solitary Micaiah
who foretold defeat.[2] Similarly, Jeremiah withstood Hananiah and
his followers who failed to recognize the hand of God in the approaching disaster.[3] After the Exile, however, when the prophetic
movement having done its work came to an end, it became possible
in retrospect to distinguish those who had spoken 'falsely' from those
who had proffered wise counsel in accordance with the purposes
of God.

The most remarkable achievement of this short-lived movement
was the establishment of ethical monotheism as a permanent contribution to the religious thought of the world in striking contrast to
the ephemeral attempts in Egypt and Persia, which, like the philosophical renaissance in Greece, left untouched the current polytheism. In Israel the restoration of the sacrificial worship in the post-
exilic community brought the prophetic ideals into relation with
the priestly tradition without reintroducing the earlier Semitic

[1] Kittel, *The Religion of the People of Israel* (Lond., 1925), pp. 136 ff.
[2] I Kings xxii. 12 ff.   [3] Jer. xxviii. 5.

cultus. The Law aimed at defining the moral demands of the God of the prophets, and an effort was made to give doctrinal expression to their ethical faith. It was a change of heart which had merited the change of divine attitude to the fortunes of the nation, and the Day of Atonement, despite its primitive setting, became an annual observance of fasting and repentance that the people might be preserved in a 'state of grace'.

The institutionalism of Judaism, in fact, gave a new permanence to the prophetic movement inasmuch as the objective worship became a means of making explicit the spiritualized piety which the outward forms enshrined. Thus, the offerings pleasing unto God remained 'a broken heart' and a 'contrite spirit', so that when the Temple was destroyed in A.D. 70 the religious life of the Jews was not rendered inoperative. Amid all the adversity of those troublous times, consciousness of fellowship with God was never allowed to fade, or trust in His overruling providence diminished. 'Nevertheless, I am continually with thee, thou hast holden my right hand. Thou dost lead me according to thy decree, and afterwards thou dost receive me with honour.'[1]

It was this conviction which found expression in the apocalyptic schools during the closing centuries of the era, and while there was much confusion of thought concerning the manner and method by which divine vindication would be wrought, there were no doubts as to the ultimate end at the consummation. The fulfilment of these hopes in the claims of the Christ, though it was a 'stumbling-block' to the Jews and 'foolishness' to the Greeks, to those who believed Christ was the power of God and the wisdom of God. A new principle of divine life had entered the human race and the natural world by which mankind was raised to a higher order. The Mystery cults offered their initiates a blissful immortality in union with a divinity who had been restored to life, but the Christian conception of the kingdom of God was that of a particular kind of corporate life begun on earth and reaching its climax in eternity. Furthermore, it was not a closely guarded esoteric tradition as the special preserve of the few, who having been initiated were not required to exercise any further effort to make their calling and election sure. The aim of Christianity was nothing less than the individual salvation of every member of the human race since the purpose of the Incarna-

[1] Ps. lxxiii. 23 f.

tion would not be complete till the kingdoms of this world became the kingdoms of the Lord and of His Christ.

Although at first the Jewish idea of a divine catastrophic intervention was retained, it was soon abandoned in favour of a worldwide missionary enterprise carried on by human agents ready to face persecution and death in bearing witness to the hope that was in them. Where Caesar was worshipped as God, Christ had flung down His challenge, and at a time when the Empire was rapidly falling into decay, as the glory of Graeco-Roman civilization crumbled into dust, a new religious culture arose which claimed to be the spiritual heir of the ages; the climax and fulfilment of all the conflicting and converging traditions that had preceded it. For three hundred years the Church strove to render its own life and faith explicit amid the vigorous currents and cross-currents of thought and religious practice in its Jewish and pagan environment, but ultimately it prevailed because it offered what none of its rivals could bestow.

No other religious Founder, Buddha, Zoroaster, Lao-Tze, Confucius, or later Mohammed, could or did say 'Come unto me'. Gautama was content to give his disciples the Dharma and leave them to work out their own salvation not as redeemed sons of God but as creatures bound to earth by the law of *karma* till they could secure release by their own unaided efforts, and thus enter the passionless peace of *Nirvana*. Zoroaster, though a humble and high-minded man, died as a warrior in self-defence in a fire-temple, and like Mohammed, he sought to propagate his movement by military enterprise rather than by personal appeal. Confucius, in making reciprocity his guiding principle, taught the duty of recompensing injury with justice, and if Lao-Tze reversed the order by his avowal or requiting evil with goodness, he never connected this spirit of forgiveness with self-sacrificing love even to the death of the Cross to draw all men to God. On the contrary, apart from his impersonal theism, he deliberately withdrew from the troubles of his times and sought a way to Heaven in inactivity and negative quietism and irresponsibility. Mohammed, 'the seal of the prophets', not only relied on the method of force to extend his worship of the one Supreme Deity, but although he was an attractive and powerful personality and efficient organizer, he was vindictive in his dealings with the Jews, the Meccans and even his own tribesmen who refused to follow him. In his mouth the appeal of Christ to the weary and heavy laden to find in Him rest to their souls in this life and beyond the grave would sound passing strange and incongruous.

In none of the higher living religions save Christianity has salvation been offered in the same personal terms in relation to a historic individual who Himself bore men's sins and carried their sorrows, and claimed to be the unique source of a new spiritual dynamic. Jesus was not content to preach a new Gospel, and initiate a fresh institutional system. He applied the principle He declared with consistency in His own life, towards friend and foe alike, and finally He made the supreme act of self-sacrifice in laying down His life in perfect surrender to what He believed to be the will and purpose of His heavenly Father, regardless of all personal cost. Therefore, while superficial resemblances recur in the veneration of religious leaders throughout the ages, it is nevertheless true that Christianity does present in the life, character, and claims of its Founder certain fundamental features which are unique. It was these qualities, together with the evaluations put upon them by the first generation of the Church, that gave the new Faith its position in the ancient world at a critical juncture in its history.

In every religion the nature of the supernatural order it seeks to make real and accessible is the fundamental question at issue; for on that depends the whole conception of the social ethic it seeks to inculcate. Everywhere and at all times the life of a community is conditioned by the transcendent reality it accepts and translates into a system of spiritual and moral values and ethical principles. Without such a consolidating force society loses its dynamic and is in danger of disintegration because it becomes dissociated from the inspiration of faith and has no controlling unity. The life of man finds its meaning only in a community of persons, so that by its essential nature it is in reaction against self-seeking individualism, opportunism, and class consciousness. But this implies some transcendent reference since, as Professor Malinowski has pointed out, 'the dependence on higher powers implies further the mutual dependence of man on his neighbour. You cannot worship in common without a common bond of mutual trust and assistance, that is, of charity and love. If God has created man in His own image, one image of God may not debase, defile or destroy the other.'[1] Hence the supreme importance of forming the loftiest conception of Deity and the eternal world possible, for upon the collective ideas on these matters the social life of man is primarily determined, for weal or for woe.

In primitive society the mythological and ritual affirmations are often crude and even obscene, lacking ethical content because they reflect the prevailing cultural condition of thought and practice, but, nevertheless, they are the consolidating force which if removed without substituting other supernatural sanctions can but have disruptive results. At least they satisfy the spiritual needs, and in consequence are indispensable to the integration of the community, uniting all its members in a closely-knit, common, transcendent fellowship, buoyed up amid all the changes and chances of this mortal life by the conviction of an all-sustaining and controlling beneficent order adequate to the demands of a precarious environment.

With the emergence of the higher spiritual and moral concepts which characterize the more developed religions of the world, both ancient and modern, the same fundamental principles obtain adapted to the conditions of particular cultures and civilizations. If a unilinear evolution from animism through polytheism to monotheism cannot be maintained, equally it cannot be denied that the oneness of God has come to be universally accepted only in the more developed systems. Thus, while Buddhism and Jainism began by repudiating theism altogether, the founders in both cases in due course came to be worshipped virtually as gods. Confucianism, though primarily an ethical system, recognized one Supreme Being, Shang-ti or Heaven (Ti'en) exalted far above all other objects of veneration, though in practice it limited the worship of heaven to one person, namely the emperor, who performed his royal prerogative at the winter solstice. Zoroastrianism, again, acknowledged Ahura Mazda to the exclusion of all other gods, and if Angra Mainyu was an opposing cosmic power, Zoroaster had but one object of devotion who was the embodiment of truth and righteousness, Similarly, in Judaism, from the Exile onwards Yahweh was controversially proclaimed as the sole divine ruler of the universe, while Islam was if anything more explicit and rigidly monotheistic. Hinduism and Taoism, while denying personality in the ultimate

---

[1] *The Foundations of Faith and Morals* (Oxford, 1936), pp. 2 f.

concept of the universe, became often indistinguishable from polytheism and animism in practice, but metaphysically the unifying
principle was interpreted as a monism (Upanishads and Tao-teh-
Ching) or dualism (Sankhya and Yi-Ching).

The notion of incarnation recurs in devotional Hinduism and in
Mahayana Buddhism, but in a form which is quite distinct from
the Christian doctrine. Thus, Krishna and Rama are divine descents
of Vishnu, a polytheistic deity who is supposed to have had many
'avatars' including animal manifestations, none of which are ethically without reproach. In the parallel movement in Buddhism the
founder came to be regarded as one of many 'enlightened beings'
who renounced *Nirvana* in order to help mankind to save itself by
following the Middle Way in the manner accepted by a particular
sect. Some of these *Bodhisattvas* are looked upon as personal beings
in the highest state of Buddhahood; others are thought of as manifestations of the one Eternal Buddha, but all were once men seeking
release.

In striking contrast to these Oriental incarnational systems is the
Christian claim that the one holy, omnipotent, omniscient ground
of the universe was made flesh in the person of Jesus Christ in order
that the human race might thereby know once and for all what
God is like, and, aided by divine grace, be enabled to fashion its
life and conduct accordingly.[1] The divine self-disclosure vouchsafed
through the Hebrew prophets reached its climax and fulfilment, it
is claimed, in this revelation,[2] but, nevertheless, if 'in these latter
days' God is said to have 'spoken by His Son whom He has made
heir of all things', it is also maintained that 'He left not Himself
without witness' in former ages.[3] The significance of the Christian
contention lies in the particular qualities and attributes it makes the
basis of the cosmic order. The Ultimate Reality revealed in Jesus
Christ is of such a nature that if human society were ordered upon
the principles therein enshrined, most of the urgent ethical problems of the world would be solved and the deepest needs of the
human soul would be satisfied. But apart from the relative merits
of any specific system, the history of religion throughout the ages
makes it abundantly clear that in every phase of society religion
exercises a cultural function by supplying the spiritual force indispensable for the cohesion of the social fabric.

[1] John xiv. 9.   [2] Heb. i. 1 f.   [3] Acts xiv. 17.

BIBLIOGRAPHY

INTRODUCTION

Bouquet, A. C, *Comparative Religion.* new ed. 1956.

Childe, V. G., *Dawn of European Civilization,* 5th. ed. 1950.
New Light on the Most Ancient East, new ed. 1952.

Comte, A., *Cours de philosophie positive.* Paris, 1877, 4th ed.

Dawson, C., *Progress and Religion,* 1929.
The Age of the Gods. 1928.

Durkheim, E., *Elementary Forms of the Religious Life.* E.T. 1915.

Eliade, Mircea, *Patterns in Comparative Religion.* 1958.

Goldenweiser, A., *Anthropology,* New York, 1937.

Graebner, F., *Methode der Ethnologie.* Heidelberg, 1911.

Evans-Pritchard, E. E., *Sociel Anthropology,* 1951.

Hegel, G. W. F., The *Philosophy of Religion.* E.T. 1895.

Hobhouse, L. T., Wheeler, G. C., Ginsberg, M., *The Material Culture and Social Institutions of the Simpler Peoples.* 1930.

Hocart, A. M., *The Progress of Man,* 1933.

Kroeber, A. L., *Anthropology.* New York, 1923.

Lowie, R. H. *History of Ethnological Theory,* 1938.

Malinowski, B., *Foundations of Faith and Morals,* (Riddell Memorial Lecture) 1935.
Article 'Culture' in *Encyclopaedia of Social Sciences.* Vol. IV. 1931.

Marett, R. R., *Anthropology,* 1912. *The Threshold of Religion,* 1914.

Pinard, H de la Boullaye, *L'Étude comparée des religions,* 3rd. ed. 1920.

Radcliffe-Brown, A. R., 'Present Position of Anthropological Studies,' *Report of the British Association 1931.* pp. 147–171 (1932).
'On the Concept of Function in Social Science' in *American Anthropologist* New Series, xxxvii. 1935.
'On Social Structure' in *Journal of Royal Anthropological Institute* 70, 1940. *Religion and Society* (Myers Lecture, 1945. R.A.I.)

Rivers, W. H. R., *History and Ethnology,* 1929.

Smith, Sir G. Elliot, *Human History,* 1929.

Tylor, E. B., *Researches into the Early History of Mankind,* 1878;
Primitive Culture, 1871. (4th. ed. 1903).

Van der Leeuw, G., *Religion in Essence and Manifestation,* E.T. 1938.

CHAPTER I

Breuil, H., *Four Hundred Centuries of Cave Art,* Montignac, 1952.

Burkitt, M. C., *Prehistory,* Cambridge, 1927.

Durkheim, E., *Elementary Forms of the Religious Life,* 1915.

Evans-Pritchard, E. E., *Nuer Religion,* Oxford, 1956.

Flower, J. C., *The Psychology of Religion,* 1927.

Frazer, J. G., *The Golden Bough,* 3rd ed. Pt. I The Magic Art, 1917.
The Worship of Nature, 1926.
Totemism and Exogamy, 1910.

Freud, S., *Totem and Taboo,* New York, 1918.

Harrison, J. E., *Ancient Art and Ritual,* 1913.
  Epilegomena to the Study of Greek Religion, Cambridge, 1921.

James, E. O., *Prehistoric Religion,* 1957.

Levy-Bruhl, L., *How Natives Think,* 1926.
  Primitive Mentality, 1923.

Luquet, G. H., *The Art and Religion of Fossil Man,* Oxford, 1930.

Marett, R. R., *The Threshold of Religion,* 1912.

Malinowski, B., 'Magic, Science and Religion; in *Science, Religion and Reality,* 1926.

Otto, R., *The Idea of the Holy.* E.T. 1950.

Radin, P., *Primitive Religion,* 1928.

Smith, W. R., *Religion of the Semites,* 3rd. ed. 1927.

Spencer, B., and Gillen, F. J., *Native Tribes of Central Australia,* 1938; The *Arunta,* 1927.

Tyler, E. B., *Primitive Culture,* 1903.

Webb, C. C. J., *Group Theories of Religion and the Individual,* 1916.

CHAPTER II

Allier, B., *Magie et religion.* Paris, 1935.

Codrington, R. H., *The Melanesians; Studies in their Anthropology and Folklore.* Oxford 1891.

Evans-Pritchard, E. E., 'The Morphology and Function of Magic' in *American Anthropologist,* XXXI. 1929, pp. 619 ff.

Frazer, J. G., *The Golden Bough,* Part I. The Magic Art. 1917.

Firth, Raymond, 'The Analysis of Man' in *Journal of Polynesian Society,* XLIX. 1940. pp. 483 ff.

Hartland, S., *Ritual and Belief,* 1914.

Hewitt, J. N. B., 'Orenda and a Definition of Religion' in *American Anthropologist,* New Series, 1892, pp. 33 ff.

Hubert, H., and Mauss, M., 'Esquisse d'une theories genérale de la magic', in *L'Année Sociologique, VII.* 1904.

James, E. O., *The Beginnings of Religion,* new ed. 1958.

Jevons, F. B., 'Definition of Magic' in *Sociological Review,* I. 1908.
  'Magic and Religion' in *Folk-lore,* XXVIII. 1917:

Malinowski, B., *Argonauts of the Western Pacific,* 1922.
  Coral Gardens, Vol. II. 1935.
  Sexual Life of Savages in North-western Melanesia, 1932.

Marett, R. R., *The Threshold of Religion* 1914.
  Articles 'Magic' and 'Mana' in *Encyclopaedia of Religion and Ethics,* Vol. VIII.

Rivers, W. H. R., *Medicine, Magic and Religion,* 1929.

Spencer, B., and F. J. Gillen, *Native Tribes of Central Australia,* 1938.
  Northern Tribes of Central Australia, 1904.

Tylor, E. B., *Primitive Culture,* 1903.

Westermarck, E., *Ritual and Belief in Morocco,* 1926.

CHAPTER III

Gennep, A van, *Les Rites de Passage,* Paris, 1909, E.T. 1960.

Evans-Pritchard, E. E., *Witchcraft, Oracles and Magic among the Azande,* Oxford, 1937.

Firth, Raymond, *The Work of the God in Tikopia,* 1940.
Harrison, J. E., *Ancient Art and Ritual,* 1913.
Hartland, S., *Ritual and Belief,* 1914.
Hocart, A. M., *Kingship.* Oxford, 1927.
   Kings and Councillors, Cairo, 1936.
Howitt, A. W., *Native Tribes of South-east Australia,* 1904.
James, E. O., *Primitive Ritual and Belief,* 1917.
Lang, A., Myth, *Myth/Ritual and Religion,* 1897.
Marett, R. R., *Sacraments of Simple Folk,* Oxford, 1933.
Spencer and Gillen, *Native Tribes of Central Australia,* 1938.
Webster, H., *Primitive Secret Societies,* New York, 1932.

CHAPTER IV

Blackman, A. M., *Recueil de travaux relatifs à la philologie et à l'archéologie
   égyptienne et assyriennes.* XXXIX. Paris, 1920.
   Articles, 'Priesthood' (Egyptian) and 'Worship' (Egyptian) in *Encyclopaedia
   of Religion and Ethics,* Vols. X and XII.
   Journal of Manchester Egyptian and Oriental Society, 1918–19.
   Article in *Myth and Ritual.* Oxford, 1933.
   Luxor and its Temples. 1923.
Brandon, S. G. F., *Time and Mankind,* 1951.
Breasted, J. H., *Development of Religion and Thought in Ancient Egypt,* 1914.
Budge, E. A. W., *Osiris and the Egyptian Resurrection.* 2. vols, 1911.
Cerny, J., *Ancient Egyptian Religion,* 1952.
Dhorme, E., *Les Religions de Babylonie et Assyrie,* 1945.
Engnell, I., *Studies in Divine Kingship in the Ancient Near East,* Uppsala, 1945.
Erman, A., *Handbook of Egyptian Religion,* 1907.
Frankfort, H., *Ancient Egyptian Religion,* (O.U.P. for Columbia U.P.) 1948.
   Kingship and the Gods, Chicago, 1948.
   Intellectual Adventure of Ancient Man, Chicago, 1946 (*Before Philosophy*
   Penguin, 1949).
Frazer, J. G., *Golden Bough.* Pt. IV (Dying God) Pt. V. (Adonis etc.)
Gadd, C. J., in *Myth and Ritual,* Oxford, 1933.
Gaster, T. H., *Thespis,* New York, 1950.
Gardiner, A. H., in *Journal of Egyptian Archaeology,* II. 1915.
Heidel, A., *The Babylonian Genesis,* 2nd. ed. Chicago, 1951.
Hocart, A. M., *Kingship,* Oxford, 1927.
Hooke, S. H., *Myth and Ritual,* Oxford, 1933, *Myth, Ritual and Kingship,*
   Oxford, 1958.
   Babylonian and Assyrian Religion, 1953.
James, E. O., *Seasonal Feasts and Festivals,* 1961.
Jastrow, M., *Religion of Babylonia and Assyria,* Boston, 1898.
Labat, R., *Du Caractère Religieux de la Royaulté Assyro Babylonienne,* Paris,
   1939.
Langdon, S., *Tammuz and Ishtar,* Oxford, 1914.
   Sumerian Liturgies and Psalms, Philadelphia, 1919.
   Babylonian Epic of Creation, Oxford, 1923.
Malinowski, B., *Myth in Primitive Psychology.* 1926.
Marett, R. R., *Faith, Hope and Charity in Primitive Religion,* Oxford, 1932.
Mercer, S. A. B., *The Religion of Ancient Egypt,* 1949.

Moret, A., *Du Caractère Religieux de la Royauté Pharaonique*. Paris, 1902.
  Le Rituel de Culte divin journalier en Egypte, Paris, 1902.
  Mystères Egyptians. Paris, 1913.
Murray, M. A., *The Osireion at Abydos*, 1904.
Raglan, Lord, *The Hero*, 1936.
Sethe, K., *Urgeschichte und älteste Religion der Aegypte*, Leipzig, 1930.
Thurgeau-Dangin, F., *Rituels accadiens*. Paris, 1921.

CHAPTER V

Allen, T. W., Halliday, W. R., Sykes, E. E., *The Homeric Hymns*, Oxford, 1936.
Angus, S., *The Mystery Religion and Christianity*, 1925.
Casson, S., *Macedonia, Thrace and Illyria*, Oxford, 1926.
Chadwick, H. M., *The Heroic Age*, 1912.
Childe, V. G., *The Dawn of European Civilization*, 6th. ed. 1957.
Deubner, L., *Attische Feste*. Berlin, 1932.
Emmett Bennett, *The Pylos Tablets*, Princeton, 1951.
Evans, Sir Arthur, *The Palace of Minos at Knossos*, Vols. III, IV. 1930–35.
  The Earliest Religion of Greece in the light of Cretan Discoveries 1931.
Farnell, L. R., *Cult of the Greeks States*, Vols. III. V. Oxford, 1906, 1909.
Frazer, J. G., *Golden Bough*. Pt. V. (Adonis etc.) 1914.
Guthrie, W. K. C., *The Greeks and their Gods*, 1950.
  Orpheus and Greek Religion, 1935.
Harrison, J. E., *Prolegomena to the Study of Greek Religion*, Cambridge, 1932, 3rd. ed. *Themis*, Cambridge, 1912.
James, E. O., *Cult of the Mother-goddess*, 1959.
  Seasonal Feasts and Festivals, 1961.
Kourouniotis, K., *Eleusis*, Athens, 1936.
Lobeck, C. A., *Aglophamus sive de theologie mysticae Graecorum. causis*, Leipzig. 1829.
Murray, G., *Five Stages in Greek Religion*, Oxford, 1925.
Mylonas, G., *Hymns to Demeter and Her Sanctuary at Eleusis*, St. Louis, 1942.
Myres, J. L., *Who were the Greeks?* Berkeley, 1930.
Nilsson, M. P., *Minoan-Mycenaean Religion*. 2nd. ed. Lund, 1950.
  A History of Greek Religion, Oxford, 1925.
  Greek Popular Religion, Columbia U.P. 1940.
  Griechische Feste von religiöser Bedeutung, Leipzig, 1906.
Persson, A. W., *The Religion of Greece in Prehistoric Times*, California, 1942.
Pickard-Cambridge, A. W., *Dithyramb, Tragedy and Comedy*. Oxford, 1927.
Reitzenstein, R., *Die hellenistischen Mysterienreligionen*, Leipzig, 1910.
Rhose, *Psyche*, 1925.
Rose, H. J., *A Handbook of Greek Mythology*. 1933. *Greek Religion*, 1947.
Showerman, G., 'The Great Mother of the Gods' in *Bulletin of the University of Wisconsin*, XLVIII. Madison, 1901.
Ventris and Chadwick, *Documents in Mycenaean Greek*, Cambridge, 1956.
Wace, A. J. B., *Mycenae*, Princeton, 1949.
Wissowa, G., *Religion und Kultus der Römer*, Munich, 1912.

CHAPTER VI

Anesaki, M., *A History of Japanese Religion*, 1930.
Aston, W. G., *Shinto, the Way of the Gods*, 1905.

Barth, A., *The Religions of India*. 1932.
Bühler, G., 'Laws of Manu', *Sacred Books of the East*, XXV. 1886.
Bouquet, A. C., *Hinduism*, 1950.
Deussen, P., *Philosophy of the Upnaishads*, Edin. 1906.
Eggeling, J., 'Satapatha Brahmana', *Sacred Books of the East*, XII, XXXVI.,
     XLI, XLIII.
Eliot, Sir Charles, *Hinduism and Buddhism*. 3 vols. 1921.
Farquhar, J. N., *A Primer of Hinduism*, Oxford, 1912.
Giles, H. A., *Confucianism and its Rivals*, 1918.
Heinmann, B., *Indian and Western Philosophy*, 1937.
Holtom, D. C., *The National Faith of Japan*, 1938.
Hughes, E. R., *Religion in China*, 1950.
Hume, R. E., *The Thirteen Principal Upanishads*, 2nd. ed. Oxford, 1931.
Knox, G. W., *Development of Religion in Japan*, New York, 1907.
MacNicol, N., *Living Religions of the Indian People*, 1934.
Mackay, E., *Early Indus Civilization*, 2nd. ed. 1948.
     Further Excavations in Mohenjo-daro, 2 vols. Delhi, 1938.
Marshall, J., *Mohenjo-daro amd the Indus Civilization*, 2 vols. 1931.
Piggott, S., *Prehistoric India to 1000 B.C.*, 1952.
Radhakrishnan, S., *Indian Philosophy*, 2 vols. 1927.
     The Principal Upanishads. 1952.
Soothill, W. E., *Three Religions of China*, 1913.
Thomas, E. J., *Vedic Hymns and the Song of the Lord*, 1913. new ed. 1959.
Waley, A., *The Analects of Confucius*, 1938.
     The Way and its Power, 1934.
Wheeler, Sir R. E. M., *The Cambridge History of India*. Supplementary Volume,
     1953.
Wheeler, P., *The Sacred Scriptures of the Japanese*, 1953.

CHAPTER VII

Conze, E., *Buddhism; it essence and development*, 1951.
     Buddhist Wisdom Books: Diamond Sutra and the Heart Sutra, 1958.
     Buddhist Texts through the Ages, 1954.
Davids, Mrs Rhys, *Buddhism* 1934.
     Manual of Buddhism, 1932.
Edgerton, F., *The Bhagavadgita*, 1944.
Eliot, Sir Charles, *Japanese Buddhism*, 1935.
Garbe, R., *Die Sankhya-Philosophie*, Leipzig, 1894.
Griffiths, R. T. A., *Ramayana*, Benares, 1874.
Horner, I. B., *The Early Buddhist Theory of Man Perfected*, 1936.
Humphreys, C., *Buddhism*, 1951.
Linsson, R., *Living Zen*, 1958.
Monier-Williams, M., *Hinduism*, 1891. 4th. ed.
Pratt, J. B., *The Pilgrimage of Buddhism*, 1928.
     India and its Faiths, 1916.
Radhakrishnan, S., *The Bhagavadgita* 5th. ed., 1956.
Smith, F. H., *The Buddhist Way of Life*, 1951.
Stenilber-Oberlin, E., and Kumi Matsuo, *The Buddhist Sects of Japan*, 1937.
Thomas, E. T., *The History of Buddhist Thought*, 1933.
     The Earliest Buddhist Scriptures, 1935.
     The Song of the Lord, 1931.

CHAPTER VIII

Bell, R., *The Qur'an.* 2 vols. 1937–39.
Breasted, J. H. *The Development of Religion and Thought in Ancient Egypt,* 1912.
Budge, E. A. W., *Tutankhamen, Amenism, Atenism and Egyptian Monotheism,* 1923.
Cumont, F., *Les Mystères de Mithra.* Paris, 1913.
Darmesteter, J., *Zend Avesta,* Sacred Books of the East. IV. 1895.
Dhalla, M. N., *Zoroastrian Theology.* New York, 1914.
    History of Zoroastrianism, 1938.
Duchesne-Guillemin, J., *The Western Response to Zoroaster,* Oxford, 1958.
Erman, A., *Handbook of Egyptian Religion,* 1912.
Gibbs, H. A. R., *Mohammedanism,* 2nd. ed. Oxford, 1953.
Guillaume, A., *The Traditions of Islam,* Oxford, 1924.
    Islam, 1954.
Macdonald, D. B., *Muslim Theology,* 1903.
Masani, R. P., *The Religion of the Good Life,* 1938.
Moulton, J. H., *Early Zoroastrianism,* 1913.
James, E. O., *The Concept of Deity,* 1950.
    The Old Testament in the light of Anthropology, 1934.
Lang, A., *The Making of Religion,* 1898.
Lods, A., *Israel, to the Middle of the Eighth Century B.C.,* 1932.
    The Prophets and the Rise of Judaism, 1937.
Oesterley, W. O. E., and Robinson, T. H., *History of Israel,* Oxford, 1932. 2 vols. *Hebrew Religion,* 1930.
Palmer, E. H., *The Qur'an,* Oxford, 1928.
Radin, P., *Monotheism among Primitive Peoples,* 1924.
Rodwell, J. M., *The Koran,* 1953.
Pettazzoni, R., 'Monotheismus und Polytheismus' in *Die Religion in Geschichte und Gegenwart,* IV. 1930.
Schmidt, W., *Der Ursprung der Gottesidee,* 1912 ff. 10 vols, *Origin and Growth of Religion,* 1931.
Smith, W. R., *Religion of the Semites,* 1927. 3rd. ed.
Söderblom, N., *The Living God,* Oxford, 1931.
Tritton, A. S., *Islam, Belief and Practice,* 1951.
Zaehner, R. C., *Dawn and Twilight of Zoroastrianism,* 1961.

CHAPTER IX

Anelm, St., *Cur Deus Homo.*
Bicknell, E. J., *The Christian Idea of Sin and Original Sin,* 1922.
Breasted, J. H., *The Development of Religion and Thought in Ancient Egypt,* 1912. *Dawn of Conscience,* 1934.
Bückler, A. *Studies in Sin and Atonement,* Oxford, 1928.
Budge, E. A. W., *Teaching of Amen-En-Apt,* 1924.
Cook, S. A., *The Law of Moses and the Code of Hammurabi,* 1903.
Dale, R. W., *The Atonement,* 1892, 14th. ed.
Erman, A., *The Literature of the Ancient Egyptians,* E.T. by Blackman, 1927.
Dhorme, P., *La Religion assyo-babylonienne,* Paris, 1910.
Franks, R. S., *The Atonement,* Oxford, 1934.
Gardner, W. R. W., *The Quran'ic Doctrine of Sin,* 1914.
Gray, G. B., *Sacrifice in the Old Testament,* Oxford, 1925.

Grensted, L. W., *A Short History of the Doctrine of the Atonement*, Manchester, 1920.
  The Atonement in History and in Life, 1929.
Hicks, F. C. N., *The Fullness of Sacrifice*, 1930.
Hooke, S. H., *Babylonian and Assyrian Religion*, 1953.
James, E. O., *Origins of Sacrifice*, 1933.
Jastrow, M., *Aspects of Religious Belief and Practice in Babylonia and Assyria*. 1911.
  Religion of Babylonia and Assyria, 1898.
Kennett, R. H., *Old Testament Essays*, Cambridge, 1928.
Langdon, S., *Babylonian Penitential Psalms*, Paris, 1927.
Macdonald, D. B., *Muslim Theology*. 1903.
McLeod Campbell, J., *The Nature of the Atonement*, 1856.
Moberley, R. C., *Atonement and Personality*, 1901.
Morgenstein, J., *Doctrine of Sin in Babylonian Religion*, 1905.
Moulton, J. H., *Early Zoroastrianism*, 1913.
Mozley, J. K., *The Doctrine of the Atonement*, 1915.
Oesterley, W. O. E., *Sacrifice in Ancient Israel*, 1937.
Oxenham, H. N., *The Catholic Doctrine of the Atonement*, 1869.
Rashdall, H., *The Idea of Atonement in Christian Theology*, 1919.
Sells, E., *The Faith of Islam*, 1907.
Tennant, F. R., *The Origin and Propagation of Sin*, Cambridge, 1906.
Williams, N. P., *Ideas of the Fall and of Original Sin*, 1927.
Zimmern, H., *Babylonische Busspsalmen*. Leipzig, 1885. 4th. ed.

CHAPTER X

Angus, C., *The Mystery Religions and Christianity*, 1925.
Bailey, C., *Phases in the Religion of Ancient Rome*, Oxford, 1932.
Cumont, F., *Les Religions orientales dans la Paganisme romain*. Paris, 1909.
  Textes et Monuments relatifs aux Mystères de Mithra. Bruxelles, 1896–99.
Dieterich, A., *Eine Mithrasliturgie*, Leipzig, 1903.
Dill, S., *Roman Society from Nero to Marcus Aurelius*, 2nd ed. 1905.
Dix, G., *The Shape of the Liturgy*, 1945.
Evans-Pritchard, E. E., *The Meaning of Sacrifice among the Nuer* (Myres Lecture) Journal of Royal Anthropological Institute, 84. 1954.
Farnell, L. R., 'Sacrificial Communion' *The Hibbert Journal*, II. 1905.
Fowler, W. Warde, *Religious Experience of the Roman People*, 1911.
Gayford, S. C., *Sacrifice and Priesthood: Jewish and Christian*, 1925.
Gaven, F., *The Jewish Antecedents of the Christian Sacraments*. 1928.
Gray, G. B. *Sacrifice in the Old Testament*, Oxford, 1925.
Guthrie, W. K. C., *Orpheus and Greek Religion*, 1935.
Hicks, F. C. N., *The Fullness of Sacrifice*, 1930.
Hubert, H., and Mauss, M., 'Essai sur la nature et la fonction du sacrifice, *L'Année Sociologique*, 2. 1898, pp. 29 ff.
James, E. O., *Origins of Sacrifice*, 1933.
  Nature and Function of Priesthood, 1955.
  Sacrifice and Sacrament, 1961.
Jeremias, J., *Die Abendmahlsworte Jesu*. Göttingen, 1935.
Kennedy, H. A. A., *St, Paul and the Mystery Religions*, 1913.
Leitzmann, H., *Messe und Herrenmahl, eine studie sur geschichte der Liturgie*, Bonn, 1926.

Loisy, A. F., *Les Mystères paiens et le mystère Chretien*, Paris, 1914.
Nock, A. D., *Conversion*, Oxford, 1935.
Oesterley, W. O. E., and Box, G. H., *The Religion and Worship of the Synagogue*, 1911.
   The Jewish Background of the Christian Liturgy, Oxford, 1925.
   Sacrifices in Ancient Israel., 1937.
Pedersen, Johs. *Israel; its Life and Culture*, Copenhagen, 1926.
Reitzenstein, R., *Die Hellenistischen Mysteriereligionen*, Leipzig, 1910.
Smith, W. R., *The Religion of the Semites*, 3rd. ed. 1927.
Taylor, V., *Jesus and His Sacrifice*, 1937.
Tylor, E. B., *Primitive Culture*, 1913.
Articles in *The Encyclopaedia of Religion and Ethics* 'Sacrifice' Vol. XI.

CHAPTER XI

Altheim, F., *A History of Roman Religion*, E.T. by E. Mattingly, 1938.
Anesaki, M. ,*Nichiren, the Buddhist Prophet*, Camb. Mass. 1916.
Bailey, C., *Phases in the Religion of Ancient Rome*, Oxford, 1932.
Blackman, A. M., Article 'Worship' (Egyptian) in *Encylopaedia of Religion and Ethics*. vol. XII.
Brightman, F. E., *Liturgies Eastern and Western*, Oxford, 1896.
Duchesne, L. *Christian Worship*, 1903.
Farnell, L. R., *The Evolution of Religion*, 1905.
   Higher Aspects of Greek Religion, 1912.
Fortescue, A., *The Mass, A Study of the Roman Liturgy.* 1912.
Fowler, W. Warde, *The Religious Experience of the Roman People*, 1911.
Frere, W. H., *Principles of Religious Ceremonial*, 1906.
   The Use of Sarum, Cambridge, 1898.
Gardiner, A. H., and Davies, N de G., *The Tomb of Amenemhet*, 1918.
Heiler, F., *Prayer*, Oxford, 1937, new ed.
Jacob, L., *Jewish Prayer*, 1955.
Jungmann, J. A., *The Mass of the Roman Rite*, 1959.
King, A. A., *The Liturgy of the Roman Church*, 1957.
King, L. W., *Babylonian Magic and Sorcery*, 1896.
Langdon, S., *Sumerian Liturgical Texts from Nippur*, Philadelphia, 1917.
   Sumerian Liturgies and Psalms, Philadelphia, 1919.
Lowther Clarke, W. K. C., and Harris, C., *Liturgy and Worship*, 1932.
Marett, R. R., 'From Spell to Prayer' in *Folk-Lore*, XV. 1904.
Montefiore, G. C., *Judaism and St Paul*, 1914.
Myhrman, D. W., *Babylonian Hymns and Prayers*, Philadelphia, 1910.
Oesterley, W. O. E., and Box, G. H., *The Religion and Worship of the Synagogue*, 1911.
Parrinder, G., *Worship in the World's Religions*, 1961.
Schmidt,W., *High Gods of North America*, Oxford, 1933.
Scrawley, J. H., *The Early History of the Liturgy*, Cambridge, 1913.
Suzuki, D. T., *Outlines of Mahayana Buddhism*, 1907.
Underhill, E., *Worship*, 1937.
Warren, F. C., *Liturgy and Ritual of the Ante-Nicene Church*, 1897.
Woolley, R. M., *The Liturgy of the Primitive Church*, Cambridge, 1910.

CHAPTER XII

Articles 'Prayer' and 'Worship' in *Encyclopaedia of Religion and Ethics*; *Jewish Encyclopaedia, Encyclopaedia of Islam*, and *Catholic Encyclopaedia*.

Boule, H., *Fossil Man* Edin. 1923.

Budge, E. A. W., *The Book of the Dead*, new ed. 1951.
The Book of the Opening of the Mouth, 1909.
The Egyptian Heaven and Hell, 1906.

Burnet, J., *The Socratic Doctrine of the Soul*, 1916.

Charles, R. H., *Eschatology; A Critical History of the Doctrine of the Future Life*, 1913.

Crawley, A. E., *The Idea of the Soul*, 1909.

Dawson, W. R., and Elliot Smith, G., *Egyptian Mummies*, 1924.

Farnell, L. R., *Greek Hero Cults and Ideas of Immortality*, Oxford, 1921.

Frazer, J. G., *The Belief in Immortality*, 1913, 2 vols,
The Fear of the Dead in Primitive Religion, 1933–6.

James, E. O., *Prehistoric Religion*, 1957.

Kruijt, A. C., *Het Animisme in den Indischen Archipel*. Hague, 1906.

Lods, A., *La Croyance a la Vie Future et le Culte des Morts dans L'Antiquités Israelite*, Paris, 1906.

Macalister, R. A. S., *A Text-book of European Archaeology*, Cambridge, 1921.

Macdonald, D. B., *Muslim Theology*, 1903.

Moore, C. H., *Ancient Beliefs in the Immortality of the Soul*, 1931.

Moore, G. F., *Judaism*, Cambridge, 1927.

Nilsson, M. P., *Minoan-Mycenaean Religion*, Lund. 1950.
Homer and Mycenae, 1933.

Oesterley, W. O. E., *Immortality and the Unseen World*, 1921.

Pedersen, Johs. *Israel; its Life and Culture*, Copenhagen, 1926.

Rhode, E., *Psyche*, 1925.

Seth Pringle-Peterson, A., *The Idea of Immortality*, Oxford, 1922.

Taylor, A. E., *The Christian Hope of Immortality*. 1938.

Index